MW00965838

Greek Religious Terminology—Telete & Orgia

Religions in the Graeco-Roman World

Editors

H.S. Versnel

D. Frankfurter

J. Hahn

VOLUME 169

Greek Religious Terminology— Telete & Orgia

A Revised and Expanded English Edition of the Studies by Zijderveld and Van der Burg

By

Feyo L. Schuddeboom

BRILL

LEIDEN • BOSTON
2009

This book is printed on acid-free paper.

Library of Congress Cataloging-in-Publication Data

Schuddeboom, Feyo.
  Greek religious terminology : telete, orgia : a revised and expanded English edition of the studies by Zijderveld and Van der Burg / by Feyo L. Schuddeboom.
      p. cm. – (Religions in the Graeco-Roman world, ISSN 0927-7633 ; v. 169)
  Includes bibliographical references and indexes.
  ISBN 978-90-04-17813-7 (hardback : alk. paper)
  1. Telete (The Greek word) 2. Orgia (The Greek word) 3. Greek language–Semantics. I. Zijderveld, Cornelis. Telete. II. Burg, Nicolaas Marius Henricus van der, 1902-1963. Aporreta-dromena-orgia. III. Title. IV. Series.

  PA430.T4S38 2009
  485–dc22

                                                                      2009029149

ISSN 0927-7633
ISBN 978 90 04 17813 7

Copyright 2009 by Koninklijke Brill NV, Leiden, The Netherlands.
Koninklijke Brill NV incorporates the imprints Brill, Hotei Publishing,
IDC Publishers, Martinus Nijhoff Publishers and VSP.

All rights reserved. No part of this publication may be reproduced, translated, stored in
a retrieval system, or transmitted in any form or by any means, electronic, mechanical,
photocopying, recording or otherwise, without prior written permission from the publisher.

Brill has made all reasonable efforts to trace all right holders to any copyrighted material used
in this work. In cases where these efforts have not been successful the publisher welcomes
communications from copyright holders, so that the appropriate acknowledgements can be
made in future editions, and to settle other permission matters.

Authorization to photocopy items for internal or personal use is granted by Koninklijke Brill NV
provided that the appropriate fees are paid directly to The Copyright Clearance Center,
222 Rosewood Drive, Suite 910, Danvers, MA 01923, USA.
Fees are subject to change.

PRINTED IN THE NETHERLANDS

IN MEMORIAM PATRIS
WALTER ARNOLD SCHUDDEBOOM
19 Jun. 1933 – 5 Aug. 2009

CONTENTS

INDICES

NOTE ON THIS EDITION

This book examines the use of two semantically related Greek religious terms: τελετή and ὄργια. The work consists of three parts.

Part One is a revised edition of C. Zijderveld, *Τελετή: Bijdrage tot de kennis der religieuze terminologie in het Grieksch* (1934). The literary sources have been supplemented with more than sixty new additions. The inscriptions have been moved to a new chapter in Part Three.

Part Two contains a revised edition of N.M.H. van der Burg, Ἀπόρ-ρητα - δρώμενα - ὄργια: *Bijdrage tot de kennis der religieuze terminologie in het Grieksch* (1939). Of this tripartite study, only the third part, where ὄργια is examined, has been retained. The literary sources have been supplemented with more than seventy new additions. Attestations of the loanword *orgia* in Latin literature have been collected in a new chapter by F.L. Schuddeboom.

Part Three contains a collection of the epigraphical evidence by F.L. Schuddeboom in two new chapters (τελετή and ὄργια). False and dubious attestations are presented separately in an appendix, as are the occurrences of the proper name Telete in inscriptions.

PREFACE

The study of the word τελετή was first suggested to me by Professor Kevin Clinton ten years ago, when I was a visiting graduate student at Cornell University: I had shown a keen interest in the study of mystery religions and the standard work on τελετή by Cornelis Zijderveld happened to be written in my native tongue.[1] At that time, however, my course work at Cornell and preparations for my Master's thesis precluded me from progressing beyond a preliminary inventory of the literary sources and some very tentative conclusions. During the years that followed, other duties and activities kept me from further pursuing the project.

In January 2006, I finally decided that, rather than starting *ab ovo*, one should prepare an updated, English edition of Zijderveld's seminal work, including a new chapter on inscriptions. When I set about working on the project, it soon became apparent that one should also include the term ὄργια and its cognates, because these are so often found in the same or similar context as τελετή. My task was made easier by the fortuitous circumstance that there was already a study of the term ὄργια by another compatriot of mine, Nicolaas van der Burg,[2] who had used very much the same modus operandi as Zijderveld.[3]

At the heart of this book, therefore, there is a new edition of Zijderveld's study of τελετή (Part One) and Van der Burg's study of ὄργια (Part Two). In addition, I have collected the attestations of the loanword *orgia* in Latin literature (Part Two, Chapter Ten) and of τελετή and ὄργια in inscriptions (Part Three).

Several years after the publication of Zijderveld's dissertation, Otto Kern wrote a highly critical review of it in *Gnomon*.[4] Two of Kern's principal complaints concerned the fact that the treatment of the epigraphical evidence was unsystematic and incomplete, and that the book was written in Dutch (albeit with an English summary). The present edition aims

---

[1] C. Zijderveld, *Τελετή. Bijdrage tot de kennis der religieuze terminologie in het Grieksch* (1934).

[2] N.M.H. van der Burg, Ἀπόρρητα - δρώμενα - ὄργια. *Bijdrage tot de kennis der religieuze terminologie in het Grieksch* (1939).

[3] In fact, his work is in many ways a supplement to Zijderveld, as Van der Burg himself indicated, *op. cit.* 2.

[4] O. Kern, *Gnomon* 15 (1939) 198–202.

to address these concerns: the language of the book is now English (Kern had suggested Latin) and the epigraphical evidence is presented in new chapters in a clear and systematic way.

One piece of criticism I have not attempted to mitigate is the reproach that Zijderveld's analysis is too superficial. While few will nowadays accept the postulation of a more or less linear development of the meaning of the words τελετή and ὄργια, Zijderveld's main thesis, that τελετή is *not* in the first place an initiation into the mysteries, is still very valid and has, in my opinion, not received the attention it deserves. Moreover, as annotated collections of sources, the works of Zijderveld and Van der Burg remain invaluable for anyone who wishes to see where and how the Greeks used τελετή and ὄργια. Why the Greeks used the terms precisely in these contexts and not in others, is a question best reserved for another book.

Brief History of Scholarship

The first serious attempts to study the terms τελετή and ὄργια in a systematic manner were undertaken by Cornelis Zijderveld and Nicolaas van der Burg in the 1930s. Both scholars were trained at the University of Utrecht and each wrote his doctoral dissertation on Greek religious terminology. These two dissertations still serve, not merely as starting points, but as standard works for the study of the words τελετή and ὄργια in Greek literature.

In spite of criticism that its analysis lacks depth and despite its being outdated in several respects, Zijderveld's dissertation has remained the standard work on the term τελετή. It examines the use of τελετή before Alexander, after Alexander, and in Jewish and Christian authors. Zijderveld distinguished between religious ceremonies in general, religious acts of a special character, symbolic acts (mysteries), religious sects, magic rites, and metaphorical uses.[5]

Van der Burg's dissertation was conceived as a supplement to Zijderveld's dissertation and follows more or less the same methodology. The third part of the dissertation examined the use of ὄργια and several cognates before Alexander and after Alexander (Jewish and Christian authors were left out of consideration). Van der Burg distinguished be-

---

[5] Cf. also F.M.J. Waanders, *The History of τέλος and τελέω in Ancient Greek* (1983) 156–159, who cites Zijderveld and lists several illustrative occurrences of the term τελετή.

tween religious ceremonies in general, ceremonies for certain gods, purification ceremonies, mysteries, and metaphorical uses.

In 1980, Ken Dowden studied the nature of the τελετή at the Eleusinian mysteries in depth.[6] Among other things, he showed conclusively
that the *mystai* and *epoptai* actually participated in the same ceremony
(the τελετή), which was, therefore, not a distinct stage preceding the
ἐποπτεία.

In 1987, Giulia Sfameni Gasparro revisited several classical authors
where the term appears, thus reviving the discussion how τελετή is used
and what the various uses have in common.[7] She discussed several pre-
dominant contexts: Eleusinian mysteries, Dionysiac rites, Thesmophoria,
Corybantism, and Orphic rites, but was rightly cautious to reach any firm
new conclusions about what exactly makes a rite a τελετή. Instead, she
emphasized once again that τελετή is a rite of a special character.

In 1992, André Motte and Vinciane Pirenne-Delforge studied the
word ὄργια and its cognates in the literary sources.[8] They identified five
different contexts: Demeter (mysteries and Thesmophoria), Dionysus,
Megaloi Theoi of Samothrace, Aphrodite and the Muses, and rites in a
more general sense. They concluded, among other things, that the notion
of sacred mysteries entailed a sort of communion with the deities for
whom ὄργια were celebrated. This also explains how certain Christian
and Jewish authors could use the term for their own celebrations.

One thing the aforementioned studies have in common is that they
have all relied very heavily on literary sources, largely ignoring the epigraphical evidence. Zijderveld merely consulted the indices of Dittenberger's and Kaibel's selections of Greek inscriptions[9] and included only
two other inscriptions.[10] Van der Burg did not take the epigraphical evidence into account at all. Sfameni Gasparro limited her discussion to

---

[6] K. Dowden, Grades in the Eleusinian Mysteries, *RHR* 197 (1980) 409–427.

[7] G. Sfameni Gasparro, Ancora sul termine telete: osservazioni storico-religiose, in:
Filologia e Forme Letterarie, ed. C. Questa, vol. 5 (1987) 137–152.

[8] A. Motte & V. Pirenne-Delforge, Le mot et les rites. Aperçu des significations de
orgia et de quelques dérivés, *Kernos* 5 (1992) 119–140.

[9] Cf. O. Kern, *Gnomon* (1939) 198–202, 200, who criticizes Zijderveld for having
limited himself to the inscriptions published by Dittenberger (*OGIS* and *Syll.*³) and Kaibel
(*EG*).

[10] *IG* III 713 and *IG* II² 1234; the fact that Zijderveld uses the old reference to *IG* III
indicates that he probably did not consult *IG* II² but copied these two inscriptions from
unnamed sources.

Greek literature of the classical period, while Motte & Pirenne-Delforge focused on the literary sources and referred to only a handful of the best-known inscriptions.

Principles of Revision

The works of Zijderveld and Van der Burg contain information that is fundamental to the study of various aspects of Greek and Roman religion. My primary aim in preparing this edition has been to make that information up to date and available to a much wider audience. The revision has therefore consisted of translating the relevant chapters into English, making countless minor editorial improvements, adding more than one hundred and forty Greek and Latin literary attestations previously not included, adding new chapters illustrating the use of τελετή and ὄργια in inscriptions, and, last but not least, providing translations of the Greek and Latin texts.

The two dissertations are obviously products of their time. This means that they inevitably contain some antiquated notions, both in the field of linguistics and that of religion. For reasons of economy, I have decided against completely rewriting the old chapters. By and large, I have preserved the original structure and wording but corrected obvious mistakes of fact and interpretation. By the same token, I do not provide a fully updated bibliography. Instead, I have occasionally suggested further reading that I found particularly relevant. Needless to say, this method of selection has involved a certain measure of subjectivity.

To avoid a multitude of unsightly brackets, I have refrained from indicating minor changes and new sources in the text of Parts One and Two. Only where I diverge significantly from the original author's point of view, do I mark words as my own ('FLS') in a footnote. A list of all the new Greek literary sources is to be found below, following this Preface.

Collection of Sources

For the collection of literary texts, I have used the Thesaurus Linguae Graecae (TLG), the Bibliotheca Teubneriana Latina (BTL) and the Library of Latin Texts (CLCLT). For papyri, I have searched the Duke Databank of Documentary Papyri (DDBDP) and the Catalogue of Para-literary Papyri (CPP). For Greek inscriptions, I have consulted the

Packard Epigraphical Database and the *Supplementum Epigraphicum Graecum* (*SEG*), up to and including *SEG* LIV 2004 (published 2008). For Latin inscriptions, I have used the Epigraphische Datenbank Frankfurt (EDCS).

Delimitation of the Material

For literary sources, I have taken the chronological limits of Zijderveld and Van der Burg as a starting point and have supplemented their material accordingly. The attestations in the principal Greek and Latin authors should now be complete up to 200 AD, except for the fragments. Sources after 200 AD have been included if they are of particular interest. Of the Jewish and Christian authors, I have revised the old and added new material only for Philo Judaeus, Clement of Alexandria and Prudentius.

I have not included Van der Burg's chapters on ἀπόρρητα and δρώμενα, because, unlike τελετή and ὄργια, these terms are predominantly used in non-religious contexts and are therefore not religious terms per se.

For the epigraphical evidence, I have adopted the conventional chronological limit of *SEG* to inscriptions up to 800 AD.

Translation and Transliteration

The translations of the Greek and Latin texts are my own (except where noted otherwise). They have no literary aspiration, but are intended to clarify my interpretation of the texts for those who read Greek and Latin, and to make a significant portion of the material accessible for those who do not. In many cases, I have benefited from existing translations, especially from the Loeb Classical Library. (If a turn of phrase is reminiscent of an earlier edition, this is therefore either due to coincidence—there are only so many ways to translate a word or phrase correctly—or because I found an English expression I could not improve.)

To avoid repeated paraphrases, the words mystic, mystery, mysteries and orgies are used in their classical sense: mystic is belonging to the mysteries; mysteries are mystery rites, i.e. the special ceremonies of the *mystai*; orgies are wild, ecstatic rites. Certain words that have no real equivalent in English, such as thyrsus and thiasos—'wand' and 'band' do not quite cover their respective meanings—are left untranslated.

I have adopted the Latinized/Anglicized spelling for most Greek names and placenames, but will occasionally depart from this practice when the direct transliteration from the Greek is more easily recognized (e.g. for the Greek islands and certain epithets).

When referring to literary sources, I use the word 'place' to indicate a passage in a text.

Acknowledgments

I owe a debt of gratitude to the series editor, Prof. H.S. Versnel, for his interest in this work and for his critical suggestions in the texts pertaining to magic. I am also very grateful to Professor Sarah Iles Johnston, who read the whole manuscript and suggested several key improvements, and Dr. Johan Strubbe, who read Part Three and saved me from numerous errors.

Many people have supported me at the various stages of writing. I would like to thank the following in particular: Professor Kevin Clinton for his continuing interest and for sending me the first volume of *I.Eleusis*; Diederik Burgersdijk for lending me his critical yet sympathetic ear on more than one occasion; Maithe Hulskamp for moral support and for contextualizing the medical texts for me; Eran Lupu for friendship and advice; Cisca Hoogendijk, Brian Muhs, Marja Bakker and Alette Bakkers at the Leiden Papyrological Institute for guiding me to the papyrological databases like true mystagogues; Kornelia Dirichs, for sending me a copy of Heberdey-Kalinka, no. 28 (which was nowhere to be found in the Netherlands); and Ania Lentz-Michaelis for her meticulous correction of the manuscript. Responsibility for any imperfections in the text rests, of course, with me alone.

For permission to reproduce the photograph of the mosaic from the Dionysus Room at Zeugma, I am much obliged to Mehmet Önal, Assistant Director of the Gaziantep Museum.

Feyo Schuddeboom
January 2009

LIST OF NEW GREEK LITERARY SOURCES

τελετή

Achilles Tatius
  Leuc. et Cit. 1.2
Aristides
  Or. 1.44
  Or. 1.330
  Or. 1.341
  Or. 1.342
  Or. 2.52
  Or. 2.56
  Or. 49.48
Aristides Quintilianus
  2.6
  3.25
  3.27
Clement of Alexandria
  Strom. 2.20.106.1
[Demosthenes]
  Neaer. 113
Dio Chrysostom
  Or. 36.39
Diodorus Siculus
  3.62.8
  8.15.3
Dionysius of Halicarnassus
  Ant. Rom. 2.19.2
Galen
  UP 1.418 Helmr.
Hesychius
  s.v. λύσειοι τελεταί
Maximus of Tyre
  32.7
Nonnus
  Dion. 16.400
  Dion. 48.880
  Dion. 48.886
Orphica

Hymn. 35.7
Hymn. 38.6
Hymn. 42.11
Hymn. 52.3
Hymn. 54.4
Hymn. 54.7
Hymn. 76.7
Hymn. 77.10
Papyri
  P.Gurôb 1.3
  PGM 4.26
  PGM 4.2889
  PGM 7.862
  PGM 7.872
  PGM 12.95
  PGM 12.307
  PGM 13.230
Pausanias
  2.12.5
  4.1.7
  4.1.9
  4.33.5
  8.9.8
Philostratus
  Her. 28.11
  Her. 52.3
Phlegon
  Olymp. fr. 1.6
Pindar
  fr. 131a
  fr. 346b
Plato
  Leg. 870d
Plutarch
  Mor.
  Def. or. 415a

Def. or. 417b
Fac. lun. 942d
Is. et Os. 360f
Is. et Os. 369b
Is. et Os. 382e
Tranq. anim. 477d
Garr. 505f
Vit.

Demetr. 26.4 (900f)
Phoc. 28.2 (754b)
Rom. 11.1 (23d)
Polyaenus
  Strat. 7.5.1
  Strat. 8.4.1
Theon of Smyrna
  Util. math. 14.18 ff.

ὄργια

Achilles Tatius
  Leuc. et Cit. 4.1
Aelian
  NA 9.66
Apollonius Rhodius
  2.907
Aristides Quintilianus
  2.6
  3.21
Callimachus
  Aet. fr. 63
Clement of Alexandria
  Paed. 2.8.73.1
  Paed. 2.10.96.2
  Protr. 1.3.1
  Protr. 2.12.2
  Protr. 2.13.1
  Protr. 2.13.3
  Protr. 2.13.4
  Protr. 2.14.2
  Protr. 2.19.1
  Protr. 2.22.3
  Protr. 2.22.4
  Protr. 2.22.7
  Protr. 7.74.3
  Protr. 12.119.1
Dionysius of Halicarnassus
  Comp. 4 (fr. Euphronius)
Herodian
  1.11.2
  5.5.4
  5.7.2

Hippocrates
  Ep. 27.195
Homeric hymns
  Ap. 389
Iamblichus
  VP 17.74
  VP 17.77
  VP 28.146
  VP 32.228
[Lucian]
  Philop. 10
Maximus of Tyre
  24.5
  26.2
  32.7
Mesomedes
  Hymn. Is. 4
[Oppian]
  Cyn. 4.249
Orphica
  Argon. 31
  Hymn. 6.4
  Hymn. 6.11
  Hymn. 31.5
  Hymn. 52.5
  Hymn. 54.10
  Frag. 350 Bernabé
Philo
  Abr. 122
  Cher. 94
  Det. pot. ins. 143
  Ebr. 146

LIST OF ABBREVIATIONS

Bolkestein, *Charakter der Deisidaimonia* = H. Bolkestein, *Theophrastus' Charakter der Deisidaimonia als religionsgeschichtliche Urkunde*, RGVV 21.2 (1929).

Burkert, *Greek Religion* = W. Burkert, *Greek Religion* (1985) (German original 1977).

Burkert, *Homo Necans* = W. Burkert, *Homo Necans: The Anthropology of Ancient Greek Sacrificial Ritual and Myth* (1983) (German original 1972).

Clinton, *Sacred Officials* = K. Clinton, *The Sacred Officials of the Eleusinian Mysteries*, TAPhS NS, 64.3 (1974).

Clinton, *I.Eleusis* = K. Clinton, *Eleusis. The Inscriptions on Stone: Documents of the Sanctuary of the Two Goddesses and Public Documents of the Deme*, vol. 1 (2005).

*DDD*² = K. van der Toorn, B. Becking, P.W. van der Horst (eds.), *Dictionary of Deities and Demons in the Bible* ²(1999).

Deubner, *Attische Feste* = L. Deubner, *Attische Feste* (1932).

Dieterich, *Kleine Schriften* = A. Dieterich, *Kleine Schriften* (ed. R. Wünsch) (1911).

Farnell, *Cults* = L.R. Farnell, *The Cults of the Greek States*, 4 vols. (1896–1909).

Graf & Johnston, *Ritual Texts* = F. Graf, S.I. Johnston, *Ritual Texts for the Afterlife: Orpheus and the Bacchic Gold Tablets* (2007).

Harrison, *Prolegomena* = J.E. Harrison, *Prolegomena to the Study of Greek Religion* (1903).

Jaccottet, *Choisir Dionysos* = A.F. Jaccottet, *Choisir Dionysos: les associations dionysiaques ou la face cachée du dionysisme*, 2 vols. (2003).

Kaltsas, *NMΓλυπτά* = N. Kaltsas, *Εθνικό Αρχαιολογικό Μουσείο: Τα Γλυπτά* (2001).

LSAM = F. Sokolowski, *Lois sacrées de l'Asie Mineure* (1955).

LSCG = F. Sokolowski, *Lois sacrées des cités grecques* (1969).

LSS = F. Sokolowski, *Lois sacrées des cités grecques. Supplément* (1962).

Lupu, *NGSL* = E. Lupu, *Greek Sacred Law: A Collection of New Documents*, RGRW 152 (2005).

Nilsson, *Feste* = M.P. Nilsson, *Griechische Feste von religiöser Bedeutung mit Ausschluss der attischen* (1906).

*OCD*³ = S. Hornblower, A. Spawforth (eds.), *The Oxford Classical Dictionary* ³(1996).

Orph. frag. … Bernabé = A. Bernabé (ed.), *Poetae Epici Graeci*. II *Orphicorum et Orphicis similium testimonia et fragmenta*, 3 fasc. (2004–2007).

PGM = K. Preisendanz et al. (eds.), *Papyri graecae magicae*, 2 vols. [2](1973–1974).

Rohde, *Psyche* = E. Rohde, *Psyche: Seelenkult und Unsterblichkeits-glaube der Griechen* (1894).

Stengel, *Kultusaltertümer*[3] = P. Stengel, *Die griechischen Kultusaltertümer* [3](1920).

Wächter, *Reinheitsvorschriften* = Th. Wächter, *Reinheitsvorschriften im griechischen Kult*, RGVV 9.1 (1910).

Wilamowitz, *Glaube* = U. von Wilamowitz Moellendorf, *Der Glaube der Hellenen*, 2 vols. (1931–1932).

PART ONE

TEΛETH IN LITERARY SOURCES

CHAPTER ONE

INTRODUCTION

Where it is true for every area of classical philology that, before all else, it is necessary to determine what meaning the Ancients attached to a certain term and what associations such a term evoked in them, this is especially cogent in the study of Greek religion. After all, writings of professional theologians have not come down to us from antiquity; a systematic theology never even existed in Greece, if we discount Orphism and the philosophical schools; consequently, definitions or explanations of religious and sacral terms by contemporaries have hardly survived at all. At times, explanations by scholiasts and lexicographers may be helpful, but more often they are incorrect or based on the usage of a single group of authors. As a result, we are compelled to derive the meaning— and the evolution of the meaning—of religious terms from their use by the ancient authors. The axiom *verba valent usu* is particularly valid in this matter; due to incorrect etymologies, sometimes already pronounced by the Ancients themselves, very significant but historically unsupported theories have arisen about the meaning of certain religious terms.

A study of the attestations of τελετή reveals that the term developed differently from what is usually presented.[1] In general, the following evolution of the meaning is presumed:[2]

τελετή is 1) fulfilment, completion;
2) completion by initiation into the mysteries,
3) the mysteries themselves;
4) ceremony, religious festival.

In other words, the impression is given that the word in its sacral sense originally referred only to the mysteries, and that the meaning was later extended to 'religious festival' in general. To be sure, τελετή often refers to the mysteries. And since these played such an important role in Greek

---

[1] For a comparable study of the word δεισιδαιμονία, see P.J. Koets, *Δεισιδαιμονία: A contribution to the knowledge of the religious terminology in Greek* [sic] (1929).
[2] Cf. the lexica (discussed below).

religiosity, this meaning has been placed in the forefront—wrongly, I believe. For example, Jane Harrison in her article, 'The meaning of the word τελετή' (*Class. Rev.* 1914, 36), states that in τελετή ('becoming perfect') there is nothing to be found but "the world-wide rite of adolescence". In my opinion, she starts from the wrong assumption that τελετή primarily means 'initiation into the mysteries'.

Before examining the use of the term in Greek literature and inscriptions, let us have a look at some of the explanations of the word given by grammarians and lexicographers.

Perhaps Plato, *Phdr.* 249c, already intends to give an etymology of τελετή when he connects it to τέλειος: complete, perfect. In any case, from the use of the word in Plato, the view can easily arise that τελετή was the rite of becoming perfect. This notion also underlies the conception of τέλος as marriage ceremony, which is found, for instance, in Hesychius, s.v. προτέλεια: τέλος γάρ ὁ γάμος ἀπὸ τοῦ εἰς τελειότητα ἄγειν: "For marriage is a *telos*, because it leads to completion."[3] The same explanation appears again in the seventh century AD, in Maximus Confessor. Such a view is, of course, facilitated by the fact that τελετή had become a standard term in the mysteries and in *that* context this explanation was self-evident.[4] Significant though it may be, I believe a meticulous study of the use of the term will make us reject this explanation.

Chrysippus' explanation of τελεταί as the knowledge to which one comes last (see below, p. 39) does not appear to find any support in other sources.

More profound is Plutarch's explanation fr. *De anima*, connecting τελετή with τελευτή (death), and τελεῖσθαι with τελευτᾶν: these terms were intended to express the liberation of the soul from the prison of the body.[5]

---

[3] Marriage is also called τελετή in Menander rhetor, Περὶ ἐπιδεικτικῶν, Spengel, *Rhetores Graeci* III, 404 ff.: τελετὴ γάμου ("marriage ceremony") (405, 406); cf. τελοῦσι τὰ ὄργια τοῦ γάμου ("they perform the marriage rites") (409).

[4] In modern times, apparently independent from these ancient statements: Jane Harrison, *Class. Rev.* (1914) 36; G. Murray, *Four Stages of Greek Religion* (1912) 46: "These initiation ceremonies are called Teletai, 'completions': they mark the great 'rite of transition' from the immature, charming, but half useless thing, which we call boy or girl, to the τέλειος ἀνήρ, the full member of the tribe as fighter or counsellor, or to the τελεία γυνή, the full wife and mother."; V. Magnien, *Les mystères d'Eleusis* (1929) 26 n. 2: "Télété, en grec, signifie 'perfection', c'est à dire 'cérémonie par laquelle on devient parfait.'"

[5] Fr. 178 Sandbach (Stob. 5.1089 H.).

Very sober is the derivation that we first find in Athenaeus 2.12, 40d. Having remarked, with reference to a place in Euripides (fr. 327 N²), that *telos* means 'offering' (τέλος θυσίαν σημαίνει), he says:

> τελετάς τε καλοῦμεν τὰς ἔτι μείζους καὶ μετά τινος μυστικῆς παραδόσε-
> ως ἑορτὰς τῶν εἰς αὐτὰς δαπανημάτων ἕνεκα· τελεῖν γὰρ τὸ δαπανᾶν,
> καὶ πολυτελεῖς οἱ πολλὰ ἀναλίσκοντες καὶ εὐτελεῖς οἱ ὀλίγα.

> And we call *teletai* those festivals that are even bigger and come with a certain mystic tradition, because of the expenses: for *telein* is to make expenses and *polyteleis* are those who spend a lot and *euteleis* those who spend little.

So, according to Athenaeus, a τελετή goes hand in hand with a mystic tradition and the term is connected with τελεῖν, to pay, to make expenses, because such a ceremony entails huge expenses. See also Suidas, s.v.

The Etymologicum Magnum, s.v., gives this same explanation, citing a certain Horus from Thebes. In addition, it gives the explanation by Chrysippus (see above).

The Etymologicum Gudianum says, s.v. τελετή: ἡ θυσία, παρὰ τὸ τελεῖν καὶ μυεῖν, ἤγουν τελεῖσθαι καὶ μυεῖσθαι: "religious festival, after performing or being subjected to a rite or initiation."

In Bachmann's *Anecdota*, p. 383, it is briefly mentioned: τελετή· θυσία.

Hesychius, s.v. τελεταί: ἑορταί, θυσίαι, μυστήρια.

From these examples, it follows that, according to these lexicographers, τελετή, besides festival or religious rite of a simple nature, also indicates the celebration of the mysteries.

In the lexicon of Photius and in Suidas, τελετή is exclusively connected to mysteries: s.v. τελετή: θυσία μυστηριώδης; s.v. μυστήρια: τελεταί.

Suidas gives s.v. λύσιοι τελεταί: αἱ Διονύσου: "the rites of Dionysus."[6] See also Hesychius, s.v. λύσειοι τελεταί: οὕτως ἐλέγοντό τινες τελεταί, ἐπεὶ καὶ Λύσιος ἐλέγετο Διόνυσος: "Some rites are called *luseioi teletai*, since Dionysus is also called Lysios."

Hesychius, s.v. ἀρκτεία (consecration of girl priestesses of Artemis at Brauron), calls this ceremony a τελετή.[7]

To what extent these divergent remarks are correct or incorrect, only a meticulous study of the use of the term in literature and inscribed documents can teach us.

---

[6] Photius also has this explanation.

[7] Cf. Deubner, *Attische Feste*, 207 n. 2, with references to other attestations of ἀρκτεύ-ειν.

CHAPTER TWO

THE USE OF ΤΕΛΕΤΗ UP TO ALEXANDER

The connection of τελετή with the words τελεῖν, τέλος and τελευτή is evident. In the three nouns τέλος, τελετή and τελευτή, we see three *nomina actionis* formed in different ways, but originally with the same meaning: completion, performance. The meanings of the three words have, however, diverged in the course of time. Τελευτή has come to indicate the finishing, the end of an action, while τελετή denotes the act itself. Τέλος is often the same as τελευτή, but in many instances its meaning has developed much further; for example, it is frequently synonymous with τελετή.[1]

In HOMER, we do not find τελετή. Τελεῖν, to perform, is said of various acts, also of ceremonies, e.g. *Il.* 24.660: τάφον τελεῖν ('to perform a burial') *Od.* 4.7: ἐκτελεῖν γάμον ('to perform a marriage ceremony'). For the performance of religious rites, offerings etc. the verb ῥέζειν, ἔρδειν is used much more often. The underlying root, ϝεργ, has also formed the word ὄργια, which has developed in a similar way as τελετή.

At the end of the pseudo-Homeric *Batrachomyomachia*, we read (305):

καὶ πολέμου τελετὴ μονοήμερος ἐξετελέσθη.

And the single-day ceremony of the war was ended.

Τελετή here is the waging of the war, and therefore has a very general meaning. This is the only place, as far as I know, where the word does not refer to a religious rite.[2] Unfortunately, the date of this poem is far from certain.[3] If the poem is itself of a relatively recent date, the parodist

---

[1] For such differentiations of meaning, see M. Bréal, *Essai de sémantique* (1897) 26; for an excellent study of the word τελός, see F.M.J. Waanders, *The History of τέλος and τελέω in Ancient Greek* (1983).

[2] Ludwich's translation "die eintägige Geheimfeier" is untenable. See A. Ludwich, *Die Homerische Batrachomachia* [sic] (1896) 424. Waanders' translation, "the festival of the one-day war", on the other hand, rightly emphasizes the grand scale and solemnity of the conflict and does not require the postulation of a unique non-religious usage of the term; for this reason, I believe it should probably be preferred to Zijderveld's interpretation, FLS. See Waanders (1983) 157 § 154.

[3] According to H. Wolke, *Untersuchungen zur Batrachomyomachia* (1978) 46–70,

possibly used terms derived from an old epic; in any event, it is likely that
such a general meaning stood at the beginning of the development.

In Pindar, we find the term: *Ol.* 3.41. The house of the Emmenids
became famous by favour of the Dioscuri:

> ὅτι πλείσταισι βροτῶν
> ξεινίαις αὐτοὺς ἐποίχονται τραπέζαις,
> εὐσεβεῖ γνώμᾳ φυλάσσοντες μακάρων τελετάς.

> because most of all mortals, they tend to them with hospitable tables and
> maintain with pious mind the rites in honour of the blessed.

This refers to the *theoxenia* that were held at Agrigentum for the Dioscuri.[4] So these belong to the τελεταί.[5]

Ol. 10.53. Having recounted how Heracles founded the Olympic
games, the poet says:

> ταύτα δ᾽ ἐν πρωτογόνῳ τελετᾷ
> παρέσταν μὲν ἄρα Μοῖραι σχεδὸν
> ὅ τ᾽ ἐλέγχων μόνος
> ἀλάθειαν ἐτήτυμον
> Χρόνος.

> And at this first performance, the Moirai were present nearby, and Chronos, who alone tests the genuine truth.

So the term τελετά refers here to the performance of games, contests.
The verb τελεῖν is frequently used in that context, e.g. *Pyth.* 4.165: τοῦτον ἄεθλον ἑκὼν τέλεσον; cf. also Strabo 3.3.7: τελοῦσι … ἀγῶνας;
Athenaeus 13.90 (Nicias, *FHG* IV, 463): ἐπιτελεῖται … ὁ ἀγών; Ditt. *Syll.*[3]
738.5: συντελεῖσθαι τὸν ἀγῶνα; Diod. 3.64.7: ἀγῶνας συντελεῖν.

We should keep in mind that the Olympic games, like almost all public
competitions, are dedicated to the gods.[6] They are religious ceremonies,

---

the poem is certainly later than archaic and most likely dates from the Hellenistic
period. J. Wackernagel, *Sprachliche Untersuchungen zu Homer* (1916) 189, places it in the
Alexandrian era, as does v. Herwerden, *Mnem.* 10 (1882) 163; Ludwich, *Die Homerische
Batrachomachia* (1896) 25, considers the beginning of the fifth century. Cf. also Schmid-
Stählin I, 1, 228 ff.

[4] Cf. Nilsson, *Feste*, 419.
[5] Cf. the scholiast: τελετὰς νῦν τὰς ἑορτάς, οὐ γὰρ τὰ ὄργια.
[6] Cf. Stengel, *Kultusaltertümer*[3] 191 ff.

but since they are open to the general public, they are markedly different from what is later understood by τελετή, e.g. in the Hellenistic era.[7]

Pindar also refers to other religious festivals, also of a general nature, as τελεταί: *Pyth.* 9.97, where he sings about Telesicrates:

πλεῖστα νικάσαντά σε καὶ τελεταῖς
ὡρίαις ἐν Παλλάδος εἶδον.

Very often I also saw you as victor in the yearly festivals of Pallas.

As is well known, the Panathenaea festival included games held in honour of the goddess.[8] These may have been called τελεταί, performances, but it is equally possible that here the poet has the whole festival in mind.

Likewise: *Nem.* 10.34:

ὕπατον δ' ἔσχεν Πίσα
Ἡρακλέος τεθμόν· ἀδεῖαί γε μὲν ἀμβολάδαν
ἐν τελεταῖς δὶς Ἀθηναίων νιν ὀμφαὶ
κώμασαν.

Pisa (ancient name of Olympia) holds the highest decoration, of Heracles, but as a prelude sweet voices of Athenians have celebrated him (Theaeus) twice at their festivals.[9]

In other words, the wrestler Theaeus, to whom the ode is dedicated, has not yet won a victory at Olympia, but, as a prelude to an Olympic victory, he has twice won in the Panathenaea in Athens.

In the fragments of Pindar's *Dithyrambs*, preserved in papyri, we find τελετά/τελεταί several times: frr. 70a.33, 70b.6, 346b.5, 70c.6?. In frr. 70a and 70c, the context is insufficient to shed light on the nature of the rite involved (except that the general context of the Dithyrambs is Dionysian). The other two fragments are more informative.

Fr. 70b,[10] a dithyramb entitled Ἡρακλῆς ἢ Κέρβερος Θηβαίοις, begins with several lines about the new technique of dithyrambs. After a small lacuna, there are the words:

---

[7] The view that all competitions had their origin in funeral games, and symbolized the struggle between life and death, is found, for instance, in W. Brede Kristensen, *Het leven uit den dood* (1926) 238. Even if this were true, I believe that at the Olympic games, at least, this origin is no longer consciously felt. *Ol.* 10.53 is, in my view, no more an example of τελετή in the sense of 'symbolic act' than *Pyth.* 9.97 (where τελεταί is the Panathenaea).

[8] See e.g. Burkert, *Greek Religion*, 232–233.

[9] I follow Donaldson in the explanation of ἀμβολάδαν. Cf. L.R. Farnell, *The Works of Pindar* II (1932) 320.

[10] *P.Oxy.* 1604; see also Farnell, *The Works of Pindar* I, 171; II, 421; S. Lavecchia, *Pindari Dithyramborum Fragmenta* (2000) 30–31, 135–137.

> [.... ε]ἰδότες
> οἵαν Βρομίου̣ [τελε]τάν
> καὶ παρὰ σκᾶ[πτ]ον Διὸς Οὐρανίδαι
> ἐν μεγάροις ἵσταντι.

knowing what a festival of Bromios the children of Uranus hold also by Zeus' sceptre in his palace.

This is followed by a description of the ecstatic ritual, in which a number of Olympian gods take part, accompanied by the sound of cymbals and castanets. The same rites, therefore, that Euripides repeatedly calls τελεταί in the *Bacchae* (see below), rites of an unusually wild character that go against the Greek sense of sobriety and composure.

Fr. 346b,[11] which, according to some scholars, may belong to the same dithyramb,[12] tells how Heracles was the first foreigner to be initiated at Eleusis.

> Ἐλευσίνοθε Φερσεφόναι Ματρί̣ τε χρυσοθρόνωι
> θῆ[κέ τ' ἀστ]οῖσιν τελετάν.

At Eleusis, he (Eumolpus?) set up a festival in the city for Persephone and the Mother with her golden throne.

So here, τελετά presumably refers to the Eleusinian mysteries.

In the fragments of the *Threni*, we find the word in fr. 131a:

> ὄλβιοι δ' ἅπαντες αἴσᾳ λυσιπόνων τελετᾶν.

Blessed are all with the good fortune of rites that deliver from toil.

This undoubtedly refers to the mystery rites of Dionysus.

So the use of τελετή in Pindar's victory odes points towards a rather general meaning: religious rite or ceremony of any nature: Panathenaea, Olympic games, theoxenia. On the other hand, the fragments of the Pindaric *Dithyrambs* and *Threni*, if they indeed belong to Pindar, show that he also used the term for mysteries and Dionysiac rites.

In the tragedians AESCHYLUS and SOPHOCLES, we do not find τελετή used once. We can, of course, by no means infer from this that they avoided the word; it is quite possible that it appeared in one or more of the many lost tragedies.

---

[11] *P.Oxy.* 2622.
[12] See H. Lloyd-Jones, *Maia* 19 (1967) 206–229; M.J.H. van der Weiden, *The Dithyrambs of Pindar* (1991) 98; S. Lavecchia, *ZPE* 110 (1996) 1–26.

This is all the more likely if we consider how τέλος is indeed used in the sacral sense: Aesch. *Supp.* 121 has the chorus of Danaids promise to the gods, in case they are saved:

> θειοῖς δ᾽ ἐναγέα τέλεα πελομένων καλῶς
> ἐπίδρομ᾽, ὁπόθι θάνατος ἀπῇ.

> If things turn out well, sacred thank-offerings will come to the gods, if only death be absent.

and *Supp.* 810:

> τέλεα δέ πως πελόμενά μοι
> λύσιμά τ᾽ ἄχιμα τ᾽ ἔπιδε, πάτερ.

> See to it, father (Zeus), that my offerings are delivering and soothing to me.

In fr. 387 N² ἔφριξ᾽ ἔρως δὲ τοῦδε μυστικοῦ τέλους the word τέλος does appear to refer to mysteries. The verse is cited by the scholiast to Sophocles *Oed. Col.* 1050, as an example for his claim: τέλη δὲ τὰς τελετάς. See below.

In Sophocles, *Trach.* 238, we read about τέλη ἔγκαρπα, fruit offerings that Heracles is about to make to Zeus, while *Ant.* 143 mentions πάγ-χαλκα τέλη, offerings of arms, made by the besiegers of Thebes to Zeus Tropaeus.

In my view, the verb τελεῖν, to offer, dedicate to the god, underlies τέλος in all these cases. It seems unnecessary to me to interpret τέλος as tribute, tax, as von Wilamowitz does at Aesch. *Supp.* 121: ἐναγέα τέλεα: "die heiligen Steuer"[13] and Jebb, Soph. *Ant.* 143: πάγχαλκα τέλη: "tributes of panoplies". In my view, in reading tribute, one uses a metaphor the poet did not intend.

A sacred rite is also referred to as τέλος in a number of other places in Sophocles, but now of a different nature than in the examples cited above.

In Soph. *OC* 1050, the chorus wishes to be present at the certain victory that the Attic troops will win over the Theban abductors of Ismene. This may take place on the beach at Eleusis:

> οὗ πότνιαι σεμνὰ τιθηνοῦνται τέλη
> θνατοῖσιν, ὧν καὶ χρυσέα
> κλὴς ἐπὶ γλώσσᾳ βέβακε προσπόλων Εὐμολπιδᾶν.

---

[13] U. von Wilamowitz, *Aischylos: Interpretationen* (1914) 32.

where the holy goddesses retain the solemn rites for mankind; and of these
rites a golden key has been pressed onto the mouth by the priests from the
house of Eumolpus.

The τέλη that occur here are the παννυχίδες, nocturnal torch processions, in remembrance of Demeter's search for her daughter, Persephone,
cf. Eur. *Ion* 1074, and also Ar. *Ran.* 342, where this festival is called τελετή. So here, τέλος refers to a religious act of a special nature, a part of the
Eleusinian mystery rites, which were only open to the initiates.

The same is the case in Soph. fr. 753 Nauck² (Pearson 837):

> ὡς τρισόλβιοι
> κεῖνοι βροτῶν, οἳ ταῦτα δερχθέντες τέλη
> μόλωσ᾿ ἐς Ἅιδου· τοῖσδε γὰρ μόνοις ἐκεῖ
> ζῆν ἔστι, τοῖς δ᾿ ἄλλοισι πάντ᾿ ἔχειν κακά.

> since thrice blessed are those mortals who go to Hades having beheld these
> rites: for they alone are allowed to be alive there, while others have all kinds
> of misery.

From these examples, it is apparent that τέλος, and therefore, in all
likelihood, also τελετή, could denote various sacred rites for Aeschylus
and Sophocles.

EURIPIDES uses the word in two of his plays: in the *Iph. Taur.* and, several
times, in the *Bacchae*.

In *IT* 959, Orestes recounts to his sister, Iphigenia, what happened
to him on his flight from the Erinyes in Athens, after he had killed his
mother to avenge his father: none of his guest-friends would receive him
because he was hated by the gods. Yet some were ashamed and gave him
a meal at a separate table, though they did not speak to him, and each
had an individual cup.

> κλύω δ᾿ Ἀθηναίοισι τἀμὰ δυστυχῆ
> τελετὴν γενέσθαι κἄτι τὸν νόμον μένειν
> χοῆρες ἄγγος Παλλάδος τιμᾶν λεών.

> And I hear that, for the Athenians, my ill fortune became a sacred rite and
> that the custom remained for Pallas' people to worship the drinking cup.

Every Athenian would immediately have understood that these verses
refer to the drinking contest on the second day of the Anthesteria, the
Choes festival.[14] So τελετή here refers to a festival that is open to all

---

[14] Cf. A. Mommsen, *Feste der Stadt Athen* (1898) 395; Deubner, *Attische Feste*, 98.

citizens, in which, however, there is a deviation from the prevailing custom.[15] It will become apparent below that the term τελετή is used for deviating customs and complex ritual in particular.

In the *Bacchae*, the word occurs several times, and here, as in Pindar, *Dith. Heracles* 5 (see above), it denotes a very special kind of sacred rites: the wild Dionysiac festivals that met such fierce resistance from Pentheus. The passages in question are:

Bacch. 22. Prologue of Dionysus, who mentions the countries he visited:

ἐς τήνδε πρῶτον ἦλθον Ἑλλήνων πόλιν,
τἀκεῖ χορεύσας καὶ καταστήσας ἐμὰς
τελετάς, ἵν᾿ εἴην ἐμφανὴς δαίμων βροτοῖς.

To this city of the Greeks I came first, having held choral dances over there and having established my rites, so that my divinity would be evident to mankind.

The τελεταί here are the ecstatic Bacchic rites; it may be noted that the word here turns into: ever-recurring sacred act, official sacred festival. Incidentally, this was already the case in Pindar, where the Olympic games and Panathenaea are called τελεταί (see above), and this meaning also often occurs in later sources.

Τελετή has this same meaning *Bacch.* 260, where Pentheus says to Tiresias:

εἰ μή σε γῆρας πολιὸν ἐξερρύετο,
καθῆσ᾿ ἂν ἐν βάκχαισι δέσμιος μέσαις,
τελετὰς πονηρὰς εἰσάγων.

If your grey old age did not protect you, you would now be sitting in the dungeon with your bacchantes for introducing depraved rites.

also verse 465, where Pentheus asks Dionysus:

πόθεν δὲ τελετὰς τάσδ᾿ ἄγεις ἐς Ἑλλάδα;

Whence are you bringing these rites to Greece?

---

[15] Stengel, *Kultusaltertümer*³ 239: "Jeder erhielt eine eigene Kanne (χοῦς) die nicht, wie es sonst üblich war, aus einem gemeinsamen Mischkrug gefüllt wurde."

In this context, it should be noted that these turbulent rites, which are presented as being of non-Greek origin,[16] are preferably called τελεταί or ὄργια, or also ὀργιασμοί, rarely ἑορταί.[17]

Bacch. 73 brings forward yet another characteristic of these rites:

ὦ μάκαρ ὅστις εὐδαίμων,
τελετὰς θεῶν εἰδώς,
βιοτὰν ἁγιστεύει,
καὶ θιασεύεται ψυχὰν
ἐν ὄρεσσι βακχεύων
ὁσίοις καθαρμοῖσιν,
τά τε ματρὸς μεγάλας ὄρ-
για Κυβέλας θεμιτεύων,
ἀνὰ θύρσον τε τινάσσων,
κισσῷ τε στεφανωθεὶς
Διόνυσον θεραπεύει.

O blessed is he, who, fortunate and knowing the rites of the gods, lives a pure life and joins the thiasos with his soul, revelling in the mountains in hallowed purifications, and who, complying with the mysteries of the great mother, Cybele, and brandishing the thyrsus and wreathed with ivy, serves Dionysus.

So knowing, i.e. having participated in these rites, entails a pure life.[18] We see how, several lines on, the term καθαρμοί is used, which is to be regarded here as a further specification of the nature of these τελεταί: cleansing rites. This cleansing is apparently also to be understood as moral purification, given the expression βιοτὰν ἁγιστεύειν ('to live a pure life'). The morally uplifting force of the Dionysian ceremonies is clearly revealed in the cited passage in Aristophanes.[19]

---

[16] The notion put forward by some historians of religion, most notably E. Rohde, that, historically, Dionysus was a new arrival in the Greek pantheon has been dispelled by the decipherment of Linear B: Dionysus already appears in Mycenaean texts from Pylos and Chania. Cf. Burkert, *Greek Religion*, 162. For the text from Chania, see E. Hallager et al., New Linear B Tablets from Khania, *Kadmos* 31 (1992) 61–87. FLS.

[17] Diod. 1.22.6 contrasts the Διονυσιακαὶ ἑορταί, phallic processions, with the turbulent ὀργιασμοί.

[18] Cf. Eur. fr. 472.9 N² and especially Ar. *Ran.* 454: Μόνοις γὰρ ἡμῖν ἥλιος | καὶ φέγγος ἱερόν ἐστιν, | ὅσοι μεμυήμεθ᾽ εὐ|σεβῆ τε διήγομεν | τρόπον περὶ τοὺς ξένους | καὶ τοὺς ἰδιώτας. "For we alone, who have been initiated (*memyemetha*) and who have maintained the way of righteousness towards strangers and common men, have sun and sacred daylight."

[19] See previous footnote.

In verse 238 of this play, yet another characteristic of these festivals is pointed out: there they are called εὔιοι τελεταί, cheering festivals of Bacchus.

So we see that Euripides uses τελετή in the sense of: *special rite*, i.e. one that more or less deviates from the norm. He also appears to use τέλος in this sense: in *Med.* 1381, Medea declares:

> γῇ δὲ τῇδε Σισύφου
> σεμνὴν ἑορτὴν καὶ τέλη προσάψομαι
> τὸ λοιπὸν ἀντὶ τοῦδε δυσσεβοῦς φόνου.

And in this land of Sisyphus I shall hereafter establish a solemn festival and rites to atone for this unholy murder.

We happen to know that a very special rite existed in Corinth, reportedly as reconciliation for the death of Medea's children.[20] Corinthian children, in mourning clothes and with shaven heads, sang lamentations for Medea's children on the occasion of a festival of Hera. It seems that Euripides refers to the festival as ἑορτή, to the special rites as τέλη.[21]

And when it is said of Hippolytus that he goes σεμνῶν ἐς ὄψιν καὶ τέλη μυστηρίων, *Hipp.* 25 ("to the viewing and rites of solemn mysteries"), these are the rites of the Eleusinian mysteries, as in Soph. *OC* 1050.

In addition, τέλος in Euripides means 'offering': fr. 327.4 N² (Stob. 5.801 Hense 14):

> ἐγὼ δὲ πολλάκις σοφωτέρους
> πένητας ἄνδρας εἰσορῶ τῶν πλουσίων
> καὶ θεοῖσι μικρὰ χειρὶ θύοντας τέλη
> τῶν βουθυτούντων ὄντας εὐσεβεστέρους

And I often see poor men who are wiser and more pious than the rich, even though they make small offerings of sacrificial animals to the gods.

Athenaeus (2.12, 40d) comments: σημαίνει ὧδε τὸ τέλος τὴν θυσίαν: "*telos* thus means 'offering'."

---

[20] Cf. Philostratus, *Heroic.* 20.24: ὁπόσα οἱ αὐτοὶ (sc. Κορίνθιοι) δρῶσιν ἐπὶ τοῖς τῆς Μηδείας παισίν … θρήνῳ εἴκασται τελεστικῷ τε καὶ ἐνθέῳ.

[21] Cf. Nilsson, *Feste*, 57 ff.; 60: "Vielleicht hatten die Korinthischen Kinder wie die Arrephoren Geheimriten aus zu führen. Eur. Med. 1382 nennt das Fest τέλη; darauf ist weniger Wert zu legen, weil das Wort bei einem Tragiker einfach Opfer bedeuten kann, mehr darauf, dass Philostratos a.a.O. den Threnos τελεστικός τε καὶ ἔνθεος nennt. Mehr als eine Vermutung läszt aber auch diese Stelle nicht zu."

See also fr. 773.51 N², where τέλος refers to the marriage ceremony: ὁρίζεται δὲ τόδε φάος γάμων τέλος ("This light marks out the marriage ceremony").

In ARISTOPHANES, the term τελετή is used in various contexts. In view of our findings, I would like to divide the examples into two groups, where τελετή means respectively:

A. Religious ceremony of a general nature.
B. Religious act or ceremony of a special, symbolic or mysterious nature.

Of course, the line cannot always be drawn sharply and I am aware of the shortcomings of this method, which, however, is not to be avoided if one wishes to capture the living language in a framework.

A. Religious ceremony of a general nature.

Vesp. 875:

> ὦ δέσποτ᾽ ἄναξ, γεῖτον, ἀγυιεῦ, τοὐμοῦ προθύρου προπύλαιε,
> δέξαι τελετὴν καινὴν, ὦναξ, ἣν τῷ πατρὶ καινοτομοῦμεν.

> O master, neighbour, Aguieus, who stands before the gate of my entrance hall, accept this fresh offering, my lord, which we cut fresh for my father.

This is about the offering Bdelycleon makes before the improvised court session begins, in imitation of the real heliaea, which were always preceded by an incense offering and a prayer.[22]

Τελετή also means 'offering' in *Pax* 413, where Trygaeus explains to Hermes why the sun and the moon are bent on betraying Greece to the Persians:

> ἙΡ. ἵνα δὴ τί τοῦτο δρᾶτον; ΤΡ. ὁτιὴ νὴ Δία
> ἡμεῖς μὲν ὑμῖν θύομεν, τούτοισι δὲ
> οἱ βάρβαροι θύουσι. διὰ τοῦτ᾽ εἰκότως
> βούλοιντ᾽ ἂν ὑμᾶς πάντας ἐξολωλέναι
> ἵνα τὰς τελετὰς λάβοιεν αὐτοὶ τῶν θεῶν.

> HERM.: Why would they do that? TRYG.: Because we sacrifice to you, while the Persians sacrifice to them. So of course they would like you all destroyed, so that they themselves could receive the offerings of the gods.

---

[22] Cf. J.H. Lipsius, *Das Attische Recht und Rechtsverfahren* III (1915) 904.

From the context, it is clear that here cult acts that profit the gods are meant; these can only be the offerings, which, incidentally, is also apparent from the preceding θύομεν.[23]

Perhaps even more general is the meaning of τελετή in this comedy, verse 419. When Hermes delivers Eirene to the Greeks, Trygaeus promises to shower him with honours:

καὶ σοὶ τὰ μεγάλ᾿ ἡμεῖς Παναθήναι᾿ ἄξομεν
πάσας τε τὰς ἄλλας τελετὰς τὰς τῶν θεῶν·
Μυστήρι᾿ Ἑρμῇ, Διπολίει᾿, Ἀδώνια.

And we will celebrate the great Panathenaea in your honour and all the other festivals of the gods: Mysteries, Dipolieia, Adonia, all for Hermes.

An instructive source for our research! Aristophanes regards as τελεταί: the Panathenaea (cf. Pind. *Pyth.* 9.97, above), the Eleusinian mysteries (which have to be kept in mind every time μυστήρια are mentioned in Athens without further specification), the Dipolieia[24] and the Adonia.[25] Festivals, therefore, of very different characters, i.e. where the rites in honour of the deity are of varying nature.

The rite of the Panathenaea is of a rational character, the whole population took part in it.[26]

The Eleusinian mysteries are shrouded in respectful secrecy; their meaning was certainly not clear to everyone.

The Dipolieia (or Bouphonia) differentiate themselves by the well-known trial against the axe by which the sacrificial bull had been killed.[27] This ceremony drew attention because of its ritual, which was ancient.

The Adonia were characterized by a display of great joy, followed by deep mourning. Nilsson observes: "Sie sind einer von den vielen Gebräuchen, die die Phasen der Vegetation begleiten und durch magische Mittel einen Einfluss auf sie einzuüben suchen."[28]

---

[23] Cf. also M. Gronewald, *ZPE* 45 (1982) 64–69.

[24] Cf. Deubner, *Attische Feste*, 158 ff.; Van Straten, *Hiera Kala* (1995) 51–52.

[25] Cf. Nilsson, *Feste*, 384; Deubner, *Attische Feste*, 220.

[26] Cf. Stengel, *Kultusaltertümer*³ 223.

[27] Cf. Burkert, *Homo Necans*, 136–143; Deubner, *Attische Feste*, 188 ff.; Stengel, *Kultusaltertümer*³ 249. As is evident from Ar. *Nub.* 984: ἀρχαῖά γε καὶ Διπολιώδη κτλ., this ceremony was already regarded as bizarre, typically old-fashioned, in the fifth century BC. Διπολιώδης is used there in the sense of: old-fashioned.

[28] Nilsson, *loc. cit.* ("These are one of the many customs that accompany the phases of vegetation and attempt to exert influence on them by magic means"); cf. Stengel, *Kultusaltertümer*³ 251.

This is therefore an example of how τελετή may refer to various religious ceremonies at the same time, both the ones indicated under A., and those under B.

In *Ran.* 368, the term τελεταὶ Διονύσου refers to the Dionysia, celebrated yearly in Athens with contests by dramatic poets:

> εὐφημεῖν χρὴ καξίστασθαι τοῖς ἡμετέροισι χοροῖσι …
> (ὃς) τοὺς μισθοὺς τῶν ποιητῶν ῥήτωρ ὢν εἶτ᾽ ἀποτρώγει
> κωμῳδηθεὶς ἐν ταῖς πατρίοις τελεταῖς ταῖς τοῦ Διονύσου.

> Let him be silent and stand aside from our choral dances who as a speaker (in the public assembly) cuts back on the prizes of the poets for being ridiculed at the traditional festivals of Dionysus.

This use of τελεταί for such a generally celebrated festival as the Dionysia, may be compared to its use for the Panathenaea.

Although it is in itself quite possible that the performances of plays were called τελετή (anything executed with a certain degree of ceremony can be called so), I believe that the whole festival is meant here and not just the dramatic performances.

B. Religious ceremony of a special, symbolic or mysterious nature.

In *Nub.* 298, the chorus of Clouds sings:

> Παρθένοι ὀμβροφόροι,
> ἔλθωμεν λιπαρὰν χθόνα Παλλάδος, εὔανδρον γᾶν
> Κέκροπος ὀψόμεναι πολυήρατον,
> οὗ σέβας ἀρρήτων ἱερῶν, ἵνα
> μυστοδόκος δόμος
> ἐν τελεταῖς ἁγίαις ἀναδείκνυται.

> Rain-bringing virgins, let us go to the splendid land of Pallas, raising good men to see the lovely land of Cecrops, where there is respect for secret rites, where the house that receives the initiates is opened at sacred festivals.

The poet is, of course, speaking of the Eleusinian mysteries. He calls them:

1. ἄρρητα ἱερά: secret religious rites.
2. ἅγιαι τελεταί: sacred rites.

Ἱερά and τελεταί are synonyms here: religious rites. The special character of these acts is indicated by the adjectives ἄρρητος and ἅγιος. As it often does, ἅγιος here has the meaning: that which one approaches only with great deference, sacred.[29]

We are also taken into the realm of the Eleusinian mysteries: *Ran.* 340. There the chorus sings:

ἔγειρε· φλογέας λαμπάδας ἐν χερσὶ γὰρ ἥκει τινάσσων
Ἴακχ᾿ ὦ Ἴακχε,
νυκτέρου τελετῆς φωσφόρος ἀστήρ.

Wake up, for he has come brandishing flaming torches in his hands, Iacchus o Iacchus, the light-bringing star of the nocturnal rite.

Τελετή here is the same as τέλος, Soph. *OC* 1050: the nocturnal torch procession, part of the Eleusinian mysteries.

In this same comedy, the expression τελετή also appears in connection with the Orphic doctrine: *Ran.* 1030, where Aeschylus stresses to Dionysus the great value of poets:

σκέψαι γὰρ ἀπ᾿ ἀρχῆς
ὡς ὠφέλιμοι τῶν ποιητῶν οἱ γενναῖοι γεγένηνται.
Ὀρφεὺς μὲν γὰρ τελετάς θ᾿ ἡμῖν κατέδειξε φόνων τ᾿ ἀπέχεσθαι.

See how useful the genuine poets have been for us from the beginning, for Orpheus taught us the rites and abstinence from slaughtered food.

In connection with a remark in Suidas, s.v. Ὀρφεύς: Τελετάς· ὁμοίως δέ φασι καὶ ταύτας Ὀνομακρίτου ("The poems of Onomacritus are also called Teletai"), Abel believes that there was an Orphic poem entitled Τελεταί.[30] Although he does not mention Ar. *Ran.* 1030, one could consider a didactic Orphic poem there too. Kern, however, doubts the existence of such a poem, as did Gruppe before him.[31]

Be this as it may, I do not believe we should think of a written legacy of Orpheus here. At Ar. *Ran.* 1030, τελεταί, in my view, simply refers to the rites which promise a better fate in the afterlife, performed by the Orphic priests.[32] Apart from the question of what these rites consisted of, we may presume that they were always performed in the same way, according to

---

[29] For the meaning of ἅγιος, see E. Williger, *Hagios*, RGVV 19.1 (1922) 72: "Dagegen wird Nub. 302 ff. wo die Weihen ἅγιαι genannt werden die Annahme nahe gelegt, dass bei dem Wort an die in den Mysterien besonders lebendige Scheu gedacht ist." The predicate ἅγιος definitely distinguishes these τελεταί from others.

[30] E. Abel, *Orphica* (1885) 224 ff.

[31] Kern, *Orph. frag.* p. 315; O. Gruppe, *Die griechischen Culte und Mythen* I (1887) 639. Nonetheless, Kern gives three fragments under the heading Τελεταί (frr. 301–303).

[32] Cf. e.g. Plut. *Apophth. Lacon.* 224e (*Orph. frag.* 653 Bernabé; t. 203 Kern). Orpheus is later regarded as the founder and expert of mysteries in general, cf. Diod. 1.23.6.

a set ritual. I believe that here Aristophanes meant to say that the nature
and correct order of these rites were revealed by Orpheus—they were
presumably recorded later. Such descriptions of Orphic rites would have
included the books that Orphic priests, according to Plato,[33] adduce in
multitude and according to which they sacrifice. It is quite possible that
these books were called Τελεταί.

It is to be expected that, in the case of somewhat complicated ceremonies, the course of the rites was recorded. In the mysteries of Andania, for example, use was made of written regulations.[34] Especially when
magic is involved, as was the case in at least part of the rites of Orphic
beggar priests, in which success depends entirely on the accuracy with
which the rites are performed, it must have been necessary to put them
down in writing.

A related type of ritual may be traced in *Vesp.* 119–122, where Xanthias
tells about the heliast illness by which Philocleon was affected. His son,
Bdelycleon, has already tried all sorts of things to cure him:

> μετὰ ταῦτ᾽ ἐκορυβάντιζε. ὁ δ᾽ αὐτῷ τυμπάνῳ
> ᾄξας ἐδίκαζεν εἰς τὸ Καινὸν ἐμπεσών.
> ὅτε δῆτα ταύταις ταῖς τελεταῖς οὐκ ὠφέλει
> διέπλευσεν εἰς Αἴγιναν.

> After that, he took him to the Corybantes, but before long he was back,
> giving judgment at the New Market, tympanon and all. When he clearly
> did not find benefit in these rites, he sailed across to Aegina.

So τελεταί here refers to the rites performed by the Corybantes. We know
that these rites were distinguished by a very impressive and fascinating
character. Apart from the dull sound of the tympana and the ecstatic
dances, the so-called θρόνωσις or θρονισμός was an important element
of this ritual and, as is also apparent from this passage, miraculous
healing power was ascribed to it all, especially in the case of mental
illness.[35]

---

[33] *Resp.* 364e; Dem. *De cor.* 259, where Dem. reproaches Aeschines: τῇ μητρὶ τελούσῃ
τὰς βίβλους ἀνεγίγνωσκες. Wilamowitz, *Glaube* II, 193: "τελεταί gab es, die von Orpheus
stammen sollten, also Anweisungen, sich durch besondere Weihungen zu reinigen und
gegen Unheil zu schützen."
[34] Paus. 4.26.8. Written regulations are apparently also referred to when there is
mention of the νόμος τελετῆς (Aelian, fr. 10); Suidas, s.v. μέγαρον (Adl. I, 344).
[35] For Corybantes, see Preller-Robert, *Gr. Myth.*, 655, and Immisch, in Roscher, *Lex.*
II, 1587 ff.; and for their healing power: Rohde, *Psyche* II, 48 n. 1.

It may not be superfluous to point out that the preceding passage tells how Bdelycleon first attempted to cure his father by rational means: αὐτὸν ἀπέλου καὶ ἐκάθαιρε, which van Leeuwen translates: "aqua frigida et purgatione alvi patrem sanare conatus est." These were tried and tested methods of refreshing someone's head! When that does not help, the son tries the Corybantes, who attempt to cure the patient by certain rites (τελεταί), the meaning of which escapes the layman. One might compare how, nowadays, people who can no longer be helped by the doctor sometimes turn to magnetizers and such, who attempt to cure them from their illnesses through mysterious gestures. Even hypnosis appears to have been practised by the Corybantes. Cf. *Vesp.* 8, with van Leeuwen's commentary.

It is worth noting that, to my knowledge, Aristophanes does not use τέλος in the sacral sense. He does use the verb τελεῖν in this sense, but, in my view, this always refers to a special type of cult act, corresponding to τελετή, meaning B.

See, for example, *Nub.* 258. This is the passage where Strepsiades, who is about to be initiated into philosophy, has been given a wreath on his head. He is afraid he will be sacrificed, but Socrates puts him at ease:

οὔκ, ἀλλὰ πάντας ταῦτα τοὺς τελουμένους
ἡμεῖς ποιοῦμεν.

No (you won't be sacrificed), but we do this to all who are subjected to our initiation rites.

I agree with Dieterich[36] that this scene is a parody on the rites of the Corybantes, the Orphic rites, or the Eleusinian mysteries.

Τελεῖν is here: to celebrate special sacred acts that are always performed in the same way, and in particular those by which someone becomes a member of a community that was hitherto closed to him, in other words: to initiate.

The same is true for τελεῖν in *Ran.* 357. Excluded from the mysteries is, joci causa, ὅστις … μηδὲ Κρατίνου τοῦ ταυροφάγου γλώττης βακχεῖ' ἐτελέσθη: "whoever has not been initiated into the Bacchic rites of bull-eating Cratinus."

From these examples, it is apparent that one construed, with a double accusative: τελεῖν τινα τὰ βακχεῖα (τὰς τελετάς, τὰ ὄργια etc.): to perform certain (initiation) ceremonies on someone, and hence: τελεῖν τινα, which can therefore mean, among other things, 'to initiate someone'.

---

36 Dieterich, *Kleine Schriften*, 119.

HERODOTUS studied the religion of Egypt with great interest. He is inclined to identify numerous Egyptian gods with Greek ones and in certain religious festivals he sees the prototypes of some Greek ones. For example, in 2.171, he speaks about a lake in the vicinity of the kings' graves at Saïs.

> ἐν δὲ τῇ λίμνῃ ταύτῃ τὰ δείκηλα τῶν παθέων αὐτοῦ νυκτὸς ποιεῦσι, τὰ καλέουσι μυστήρια Αἰγύπτιοι. περὶ μέν νυν τούτων εἰδότι μοι ἐπὶ πλέον ὡς ἕκαστα αὐτῶν ἔχει, εὔστομα κείσθω. καὶ τῆς Δήμητρος τελετῆς πέρι, τὴν οἱ Ἕλληνες Θεσμοφόρια καλέουσι, καὶ ταύτης μοι πέρι εὔστομα κείσθω, πλὴν ὅσον αὐτῆς ὁσίη ἐστὶ λέγειν. αἱ Δαναοῦ θυγατέρες ἦσαν αἱ τὴν τελετὴν ταύτην ἐξ Αἰγύπτου ἐξαγαγοῦσαι καὶ διδάξασαι τὰς Πελασγιώτιδας γυναῖκας. μετὰ δὲ ἐξαναστάσης πάσης Πελοποννήσου ὑπὸ Δωριέων ἐξαπώλετο ἡ τελετή, οἱ δὲ ὑπολειφθέντες Πελοποννησίων καὶ οὐκ ἐξαναστάντες Ἀρκάδες διέσῳζον αὐτὴν μοῦνοι.

> On this lake, they reenact his sufferings (i.e. of Osiris) at night; the Egyptians call this Mysteries. While I know more about these things, how everything happens there, I must keep a respectful silence. Let me also keep a respectful silence about the rite of Demeter, which the Greeks call Thesmophoria. It was the daughters of Danaus who brought this rite from Egypt and taught it to the Pelasgian women. But afterwards, when the whole Peloponnese had been depopulated by the Dorians, this rite was lost. Only the Arcadians, who were left behind and were not forced to emigrate, preserved it.

At this festival of Osiris, his fortunes and Isis' search for him will have been portrayed. This reminds Herodotus of Eleusis, and he uses the word μυστήρια. Egyptian religion, however, probably does not know mysteries in the Greek sense: a gradual becoming acquainted with certain acts with symbolic meaning. This Egyptian ceremony was open to all, but undoubtedly had symbolic meaning.[37]

Herodotus calls the Thesmophoria τελεταὶ Δήμητρος, because these, too, have a symbolic meaning, which meanwhile was no longer entirely clear to the Greeks themselves, just as they still present great problems for modern scholarship.[38] They stand out by their striking ritual.[39]

---

[37] Cf. A. Wiedemann, *Herodots zweites Buch* (1890) ad locum; for Herodotus' view on the mysteries, see C. Sourdille, *Hérodote et la religion de l'Égypte* (1910) chap. VII.

[38] Cf. e.g. Harrison, *Prolegomena*, 120 ff.

[39] Cf. H.S. Versnel, *Inconsistencies in Greek and Roman Religion. 2. Transition and Reversal in Myth and Ritual*, SGRR 6.2 (1993) 235–260; Burkert, *Greek Religion*, 242–246; Stengel, *Kultusaltertümer*[3] 231 ff.

In Hdt. 4.79, we read the following about the Scythian king Scylas, who regarded the Greeks with favour:

ἐπείτε δὲ ἔδεέ οἱ κακῶς γενέσθαι, ἐγίνετο ἀπὸ προφάσιος τοιῆσδε. Ἐπεθύμησε Διονύσῳ Βακχείῳ τελεσθῆναι· μέλλοντι δέ οἱ ἐς χεῖρας ἄγεσθαι τὴν τελετὴν ἐγένετο φάσμα μέγιστον. [His splendid palace at Borysthenes is hit by lightning and burns down.] Σκύλης δὲ οὐδὲν τούτου εἴνεκα ἧσσον ἐπετέλεσε τὴν τελετήν.

Since it was inevitable that he would fare ill, this happened for the following reason. He wished to subject himself to the rites of Dionysus. Just as he was about to begin the ceremony, a great portent occurred. Nonetheless, Scylas performed the ceremony.

This is about the wild, ecstatic Bacchic cult (cf. farther down: βακχεύειν), which is repeatedly called τελετή by Euripides. Noteworthy here is the passive τελεσθῆναι beside the active ἐπετέλεσε τελετήν, and also ἐς χεῖρας ἄγεσθαι τὴν τελετήν. This shows that the participants were subjected to rites, but also performed certain rites themselves.

ANDOCIDES, *De mysteriis* (399 BC), relates how the event occurred for which he had been indicted: he was alleged to have participated in the mysteries without being eligible and to have laid down his ἱκετηρία (olive branch bound with wool), an offence punishable by death. For this he was indicted, Andoc. *De myst.* 15 (1.111):

ἐπειδὴ γὰρ ἤλθομεν Ἐλευσινόθεν καὶ ἡ ἔνδειξις ἐγεγένητο, προσῄει ὁ βασιλεὺς περὶ τῶν γεγενημένων Ἐλευσῖνι κατὰ τὴν τελετήν, ὥσπερ ἔθος ἐστίν, οἱ δὲ πρυτάνεις προσάξειν ἔφασαν αὐτὸν πρὸς τὴν βουλήν, ἐπαγγεῖλαί τ᾽ ἐκέλευον ἐμοί τε καὶ Κηφισίῳ παρεῖναι εἰς τὸ Ἐλευσίνιον.

For when we came from Eleusis and the indictment had been issued, the *basileus* went (to the *prytaneis*) to discuss what had happened at Eleusis during the performance (of the mysteries), as is customary; and the *prytaneis* said they would take him to the council and commanded to tell me and Cephisius to be present in the Eleusinium.

So it appears to have been the custom that, after the festival at Eleusis, the *basileus* in charge of supervising the festival made a report of the events to the *prytaneis*.[40]

It will be shown that there is also mention of τελετή μυστηρίων in other orators: performance of the mysteries. When it is entirely clear

---

[40] Cf. A.D.J. Makkink, *Andokides' eerste rede* (1932) 286; A. Mommsen, *Feste der Stadt Athen* (1898) 248.

from the context, as in this passage by Andocides, which 'performance' is meant, the adjunct μυστηρίων is left out.

Likewise, Isocrates, *Panegyricus* 28 (46a), leaves no doubt as to which τελετή is meant.

> Δήμητρος γὰρ ἀφικομένης εἰς τὴν χώραν, ὅτ᾽ ἐπλανήθη τῆς Κόρης ἁρπασθείσης, καὶ πρὸς τοὺς προγόνους ἡμῶν εὐμενῶς διατεθείσης ἐκ τῶν εὐεργεσιῶν, ἃς οὐχ οἷόντ᾽ ἄλλοις ἢ τοῖς μεμυημένοις ἀκούειν, καὶ δούσης δωρεὰς διττάς, ἅπερ μέγισται τυγχάνουσιν οὖσαι· τούς τε καρπούς, οἳ τοῦ μὴ θηριωδῶς ζῆν ἡμᾶς αἴτιοι γεγόνασι, καὶ τὴν τελετήν, ἧς οἱ μετασχόντες περί τε τῆς τοῦ βίου τελευτῆς καὶ τοῦ σύμπαντος αἰῶνος ἡδίους τὰς ἐλπίδας ἔχουσιν.

> When Demeter came to our land, wandering after the rape of Kore, and, well-disposed towards our ancestors because of kindnesses, which none other than the initiates may hear, gave these two gifts that are the greatest: crops, which have enabled us not to live like animals, and the sacred rite, which offers to those who participate in it sweeter hopes, not just for the end of life but for all eternity.

This same rite is called ὄργια in the Homeric Hymn to Demeter. There the goddess says (*Hymn. Dem.* 274):

> ὄργια δ᾽ αὐτὴ ἐγὼν ὑποθήσομαι ὡς ἂν ἔπειτα
> εὐαγέως ἔρδοντες ἐμὸν νόον ἱλάσκοισθε.[41]

> And I myself will teach my mysteries, so that hereafter, by performing them righteously, you may win the favour of my heart.

Just as ἔρδειν and ὄργια refer to ritual acts here, one may likewise speak of τελεῖν and τελετή.

Though Isoc. *Paneg.* 157 (73d), too, could leave no doubt as to which ceremony is meant, the orator has superfluously added μυστηρίων here. This passage talks about the the Athenians' eternal hatred against the Persians:

> Εὐμολπίδαι δὲ καὶ Κήρυκες ἐν τῇ τελετῇ τῶν μυστηρίων διὰ τὸ τούτων μῖσος καὶ τοῖς ἄλλοις βαρβάροις εἴργεσθαι τῶν ἱερῶν ὥσπερ τοῖς ἀνδροφόνοις προαγορεύουσιν.

---

[41] Cf. also 473–476: ἡ δὲ (Δημήτηρ) κιοῦσα θεμιστοπόλοις βασιλεῦσιν δεῖξε ... δρησμοσύνην θ᾽ ἱερῶν, καὶ ἐπέφραδεν ὄργια πᾶσιν.

Because of that same hatred the Eumolpidae and the Kerykes declare in the
performance of the mysteries, that even other foreigners (i.e. non-Greeks)
are barred from the holy festivals, just like murderers.

Μυστήρια and ἱερά are the holy institutions here; τελετή is their performance.

DEMOSTHENES, *Aristog.* 1.11, sketches the subversive behaviour of Aristogiton and his companions, and urges the judges to render a just but
severe judgment and, in doing so, hold in esteem Εὐνομία, who holds
justice dear. In the same measure, they should respect:

> τὴν ἀπαραίτητον καὶ σεμνὴν Δίκην, ἣν ὁ τὰς ἁγιωτάτας ἡμῖν τελετὰς
> καταδείξας Ὀρφεὺς παρὰ τὸν τοῦ Διὸς θρόνον φησὶ καθημένην πάντα
> τὰ τῶν ἀνθρώπων ἐφορᾶν.

> inexorable and solemn Justice, who sits next to the throne of Zeus and
> oversees all the works of men, as Orpheus, the revealer of our most sacred
> mysteries, tells us.

Again, the τελεταί that Orpheus showed (revealed). Cf. Ar. *Ran.* 1030,
above. Moreover, the rites revealed by Orpheus are qualified here as
ἁγιώταται. There are religious rites of various nature, but according to
the author, those of Orpheus are the holiest.

In ps. Demosthenes, *In Neaeram* 104, the word occurs in a context that
can contribute to our understanding of what the Greeks of the fifth and
fourth centuries imagined with this word. A decree of the Athenians is
cited about the inhabitants of Plataea, who are given Athenian citizen-
ship:

> Ἱπποκράτης εἶπεν, Πλαταιέας εἶναι Ἀθηναίους ἀπὸ τῆσδε τῆς ἡμέρας,
> ἐπιτίμους καθάπερ οἱ ἄλλοι Ἀθηναῖοι, καὶ μετεῖναι αὐτοῖς ὧνπερ Ἀθη-
> ναίοις μέτεστι πάντων, καὶ ἱερῶν καὶ ὁσίων, πλὴν εἴ τις ἱερωσύνη ἢ τελε-
> τή ἐστιν ἐκ γένους, μηδὲ τῶν ἐννέα ἀρχόντων, τοῖς δ' ἐκ τούτων.

> Hippocrates proposed that, from this day forth, the Plataeans be Athenians
> with the same civil rights as the other Athenians, and share in everything in
> which the Athenians share, both sacred and profane, unless a priesthood
> or *telete* belongs to a clan; nor may they be one of the nine archons, but
> their descendants may.

An exception is therefore made for priesthood or service, practised by
reason of birth; ἱερωσύνη concerns leading such services as a priest,
τελετή participating in it (as a 'member of the congregation', one might

say). This concerns a clan cult, as Prof. Bolkestein[42] also notes, citing Photius, s.v. ὀργεῶνες: πρῶτοι ὀργίων καὶ τελετῶν συγγενικῶν ("first of hereditary rituals and rites"). We note that τελετή here indicates a religious rite (institutionalized) of an exclusive nature. One may also be reminded that the Eleusinian mysteries, which are repeatedly called τελετή (-ταί), were originally a clan cult.[43] But the characteristic element of such a cult is not its secretive nature, but the fact that participation is limited to the members of the family.

We find the word again later in the same oration, § 113, where it is said that the reputation of free Athenian women will fall to the level of courtesans if they be allowed to bear children to whomever they please and still τελετῶν καὶ ἱερῶν καὶ τιμῶν μετέχειν τῶν ἐν τῇ πόλει ("participate in the rites and religious ceremonies and worship in the city").

How the verb τελεῖν in Demosthenes can have the meaning: to perform a ritual act, is clear from *De corona* 259, where Aeschines is reviled by Demosthenes:

> ἀνὴρ δὲ γενόμενος τῇ μητρὶ τελούσῃ τὰς βίβλους ἀνεγίγνωσκες καὶ τἄλλα συνεσκευωροῦ, τὴν μὲν νύκτα νεβρίζων καὶ κρατηρίζων καὶ καθαίρων τοὺς τελουμένους κἀπομάττων τῷ πηλῷ καὶ τοῖς πιτύροις, καὶ ἀνιστὰς ἀπὸ τοῦ καθαρμοῦ κελεύων λέγειν· ἔφυγον κακόν, εὗρον ἄμεινον.

> And having reached manhood, you used to read the (sacred) books and look after the rest for your mother when she performed the rite. During the night, you distributed fawn-skins, mixed wine, cleansed those who undergo the ritual and wiped them off with clay and bran, and after the purification, you made them stand up and urged them to say: "I have escaped evil, I have found better."

The activities of Aeschines as helper of his mother, the Sabazius priestess, are all τελεταί; those on whom they are performed are called: τελούμε-νοι. That τελεῖν must not be translated here as 'to initiate' has been clearly demonstrated by Prof. Bolkestein[44] with reference to Theophr. *Deis.* § 12: the δεισιδαίμων goes to the Orphic priests every month, τελεσθησόμε-νος ("to have the rites performed on him"). In this same invective against Aeschines, Demosthenes says, 265: ἐδίδασκες γράμματα, ἐγὼ δ᾽ ἐφοί-των· ἐτέλεις, ἐγὼ δ᾽ ἐτελούμην: "You practised the (despised) profession

---

[42] Bolkestein, *Charakter der Deisidaimonia*, 54.
[43] Cf. Stengel, *Kultusaltertümer*³ 170 ff.
[44] Bolkestein, *Charakter der Deisidaimonia*, 50.

of schoolteacher, I went to school. You performed the sacred rites, I had them performed on me (by you and the likes of you)."

The word Ὀρφεοτελεστής must therefore be explained as: 'he who performs the rites handed down by Orpheus'. Likewise, τελεστήρ,[45] τελε-στής:[46] 'he who performs the ceremonies'. The τελεστήριον is the building where the sacred rite takes place.

In PLATO, the word is used numerous times, always in the sense of: *special religious act*, often in a more or less metaphorical sense, to indicate the working of the Platonic Ideas. A classification of the examples does not seem necessary to me.[47]

In *Prot.* 316d, Plato has Protagoras speak of the σοφιστικὴ τέχνη. The practitioners of this art have always been exposed to the envy and animosity of many; for this reason, they have hidden their aspiration behind all sorts of forms:

> (ἐγὼ δὲ … φημὶ) τοὺς δὲ μεταχειριζομένους αὐτὴν … πρόσχημα ποιεῖ-σθαι καὶ προκαλύπτεσθαι, τοὺς μὲν ποίησιν, οἷον Ὅμηρόν τε καὶ Ἡσί-οδον καὶ Σιμωνίδην, τοὺς δὲ αὖ τελετάς τε καὶ χρησμῳδίας, τοὺς ἀμφί τε Ὀρφέα καὶ Μουσαῖον· ἐνίους δέ τινας ᾔσθημαι καὶ γυμναστικήν … μουσικὴν δὲ Ἀγαθοκλῆς τε ὁ ὑμέτερος πρόσχημα ἐποιήσατο.

> I am saying that those who practised it disguised and concealed it, some-times as poetry, like Homer, Hesiod and Simonides, sometimes as rites and prophecies, as did Orpheus and Musaeus and their crowd; and sometimes even, I have noticed, as athletics; and your own Agathocles used the pre-tence of music.

So Protagoras claims here that the Orphics are nothing but Sophists in disguise. In the uncomprehended rites (τελεταί) and the obscure orac-ular responses of the Orphics, a secret meaning was therefore hidden, according to Protagoras: the same that the Sophists pursue: practical use for mankind. We can safely assume that many visited Orphic priests for this reason alone, and not out of a deeply felt religious need, especially since the benefit extends beyond this lifetime.[48] And it is only natural that a Sophist like Protagoras takes this view of Orphic rites (τελεταί),

---

[45] E.g. *IG* IV 757.
[46] E.g. Origen *Cels.* 8.48. Cf. also F. Poland, *Geschichte des griechischen Vereinswesens* (1909) 41.
[47] I list the places chronologically, after E. Zeller, *Grundriss der Geschichte der griechi-schen Philosophie*[12] (1920) 140.
[48] Cf. *Resp.* 364e.

which, after all, would otherwise be deprived of meaning. He therefore
puts them on a par with music and physical training.

In *Euthyd.* 277d, Socrates tells how two Sophists, in whose company
Euthydemus also is, are trying to confuse a curious youth with trick
questions. When Socrates notices the youth is about to lose his senses,
he consoles him with these words:

> ὦ Κλεινία, μὴ θαύμαζε εἴ σοι φαίνονται ἀήθεις οἱ λόγοι, ἴσως γὰρ οὐκ
> αἰσθάνῃ οἷον ποιεῖτον τὼ ξένω περὶ σέ· ποιεῖτον δὲ ταὐτὸν ὅπερ οἱ ἐν
> τῇ τελετῇ τῶν Κορυβάντων, ὅταν τὴν θρόνωσιν ποιῶσιν περὶ τοῦτον ὃν
> ἂν μέλλωσι τελεῖν.

> Don't be confused, Cleinias, if the words seem unusual to you. Perhaps you
> do not realize what the two guests are doing to you: they are doing the same
> as those in the rite of the Corybantes do when they perform the *thronosis*
> (enthronement ceremony) around the person on whom they are about to
> perform the rite.

So the Sophist pedagogues' confusing questions are compared to the
rite (τελετή) to which one is subjected by the Corybantes; it is apparent
from this analogy by Plato that this rite is not understood by the person
subjected to it, that he may even be confused by it, which will refer to the
dull, fascinating sounds of the tympana and cymbals that the Corybantes
produced while dancing around the person involved. They also appear
to have performed armed dances. Dio Chrysostom, *Or.* 12.33, says about
this:

> εἰώθασιν ἐν τῷ καλουμένῳ θρονισμῷ καθίσαντες τοὺς μυουμένους οἱ
> τελοῦντες κύκλῳ περιχορεύειν.[49]

> In the so-called *thronismos* (enthronement ceremony) the ones perform-
> ing the rite always make the initiands sit down, and dance around them in
> a circle.

So here, the religious act indicated by τελετή is one of a special, uncomprehended nature.

As Bolkestein has argued,[50] *Symp.* 202e teaches us that Plato does not
see a fundamental distinction between magic and religion the way we
now do. It is said here that the δαιμόνιον plays a vital role as mediator
between the world of humans and that of the gods:

---

[49] For depiction of this ceremony on an ivory chest in the Sammlung Palagi, see
Roscher, *Lex.* II, 1618, fig. 4.

[50] Bolkestein, *Charakter der Deisidaimonia,* 57 n. 2.

διὰ τούτου καὶ ἡ μαντικὴ πᾶσα χωρεῖ καὶ ἡ τῶν ἱερέων τέχνη τῶν τε
περὶ τὰς θυσίας καὶ τελετὰς καὶ τὰς ἐπῳδὰς καὶ τὴν μαντείαν πᾶσαν
καὶ γοητείαν.

The whole art of divination works through it, as does the trade of the priests
and others who occupy themselves with sacrifices, sacred rites (*teletai*),
incantations, the whole art of divination, and sorcery.

Here τελεταί is used to indicate those religious rites, of which the sense
was no longer, or only partially clear, in contrast to the θυσίαι, the offerings. In current specialized literature, ἐπῳδαί, incantations, are generally ranged under the label magic. I am under the impression that there
is a certain climax in the sequence: θυσίαι, τελεταί, ἐπῳδαί. One might
say that the placement of τελεταί between θυσίαι and ἐπῳδαί here is, in
a certain sense, symbolic for the evolution of the meaning of the word:
in the oldest sources, it is the general indication of a cult act, and often
similar in meaning to θυσία. Later, it is used more and more to indicate uncomprehended religious rites and we shall see that, at least in later
times, it can also mean incantation.

In *Symp.* 215c, Alcibiades compares Socrates to the oboe-player Olym-
pus, who enchants people with his playing, which he has learnt from
Marsyas:

τὰ οὖν ἐκείνου … μόνα κατέχεσθαι ποιεῖ καὶ δηλοῖ τοὺς τῶν θεῶν τε
καὶ τελετῶν δεομένους διὰ τὸ θεῖα εἶναι.

Only his songs make one possessed, and, by being of divine origin, point
out those who need the gods and the sacred rites.

With Rohde,[51] we recognize in these θεῶν τε καὶ τελετῶν δεόμενοι the
same figures that are called κορυβαντιῶντες in 215e. The rites meant
here are therefore those of the Corybantes discussed above.

In *Phaedo* 69c, Socrates has voiced his suspicion that virtues, and also
φρόνησις, are nothing but a καθαρμός, a cleansing of the ἡδοναί and
φόβοι.[52] This expression καθαρμός seems to remind him of certain ritual
customs that bring about purification:

καὶ κινδυνεύουσι καὶ οἱ τὰς τελετὰς ἡμῖν οὗτοι καταστήσαντες οὐ φαῦ-
λοί τινες εἶναι, ἀλλὰ τῷ ὄντι πάλαι αἰνίττεσθαι ὅτι ὃς ἂν ἀμύητος καὶ
ἀτέλεστος εἰς Ἅιδου ἀφίκηται ἐν βορβόρῳ κείσεται, ὁ δὲ κεκαθαρμένος

---

[51] Rohde, *Psyche* II, 48 n. 1.
[52] Protagoras also claims that Orphism and such are nothing but philosophy in a mystic form. Plato, *Prot.* 316d. See also H. Leisegang, Griechische Philosophie als Mysterion,
PhilWoch Aug. 1932 (= *Festschrift Poland*), 245.

τε καὶ τετελεσμένος ἐκεῖσε ἀφικόμενος μετὰ θεῶν οἰκήσει. εἰσὶν γὰρ δή, ὥς φασιν οἱ περὶ τὰς τελετάς, ναρθηκοφόροι μὲν πολλοί, βάκχοι δέ τε παῦροι· οὗτοι δ᾽ εἰσὶν κατὰ τὴν ἐμὴν δόξαν οὐκ ἄλλοι ἢ οἱ πεφιλοσοφη- κότες ὀρθῶς.

And it is likely that those who instituted the *teletai* for us are also no fools, but long ago already wished to indicate truthfully that he who comes to Hades uninitiated and without having had cleansing rites performed on him, will lie in the mud, but that those who arrive there, having submitted to the cleansing rites and other ceremonies, will live with the gods. For, as those concerned with the *teletai* say, "There are many narthex-bearers, but bacchi are few." The latter are, in my opinion, none other than those who have practised philosophy in the right way.

What τελεταί are meant here? I believe that, with the first τελεταί, Plato thinks of all τελεταί (ritual acts) that have a special effect (we saw above that the word tends to evolve in that direction), so also the Eleusinian cult and such. Then he mentions several terms (ἐν βορβόρῳ κείσεται and the cited verse) that point towards Orphism. Be this as it may, it is clear that τελεταί here are cleansing rites.

Resp. 364e. The poets are rebuked because they appear to have had a strange notion of the justice of the gods, who, according to them, give many good people a difficult life, and vice versa. Such poets are also invoked by beggar priests and diviners, who trick us into believing that the gods have given them the power to purge (ἀκεῖσθαι), by means of θυσίαι and ἐπῳδαί, a transgression of ours, or even of our ancestors μεθ᾽ ἡδονῶν τε καὶ ἑορτῶν: in merry festivals. In this context, they cite Hom. *Il.* 9.497: λιστοὶ δέ τε καὶ θεοὶ αὐτοί: "The gods themselves may be moved (by prayer)." Plato continues (364e):

βίβλων δὲ ὅμαδον παρέχονται Μουσαίου καὶ Ὀρφέως, Σελήνης τε καὶ Μουσῶν ἐκγόνων, ὥς φασι, καθ᾽ ἃς θυηπολοῦσιν, πείθοντες οὐ μόνον ἰδιώτας ἀλλὰ καὶ πόλεις, ὡς ἄρα λύσεις τε καὶ καθαρμοὶ ἀδικημάτων διὰ θυσιῶν καὶ παιδιᾶς ἡδονῶν εἰσι μὲν ἔτι ζῶσιν, εἰσὶ δὲ καὶ τελευτή- σασιν, ἃς δὴ τελετὰς καλοῦσιν, αἳ τῶν ἐκεῖ κακῶν ἀπολύουσιν ἡμᾶς, μὴ θύσαντας δὲ δεινὰ περιμένει.

And they arrive with a mass of books by Musaeus and Orpheus, who, they say, descend from Selene and the Muses, and perform offerings according to these books, while they thus convince not only private persons but also states, that there is redemption and cleansing of misdeeds by means of offerings and merry festivals, both for the living and for those who have already died, which they call *teletai*; these deliver us from torments in the afterlife, but if we do not make these offerings, a terrible fate awaits us.

So the θυσίαι and ἡδοναὶ παιδιῶν that purge away transgressions were apparently referred to as τελεταί by the Orphics themselves. They were complex rituals, so complex, in fact, that written instructions were used. The scholiast comments at βίβλων: περὶ ἐπῳδῶν καὶ καταδέσμων καὶ καθαρσίων καὶ μειλιγμάτων ("books about incantations and binding spells and purifications and propitiations"). So this is yet another example of τελετή in the sense of a religious rite of a special, uncomprehended character, aiming at a very particular effect, in this case, to cleanse of transgressions.[53] For such books containing the regulations of the offerings and other ceremonies, see above, p. 20.

The argument about the untenability of this view about the gods continues more or less like this: if the gods can truly be mollified by such means, one could enjoy oneself most if one first gave free rein to one's sinful desires and later, by means of prayers and other rituals, persuaded the gods that one should escape punishment. *Resp.* 366a:

> ἀλλὰ γὰρ ἐν Ἅιδου δίκην δώσομεν ὧν ἂν ἐνθάδε ἀδικήσωμεν, ἢ αὐτοὶ ἢ παῖδες παίδων. ἀλλ᾽, ὦ φίλε, φήσει λογιζόμενος, αἱ τελεταὶ αὖ μέγα δύνανται καὶ οἱ λύσιοι θεοί, ὡς αἱ μέγισται πόλεις λέγουσι καὶ οἱ θεῶν παῖδες ποιηταὶ καὶ προφῆται τῶν θεῶν γενόμενοι, οἳ ταῦτα οὕτως ἔχειν μηνύουσιν.

> But we will suffer punishment in Hades anyway for the wrongs that we have committed here, either we ourselves or our children's children. 'But, dear friend,' he who reasons logically will say, 'the *teletai* on the other hand have much influence, and the gods who bring deliverance (from guilt), as the greatest states say, and also the sons of the gods, who have become poets and prophets of the gods, say that this is so.'

After the preceding passage, it is clear that here Orphic (and similar) cleansing ceremonies are meant by τελεταί. With the words ὡς αἱ μέγισται πόλεις λέγουσι, the author thinks of the Eleusinian mysteries, which enjoyed great fame in Athens and also promised great privileges in the afterlife. The poet-prophets of divine origin are figures like Orpheus, the son of Apollo, and Eumolpus, the son of Poseidon.[54]

In *Phaedrus* 244e, Socrates connects the word μανία to μαντική, and this μανία, madness, is praised as a great blessing, for which we have the gods to thank; this μανία also finds the proper defence in distressful times and in case of illnesses sent by the gods:

---

[53] O. Gruppe, *Die griechischen Culte und Mythen* I (1887) 639 seems to conclude from this place that the books are called τελεταί. But cf. Rohde, *Psyche* I, 112 n. 3.

[54] Cf. Apollodorus, *Bibl.* 3.15.4.

ἀλλὰ μὴν νόσων γε καὶ πόνων τῶν μεγίστων, ἃ δὴ παλαιῶν ἐκ μηνιμά-
των ποθὲν ἔν τισι τῶν γενῶν ἡ μανία ἐγγενομένη καὶ προφητεύσασα, οἷς
ἔδει ἀπαλλαγὴν ηὕρετο, καταφυγοῦσα πρὸς θεῶν εὐχάς τε καὶ λατρεί-
ας, ὅθεν δὴ καθαρμῶν τε καὶ τελετῶν τυχοῦσα ἐξάντη ἐποίησε τὸν ἑαυ-
τῆς ἔχοντα πρός τε τὸν παρόντα καὶ τὸν ἔπειτα χρόνον, λύσιν τῷ ὀρθῶς
μανέντι τε καὶ κατασχομένῳ τῶν παρόντων κακῶν εὑρομένη.

But surely, when from some place or other the greatest diseases and distress
occurred in some of the families, presumably because of some ancient
guilt, this madness, by arising and giving prophesies, delivered those who
needed it, because it sought refuge in prayers and service to the gods, from
whence it drew purifications and other rites (*teletai*), and it made him who
took part in them safe for the present and for the future, delivering him
who is properly mad and possessed from his present misery.

It appears that Socrates here makes allusions to the pollution of a clan,
so common in myth, which must then be expiated, on the instructions
of a seer, as was the case in the house of Laius.[55] But, in historical time,
too, we know of pollutions that must be removed, for example, Thuc. 5.1,
where there is mention of the pollution of the Delians, who had been
consecrated too early, i.e. before they had been cleansed of an old guilt
(παλαιὰ αἰτία). For this reason, they are driven out by the Athenians.
Thuc. 3.104 also mentions a cleansing by the Athenians of Delos, κατὰ
χρησμόν τινα ("in accordance with an oracle"). The measures, carefully
executed at the recommendation of an oracle, are called καθαρμοὶ καὶ
τελεταί. The word τελεταί again implies the solemn, precise character of
such rites and also the designation for a very specific effect.

In his splendid prose poem about what happens to the soul in the
world of Ideas and on earth, Plato, *Phdr.* 249b, says that the soul of
the wise man grows wings, because it, drawn by memory, continuously
yearns for the world of the gods and is therefore regularly in contact with
the world of divine Ideas:

τοῖς δὲ δὴ τοιούτοις ἀνὴρ ὑπομνήμασιν ὀρθῶς χρώμενος, τελέους ἀεὶ
τελετὰς τελούμενος, τέλεος ὄντως μόνος γίγνεται.

Only if someone is able to use such reminders correctly, does he become
truly perfect, by having perfect rites continuously performed on him.

Τελετάς here is the so-called internal object of τελεῖν, and is used so
that the adjective τέλεος may be added: τελέους τελετὰς τελεῖσθαι is a
stronger expression than τελέως τελεῖσθαι. Τελεῖν is here, as so often:

---

[55] Cf. Stallbaum ad locum.

to perform a ritual act on someone; and τελετή is the corresponding nomen actionis: the ritual act, and again one of a special nature and with a special effect: the soul that submits to it grows wings, i.e. is cleansed of the burdening substance and is lifted up. It is clear that Plato, when he speaks thus, has the Eleusinian mysteries in mind, where the 'viewing' (ἐποπτεία) had a powerful effect on the participants. Viewing the Ideas has a powerful effect on the human soul as well and is therefore called τελετή here.

Plato apparently gives his opinion that τελετή means 'becoming perfect' (τελέους τελετὰς τελούμενος τέλεος γίγνεται) but this need not be a reason for us to follow him in this regard.

In the same passage, *Phdr.* 250b, Socrates explains how justice and wisdom here on earth are but weak reflections of the Ideas of these virtues up there. "Then they were splendid in appearance, when the souls, with a blissful host, with Zeus or other gods, rejoiced in this beatific sight (μακαρίαν ὄψιν τε καὶ θέαν) of the Ideas and they underwent the ritual act, which one may rightly call the most beatific of all (καὶ ἐτελοῦντο τῶν τελετῶν ἣν θέμις λέγειν μακαριωτάτην)."

Again, τελετή here is the same as above: the act, consisting of ὄψις and θέα, that causes one to become blessed. So here, μακάριος is 'beatific'; it signals the effect to which τελετή so often refers, as we have seen.

So also at *Phdr.* 253c, where it is argued how ἔρως, desire, induces the growth of soul wings in him who is stricken by love:

προθυμία μὲν οὖν τῶν ὡς ἀληθῶς ἐρώντων καὶ τελετή, ἐάν γε διαπρά-
ξωνται ὃ προθυμοῦνται ᾗ λέγω, καλή τε καὶ εὐδαιμονικὴ ὑπὸ τοῦ δι'
ἔρωτα μανέντος φίλου τῷ φιληθέντι γίγνεται, ἐὰν αἱρεθῇ.

Thus the desire of true lovers and the rite that makes beautiful and happy, at least if they attain what they desire in the way described by me, are created by the love-crazed lover in the loved one when he surrenders.

The emphasis in τελετή on its effect is very strong here, as is indicated by the words καλή τε καὶ εὐδαιμονική.

By songs, so the Athenian recommends in *Leges* 664a–666e, one must ἐπᾴδειν the truth to the citizens; however, the older people get, the less they tend to sing; and yet it is precisely older people, who, after all, surpass others in understanding and the power of persuasion, who could attain the most beneficial results by their singing. For this reason, it is recommended that youths abstain from wine until the age of 18; from the age of 18 to 30, moderate use of wine is permitted (666b):

τετταράκοντα δὲ ἐπιβαίνοντα ἐτῶν ἐν τοῖς ξυσσιτίοις εὐωχηθέντα καλεῖν τούς τε ἄλλους θεοὺς καὶ δὴ καὶ Διόνυσον παρακαλεῖν εἰς τὴν τῶν
πρεσβυτέρων τελετὴν ἅμα καὶ παιδιάν, ἣν τοῖς ἀνθρώποις ἐπίκουρον
τῆς τοῦ γήρως αὐστηρότητος ἐδωρήσατο τὸν οἶνον φάρμακον, ὥστε
ἀνηβᾶν ἡμᾶς.

But when he has reached the age of forty, he should party with his table
companions and not only invoke the other gods, but especially call Dionysus to what is, at the same time, the ceremony and relaxation of older
men. For this reason, he (Dionysus) has given wine to the people, as an
aid against the stiffness of old age, a magic potion that makes us young
again.

Here we have another example of how, in Plato, the term τελετή especially
indicates the effect of the action. Plato may have thought here of the
orgiastic cult of Dionysus, in which the god was invoked to appear
at the festival;[56] possibly also of Orphic rites. The surviving Orphic
hymns frequently end with words like: βαῖνε γεγηθὼς | ἐς τελετὴν ἁγίαν
πολυποίκιλον ὀργιοφάνταις.[57]

In *Leg.* 738c, Plato says that the founder of a state must not make
any changes to the religious institutions that already exist; these may
have evolved in different ways: sometimes παλαιοὶ λόγοι led to their
foundation:

οὐδεὶς ἐπιχειρήσει κινεῖν νοῦν ἔχων ὅσα ἐκ Δελφῶν ἢ Δωδώνης ἢ παρ'
Ἄμμωνος ἤ τινες ἔπεισαν παλαιοὶ λόγοι ὁπῃδή τινας πείσαντες, φασμά-
των γενομένων ἢ ἐπιπνοίας λεχθείσης θεῶν, πείσαντες δὲ θυσίας τελεταῖς συμμείκτους κατεστήσαντο.

No sensible person will attempt to change what the oracles of Delphi,
Dodona and Ammon or some old myths established, persuading people
one way or another, because of apparitions or because of some reported
divine inspiration; these things persuaded them and led to the foundation
of sacrifices, mixed with ritual acts.

The distinction between θυσίαι and τελεταί appears to me to lie in the
uncomprehended and therefore, perhaps, mysterious nature of some rites
that occurred in the offerings. Compare, for example, the Bouphonia in
Athens, which Aristophanes therefore calls τελετή.[58]

Leg. 815c discusses different kinds of dances. Between war dances
and peace dances is a type of dance that belongs to neither category,

---

[56] Cf. Eur. *Bacch.* 583: μόλε νυν ἡμέτερον ἐς θίασον, ὦ Βρόμιε.
[57] *Hymn. Orph.* 6.10–11.
[58] See above, p. 17.

namely that in which people imitate bacchantes, nymphs, Pans, etc. περὶ καθαρμούς τε καὶ τελετάς τινας ἀποτελούντων "while they perform this dance in cleansing and (other) rites." We have already seen this use of τελετή, e.g. in Euripides' *Bacchae*; they are the ecstatic rites of the followers of Dionysus.

Leg. 870d mentions a story ἐν ταῖς τελεταῖς that people guilty of homicide are punished in Hades and those who return again to earth will meet their just end here. Evidently τελεταί here refers to a special religious ceremony teaching the transmigration of the soul.

Leg. 908d is about different kinds of ἀσέβεια. There are atheists who openly profess their godlessness and demonstrate this in their lives but are nevertheless virtuous. This type is the least dangerous. But another type of atheist has the same conviction but hides it carefully; they often enjoy an excellent reputation but are full of guile; this category produces many diviners (μάντεις) and people who practise sorcery, and sometimes also τύραννοι καὶ δημηγόροι καὶ στρατηγοί, καὶ τελεταῖς δὲ ἰδίαις ἐπιβεβουλευκότες κτλ.: "tyrants, demagogues, generals and those who are against special religious customs."[59]

A class, therefore, of people who are intent on gaining influence on their fellow citizens in all kinds of cunning ways. There are swindlers in political affairs, tyrants and demagogues; in military affairs, generals; and in the field of religion, those who are bent on creating special religious circles, in order to bind a number of people to themselves: sectarians.

Recapitulating the use of our term in Plato, it is striking that it is always used to indicate a special religious act. Several times we observe that Plato used it for a rite or ceremony that has a certain *effect*; τελετή also appeared to mean this effect itself.[60]

In HIPPOCRATES, *De morbo sacro* 1.71 (6.360 Littré),[61] the author speaks of certain people who pretend to be able to bring down the moon, eclipse the sun, influence the weather and such miracles. Whether they claim to do these things "by means of rites or by means of some other knowledge or practice" (εἴτε καὶ ἐκ τελετέων εἴτε καὶ ἐξ ἄλλης τινὸς γνώμης καὶ μελέτης), the author certainly thinks they are atheists. After

---

[59] We also find this warning against private cult communities (ἴδια ἱερά) in Arist. *Pol.* 6.4 (1319b).

[60] Plato, *Phdr.* 253c.

[61] J. Jouanna, *Hippocrates* (1999) 412, dates this work to the second half of the fifth century BC.

all, if they can do all these things, they are more powerful than the gods themselves. I would say that the τελεταί here refer to *magic acts*, which is also apparent from what follows: εἰ γὰρ ἄνθρωπος μαγεύων τε καὶ θύων σελήνην τε καθαιρήσει κτλ.: "For if a man will bring down the moon by magic or sacrifice ..."[62]

ARCHYTAS, fr. 1 DK, speaking about harmony, says that a fast movement produces a higher tone, a slow one, a lower tone.

> ἀλλὰ μὰν καὶ τοῖς ῥόμβοις τοῖς ἐν ταῖς τελεταῖς κινουμένοις τὸ αὐτὸ συμβαίνει· ἁσυχᾷ μὲν κινούμενοι βαρὺν ἀφιέντι ἆχον, ἰσχυρῶς δέ ὀξύν.

> The same also happens with the rhomboi that are moved in the ceremonies. When moved gently, they give off a deep sound, but when vigorously, a piercing sound.

The rhombos was used in ceremonies of various nature.[63] The instrument consisted of a little oval plank, swung around on a string. It was used by the Orphics (cf. Clem. Al. *Protr.* 2.17–18), but, in Theoc. *Id.* 2, it was also used by the sorceress who tries to get her absconded lover back by magic rites.

When ARISTOTLE, *Rhet.* 2.24.2 (1401a 15), says: τὰ γὰρ μυστήρια πασῶν τιμιωτάτη τελετή ("for the mysteries are the most respected ceremony of all"), one could take this as an example of how, even in this period, the word still has its more general meaning: 'religious ceremony'.

In *Rhet.* 3.18 (1419a 3), τελετή refers to the worship of Soteira, which was presumably secret, as is apparent from the context.

Conclusion

If we now attempt to form a mental image of the meaning of τελετή before the age of Alexander, it is essentially as follows.

The original, general meaning: performance, without a sacral connotation, appears to be attested only at *Batrachom.* 305.

---

[62] This shows that offerings, too, could be of a magical nature.

[63] For the rhombos, cf. A. Lang, in *Encyclopaedia of Religion and Ethics*, s.v. bull-roarer (esp. ethnological data); R. Pettazoni, *I misteri* (1924). Cf. also Ovid, *Fasti* 2.575; Preisendanz, *PGM* 4.2295. For a depiction of the rhombos, see Daremberg-Saglio, *Dictionnaire* IV, 863.

In Pindar, it is performance of a religious act, in whatever shape or form: e.g. theoxenia (*Ol.* 3.41), also regularly recurring ceremonies for the gods: religious festivals (Panathenaea, Olympic games).

A so-called orgiastic cult act is also called τελετή, as is evident from the dithyrambic fragment from Oxyrhynchus, entitled *Heracles* (fr. 70b).

In the tragedians, we find τέλος for offering and other ritual acts, also for mystery rites (Soph. fr. 753 N²). Possibly there is a slight tendency to use the word τελετή for religious acts of a special nature, i.e. those that are bound by strict regulations and have symbolic meaning. For example, in Euripides, for the Choes festival with its deviating ritual and for the wild Bacchic rituals.

The same is true for Aristophanes. There it is: offering (*Pax* 413, *Vesp.* 875); the Dipolieia, Adonia etc. (*Pax* 419) and also secret ceremonies, like those conducted by Orphics and those of the Eleusinian mysteries (*Nub.* 304, *Vesp.* 121, *Ran.* 1032).

The ritual of mysteries was certainly bound by very specific regulations. They are therefore understandably called τελετή (τελεταί). In the orators, we find the expression τελετὴ τῶν μυστηρίων (Isoc. *Paneg.* 157 (73d)), but in Athens, τελετή can also be used without further specification to refer to the mysteries, i.e. those at Eleusis (Isoc. *Paneg.* 28 (46a)).

In ps. Demosthenes, *Neaer.* 104 (quoting from a decree of the Athenians), τελετή means 'clan cult'.

From the use in Plato, it appears that τελετή, in his time, referred in particular to the sort of rites from which a powerful effect emanates on the person who submits to it (τελεῖται), usually a cleansing effect. For example, the word is often used together with καθαρμός (e.g. *Leg.* 815). He also uses the word for Orphic practices that deliver from guilt, even after death (*Resp.* 366a). These τελεταί are purely magic acts, i.e. such by which the gods are compelled to confer a certain favour. Cf. also Hippoc. *Morb. sacr.* 1.71. Furthermore, he calls the elevating effect of the world of Ideas on the human soul τελέους τελετάς (*Phdr.* 249c).

A place in Archytas (fr. 1 DK) also appears to give τελετή in the sense of magic act. Finally, Aristotle perhaps teaches us that the more general meaning, religious ceremony in the neutral sense, is also still current. (*Rhet.* 2.24.2 (1401a 15)).

CHAPTER THREE

THE USE OF ΤΕΛΕΤΗ AFTER ALEXANDER

In the introduction to the laws of CHARONDAS, handed down by Stobaeus (4.150 Hense), we find a metaphorical use of the term τελετή that clearly shows how the author thinks in particular of the *effect* emanating from it.

For one should, they say, have no contact with disreputable people, but seek good company:

> τελεῖσθαι τε τὴν μεγίστην καὶ τελειοτάτην τελετήν, ἀνδραγαθίαν, μιμου-
> μένους ἐπ' ἀληθείᾳ καὶ κτωμένους τὴν ἀρετήν· οὐδεὶς γὰρ ἀνὴρ τέλειος
> ἄνευ ταύτης.

> and undergo the greatest and most perfect *telete*, righteousness, imitating
> in truth and acquiring goodness; for no man is complete without that.

So ἀνδραγαθία, righteousness, is here imagined as a τελετή, an inspiring force that also turns others into ἀγαθοί. The expression τελεῖσθαι τὴν μεγίστην καὶ τελειοτάτην τελετήν is reminiscent of Plato, *Phdr.* 249c. Other features, too, make it fairly certain that the piece dates from the Hellenistic period.[1]

CHRYSIPPUS, fr. 42 v. Arnim (= Plut. *De Stoic. repugn.* 1035a), gives a classification of philosophy, which, according to him, should be divided into three parts: logic, physics and ethics. He adds:

> τῶν δὲ φυσικῶν ἔσχατος εἶναι ὁ περὶ τῶν θεῶν λόγος (sc. δοκεῖ μοι), διὸ
> καὶ τελετὰς ἠγόρευσαν τὰς τούτου παραδόσεις.

> The utmost of physics is in my opinion the statement about the gods; and
> therefore they proclaimed the *teletai* as the handing down of this.

Here we have a new and noteworthy explanation of the word τελετή, perhaps approximated by the translation 'end doctrine'. One may compare the familiar history of the development of the term metaphysics: τὰ μετὰ τὰ φυσικά, that which is beyond physics.[2] Incidentally, we can infer

---

[1] Cf. Niese in *RE* s.v. Charondas, III, 2182.
[2] Cf. W. Windelband, *Geschichte der abendländischen Philosophie im Altertum*[4] (1923) 174.

from this to what extent the term evoked associations of certain dogmas in this regard. To Chrysippus, the contents of the τελεταί are, as we
see, mythological-philosophical statements about the gods, i.e. nothing
but the familiar Stoic allegorization of popular religion.[3] That τελεταί are
classified as philosophy is not new, as we saw above (Plato *Prot.* 316d),
where it was said that Musaeus and Orpheus and those who occupy
themselves with τελεταί, are, in fact, Sophists. Chrysippus here uses the
term as a full synonym for *doctrine*, a use we will encounter several more
times.

Etymologicum Magnum, s.v. τελετή, quotes this same passage by
Chrysippus, though not verbatim (= fr. 1008 Arnim):

> Χρύσιππος δέ φησι τοὺς περὶ τῶν θείων λόγους εἰκότως καλεῖσθαι
> τελετάς· χρῆναι γὰρ τούτους τελευταίους καὶ ἐπὶ πᾶσι διδάσκεσθαι, τῆς
> ψυχῆς ἐχούσης ἔρμα καὶ κεκρατημένης καὶ πρὸς τοὺς ἀμυήτους σιωπᾶν
> δυναμένης.

> Chrysippus says that statements about the gods are naturally called *tele-
> tai*, for they must be taught last and in addition to all, when the soul has
> a solid basis and is strong and is able to keep silent towards the uniniti-
> ated.

From the last remark about the ἀμύητοι, it is apparent that this Stoic
theology was not intended for everyone. Hence, besides the religious
teachings of philosophers, in other words τελεταί, there was one theology
for statesmen and another for poets.

A contemporary of Chrysippus, Neanthes, appears to have followed the
example of Stesimbrotus[4] in compiling a work entitled Περὶ τελετῶν.
It is clear from the fragments that, like the work of the same name by
Stesimbrotus, it discussed the myths underlying the different cult acts of
mysteries, and possibly also their meaning, their symbolism. Here are
those fragments.

In the Etymologicum Magnum, s.v. Ἰδαῖοι, we find a mythological
explanation of the name Idaean Dactyls (Ἰδαῖοι Δάκτυλοι), citing Stesimbrotus' Περὶ τελετῶν.

---

[3] Cf. E. Zeller, *Grundriss der Geschichte der griechischen Philosophie*[12] (1920) 275.
[4] For Stesimbrotus and Neanthes and other such authors, cf. A. Tresp, *Fragmente der
griechischen Kultschriftsteller* (1914) 15.

The same lexicon, s.v. Βριτόμαρτις,[5] mentions: Νεάνθης ἐν τῷ πρώτῳ Περὶ τελετῶν φησί ... "In the first book of *On Sacred Rites*, Neanthes says ..." This is followed by an explanation of the name Britomartis.

Athenaeus, 9.18, 376a, recounts why the boar is worshipped on Crete, and also refers to Neanthes' Περὶ τελετῶν.[6]

From this same work, Athenaeus, 13.78, 602d, derives the story of the noble deed of a certain Cratinus from Athens.[7] As a boy, this man had apparently volunteered when the καθαρτής Epimenides needed human blood for the ritual cleansing of the city from an ancient pollution.

As is evident from this latest example, this work by Neanthes also discussed the ritual cleansing of cities and peoples, which as we already saw in Plato, *Phd.* 244e, are also called τελεταί.

Whether Aristotle wrote a work called Τελεταί (mentioned Schol. Ap. Rhod. 4.973, p. 511, 21 Keil) must be doubted.[8]

Suidas, s.v. Ἀριγνώτη, also mentions a book of Τελεταὶ Διονύσου.[9] Such writings will have been of similar content to Neanthes' work, like those entitled Περὶ μυστηρίων.[10]

We also have Athenaeus to thank for a passage from the scholar POLE-MON, who lived around 200 BC, where the term τελετή occurs (11.56, 478c = fr. 88 Pr). Discussing all kinds of special dinnerware, Athenaeus turns to the κότυλος, a cup used for ritual acts. According to him, Polemon says in his treatise Περὶ τοῦ Δίου Κῳδίου:

> μετὰ δὲ ταῦτα τὴν τελετὴν ποιεῖ καὶ αἱρεῖ τὰ ἐκ τῆς θαλάμης καὶ νέμει ὅσοι ἄνω τὸ κέρνος περιενηνοχότες.

> After that, he performs the sacred act and takes the objects out of the sacred shrine and distributes them to those who have carried the *kernos* around high.

This kernos is a cup composed of many small cups; according to Polemon it contained no less than seventeen different ingredients, which are

---

[5] *FGrHist* II, 84, fr. 14.

[6] *FGrHist* II, 84, fr. 15.

[7] *FGrHist* II, 84, fr. 16.

[8] Fr. 10 Rose, who, however, reads Ἀριστοκλῆς instead of Ἀριστοτέλης. Cf. A. Tresp, *Fragmente der griechischen Kultschriftsteller* (1914) 173.

[9] See also Harpocration, s.v. νεβρίζων.

[10] Cf. A. Tresp, *Fragmente der griechischen Kultschriftsteller* (1914) 15.

all mentioned by name. We know the κερνοφορία was one of the ceremonies at the lesser mysteries at Agrae.[11] It possibly had symbolic meaning.

Considerable parts of DIONYSIUS SCYTOBRACHION's works about Amazons and Argonauts have survived in Diodorus Siculus.

Diod. 3.55.9 (*FGrHist* I, 32, fr. 7) is extracted from his History of the Amazons. The Mother of the gods made her sons, the Corybantes, live on Samothrace:

ἐξ οὗ δ' εἰσὶ πατρὸς ἐν ἀπορρήτῳ κατὰ τὴν τελετὴν παραδίδοσθαι.

From which father they descended, was supposedly passed down in a secret in the rite (of the Samothracian mysteries).

Diod. 4.43.1 (*FGrHist* I, 32, fr. 14) also comes from the work of Dionysius Scytobrachion, according to Jacoby, but appears to have been slightly edited by Diodorus.[12] When the Argonauts are scourged by a storm and the leaders despair of their rescue, it is said that:

Ὀρφέα, τῆς τελετῆς μόνον τῶν συμπλεόντων μετεσχηκότα, ποιήσασθαι τοῖς Σαμόθραξι τὰς ὑπὲρ τῆς σωτηρίας εὐχάς.

Orpheus, who alone of the men sailing together had participated in the rite, prayed to the Samothracian gods for their safety.

The Samothracian gods are invoked especially in case of danger at sea.[13] The fact that Orpheus here performs the prayers, because he alone had participated in the τελετή of Samothrace, could indicate that prayer formulas, known only to the initiated, existed to ensure the help of these gods. We know little about the Samothracian rites; we do know that a dog was sacrificed to Hecate and the Cabiri, which is certainly indicative of a deviating rite.[14]

---

[11] Cf. Scholion to Plato *Gorg.* 497c: ἐν οἷς πολλὰ μὲν ἐπράττετο αἰσχρά, ἐλέγετο δὲ πρὸς τῶν μυουμένων ταῦτα· ἐκ τυμπάνου ἔφαγον, ἐκ κυμβάλου ἔπιον, ἐκερνοφόρησα, κτλ. For the kernos, see also Harrison, *Prolegomena*, 158 ff., where one also finds a picture of it. According to P. Foucart, *Les mystères d'Eleusis* (1914) 383 the scholiast here confuses Eleusis with the cult of Cybele.

[12] Cf. Jacoby, *FGrHist* I, 515.

[13] Cf. Theophr. *Char.* 25.2.

[14] Cf. Nilsson, *Feste*, 399; a red-figure lekythos, 5th c. BC, from Athens (NM 1695) shows a woman sacrificing a puppy, presumably to Hecate (three torches), see M. Dillon, *Girls and Women in Classical Greek Religion* (2002) 246, 247 fig. 8.1.

In citing other places from Diodorus, we should also be aware at all times that his work is only a compilation of older sources,[15] so that the quotations may be from various periods. Τελετή appears in various nuances in Diodorus.

A. τελετή is a cult act of a special nature.

In 1.22.6–7, we read how Isis instituted phallus worship in the rites for Osiris-Dionysus:

> ἔν τε γὰρ τοῖς ἱεροῖς εἴδωλον αὐτοῦ κατασκευάσασαν τιμᾶν καταδεῖξαι καὶ κατὰ τὰς τελετὰς καὶ τὰς θυσίας τὰς τῷ θεῷ τούτῳ γινομένας ἐντιμότατον ποιῆσαι καὶ πλείστου σεβασμοῦ τυγχάνειν. διὸ καὶ τοὺς Ἕλληνας, ἐξ Αἰγύπτου παρειληφότας τὰ περὶ τοὺς ὀργιασμοὺς καὶ τὰς Διονυσιακὰς ἑορτάς, τιμᾶν τοῦτο τὸ μόριον ἔν τε τοῖς μυστηρίοις καὶ ταῖς τοῦ θεοῦ τούτου τελεταῖς τε καὶ θυσίαις, ὀνομάζοντας αὐτὸ φαλλόν.

> Having prepared an idol of it in the sanctuaries, she introduced its worship and made it the object of the highest honour and reverence in the rites and offerings accorded to that god. And for this reason, the Greeks, too, having received the celebrations of orgies and Dionysiac festivals from Egypt, honour that member in the mysteries and rites and offerings of that god, calling it 'phallus'.

It seems to me that τελετή here should not be regarded as a secret festival. The expression Διονυσιακαὶ ἑορταί appears to be used for the same phenomenon here and the word ἑορτή hardly ever means 'exclusive ceremony': it is the normal word for a public religious festival. It seems quite possible to me that, in using the word τελετή here, the author was thinking of the phallus procession which was held in Athens in honour of Dionysus.[16]

Our term is used in a similar context in 1.88.2, where it its said that not only Egypt, but also many other peoples have held genitals sacred in their religious rites: τὸ αἰδοῖον καθιερωκέναι κατὰ τὰς τελετάς.

Likewise 4.6.4, where we read that Priapus is worshipped, not only at the Διονυσιακαὶ τελεταί, but also at nearly all other τελεταί, and that he is carried along with laughter and pleasantry at the sacrifices. Now Priapus had become well known everywhere in the third century and

---

[15] For Diodorus and his sources, see Schwarz, *RE* V, 669 ff.

[16] Cf. Stengel, *Kultusaltertümer*[3] 235 ff.

was often identified with other ithyphallic deities. Such gods were, for example, seen at the Dionysia,[17] Haloa,[18] and Artemis cults.[19]

So the author could have had such ceremonies in mind with τελεταί. Certainly the ithyphallic rites did not cause such a stir as they would today; yet they were presumably felt as deviating from the usual ceremonies and are therefore called τελεταί,[20] possibly also because they were regarded as symbolic acts for fertility.

5.77.3. With reference to the view that some gods were born on Crete, the Cretans say: τὰς δὲ τιμὰς καὶ θυσίας καὶ τὰς περὶ τὰ μυστήρια τελετὰς ἐκ Κρήτης εἰς τοὺς ἄλλους ἀνθρώπους παραδεδόσθαι ("that honours, offerings and mystery rites have been handed down from Crete to the rest of mankind"). Their strongest evidence for this is that the τελετή at Eleusis, like that on Samothrace and in Thrace with the Cicones, tends to be handed down in secret: μυστικῶς παραδίδοσθαι, while in Cnossus, on Crete, it is customary of old to hand down these τελεταί openly to all: φανερῶς τὰς τελετὰς πᾶσι παραδίδοσθαι. What is true of this claim of the Cretans, is immaterial; but it is clear from this example that, at least in this period, the aspect of secrecy is not essential for a τελετή, because, whether it is celebrated in secret (μυστικῶς) or openly (φανερῶς), it is in both cases called τελετή.[21]

B. We can point to several places in Diodorus where τελετή evidently already has the narrower meaning of: secret religious act. But the line cannot always be sharply drawn.

1.20.6. After the apotheosis of Osiris, Isis and Hermes (Thoth) begin to make an offering to him: τούτους δὲ καὶ τελετὰς καταδεῖξαι καὶ πολλὰ μυστικῶς εἰσηγήσασθαι ("they revealed the rites and introduced many things in secret").[22]

---

[17] Cf. Deubner, *Attische Feste*, 135 ff.

[18] Cf. Deubner, *Attische Feste*, 63 ff.; Dillon (2002) 120–124.

[19] Cf. Deubner, *Attische Feste*, 133 n. 2.

[20] For the worship of Priapus, see Wilamowitz, *Glaube*, 232 ff.; H. Herter, *De Priapo*, RGVV 23 (1932) 8 and passim. Cf. also Philostr. *Vita Ap.* 6.20.

[21] Because she translates τελετή as 'mysteries' here, Harrison, *Prolegomena*, 154 arrives at the curious statement: "In Crete … the mysteries … were not mysterious." Due to the same misconception, Farnell, *Cults* III, 130a, says of this place: "the odd statement of Diod. Sic. V, 77 … is self-contradictory."

[22] I doubt whether the verb καταδείκνυμι, which occurs so often in such a context, means 'to institute', as Jan Gonda would have it (*Δείκνυμι: Semantische studie over den*

In 1.23, τελετή appears several times in the story of how Orpheus brought secret rites from Egypt to Greece (Thebes). Twice we see the combination τελετὴ (-ταὶ) καὶ μυστήρια. The word here refers to the indigenous nocturnal festivals of Dionysus at Thebes, which had a very special character, cf. Euripides *Bacchae*. In §6, there is mention of the great reputation that Orpheus later enjoyed with the Greeks ἐπὶ μελῳδίᾳ καὶ τελεταῖς καὶ θεολογίαις ("because of his singing, rites, and theologies"). It is clear that special, secret cult acts are meant here. The θεολογίαι must then be the accompanying instruction and statements given by him, that were themselves also called τελεταί.[23] The same words also appear in the same context in 4.25.3: ἔν τε ταῖς θεολογίαις καὶ ταῖς τελεταῖς καὶ ποιήμασι καὶ μελῳδίαις ("in his theologies, his rites, poems and songs").

Similarly, 1.29.2 and 3, the combination αἱ τελεταὶ καὶ τὰ μυστήρια ("the rites and mysteries") is used of the Eleusinian mysteries.

In 1.96.4, it is said that Orpheus brought the μυστικαὶ τελεταί from Egypt. The addition of the adjective μυστικός does not necessarily imply that here, τελετή is still used in its general meaning, ritual act of any nature, even less because, in §5, τελεταί is used without further specification to indicate the mysteries of Dionysus-Osiris and those of Demeter-Isis. We must, however, keep in mind that Herodotus already began to see the prototype of Greek mysteries[24] in certain Egyptian ceremonies, and we find this notion again in Diodorus and Plutarch. It is most likely, however, that mysteries in the Greek sense did not exist in Egypt.[25] All Egyptian religious acts were, however, performed with meticulous care and there was often a certain underlying dogma, which was also the case in the Greek mysteries. So it should not surprise us that both are repeatedly called τελεταί.

3.63.2 speaks of Dionysus as τὰ μυστήρια καὶ τελετὰς καὶ βακχείας εἰσηγησάμενον ("having introduced his mysteries and rites and bacchanals").

The word occurs again in more or less the same sense in the following five places:

Indo-Germaanschen wortel deik-, 1929, 111). I believe that it is rather 'to reveal', i.e. actually demonstrate. Cf. *Hymn. Dem.* 474 and below, p. 121.

[23] Cf. above, p. 20.

[24] Cf. above, Hdt. 2.171.

[25] Cf. C. Sourdille, *Hérodote et la religion de l'Égypte* (1910) chap. VII.

3.64.7: καταδεῖξαι δὲ καὶ τὰ περὶ τὰς τελετὰς καὶ μεταδοῦναι τῶν μυστηρίων τοῖς εὐσεβέσι τῶν ἀνθρώπων: "He (Dionysus) also taught the celebration of his rites and shared his mysteries with pious men."

3.65.2: τὰς δὲ τελετὰς καὶ τὰ μυστήρια φθορᾶς ἕνεκα τῶν ἀλλοτρίων γυναικῶν καταδεικνύειν: "(Some claimed) he was introducing his rites and mysteries in order to seduce the wives of other men."

3.74.1: καταδεῖξαι δὲ τὰς τελετάς: "He revealed the mysteries."

3.74.2: ἐνεργῆσαι δ' ἐπὶ πλέον καὶ τὰ περὶ τοὺς ὀργιασμούς, καὶ τελετὰς ἃς μὲν μεταθεῖναι πρὸς τὸ κρεῖττον, ἃς δὲ ἐπινόησαι: "He went above and beyond in performing the celebration of orgiastic rites and, with regard to mysteries, he improved some and invented others."

4.25.1: παρῆλθεν εἰς τὰς Ἀθήνας καὶ μετέσχε τῶν ἐν Ἐλευσῖνι μυ-στηρίων, Μουσαίου τοῦ Ὀρφέως υἱοῦ τότε προεστηκότος τῆς τελετῆς: "He went to Athens and participated in the mysteries at Eleusis, while Musaeus, son of Orpheus, was in charge of the rite at that time."

The performance of the mysteries of Samothrace is called τελετή in 5.48.4 (and 5), where it is said that Zeus revealed the rite of the mysteries to his son Iasion.

> τὸν δὲ Δία βουληθέντα καὶ τὸν ἕτερον τῶν υἱῶν τιμῆς τυχεῖν, παρα-δεῖξαι αὐτῷ τὴν τῶν μυστηρίων τελετήν, πάλαι μὲν οὖσαν ἐν τῷ νήσῳ, τότε δέ πως παραδοθεῖσαν, ὧν οὐ θέμις ἀκοῦσαι πλὴν τῶν μεμυημένων. δοκεῖ δ' οὗτος πρῶτος ξένους μυῆσαι καὶ τὴν τελετὴν διὰ τοῦτο ἔνδοξον ποιῆσαι. [5] μετὰ δὲ ταῦτα Κάδμον τὸν Ἀγήνορος κατὰ ζήτησιν τῆς Εὐ-ρώπης ἀφικέσθαι πρὸς αὐτούς, καὶ τῆς τελετῆς μετασχόντα γῆμαι τὴν ἀδελφὴν τοῦ Ἰασίωνος Ἁρμονίαν, οὐ καθάπερ Ἕλληνες μυθολογοῦσι, τὴν Ἄρεος.

> But Zeus wished that the other of his sons (Iasion) would also receive honour and so he revealed to him the rite of the mysteries, which had existed of old on the island but was at that time handed over to him, so to speak; it is not permitted, however, for anyone except the initiated to hear about them. And he appears to have been the first to initiate strangers and thereby make the rite famous. After this, Cadmus, the son of Agenor, arrived there on his quest for Europa and, having participated in the mystery rite, married Harmonia, who was the sister of Iasion and not, as the Greeks tell in their stories, the daughter of Ares.

Cf. also 5.49.5–6:

> καὶ τὰ μὲν κατὰ μέρος τῆς τελετῆς ἐν ἀπορρήτοις τηρούμενα μόνοις παραδίδοται τοῖς μυηθεῖσι· διαβεβόηται δ' ἡ τούτων τῶν θεῶν ἐπιφά-νεια καὶ παράδοξος ἐν τοῖς κινδύνοις βοήθεια τοῖς [6] ἐπικαλεσαμένοις τῶν μυηθέντων. γίνεσθαι δέ φασι καὶ εὐσεβεστέρους καὶ δικαιοτέρους

καὶ κατὰ πᾶν βελτίονας ἑαυτῶν τοὺς τῶν μυστηρίων κοινωνήσαντας. διὸ καὶ τῶν ἀρχαίων ἡρώων τε καὶ ἡμιθέων τοὺς ἐπιφανεστάτους πεφιλοτιμῆσθαι μεταλαβεῖν τῆς τελετῆς.

The particulars of the rite are guarded among the secrets and are transmitted only to the initiated; but the epiphany of these gods is legendary, especially their marvellous rescue of initiates who call upon them when in danger. They also say that those who have shared in their mysteries become both more pious and more righteous and better in every respect. For this reason, the most famous of the ancient heroes and demi-gods were eager to take part in the mystery rite.

8.15.3 tells us that we should worship the gods with great zeal, because:

οὐ μόνον τοὺς εὐσεβεῖς ἐν τῷ ζῆν εὖ ποιοῦσιν, ἀλλὰ καὶ μετὰ τὸν θάνατον· εἰ δὲ καὶ ταῖς τελεταῖς, διαγωγὴν μετ᾽ εὐφημίας ἡδείας εἰς ἅπαντα τὸν αἰῶνα παρασκευάζουσιν.

They are not only beneficial to the pious in life but also after death; and if we believe in the mysteries, they also provide a pleasant life with dignity for all eternity.

In 20.110.1, it is said of Demetrius that he hastened to be initiated and receive the rite at Eleusis: ἔσπευδε μυηθῆναι καὶ καταλαβεῖν τὴν ἐν Ἐλευσῖνι τελετήν.

In various places, the word is used in the same breath as ὄργια. It is difficult to point to a difference in meaning. This is very evident in 3.65.6. Some say that Dionysus taught Charops the acts of the sacred rites: διδάξαι (τὸν Χάροπα) τὰ κατὰ τὰς τελετὰς ὄργια, and that Charops' son, Oeager, received the mysteries that have been handed down in the rites: παραλαβεῖν ... τὰς ἐν τοῖς μυστηρίοις παραδεδομένας τελετάς. The son of this Oeager was Orpheus, of whom it is said that:

μαθόντα παρὰ τοῦ πατρός ... πολλὰ μεταθεῖναι τῶν ἐν τοῖς ὀργίοις· διὸ καὶ τὰς ὑπὸ τοῦ Διονύσου γενομένας τελετὰς Ὀρφικὰς προσαγορευθῆναι.

having learnt (the rites) from his father, he changed many of the things in the mysteries (orgia): therefore the rites (teletai) of Dionysus are called Orphic.

Certainly τελεταί and ὄργια both refer to sacred acts and are both also used as synonyms of μυστήρια to indicate the cult as an institution.

Cf. also 5.75.4. (Διόνυσον) Ὀρφεὺς κατὰ τὰς τελετὰς παρέδωκε διασπώμενον ὑπὸ τῶν Τιτάνων. "In the sacred acts, Orpheus passed down how Dionysus was rent apart by the Titans."

3.62.8. Diodorus is talking about the stories about the dismemberment and restoration of Dionysus:

> σύμφωνα δὲ τούτοις εἶναι τά τε δηλούμενα διὰ τῶν Ὀρφικῶν ποιημά-
> των καὶ τὰ παρεισαγόμενα κατὰ τὰς τελετάς, περὶ ὧν οὐ θέμις τοῖς ἀμυ-
> ήτοις ἱστορεῖν τὰ κατὰ μέρος.

> And in agreement with these (stories) are the things that are revealed in the Orphic poems and introduced in their rites, of which recounting in detail to the uninitiated is not permitted.

C. In a couple of places, the meaning of τελετή leans towards 'magic act'.

5.64.4. Some, including Ephorus, say that the so-called Idaean Dactyls originated from Phrygia; they had reportedly come to Europe with a certain Mygdon, and initially practised τάς τε ἐπῳδὰς καὶ τελετὰς καὶ μυστήρια there as γόητες ('sorcerers'); in particular, they made a big impression on the people around Samothrace. At that time, Orpheus, too, was supposedly their student and brought the τελεταί to Greece for the first time.

Presumably, the τελεταί of Orpheus referred to here are the same as those mentioned by Plato, *Resp.* 364e. This is clearly pointed out by the term ἐπῳδαί: the incantations that accompanied the acts that can cleanse a person, yes even his ancestors, from pollution.

5.64.7. Among these Dactyls was also a Heracles, who is not the same, however, as Alcmene's son. This is demonstrated by the fact that:

> πολλὰς τῶν γυναικῶν ἔτι καὶ νῦν λαμβάνειν ἐπῳδὰς ἀπὸ τούτου τοῦ
> θεοῦ καὶ περιάμματα ποιεῖν, ὡς γεγονότος αὐτοῦ γόητος καὶ τὰ περὶ τὰς
> τελετὰς ἐπιτετηδευκότος· ἃ δὴ πλεῖστον κεχωρίσθαι τῆς Ἡρακλέους
> συνηθείας τοῦ γεγονότος ἐξ Ἀλκμήνης.

> to this day, many women still derive incantations from this god and make amulets of him, since he had become a sorcerer and had invented the things in the (magic) rites. These things are completely foreign to the nature of Heracles the son of Alcmene.

STRABO was rather sceptical of religious customs of a special nature.[26] In 4.4.6, he mentions an island that lies in the Ocean, in front of the estuary of the Liger, where Samnite women live in seclusion, as related by Posidonius. The author describes these women as:

---

[26] Cf. P.J. Koets, Δεισιδαιμονία (1929) 63.

Διονύσῳ κατεχομένας καὶ ἱλασκομένας τὸν θεὸν τοῦτον τελεταῖς τε καὶ ἄλλαις ἱεροποιίαις ἐξηλλαγμέναις.

possessed by Dionysus and appeasing that god with *teletai* and other deviating sacred acts.

Men are not allowed on the island. One of the sacred acts is subsequently described: once a year the women demolish the roof of the temple and rebuild it before sunrise. Every woman must do her share of the work. She who drops her load is rent apart and carried around the temple amid cheers. So here is a custom that shows great similarity to Bacchic rites where animals were rent apart, which were also performed by women. The meaning of τελεταί: deviating, sensational rites, is clearly accentuated here by what follows as a synonym: ἄλλαι ἱεροποιίαι ἐξηλλαγμέναι, other eccentric cult acts. The word ἱεροποιία, as a general, neutral term for sacred acts, here requires the further specification with the adjective ἐξηλλαγμένος, which is unnecessary in the case of τελετή.[27]

10.3.10 the author argues that music is of divine origin:

οἱ μὲν οὖν Ἕλληνες οἱ πλεῖστοι τῷ Διονύσῳ προσέθεσαν καὶ τῷ Ἀπόλλωνι καὶ τῇ Ἑκάτῃ καὶ ταῖς Μούσαις καὶ Δήμητρι, νὴ Δία, τὸ ὀργιαστικὸν πᾶν καὶ τὸ βακχικὸν καὶ τὸ χορικὸν καὶ τὸ περὶ τὰς τελετὰς μυστικόν.

Most Greeks therefore ascribed everything orgiastic, Bacchic or choral, and also the mystic element in the rites, to Dionysus, Apollo, Hecate, the Muses, and especially to Demeter.

So here, τελεταί are sacred acts of the mysteries. The text continues:

Ἴακχόν τε καὶ τὸν Διόνυσον καλοῦσι καὶ τὸν ἀρχηγέτην τῶν μυστηρίων, τῆς Δήμητρος δαίμονα· δενδροφορίαι τε καὶ χορεῖαι καὶ τελεταὶ κοιναὶ τῶν θεῶν εἰσι τούτων.

And both Dionysus and the first leader of the mysteries, who is a daemon of Demeter, are called Iacchus. These gods have in common tree-bearing, dances and rites.

The nature of the τελεταί is defined here by the χορεῖαι, orgiastic dances, that are mentioned in the same breath, and the δενδροφορίαι, rites in honour of Cybele, akin to the phallophoria.[28]

---

[27] In Athens, the ἱεροποιοί were sacred officials, lower than priests, responsible for the performance of various rituals. Cf. Stengel, *Kultusaltertümer*[3] 48.

[28] Cf. F. Cumont, *Les religions orientales dans le paganisme romain* [3](1929) 89.

The nuance 'magic act' is also attested in Strabo. In fr. 18 of book 7, Orpheus is called:

> ἄνδρα γόητα ἀπὸ μουσικῆς ἅμα καὶ μαντικῆς καὶ τῶν περὶ τὰς τελετὰς ὀργιασμῶν ἀγυρτεύοντα τὸ πρῶτον.

> A sorcerer who first begged by means of music and simultaneously by his divination and (exalting) acts in his rites.

In other words, the same performances that Plato, *Resp.* 364e, mentions and that have a magical character, as we have seen. The fact that Orpheus is here called γόης ('sorcerer'), points in the same direction.

Musonius Rufus, the Stoic philosopher, warns (20 end, Hense) that one should avoid luxury in the interior of one's home, because a τρυφητής ('voluptuary'), owing to his inability to endure any inconvenience, cannot perform his duties towards the state, his friends, and the gods. For he who wishes to be in right relation to the gods, must also exert himself from time to time, ὅτι θυσίας ἢ τελετὰς ἤ τινα ἄλλην ὑπηρεσίαν τελέσει τοῖς θεοῖς: "because he has to perform offerings or rites or some other service to the gods." It cannot be said with certainty what the author means here by τελεταί next to θυσίαι. Perhaps participation in religious ceremonies of a special nature?

Dionysius of Halicarnassus, speaking of the origin of the cult of the Mother of the gods in Phrygia, relates that Idaeus, a son of Dardanus, founded ὄργια καὶ τελετάς there (*Ant. Rom.* 1.61.4) that remained in Phrygia until the days of Dionysius himself. So these are the wild, Phrygian rites of Cybele.[29]

Ant. Rom. 1.68.3 gives the following account of the origin of the Samothracian mysteries:

> Χρύσην τὴν Πάλλαντος θυγατέρα γημαμένην Δαρδάνῳ φερνὰς ἐπενέγ-κασθαι δωρεὰς Ἀθηνᾶς τά τε Παλλάδια καὶ τὰ ἱερὰ τῶν Μεγάλων θεῶν διδαχθεῖσαν αὐτῶν τὰς τελετάς.

> Having married Dardanus, Chryse, the daughter of Pallas, brought the Palladia[30] and the sacred acts (*hiera*) of the Great Gods from Athens (to Arcadia) as a dowry, since she had been taught their rites (*teletai*).

---

[29] Cf. Drexler in Roscher, *Lex.* II, 2932.
[30] Holy statues or objects, consecrated to Pallas Athena.

The Arcadians, fleeing from the great deluge, supposedly settled on Samothrace, where their king, Dardanus, founded a sanctuary,

ἀρρήτους τοῖς ἄλλοις ποιοῦντα τὰς ἰδίους αὐτῶν ὀνομασίας, καὶ τὰς τελετὰς αὐτοῖς τὰς καὶ εἰς τόδε χρόνου γινομένας ὑπὸ Σαμοθρᾴκων ἐπιτελεῖν.

Making their personal names secret from the others; and he performed the rites for them that are performed by the Samothracians to this day.

On his departure for Asia Minor, Dardanus left the τελεταί on Samothrace, but took the Palladia with him. So here, τελεταί refers again to the sacred acts in honour of the Μεγάλοι θεοί, which Diod. 5.48.4 also mentioned.

According to *Ant. Rom.* 2.19.2, Roman religion is much more dignified than Greek religion. There are no loud lamentations for Persephone or Dionysus,

οὐδ' ἂν ἴδοι τις παρ' αὐτοῖς, καίτοι διεφθαρμένων ἤδη τῶν ἐθῶν, οὐ θεοφορήσεις, οὐ κορυβαντιασμούς, οὐκ ἀγυρμούς, οὐ βακχείας καὶ τελετὰς ἀπορρήτους, οὐ διαπαννυχισμοὺς ἐν ἱεροῖς ἀνδρῶν σὺν γυναιξίν, οὐκ ἄλλο τῶν παραπλησίων τούτοις τερατευμάτων οὐδέν.

And even though their morals have already been corrupted, one will see among them no being possessed by a god, no Corybantism, no begging by priests, no bacchanals or secret rites, no vigils in temples where men spend the whole night together with women, no other such marvels whatsoever.

The τελεταὶ ἀπόρρητοι are, of course, the secret rites of Greek mystery religions.

In *De compositione verborum* 25, Dionysius wishes to explain the beauty of an oration by Demosthenes.

μυστηρίοις μὲν οὖν ἔοικεν ἤδη ταῦτα, καὶ οὐκ εἰς πολλοὺς οἷά τε ἐστιν ἐκφέρεσθαι, ὥστ' οὐκ ἂν εἴην φορτικός εἰ παρακαλοίην οἷς θέμις ἐστὶν, ἥκειν ἐπὶ τὰς τελετὰς τοῦ λόγου, θύρας δ' ἐπιθέσθαι λέγοιμι ταῖς ἀκοαῖς τοὺς βεβήλους.

So these already seemed like mysteries and they cannot be disclosed to many people, so that I would not offend if I invited the right people to come to the ceremonies of the word and told the audience to shut the doors on the uninitiated.

So eloquence is compared to mysteries. Only authorized persons were allowed access to her τελεταί. A similar image is used by Aristophanes, *Ranae* 357, where there is mention of the Bacchic τελεταί of Cratinus; cf. also *Ran.* 356 γενναίων ὄργια Μουσῶν: "the rites of the noble Muses".

HERACLITUS, the Stoic author of the *Quaestiones Homericae*, who probably lived in the first century AD,[31] is very different kind of author. In his allegorical explanation of Homer, he says in 6.6 that Apollo is the sun:

> ὅτι μὲν τοίνυν ὁ αὐτὸς Ἀπόλλων ἡλίῳ καὶ θεὸς εἷς δυσὶν ὀνόμασι κοσμεῖται, σαφὲς ἡμῖν ἔκ τε τῶν μυστικῶν λόγων, οὓς αἱ ἀπόρρητοι τελεταὶ θεολογοῦσι, καὶ τὸ δημῶδες ἄνω καὶ κάτω θρυλούμενον· ἥλιος Ἀπόλλων, ὁ δέ γε Ἀπόλλων ἥλιος.

> Apollo is the same as the sun and one god is adorned with two names. This is clear to us from the mystic stories that the secret rites tell about the gods and from the popular expression that is repeated over and over again, up and down: "the sun is Apollo, Apollo the sun."

Which secret rites Heraclitus had in mind, cannot be determined.

The multiform figure of Proteus, says Heraclitus, *Quaest. Hom.* 64.4, is a curious story, εἰ μή τις οὐρανίῳ ψυχῇ τὰς ὀλυμπίους Ὁμήρου τελετὰς ἱεροφαντήσειε: "unless someone with a celestial soul should reveal Homer's Olympian *teletai* as a hierophant." So the works of Homer are τελεταί, in this context: stories of profound meaning that a man like Heraclitus reveals to us as a priest (ἱεροφαντεῖν). We saw above, that Chrysippus also called Stoic theology τελεταί, probably referring to the allegorical explanation of myths. Here, those myths themselves are called τελεταί. Here, too, the meaning comes close to 'doctrine'.

In DIO CHRYSOSTOM, there are two places where τελετή is used in a more general sense than elsewhere in his work: *Or.* 31.80 and 36.56.

In *Or.* 31.80, the orator rebukes the Rhodians for their strange policy when honouring recently deceased fellow citizens. On several occasions, the name of an old statue had been removed for this purpose and replaced by the name of the citizen to be honoured. It is inappropriate, argues Dio, that contemporaries receive the same honour as such famous men who are deemed worthy of the highest honours:

> ὧν ἔνιοι καὶ τὰς τελετὰς ἐσχήκασιν ἡρώων.

> some of whom have even received the rites of heroes.

So τελεταὶ ἡρώων are here the sacred acts, the honours for the heroes. Hero cult always occupied a special place in Greek religion. Originally,

---

[31] Cf. Christ-Schmid-Stählin II, 367.

human sacrifices supposedly took place; the special type of sacrifice, ἐναγίζειν, remains.[32]

And *Or.* 36.56, speaking of Zeus, he tells how the primordial marriage (τὸ τελειότατον λέχος) of Zeus and Hera became the origin of all life.

> τοῦτον ὑμνοῦσι παῖδες σοφῶν ἐν ἀρρήτοις τελεταῖς ῞Ηρας καὶ Διὸς εὐδαίμονα γάμον.
>
> In the secret rites, children of wise men sing of this as the blessed marriage of Hera and Zeus.

At what festivals was the marriage of Zeus and Hera celebrated thus? Inter alia at the Daedala,[33] a festival celebrated by the Plataeans on Mount Cithaeron with a very special ritual, but, as far as we know, not secret, i.e. all citizens participated in it. Pausanias (9.3.3) therefore calls it a ἑορτή. The same applies to other Hera festivals in which the ἱερὸς γάμος took place. Is an otherwise unknown festival intended here, or could ἄρρητος mean 'profound' rather than 'secret' here?

In *Or.* 36.33, Dio compares poets to the attendants of the mysteries who stand outside by the doors: τοῖς ἔξω περὶ θύρας ὑπηρέταις τῶν τελετῶν. They decorate the vestibule (of the temple where the mysteries are celebrated) and make ready the altars and the other things outside. 36.34:

> οὐκοῦν, ὡς ἔφην, τούς πλησίον ἀναστρεφομένους τελετῆς τινος πρὸς ταῖς εἰσόδοις εἰκὸς τό γε τοσοῦτον τῶν ἔνδοθεν αἰσθάνεσθαί τινος, ἤτοι ῥήματος ἐκβοηθέντος ἑνὸς μυστικοῦ ἢ πυρὸς ὑπερφανέντος.
>
> Therefore, he said, those who linger by the entrances close to some rite probably experience just as much of what goes on inside, whether it be one mystic word cried aloud or fire appearing from above.

Without a doubt, the Eleusinian mysteries are referred to here, in which a great impression was made on those present by alternating light and darkness.[34]

---

[32] Cf. Stengel, *Kultusaltertümer*[3] 138. On the practice and fiction of human sacrifice in ancient Greece, see F. Schwenn. *Die Menschenopfer bei den Griechen und Römern*, RGVV 15.3 (1915); A. Henrichs, Human Sacrifices in Greek Religion: Three case studies, in: *Le sacrifice dans l'Antiquité* (1981) 195–235; D.D. Hughes, *Human Sacrifice in Ancient Greece* (1991); P. Bonnechere, *Le sacrifice humain en Grèce ancienne*, Kernos Suppl. 3 (1994).

[33] Cf. Nilsson, *Feste*, 50; Farnell, *Cults* I, 185 mentions several places where the ἱερὸς γάμος was celebrated.

[34] Cf. Deubner, *Attische Feste*, 87.

Or. 36.39 mentions a fascinating story recited by the magi in their secret rites: ἕτερος δὲ μῦθος ἐν ἀπορρήτοις τελεταῖς ὑπὸ μάγων ἀνδρῶν ᾄδεται θαυμαζόμενος. According to this Zoroastrian story, Zeus is the first and perfect driver of the perfect chariot.

Or. 12.34 clearly shows how acts performed in the mysteries remain uncomprehended by the layman, while to the priest, each of them has a deliberate purpose. Dio explains that man can never understand the works of nature and those of the deity; for example, someone who attends a mystery festival will not come close to understanding everything, but if he has a human soul (ψυχὴ ἀνθρωπίνη), he will nevertheless suspect that everything happens with a higher purpose and design (μετὰ γνώμης καὶ παρασκευῆς σοφωτέρας). For Dio, the mysteries are a symbol of the greatest mystery of nature, the complete and truly perfect mystery rite: τὴν ὁλόκληρον καὶ τῷ ὄντι τελείαν τελετὴν, into which the whole human race is initiated (μυούμενον). This happens under many wondrous phenomena, viz. those of nature, because immortal gods are performing rites on mortals: θεῶν ἀθανάτων θνητοὺς τελούντων. The κορυφαῖος is the supreme ruler of the universe, who steers the world like a skilful helmsman.

Orphic rites are called τελεταί in *Or.* 4.90; there, Dio discusses the routine of those who engage in τὰς τελετὰς καὶ τὰ καθάρσια (rites and purifications), who claim that they can ward off the wrath of Hecate. Before the καθαρμοί, they conjure up all kinds of motley apparitions, which they claim are sent by the wrathful goddess. It is clear that this refers once again to Orphic cleansing rites. Hecate played an important role in these (Cf. *Hymn. Orph.* 1).

PLUTARCH uses the term τελετή many times. It is, however, not always easy to determine exactly what he means by it. I have tried to classify the examples:

A. Ritual act of a complicated nature, in which, however, secrecy is not required.
B. Solemn performance of the Mysteries.
C. Rites performed by Orphic priests and such.
D. Licentious festival held under the guise of religious rites.

As one will see, the demarcation lines are sometimes hard to define. We can, however, say that, to Plutarch, τελετή is always a special cult act.

A. Ritual act of a complicated nature, in which, however, secrecy is not required.

Non posse 1101e. Indeed, there is always δεισιδαιμονία in the faith of the masses, but on the other hand one finds trust, joy, and the expectation of salvation drawn from religion. For nothing brings more joy than what we accomplish ourselves and what we δρῶμεν αὐτοὶ περὶ τοὺς θεούς, ὀργιάζοντες ἢ χορεύοντες ἢ θυσίαις παρόντες καὶ τελεταῖς ("do ourselves with regard to the gods, performing rituals, dancing or attending sacrifices and rites").

Cf. also 1102c: ἢ καὶ τοὺς δεισιδαίμονας οὐ χαίροντας ἀλλὰ φοβουμένους οἴονται θυσίαις καὶ τελεταῖς ὁμιλεῖν ("So the superstitious, too, supposedly do not attend sacrifices and rites gladly, but out of fear").

In *De Herodoti malignitate* 857d, Plutarch disputes the truth of Herodotus' statement that μυστήρια δὲ καὶ τὰς περὶ Δήμητραν τελετὰς ὑπὸ τῶν Δαναοῦ θυγατέρων ἐξ Αἰγύπτου κομισθῆναι ("the mysteries and rites of Demeter were brought from Egypt by the Danaids"). This probably concerns the Thesmophoria, cf. Hdt. 2.171.

In *Is. et Os.* 361e, the term is again used to indicate Egyptian ceremonies. Isis has created a lasting memory of the adventures of Osiris and herself ταῖς ἁγιωτάταις ἀναμίξασα τελεταῖς εἰκόνας καὶ ὑπονοίας καὶ μιμήματα τῶν τότε παθημάτων ("having incorporated in the holiest rites images, hidden meanings and imitations of their former sufferings").

In *Is. et Os.* 369b, we again find τελετή in the general sense of religious ceremony:

> διὸ καὶ παμπάλαιος αὕτη κάτεισιν ἐκ θεολόγων καὶ νομοθετῶν εἴς τε ποιητὰς καὶ φιλοσόφους δόξα, τὴν ἀρχὴν ἀδέσποτον ἔχουσα, τὴν δὲ πίστιν ἰσχυρὰν καὶ δυσεξάλειπτον, οὐκ ἐν λόγοις μόνον οὐδ᾽ ἐν φήμαις, ἀλλ᾽ ἔν τε τελεταῖς ἔν τε θυσίαις καὶ βαρβάροις καὶ Ἕλλησι πολλαχοῦ περιφερομένη, κτλ.

> Therefore a very old doctrine passes down from theologians and legislators to poets and philosophers, with an authorless origin, but with a strong and unfailing conviction, not just in myths and legends, but also in rituals and offerings, both abroad and in Greece.

In *Artax.* 3 (1012c), the solemn act of the inauguration of the Persian king is called τελετή: Artaxerxes rides to Pasargadae in order to be consecrated by the royal ritual: ὅπως τελεσθείη τὴν βασιλικὴν τελετήν. This ceremony consisted of donning the robe of Cyrus the Elder, consuming fig pulp and resin, and drinking sour milk! So for the greater part, these are once again strange rituals that are no longer understood.

In *Rom.* 11.1 (23d), the elaborate ritual connected to the founding of Rome is compared to a τελετή:

> ὁ δὲ Ῥωμύλος ἐν τῇ Ῥεμωρίᾳ θάψας τὸν Ῥέμον ὁμοῦ καὶ τοὺς τροφεῖς, ᾤκιζε τὴν πόλιν, ἐκ Τυρρηνίας μεταπεμψάμενος ἄνδρας ἱεροῖς τισι θεσμοῖς καὶ γράμμασιν ὑφηγουμένους ἕκαστα καὶ διδάσκοντας ὥσπερ ἐν τελετῇ.

> When Romulus had buried his brother, Remus, on the hill Remoria with his foster-fathers, he started to build his city. He sent for Etruscan men, who directed him in every regard with sacred laws and writings and instructed him, as in a *telete*.

What these Etruscan rituals evidently had in common with *teletai* is that they involved instruction (ὑφηγεῖσθαι καὶ διδάσκειν) in a complex ritual prescribed in sacred texts.

Another very illustrative place is *Thes.* 25 (12a), where it is said of games in honour of Melicertes on the Isthmus:

> ὁ γὰρ ἐπὶ Μελικέρτῃ τεθεὶς αὐτόθι νυκτὸς ἐδρᾶτο, τελετῆς ἔχων μᾶλλον ἢ θέας καὶ πανηγυρισμοῦ τάξιν.

> For the games instituted there in honour of Melicertes were conducted at night, having the form of a religious rite rather than that of a spectacle or public festival.

So the τελετή as a special, deviating ceremony is here contrasted with the normal spectacle at a public festival. It appears that a lamentation was held for the dead hero. Compare also Aelius Aristides, *Or.* 46.40, who speaks of a τελετή καὶ ὀργιασμός for Palaemon (Melicertes).[35]

B. The solemn performance of the Mysteries.

Demetr. 26 (900e): Demetrius wants to be initiated immediately and "receive the whole rite, from the lesser mysteries to the *epoptika*" (τὴν τελετὴν ἅπασαν ἀπὸ τῶν μικρῶν ἄχρι τῶν ἐποπτικῶν παραλαβεῖν). Despite the protests of the daduch, Pythodorus, the situation was resolved as follows. First, the name of the current month was changed to Anthesterion, so that Demetrius could be initiated into the lesser mysteries at Agrae.

---

[35] Cf. Nilsson, *Feste*, 439.

καὶ μετὰ ταῦτα πάλιν ἐξ Ἀνθεστηριῶνος ὁ Μουνυχιὼν γενόμενος Βοη-
δρομιὼν ἐδέξατο τὴν λοιπὴν τελετήν, ἅμα καὶ τὴν ἐποπτείαν τοῦ Δημη-
τρίου προσεπιλαβόντος.

And after that, when Mounychion had changed again from Anthesterion
to Boedromion, he received the rest of the ceremony (*telete*), as Demetrius
at the same time even participated in the *epopteia*.

This passage shows that τελετή could also be used for the entire course
of the Eleusinian mysteries, from the lesser mysteries to the *epopteia*.

Alc. 34 (210). When Decelea was occupied, all splendour was taken
away from the *telete*:

ἀφ᾽ οὗ γὰρ ἐπετειχίσθη Δεκέλεια καὶ τῶν εἰς Ἐλευσῖνα παρόδων ἐκρά-
τουν οἱ πολέμιοι παρόντες, οὐδένα κόσμον εἶχεν ἡ τελετὴ πεμπομένη
κατὰ θάλατταν, ἀλλὰ καὶ θυσίαι καὶ χορεῖαι καὶ πολλὰ τῶν δρωμένων
καθ᾽ ὁδὸν ἱερῶν, ὅταν ἐξελαύνωσι τὸν Ἴακχον, ὑπ᾽ ἀνάγκης ἐξελείπετο.
καλὸν οὖν ἐφαίνετο τῷ Ἀλκιβιάδῃ καὶ πρὸς θεῶν ὁσιότητα καὶ πρὸς
ἀνθρώπων δόξαν ἀποδοῦναι τὸ πάτριον σχῆμα τοῖς ἱεροῖς, παραπέμ-
ψαντα πεζῇ τὴν τελετὴν καὶ δορυφορήσαντα παρὰ τοὺς πολεμίους.

Ever since Decelea had been occupied and the enemy controlled the roads
to Eleusis, the *telete*, being conducted by the sea, had no splendour whatsoever. Even sacrifices and dances and many of the sacred rites (*hiera dromena*) that they used to perform on the way whenever they led out Iacchus,
had of necessity been abandoned. It therefore seemed good to Alcibiades,
both in terms of piety towards the gods and of honour with men, to return
the traditional appearance to the sacred rites (*hiera*), escorting the *telete*
by land and guarding it with his army in the face of the enemy.

It is clear from the context that τελετή here refers to the procession to
Eleusis, also including the θυσίαι etc. that belonged to the ἱερὰ δρώμενα.

Phoc. 28.2 (754b) describes how the presence of a Macedonian garrison disturbed the Eleusinian mysteries:

εἰκάδι γὰρ ἡ φρουρὰ Βοηδρομιῶνος εἰσήχθη μυστηρίων ὄντων, ᾗ τὸν
Ἴακχον ἐξ ἄστεος Ἐλευσινάδε πέμπουσιν, ὥστε τῆς τελετῆς συγχυθεί-
σης ἀναλογίζεσθαι τοὺς πολλοὺς καὶ τὰ πρεσβύτερα τῶν θείων καὶ τὰ
πρόσφατα.

For the garrison was brought in on the twentieth of Boedromion, just at the
time of the mysteries, when they carry Iacchus in procession from the city
to Eleusis. So the *telete* was ruined and many recalled old divine portents
and recent ones.

That *telete* here refers to the whole festival and not just the procession, is
also clear from what follows (28.3):

πάλαι μὲν γὰρ ἐν τοῖς ἀρίστοις εὐτυχήμασι τὰς μυστικὰς ὄψεις καὶ
φωνὰς παραγενέσθαι σὺν ἐκπλήξει καὶ θάμβει τῶν πολεμίων, νῦν δὲ
τοῖς αὐτοῖς ἱεροῖς τὰ δυσχερέστατα πάθη τῆς Ἑλλάδος ἐπισκοπεῖν τοὺς
θεούς, καὶ καθυβρίζεσθαι τὸν ἁγιώτατον τοῦ χρόνου καὶ ἥδιστον αὐτοῖς ἐπώνυμον τῶν μεγίστων κακῶν γενόμενον.

For in the past, during their greatest successes, the mystic scenes and voices
had always gone hand in hand with the terror and amazement of their
enemies; but now, at the very season of their sacred rites (*hiera*), the gods
themselves watched the saddest misfortune of Greece, the holiest of time
being profaned, and their most enjoyable festival being named in the same
breath as the greatest calamity.

De Is. et Os. 360f:

ὅσα τε μυστικοῖς ἱεροῖς περικαλυπτόμενα καὶ τελεταῖς ἄρρητα διασώ-
ζεται καὶ ἀθέατα πρὸς τοὺς πολλούς, ὅμοιον ἔχει λόγον.

Everything that is kept completely covered in mystic rituals, unspoken in
ceremonies (*teletai*), unseen by the masses, has the same reason.

Amat. 761f: ὅθεν ἀγαθὸν μέν, ὦ ἑταῖρε, τῆς ἐν Ἐλευσῖνι τελετῆς μετασχεῖν: "So it is a good thing, my friend, to participate in the rite at Eleusis."

Amat. 765a: Eros leads our souls to the truth, οἷον ἐν τελετῇ παρέστη
μυσταγωγός: "just as a mystagogue assists in the rite."

Quaest. conv. 718d. The viewing (θέα) is the objective of philosophy,
οἷον ἐποπτεία τελετῆς ("just as the viewing of the rite"). In these last two
places, one can detect the direct influence of Plato, who repeatedly uses
a similar image.[36]

See also *De Is. et Os.* 382e:

διὸ καὶ Πλάτων καὶ Ἀριστοτέλης ἐποπτικὸν τοῦτο τὸ μέρος τῆς φιλοσοφίας καλοῦσιν, καθ' ὅσον οἱ τὰ δοξαστὰ καὶ μικτὰ καὶ παντοδαπὰ
ταῦτα παραμειψάμενοι τῷ λόγῳ πρὸς τὸ πρῶτον ἐκεῖνο καὶ ἁπλοῦν καὶ
ἄυλον ἐξάλλονται καὶ θιγόντες ἀληθῶς τῆς περὶ αὐτὸ καθαρᾶς ἀληθείας οἷον ἐν τελετῇ τέλος ἔχειν φιλοσοφίας νομίζουσι.

Therefore Plato and Aristotle also call that part of philosophy *epoptikon*,
because those who pass over the conjectured, the mixed, the manifold
by means of reason and leap up to the archetype, the indivisible, the
immaterial, completely touching the pure truth about it, they believe they
have philosophy in its perfect form, like in a *telete*.

---

[36] E.g. *Phdr.* 249c.

Discussing the Cilician pirates, Plutarch comments on their strange religious customs, *Pomp.* 24.5 (631c):

> ξένας δὲ θυσίας ἔθυον αὐτοὶ τὰς ἐν Ὀλύμπῳ, καὶ τελετάς τινας ἀπορ-ρήτους ἐτέλουν, ὧν ἡ τοῦ Μίθρου καὶ μέχρι δεῦρο διασώζεται καταδει-χθεῖσα πρῶτον ὑπ' ἐκείνων.[37]

> They themselves offered strange sacrifices on Mount Olympus and performed certain secret rites, of which that of Mithras has been preserved to this day, having first been introduced by them.

Evidently, our term here refers to the strange, secret rites of certain foreign cults, including, but not necessarily limited to, mystery cults.

There is a category of lesser gods, δαίμονες, between gods and men. *De def. orac.* 415a explains:

> εἴτε μάγων τῶν περὶ Ζωροάστρην ὁ λόγος οὗτός ἐστιν εἴτε Θρᾴκιος ἀπ' Ὀρφέως εἴτ' Αἰγύπτιος ἢ Φρύγιος, ὡς τεκμαιρόμεθα ταῖς ἑκατέρωθι τελεταῖς ἀναμεμιγμένα πολλὰ θνητὰ καὶ πένθιμα τῶν ὀργιαζομένων καὶ δρωμένων ἱερῶν ὁρῶντες.

> This doctrine may come from the Zoroastrian magi or be Thracian from Orpheus, or Egyptian, or Phrygian, as we judge from the fact that, in each of those countries, of the sacred rites that are celebrated and performed, many rites of death and mourning are mixed in with the religious ceremonies.

In several passages, Plutarch declares that these δαίμονες participate in our τελεταί. E.g. *De def. orac.* 417a: "Let us not believe that our τελεταὶ καὶ ὀργιασμοί are ignored by the gods." A few lines on, we read that there are different levels of excellence among the daemons, of which the traces and signs are preserved in τελεταὶ καὶ μυθολογίαι (417b). *Ibid.* 422c, a certain Cleombrotus talks about 183 worlds that are gathered around a triangle, according to a mysterious prophet whom he once met. Inside this triangle, the πεδίον ἀληθείας was supposed to be situated. There lie the archetypes of all that is and ever will be. Of the τελεταί here on earth, the best are dreams of the ἐποπτεία καὶ τελετή there. Cleombrotus learnt all this from the prophet καθάπερ ἐν τελετῇ καὶ μυήσει: he did not support his words with a shred of evidence. In *De facie lunae* 944d,

---

[37] Mithras worship is also called τελετή by Justin, *Apol.* 1.66 and Eunapius *VS* 93 (7.3.4).

we read that the δαίμονες on the moon ταῖς ἀνωτάτω συμπάρεισι καὶ συνοργιάζουσι τῶν τελετῶν, κτλ. ("are present and participate in the highest of the sacred rites").

De fac. lun. 942c. The stranger had countless interesting meetings and experiences, ἱεροῖς τε γράμμασιν ἐντυγχάνων ἐν τελεταῖς τε πάσαις τελούμενος ("coming across sacred writings and having rites performed on him in all *teletai*"). The expression ἐν τελεταῖς τελεῖσθαι presumably refers here to initiation into mystery cults.

De lib. ed. 10e. Silence is a very good thing in its time. In Plutarch's opinion, they who instituted the μυστηριώδεις τελετάς had the pedagogic aim to teach us to be silent.

The same theme, silence is golden, recurs in Plutarch's treatise on talkativeness, *De garr.* 505f:

> ὅθεν οἶμαι τοῦ μὲν λέγειν ἀνθρώπους τοῦ δὲ σιωπᾶν θεοὺς διδασκάλους ἔχομεν, ἐν τελεταῖς καὶ μυστηρίοις σιωπὴν παραλαμβάνοντες.
>
> Hence I think we have people as teachers for speaking but gods for being silent, since we obtain silence in the celebration of the mysteries.

In *De tranquilitate animi* 477d, life itself is regarded as an initiation into the mysteries of the universe. From birth, man views the sun, the moon and the stars, the rivers and the land.

> ὧν τὸν βίον μύησιν ὄντα καὶ τελετὴν τελειοτάτην εὐθυμίας δεῖ μεστὸν εἶναι καὶ γήθους.
>
> Since life is a perfect *myesis* and *telete* of these things, it should be full of cheerfulness and joy.

Rom. 28.18 (36). Plutarch does not believe that the body of Romulus disappeared at his apotheosis. But he does believe that the ἀρεταὶ καὶ ψυχαί of people first become heroes, then daemons, and finally gods, if:

> τέλεον ὥσπερ ἐν τελετῇ καθαρθῶσι καὶ ὁσιωθῶσιν, ἅπαν ἀποφυγοῦσαι τὸ θνητὸν καὶ παθητικόν.
>
> as in an initiation rite, they complete a cleansing and sanctification, escaping all that pertains to mortality and sensation.

From Plutarch's work *De Daedalis Plataeensibus*, Eusebius made an extract in his *Praep. evang.*, from which fr. 9.1 is derived (Euseb. *Praep. evang.* 3.1). The thrust of Plutarch's argument is that, both with Greeks and with foreigners, ancient science was hidden in myths. One can observe this in particular in Orphic and Egyptian myths:

μάλιστα δὲ οἱ περὶ τὰς τελετὰς ὀργιασμοὶ καὶ τὰ δρώμενα συμβολικῶς
ἐν ταῖς ἱερουργίαις τὴν τῶν παλαιῶν ἐμφαίνει διάνοιαν.

Especially the sacred acts at the *teletai* and symbolic performances at
religious service show the persuasion of the ancients.[38]

I cannot find much difference between the meaning of τελεταί and
ἱερουργίαι, except that the term τελεταί possibly referred to rites, the
meaning of which was known to only a few, whereas ἱερουργίαι were
public and understood by all.

C. Rites performed by Orphic priests and such (e.g. mysteries of Dionysus).

Non posse 1105b. In their fear of the afterlife, some people believe that
certain τελεταὶ καὶ καθαρμοί (rites and purifications) can help them.
Cf. Plato *Resp.* 364e.

De aud. 47a. Someone who starts with philosophy must:

ὥσπερ ἐν τελετῇ ... τοὺς πρώτους καθαρμοὺς καὶ θορύβους ἀνασχό-
μενον, ἐλπίζειν τι γλυκὺ καὶ λαμπρὸν ἐκ τῆς παρούσης ἀδημονίας καὶ
ταραχῆς.

submit to the preliminary purifications and commotions, and hope something sweet and splendid will come from his present distress and confusion, just as in a *telete*.

Cf. Plato *Euthyd.* 277d (the Corybantes).

De def. or. 432c. In their dreams, our souls regain the latent ability to
predict the future:

καὶ περὶ τὰς τελετὰς[39] ἔνιαι, καθαροῦ γιγνομένου τοῦ σώματος, ἤ τινα
κρᾶσιν οἰκείαν πρὸς τοῦτο λαμβάνοντος, ἢ τὸ λογιστικὸν καὶ φροντιστι-
κὸν ἀνίεσθαι καὶ ἀπολύεσθαι τῶν παρόντων ἀλόγῳ καὶ φαντασιαστικῷ
τοῦ μέλλοντος ἐπιστρεφόμεναι.

And some do this at the mysteries, because the body is then pure, or
receives a mixture that is appropriate for it, or because reason and intellect
run free, and free themselves from the present and turn to the irrational
and fantastic of the future.

---

[38] This same notion appears in Plato, *Prot.* 316d.
[39] One manuscript has τελετάς, the others τελευτάς. We believe τελετάς is the better
reading.

Plutarch is probably thinking of the effect of Orphic or Corybantic rites.[40]

It is not entirely clear, exactly which τελεταί are intended in fr. *De anima*[41] (Stob. 5.1089 Hense):

> ὅταν ἐν τῷ τελευτᾶν ἤδη γένηται, τότε δὲ πάσχει πάθος οἷον οἱ τελεταῖς μεγάλαις κατοργιαζόμενοι. διὸ καὶ τὸ ῥῆμα τῷ ῥήματι καὶ τὸ ἔργον τῷ ἔργῳ τοῦ τελευτᾶν καὶ τελεῖσθαι προσέοικε.

> When it (the soul) comes to the point of death, it suffers something like those who participate in the great initiations (*teletai*). Therefore the word *teleutan* also resembles the word *teleisthai* and the act of dying resembles the act of being initiated.

In both cases, fear, fright, and darkness appear, followed by great joy and bliss. The reference to μεγάλαι τελεταί brings Eleusis to mind; and yet the whole atmosphere, the strong emphasis on blissful afterlife, seems to point to the Orphic σῶμα-σῆμα notion (Plato *Crat.* 400). Dieterich also deems it possible that the late Eleusinia, which are little known to us, were intended.[42]

D. Licentious festivals held under the guise of religious rites.

In *Cleom.* 33 (820d), Plutarch uses the term in a distinctly pejorative sense: it is said of Ptolemy IV that he was so loose and voluptuous that in his sober moments he tended to perform *teletai* in his palace:

> ὁ μὲν γὰρ βασιλεὺς αὐτὸς οὕτω διέφθαρτο τὴν ψυχὴν ὑπὸ γυναικῶν καὶ πότων, ὥσθ᾽, ὁπότε νήφοι μάλιστα καὶ σπουδαιότατος αὐτοῦ γένοιτο, τελετὰς τελεῖν καὶ τύμπανον ἔχων ἐν τοῖς βασιλείοις ἀγείρειν.

> For the king himself had so lost his mind to women and drinking that, whenever he was really sober and at his most serious, he used to perform *teletai* and convene them in his palace, tympanon in hand.

Used like this, *teletai* seem to be licentious festivals or orgies held under the guise of religious rites. Cf. Josephus, *Ant. Jud.* 19.1.5.

---

[40] For this divination aspect in the mysteries of Dionysus, see K.H.E. de Jong, *Das antike Mysterienwesen*[2] (1919) 198, 209.

[41] E. Maass, *Orpheus* (1895) 303–305, believes that Themistius, under whose name Stobaeus presents it, is the author; so does A. Dieterich, *Eine Mithrasliturgie* (1905) 163; Wyttenbach's view that it is Plutarch's, is, however, almost universally accepted.

[42] A. Dieterich, *Eine Mithrasliturgie* (1905) 164.

PHLEGON, a freedman of Hadrian, uses the word for the festival of the Olympic games. The Peloponnesians had suffered a plague and a loss of crops, when they decided to consult the Delphic oracle. According to Phlegon, the oracle responded, as always, in fluent hexameters (*Olymp.* fr. 1.6):

Ζεὺς ὑμῖν μῆνιν τελετῆς ἔχει ἣν διέχρησεν,
οὕνεκ' ἀτιμάζοντες Ὀλύμπια πασιάνακτος
Ζηνός· τοῦ πρῶτος μὲν ἱδρύσατο καὶ θέτο τιμὴν
Πεῖσος, καὶ μετὰ τόνδε Πέλοψ, ὅτε δὴ μόλεν αἶαν
Ἑλλάδα, θῆκε δ' ἔπειτα ἔροτιν καὶ ἔπαθλα θανόντι
Οἰνομάωι, τρίτατος δ' ἐπὶ τοῖς πάις Ἀμφιτρύωνος
Ἡρακλέης ἐτέλεσσ' ἔροτιν καὶ ἀγῶνα ἐπὶ μήτρωι
Τανταλίδηι Πέλοπι φθιμένωι, τὸν δήποθεν ὑμεῖς
λείπετε καὶ τελετήν.

Zeus holds wrath towards you because of the rite (*telete*) that he revealed by oracle, because you are dishonouring the Olympic games of Zeus, ruler of all. The first to found and institute his worship was Peisos, and after him Pelops, when he came to the land of Hellas. Pelops then established a festival (*erotis*) and contests in honour of the dead Oinomaos. And third, in addition to these two, the child of Amphitryon, Herakles, brought about a festival (*erotis*) and contest for his deceased maternal uncle, Tantalid Pelops. You are clearly abandoning this contest and the rite (*telete*).

The oracular response illustrates the dual function of the games: competition and worship. For the religious aspect, the words ἔροτις (festival) and τελετή (rite, festival) are used. The use of τελετή for the Olympic games is already found in Pind. *Ol.* 10.53.

The Platonist mathematician THEON OF SMYRNA, comparing philosophy to initiation, gives five stages of *myesis*, 14.18 ff. (Hiller):

καὶ γὰρ αὖ τὴν φιλοσοφίαν μύησιν φαίη τις ἂν ἀληθοῦς τελετῆς καὶ τῶν ὄντων ὡς ἀληθῶς μυστηρίων παράδοσιν. μυήσεως δὲ μέρη πέντε. τὸ μὲν προηγούμενον καθαρμός· οὔτε γὰρ ἅπασι τοῖς βουλομένοις μετουσία μυστηρίων ἐστίν, ἀλλ' εἰσὶν οὓς αὐτῶν εἴργεσθαι προαγορεύεται, οἷον τοὺς χεῖρας μὴ καθαρὰς καὶ φωνὴν ἀξύνετον ἔχοντας, καὶ αὐτοὺς δὲ τοὺς μὴ εἰργομένους ἀνάγκη καθαρμοῦ τινος πρότερον τυχεῖν. μετὰ δὲ τὴν κάθαρσιν δευτέρα ἐστὶν ἡ τῆς τελετῆς παράδοσις· τρίτη δὲ ⟨ἡ⟩ ἐπονομαζομένη ἐποπτεία· τετάρτη δέ, ὃ δὴ καὶ τέλος τῆς ἐποπτείας, ἀνάδεσις καὶ στεμμάτων ἐπίθεσις, ὥστε καὶ ἑτέροις, ἅς τις παρέλαβε τελετάς, παραδοῦναι δύνασθαι, δαδουχίας τυχόντα ἢ ἱεροφαντίας ἢ τινος ἄλλης ἱερωσύνης· πέμπτη δὲ ἡ ἐξ αὐτῶν περιγενομένη κατὰ τὸ θεοφιλὲς καὶ θεοῖς συνδίαιτον εὐδαιμονία.

One could say that philosophy is an initiation (*myesis*) of a true rite (*telete*) and, in truth, a bestowing of actual mysteries. There are five parts to initiation: the first (preceding) part is purification. For not everyone who wishes may participate in the mysteries, but some are told beforehand that they are excluded from them, like those who have impure hands or unintelligible speech. And those who are not excluded must still first get some purification. Second, after the purification, is the bestowing of the rite (*telete*). Third is what is called the *epopteia*. Fourth, and this completes the *epopteia*, is the wreathing and laying on of garlands, so as to be able to pass on to others the rites (*teletai*) one has received, getting the daduchy or hierophancy or some other priesthood. Fifth is the happiness that comes from these things by way of being loved by the gods and living with the gods.

The word is used in the same sense a few lines on, in 15.14. The fact that Theon viewed the *telete* and the *epopteia* as distinct stages of the mysteries of course does not mean we should follow him in this regard.[43]

For LUCIAN, who liked to pick certain religious manifestations as the object of his satire, the same holds true as was said above of Plutarch: classifying the examples where he uses our term often produces great difficulty. Just as in Plutarch, the word always seems to indicate a religious act of a special nature. In some cases it is unclear whether mysteries are intended.

A. The Eleusinian mysteries are meant in the following passages. *Demonax* 11:

τὸ τῶν μυστηρίων, ταύτην ἔφη ἔχειν αἰτίαν τοῦ μὴ κοινωνῆσαι σφίσι τῆς τελετῆς, ὅτι, ἄν τε φαῦλα ᾖ τὰ μυστήρια, οὐ σιωπήσεται πρὸς τοὺς μηδέπω μεμυημένους, ἀλλ' ἀποτρέψει αὐτοὺς τῶν ὀργίων, ἄν τε καλά, πᾶσιν αὐτὰ ἐξαγορεύσει ὑπὸ φιλανθρωπίας.

Regarding the mysteries, he said he had the following reason for not taking part in the rite with them: if the mysteries turned out to be trivial, he would not as yet keep quiet to the uninitiated but would keep them away from the ceremonies; and if they were good, he would make them known to everyone out of benevolence.

---

[43] See K. Dowden, Grades in the Eleusinian Mysteries, RHR 197 (1980) 409–427; cf. K. Clinton, Stages of initiation in the Eleusinian and Samothracian Mysteries, in: M.B. Cosmopoulos (ed.), *Greek Mysteries* (2003) 50–78, 52: "To be precise, at the Greater Mysteria there was only a single *telete* for both *mystai* and *epoptai*, but the special experience of the *epoptai* at this *telete* was referred to as *epoptika* (or *epopteia*)."

Demon. 34:

ἐτόλμησε δέ ποτε καὶ Ἀθηναίους ἐρωτῆσαι δημοσίᾳ τῆς προρρήσεως
ἀκούσας, διὰ τίνα αἰτίαν ἀποκλείουσι τοὺς βαρβάρους, καὶ ταῦτα τοῦ
τὴν τελετὴν αὐτοῖς καταστησαμένου Εὐμόλπου βαρβάρου καὶ Θρᾳκὸς
ὄντος.

When he heard the sacred proclamation, he once had the audacity to ask
the Athenians in assembly why they excluded foreigners from the rite,
while Eumolpus, who had founded them, was a foreigner from Thrace.

Pseudol. 5:

ἦν δὲ ὑπόθεσις τῷ συγγράμματι ὁ Πυθαγόρας κωλυόμενος ὑπό τινος
Ἀθηναίων, οἶμαι, μετέχειν τῆς Ἐλευσῖνι τελετῆς ὡς βάρβαρος, ὅτι ἔλε-
γεν αὐτὸς ὁ Πυθαγόρας πρὸ τούτου ποτὲ καὶ Εὔφορβος γεγονέναι.

The subject of the document was that a certain Athenian, I believe, wants
to prevent Pythagoras, as a foreigner, from participating in the rite at
Eleusis because Pythagoras himself said that he had also been Euphorbus
sometime before (i.e. in a previous incarnation).

B. They are the Bacchic festivals of the followers of Dionysus: *Dial. D.*
18.1:

εἰ δέ τις ἐπεχείρησε λοιδορήσασθαι αὐτῷ ὑβρίσας ἐς τὴν τελετήν, καὶ
τοῦτον ἐτιμωρήσατο ἢ καταδήσας τοῖς κλήμασιν ἢ διασπασθῆναι ποιήσας ὑπὸ τῆς μητρὸς ὥσπερ νεβρόν.

If anyone tries to ridicule him by offending against his rite, the god punishes him, either binding him with vines, or having him torn apart his by
his own mother like a fawn.

Also *Bacchus* 5, where the god promises to bring his followers Bacchic
ecstasy, ἢν καὶ νῦν ὡς πρότερόν ποτε τὴν τελετὴν ἐθελήσωσιν ἐπιδεῖν
πολλάκις: "if now, as before, they will often watch my rite."

C. The festival of Hecate Enodia celebrated at Aegina is called τελετή,
Nav. 15, where Lycinus recalls how he and his friends sailed across
to Aegina for the festival of Enodia: ἐς Αἴγιναν ἐπὶ τὴν τῆς Ἐνοδίας
τελετὴν. Hardly anything is known about this festival.[44]

---

[44] Cf. Nilsson, *Feste*, 398, 399.

D. In this period there are (and arise) many smaller religious circles, with rituals modelled on those of the great mysteries.[45] This is also evident from the fact that after the sensational death of Peregrinus (*Peregr.* 28), Lucian fears:

> ἦ μὴν καὶ ἱερέας αὐτοῦ ἀποδειχθήσεσθαι μαστίγων ἢ καυτηρίων ἤ τινος τοιαύτης τερατουργίας, ἢ καὶ νὴ Δία τελετήν τινα ἐπ᾿ αὐτῷ συστήσεσθαι νυκτέριον καὶ δᾳδουχίαν ἐπὶ τῇ πυρᾷ.

> that priests of his will surely be ordained, with whips or brands or such curious stuff, or—by Jove!—that a nocturnal festival will arise in his honour, and a torch procession by his grave.

The following story is told of Alexander Pseudomantis (*Alex.* 38):

> τελετήν τε γάρ τινα συνίσταται καὶ δᾳδουχίας καὶ ἱεροφαντίας, τριῶν ἑξῆς ἀεὶ τελουμένων ἡμερῶν. καὶ ἐν μὲν τῇ πρώτῃ πρόρρησις ἦν ὥσπερ Ἀθήνησι τοιαύτη· εἴ τις ἄθεος ἢ Χριστιανὸς ἢ Ἐπικούρειος ἥκει κατάσκοπος τῶν ὀργίων, φευγέτω, οἱ δὲ πιστεύοντες τῷ θεῷ τελείσθωσαν τύχῃ τῇ ἀγαθῇ.

> He established a celebration of mysteries with offices of daduch and hierophant, to be performed (annually) forever for three days in a row. And on the first day there was a proclamation, just as in Athens, that went as follows: if any atheist or Christian or Epicurean has come to spy on the rites (*orgia*), let him be off, and let those who believe in the god perform the mysteries with good fortune.

It is clear how Alexander has emulated the form of the Eleusinian mysteries.

We also learn, among other things, that the λοχεία of Leto, the birth of Apollo, the wedding of Coronis and Apollo, and the birth of Asclepius were represented on the first day; on the second day came the *epiphaneia* of Glycon, including the birth of the god.[46] On the third day, called the Day of Torches (Δᾳδίς, § 39), the love of Selene and Endymion was re-enacted by a very pretty woman named Rutilia and Alexander himself. On the basis of this information, we can form an idea of what constituted the sacred acts.

---

[45] Cf. P. Wendland, *Die hellenistisch-römische Kultur* (1907) 132; L. Friedländer, *Darstellungen aus der Sittengeschichte Roms* III[10] (1923) 312.

[46] Cf. in the Eleusinian mysteries, the call: ἱερὸν ἔτεκε πότνια κοῦρον Βριμὼ Βριμόν. ("Lady Brimo has given birth to Brimos, a holy son.") Hippol. *Haer.* 5.8.39.

Lucian uses our term metaphorically in *De merc. cond.* 1, where he says that the stories of those who have already been house philosophers are the most credible:

> διὰ πάσης ὡς εἰπεῖν τῆς τελετῆς διεξεληλυθότες καὶ πάντα ἐξ ἀρχῆς εἰς τέλος ἐποπτεύσαντες.

> since they have gone completely through the entire rite, so to speak, and have been *epoptai* entirely from the beginning to the end.

The house philosophers had to endure all kinds of unpleasantness; this brings Lucian to compare their experiences to those who are subjected to a mystery rite.[47]

E. We have seen repeatedly that the institution of a religious festival recurring at regular intervals was also called τελετή, e.g. at the Eleusinian mysteries. That the circle of regular participants in such a festival is also called τελετή, is a natural extension of the meaning, which, of course, was made completely unconsciously. One may compare the development of Latin *conventiculum* (gathering). Through 'participants in these gatherings', the meaning becomes 'sect'. I believe the use of τελετή should be explained thus at *Peregr.* 11, where the word is used to refer to Christianity. Lucian says there that the Christians still worship that man who was crucified in Palestine:

> ὅτι καινὴν ταύτην τελετὴν εἰσῆγεν ἐς τὸν βίον.

> because he introduced that new sect to the world.

So τελετή here refers to the circle of Christians participating in certain ceremonies (e.g. the Eucharist, which is sometimes also called τελετή).[48] Already in Plato (*Leg.* 908d) and in ps. Demosthenes (*Neaer.* 104), τελετή refers to a separate clan cult; in the passage from *Leges*, it is disapproved of as a reprehensible religious institution, a sect.

F. We come to a magical context when we read, *Menippus* 6, how the hero of the story tells that he hears from a magician, a student of Zoroaster, that the latter can take someone to the underworld and back by means of incantations and rites: ἐπῳδαῖς καὶ τελεταῖς. We then read how the

---

[47] We know for certain that such a rite entailed unpleasant experiences at the Corybantes (Plato *Euthyd.* 277d) and the Orphics (Plut. fr. *De anima*).
[48] Cf. Dion. Areop., *EH* 3.1.

magician takes Menippus along to the Euphrates. Menippus has brought everything needed for the rite: ὅσα πρὸς τὴν τελετὴν χρήσιμα. Then the magician invokes all daemons in a loud voice, with incomprehensible magic formulas (9): παραμιγνὺς ἅμα βαρβαρικά τινα καὶ ἄσημα ὀνόματα καὶ πολυσύλλαβα ("mixing them together with certain foreign, obscure, polysyllabic names"). We shall see below how, in the magical papyri that have preserved such incantations for us, the word τελετή is repeatedly used, as it is here, in the sense of 'magic act'.

In the spurious writings of Lucian, τελετή is also attested several times. It is uncertain from which period they date.[49] Because it is likely that the authors were imitating Lucian's parlance, it does not seem unreasonable to discuss them here.

In *Tragoedopodagra* 112, the podagra patient asks the followers of the goddess Podagra:

> τίσιν δὲ τελεταῖς ὀργιάζει προσπόλους;

> With what sacred rites does she enrapture her devotees?

Amores 24 mentions τὴν ἐν Ἐλευσῖνι τελετὴν ("the ceremony at Eleusis").

In *De saltatione* 15, it is said that not a single old τελετή is without dance, because Orpheus and Musaeus, the founders, were the best dancers of their time. And hence, says the author, the term ἐξορχεῖσθαι τὰ μυστήρια: 'to "dance out" the mysteries' (i.e. to divulge their contents). Religious acts of an exclusive and ecstatic nature are presumably intended here.

Another place, *Amores* 42, describes how some women's conduct is simply insufferable. After taking forever to make their toilet ever so minutely, they go to the service of every possible god that is their husband's undoing, for example, the 'Phrygian goddess' (Cybele) and the 'herdsman' (Attis), τελεταὶ δὲ ἀπόρρητοι καὶ χωρὶς ἀνδρῶν ὕποπτα μυστήρια ("secret rites and suspicious mysteries without men"). So this refers to the same group of rampant lesser mysteries mentioned in *Peregr.* 28 and *Alex.* 38.

In the fictitious *Letters* of ALCIPHRON, we find a letter to Glycera from Menander, who has turned down an invitation by Ptolemy I to come to

---

[49] Karl Krumbacher thinks of Byzantine imitators (*Geschichte der byzantinischen Literatur*, 1891, 91 ff.).

Egypt because he cannot be separated from Glycera; moreover, he is too attached to life in Athens:

ἐμοὶ γένοιτο τὸν Ἀττικὸν ἀεὶ στέφεσθαι κισσὸν καὶ τὸν ἐπ’ ἐσχάρας ὑμνῆσαι κατ’ ἔτος Διόνυσον, τὰς μυστηριώτιδας ἄγειν τελετάς, δραματουργεῖν τι καινὸν ταῖς ἐτησίοις θυμέλαις (4.18.16 Schepers).

If only I could always be wreathed with Attic ivy[50] and sing to Dionysus each year at the altars, celebrate mystery rites and produce a new play on stage every year.

Without a doubt the Eleusinian mysteries are meant here.

In the last book of his *Metamorphoses*, the Latin author APULEIUS several times uses the loanword *teleta* for the mysteries of Isis and Osiris. In a humorous way, he describes how Lucius cannot resist the urge to undergo expensive initiations, even when he cannot afford it.

11.22: Indidem mihi praedicat, quae forent ad usum teletae necessario praeparanda.

From these books, the high priest declared to me what things must of necessity be prepared for the performance of the initiation rite.

11.24: Dies etiam tertius pari caerimoniarum ritu celebratus et ientaculum religiosum et teletae legitima consummatio.

The third day, too, was celebrated with a similar rite of worship, with a ritual breakfast and the proper consummation of my initiation rite.

11.26: Ecce transcurso signifero circulo Sol magnus annum compleverat, et quietem meam rursus interpellat numinis benefici cura pervigilis et rursus teletae, rursus sacrorum commonet. Mirabar, quid rei temptaret, quid pronuntiaret futurum; quidni? qui plenissime iamdudum videbar initiatus.

Now the mighty sun had passed through the signs of the zodiac and completed the year, and the wakeful worship of the kind goddess once again disturbed my sleep, reminded me again of initiation, again of sacred rituals.

Naturally, Lucius was bewildered, because he had considered himself already fully initiated. As it turned out, however, he had only been initiated into the mysteries of Isis, not yet of Osiris.

---

[50] A wreath of ivy was the prize for the winning playwright or producer at the City Dionysia.

11.27: Quanquam enim conexa, immo vero unita ratio numinis religio-
nisque esset, tamen teletae discrimen interesse maximum.

For although the natures of these deities and their religions are connected,
yes actually united, there is still a very big divide between their initiation
rites.

By this time, Lucius is so poor that he has to sell the clothes off his back.

11.29: Et ecce post pauculum tempus inopinatis et usquequaque miri-
ficis imperiis deum rursus interpellor et cogor tertiam quoque teletam
sustinere.

But shortly afterwards, I was again disturbed by unexpected and continuously amazing commands of the gods, and I was forced to complete a third
initiation.

Lucius is now yearning for the mystery of Roman Isis.

11.30: Statim sacerdoti meo relatis quae videram, inanimae protinus casti-
moniae iugum subeo et lege perpetua praescriptis illis decem diebus spon-
tali sobrietate multiplicatis instructum teletae comparo largitus, omnibus
ex studio pietatis magis quam mensura rerum mearum collatis.

Having told my high priest right away what I had seen, I immediately submitted to the yoke of abstinence from meat, and from voluntary sobriety
extended the period beyond those ten days prescribed by everlasting law.
Then I bought all the necessary things for the initiation rite, considering
more the extent of my piety than the narrowness of my means.

After this third and last initiation, Osiris himself appears in Lucius's sleep
and commands him to become a successful lawyer, which he did.

AELIUS ARISTIDES, *Or.* 45.17 (8 Df; *to Sarapis*). Sarapis endowed our
soul with wisdom, which shows our kinship to the gods, who gave
the notion (ἔννοιαν) of the gods to mankind "and found sacred rites
and mysteries and all honours" (καὶ ἱερὰ καὶ τελετὰς καὶ τιμὰς πάσας
εὗρεν), and furthermore, he gave us the blessings of civilization. In
contrast to ἱερά and other honours bestowed on the gods, τελεταί will
presumably refer to mysteries here. It is quite possible that Aristides,
who was very much influenced by the Attic orators, was inspired here
by Isocrates, *Paneg.* 28, where the latter praises Demeter as the giver of
τελεταί.

Or. 2.52 (45 Df) is an extensive quote taken from Plato's *Phaedrus* 244e,
where τελετή was used in the sense of solemn religious act. Aristides
refers to these same *teletai* in § 56:

καὶ μὴν εἰ μαντικὴν μὲν ἐξ Ἀπόλλωνος ἢ καὶ Διὸς, τελετὰς δὲ ἐξ ἄλλου
του θεῶν τίθης, ποιητικὴν δ' ἐκ Μουσῶν, οὐδ' ὁ ... Ἑρμῆς ἀπορήσει
λόγων περὶ τῆς αὐτοῦ δωρεᾶς, ἀλλ' αὐτῷ τε καὶ τῷ πατρὶ προστιθεὶς
τοὺς λόγους ἀληθῆ τε καὶ δίκαια ἐρεῖ.

And if you suppose that the art of divination comes from Apollo or even
Zeus, and *teletai* from another god, and poetry from the Muses, then
Hermes will not be silent about his own gift, but will speak truthfully and
justly when he claims oratory for himself and his father.

In *Or.* 48.28 (24 Df; *Or. Sacr.* 2), τελετή is the celebration of mysteries,
or possibly initiation, After an account of the epiphany of a deity, Aristides states: σχεδὸν γὰρ ὥσπερ ἐν τελετῇ περὶ πάντα ταῦτα διήγομεν,
παρεστώσης ἅμα τῷ φόβῳ τῆς ἀγαθῆς ἐλπίδος. "We performed all this
almost like in a mystery cult, since there was good hope together with
fear." Fear, coupled with hope for the best, is, as we know, a characteristic
of many a mystery cult.

We find the same meaning in *Or.* 50.6 (26 Df; *Or. Sacr.* 4). Aristides
hears a voice in his dream. The whole incident resembled a τελετή,
"since the rituals were so divine and extraordinary" (οὕτω θείων τε καὶ
παραδόξων τῶν δρωμένων ὄντων).

Or. 49.48 (25 Df; *Or. Sacr.* 3), the word refers to initiation into the
mysteries of Sarapis. Aristides had a wonderful vision:

ἐν οἷς αἵ τε δὴ κλίμακες ἦσαν αἱ τὸ ὑπὲρ γῆς τε καὶ ὑπὸ γῆς ἀφορίζου-
σαι, καὶ τὸ ἑκατέρωθι κράτος τοῦ θεοῦ, καὶ ἕτερα ἔκπληξιν θαυμαστὴν
φέροντα, καὶ οὐδὲ ῥητὰ ἴσως εἰς ἅπαντας, ὥστε ἀσμένῳ μοι φανῆναι
σύμβολα τοῦ Ἀσκληπιοῦ. κεφάλαιον δ' ἦν περὶ τῆς τοῦ θεοῦ δυνάμε-
ως ὅτι καὶ χωρὶς ὀχημάτων καὶ χωρὶς σωμάτων ὁ Σάραπις οἷός τ' εἴη
κομίζειν ἀνθρώπους ὅπῃ βούλοιτο. τοιαῦτα ἦν τὰ τῆς τελετῆς.

in which there were ladders that bordered off the region above the earth
and below the earth, and on both sides was the power of the god, and
there were other things that brought a marvellous feeling of terror and are
perhaps not to be told to all, so I was glad to see symbols of Asclepius. And
the main point was about the power of the god: even without vehicles and
without bodies, Sarapis is able to carry men wherever he pleases. Such was
my vision of the initiation.

Or. 46.40 (3 Df). Having mentioned all kinds of sea gods, it is remarked
that Palaemon is also an important deity, and it is good "to participate in the festival in his honour and in the celebration of his rites":

τῆς τελετῆς ἐπ᾽ αὐτῷ καὶ τοῦ ὀργιασμοῦ μετασχεῖν. We know little
about his mysteries.[51]

In *Or.* 53.5 (55 Df; *Paneg. Perg.*), the last, fragmentary line mentions
the τελεταὶ καὶ μυστήρια for the Cabiri;[52] these possessed such power
that they could calm storms, it appears to have read. Their cult apparently
always retained something exotic.[53]

Our term also appears several times in the Panathenaic Oration, *Or.* 1
(13 Df).

In 1.44, the word is apparently used for religious ceremony in the more
general sense. Athena gave her name to the city of Athens and introduces
various good things: oratory, law, democracy, weapons, horsemanship.

> ἐπὶ δὲ τούτοις χορεῖαι καὶ τελεταὶ καὶ πανηγύρεις ἐπεκράτησαν ἄλλαι
> δι᾽ ἄλλων θεῶν ἐπιδημίας.

> And after that, choral dances and *teletai* and festivals came into being
> because of the arrival of other gods.

1.330 praises the Athenians for their role in the ceremony of the Eleusinian mysteries:

> τῇ μὲν γὰρ τῶν Ἐλευσινίων τελετῇ τοῖς εἰσαφικνουμένοις ἐξηγηταὶ τῶν
> ἱερῶν καὶ μυσταγωγοὶ κέκλησθε.

> For in the ceremony of the Eleusinian mysteries you have been called
> interpreters and mystagogues of the sacred rites for those who attend.

The word has this same meaning in 1.341 and 1.342:

> τὰς δ᾽ ἀρρήτους τελετάς, ὧν τοῖς μετασχοῦσι καὶ μετὰ τὴν τοῦ βίου
> τελευτὴν βελτίω τὰ πράγματα γίγνεσθαι δοκεῖ, τίς οὐκ ἂν ἐξαρκεῖν
> φαίη πᾶσιν ἓν ἀντιθεῖναι; [342] ἀλλὰ μὴν ἥ γε πρὸς τοὺς ἀνθρώπους
> ὁμιλία τίν᾽ ἐκπέφευγε τρόπον εὐεργεσίας; πρῶτον μέν γε ἡ τῶν καρπῶν
> μετάδοσις, ἔπειθ᾽ ἡ τῶν τελετῶν ἑτέρα, κτλ.

> And who would deny that the secret ceremonies, whose participants, it
> seems, have a better life after death, are sufficient by themselves to be
> matched against everything? (342) But truly, has this association with
> mankind escaped any kind of benefit? First there is the sharing of crops,
> after that another sharing, that of ceremonies, etc.

---

[51] Cf. Burkert, *Homo Necans*, 196–199; Wilamowitz, *Glaube* I, 217; II, 507; Plut. *Thes.*
25 (12a).

[52] τοῦτο μοι πρεσβύτατοι δαιμόνων ἐνταῦθα λέγονται γενέσθαι Κάβειροι, καὶ
τελεταὶ τούτοις καὶ μυστήρια, ἃ τοσαύτην ἰσχὺν ἔχειν πεπίστευται ὥστε χειμώνων τε
ἐξαισίων …

[53] Cf. Wilamowitz, *Glaube* I, 85.

Used like this, without further specification, the secret *teletai* of Athens must, of course, refer to the Eleusinian mysteries.

P.Oxy. XIII 1612.17 (Grenfell-Hunt), gives a passage from an oration against the Emperor cult. The editors of the papyrus think of the oration of a Sophist from the time of Aristides, or a fragment from a historical work like that of Cassius Dio. The novelties, according to the author, were established by someone from neighbouring Nicaea. He then says:

> … παρ' ἐκείνοις τελείσθω μόνοις, ὥσπερ παρὰ τοῖς Ἀθηναίοις τὰ τῶν Ἐλευσινίων, εἰ ⟨μὴ⟩ βουλόμεθα αὐτὸν ἀσεβεῖν τὸν Καίσαρα, ὥσπερ ἂν καὶ τὴν Δημήτραν ⟨ἀ⟩σέβ[ο]⟨ι⟩μεν {[ἄ]ν} ἐνθάδε τελοῦντες αὐτῇ τὴν ἐκεῖσε τελετήν.[54]

> Let (these rites) be performed by them alone, just as the Eleusinian festivals by the Athenians, unless we wish to be impious towards the emperor himself, just as we would also be impious towards Demeter if we performed here the sacred act that belongs there.

Indeed, the Emperor cult itself is not called a τελετή, but τελεῖν is used for its performance, and it is compared to the τελετή of Eleusis. Herodian, *Ab exc. d. Marci* 4.2.1, called the apotheosis of the emperor τελετή.

MAXIMUS OF TYRE, the not very original Platonist philosopher, in *Diss.* 2.1, talks about the worship of river gods, which is conducted for different reasons in various countries. For example, the Egyptians worshipped the Nile for its usefulness and the Athenians worshipped the Ilissus κατὰ τελετήν: in connection with their sacred rite. In Athens, the *telete*, without further specification, is always the celebration of the Eleusinian mysteries. Here it is a part thereof, at the lesser mysteries at Agrae: the bath of the *mystai* in the river Ilissus, to cleanse themselves ritually.[55] So this place is actually also an example of τελετή in the sense of καθαρμός.

Diss. 24.5 says that farmers are much more suited to religious occasions than soldiers (ἑορταῖς γε μὴν καὶ μυστηρίοις καὶ πανηγύρεσι). In general, Maximus is of the opinion that farmers were the first to establish festivals and rites for the gods:

> δοκοῦσι δέ μοι μηδὲ τὴν ἀρχὴν συστήσασθαι ἑορτὰς καὶ τελετὰς θεῶν ἄλλοι τινὲς ἢ γεωργοί, πρῶτοι δὲ μὲν ἐπὶ ληνῷ στασάμενοι Διονύσῳ

---

[54] As one can see, the text has been significantly emended to make proper sense.
[55] Cf. Deubner, *Attische Feste*, 70, who cites inter alia Polyaenus, *Strat.* 5.17: παρὰ τὸν Ἰλισσόν, οὗ τὸν καθαρμὸν τελοῦσι τοῖς ἐλάττοσι μυστηρίοις.

χορούς, πρῶτοι δὲ ἐπὶ ἅλῳ Δήμητρι ὄργια, πρῶτοι δὲ τὴν ἐλαίας γένεσιν
τῇ Ἀθηνᾷ ἐπιφημίσαντες, πρῶτοι δὲ τῶν ἐκ γῆς καρπῶν τοῖς δεδωκόσιν
θεοῖς ἀπαρξάμενοι.

And I believe that the ones who first established festivals and rites of the
gods were none other than farmers. For they were the first to perform
choral dances for Dionysus at the winepress, they instituted the threshing
festival for Demeter, they first attributed the creation of the olive to Athena
and they were the first to dedicate fruits of the field to those who have given
them, the gods.

It is difficult to determine which festivals are considered ἑορταί by Maximus and which are τελεταί, if he makes the distinction at all. The country Dionysia have a very special ritual, as do the Haloa.[56] The worship of
Athena as giver of the olive is known,[57] although, as far as I am aware, we
do not know anything about a special cult that exhibits this. The offering of first fruits at Eleusis was long a custom.[58] This type of sacrifice
was already referred to by Sophocles, *Trach.* 238, with the words τέλη
ἔγκαρπα.

Diss. 26.2 discusses whether Homer was a follower of a philosophical
school. His entire work is said to have been a carrier of ἐπιστήμη, which
some presented in the form of τελετὰς καὶ ὀργιασμούς. Compare Heraclitus 64. The meaning here is: secret doctrine.

Diss. 32.7. Maximus observes that the pleasures associated with the
worship of Dionysus have the status of a religious rite: τελετῆς χώραν
ἔχουσιν.

Diss. 37.5. Singing is useful for many things: δεινὴ δὲ καὶ ἐν ἑορταῖς
εὐφρᾶναι καὶ ἐν Διονυσίοις κωμάσαι καὶ ἐν τελεταῖς ἐπιθειάσαι. So
singing played a role in many ritual acts of a special nature, to promote
ecstasy, the ἐνθουσιασμός. Perhaps Orphic hymns are evidence of this.[59]

Diss. 39.3 discusses in particular the τελετή at Eleusis. Life is compared
to a long road to Eleusis or Babylon, τέρμα τε δὴ τῆς ὁδοῦ τὰ βασίλεια
αὐτὰ καὶ ἀνάκτορα καὶ τὴν τελετήν ("The end then is the palace itself
and the temple and the rite"). When souls arrive there, tired and painful,
καὶ ἐπιθυμοῦσαι τοῦ χωρίου καὶ ἐρῶσαι τῆς τελετῆς ("and longing for
the place and yearning for the rite"), the pain and suffering stops. τίς γὰρ

---

[56] Cf. Schol. Lucian *Dial. meret.* 7.4: ἑορτὴ Ἀθήνῃσι μυστήρια περιέχουσα Δήμητρος
καὶ Κόρης καὶ Διονύσου ... ἐν ταύτῃ καὶ τελετή τις εἰσάγεται γυναικῶν κτλ.
[57] Cf. Farnell, *Cults* I, 293.
[58] Cf. W.H.D. Rouse, *Greek Votive Offerings* (1902) 57.
[59] Cf. Dieterich, *Kleine Schriften* 69; one should also consider the term ἐπῳδή, which
was very common among the Orphics. For ἐπᾴδειν, cf. also Plato, *Leg.* 664.

ἄλλη τελετὴ μυστικωτέρα καὶ τίς ἄλλος τόπος σπουδῆς ἄξιος; ("For what other rite is more mystic and what other location more worthy of zeal?").

AELIAN, *Var. Hist.* 2.31, challenges the atheists and deists with the argument that worship of the gods is found among all foreign peoples. They have a firm belief about this: θύουσί τε καθαρῶς καὶ ἁγνεύουσιν ὁσίως, καὶ τελετὰς τελοῦσι καὶ ὀργίων φυλάττουσι νόμον ("Their sacrifice is pure and they piously avoid pollution, and they perform religious rites and preserve custom in their rituals"). I believe that here, τελεταί and also ὄργια are certain rites that are bound by fixed regulations.

VH 13.2 the βακχεῖα, the festivals of Dionysus in Mytilene, are called τελεταί.

Fr. 10 mentions τὸν τῆς τελετῆς νόμον ("the customary law of the rite") in connection with Eleusis.

ANTONINUS LIBERALIS, *Met.* 10.1 uses τελετὰς ἢ μυστήρια for the rites of Dionysus.

Likewise, the mythographic handbook attributed to APOLLODORUS, talks about the *teletai* of Dionysus.

In *Bibl.* 2.2.2, it is said about the daughters of Proetus:

> αὗται δὲ ὡς ἐτελειώθησαν, ἐμάνησαν, ὡς μὲν Ἡσίοδός φησιν, ὅτι τὰς Διονύσου τελετὰς οὐ κατεδέχοντο, ὡς δὲ Ἀκουσίλαος λέγει, διότι τὸ τῆς Ἥρας ξόανον ἐξηυτέλισαν.

> When they were grown up, they went mad, as Hesiod says, because they did not accept the rites of Dionysus but, as Acusilaus says, it was because they disparaged the wooden image of Hera.

3.5.1 explains the origin of the orgiastic rites of Dionysus:

> αὖθις δὲ εἰς Κύβελα τῆς Φρυγίας ἀφικνεῖται, κἀκεῖ καθαρθεὶς ὑπὸ Ῥέας καὶ τὰς τελετὰς ἐκμαθὼν καὶ λαβὼν παρ᾽ ἐκείνης τὴν στολὴν διὰ τῆς Θρᾴκης ἠπείγετο.

> But then he (Dionysus) arrived at the Cybela mountains in Phrygia, and there, after he had been cleansed by Rhea, he learned her rites and received the robe from her before he hurried on through Thrace.

ARTEMIDORUS wrote a book on dreams that, as a document of Greek popular religion, perhaps deserves more attention than it has enjoyed.

In 1.68, he says that legumes were barred from every *telete* and every *hieron*: πάσης τελετῆς καὶ παντὸς ἱεροῦ ἀπελήλαται. While this is certainly an exaggeration, there were nonetheless several temples and ceremonies where this was the case.[60]

4.2. The many social institutions of mankind include μυστήρια καὶ τελεταὶ καὶ πανηγύρεις καὶ ἀγῶνες ("mysteries, rites, festivals and games").

In neither of these two cases can it be said with certainty what Artemidorus means by τελεταί.

MARCUS AURELIUS, *Med.* 9.30, warns that we should, in particular, realize that everything is relative: just look at the countless mobs and their countless τελετάς. It seems to me that τελετή here means 'religious movement'.[61]

The physician GALEN, *De usu part.* 17.1 (2.448 Helmreich; 4.361 Kühn), uses our term in a metaphorical sense. According to him, all religious people had to be initiated into the mystery (χρὴ τελεῖσθαι τὴν τελετὴν) that exists in the knowledge of the use of our limbs. This does not resemble the Eleusinian and Samothracian mysteries (ὄργια) at all, for those are obscure in indicating their doctrine, while nature's ὄργια are manifest in all that lives.

De usu part. 7.14 (1.418 Helmreich; 3.576 Kühn) has τελετή as the special rite of a mystery cult, first literally and then metaphorically:

> πρόσσχες τοίνυν ἤδη μοι τὸν νοῦν μᾶλλον, ἢ εἴ ποτε μυούμενος Ἐλευσί-
> νια καὶ Σαμοθράκια καὶ ἄλλην τινὰ τελετὴν ἁγίαν ὅλος ἦσθα πρὸς τοῖς
> δρωμένοις τε καὶ λεγομένοις ὑπὸ τῶν ἱεροφαντῶν, μηδέν τι χείρω νομί-
> σας ταύτην ἐκείνων εἶναι τὴν τελετήν, μηδ' ἧττον ἐνδείξασθαι δυναμέ-
> νην ἢ σοφίαν ἢ πρόνοιαν ἢ δύναμιν τοῦ τῶν ζῴων δημιουργοῦ, καὶ μά-
> λισθ' ὅτι τὴν τελετὴν ταύτην, ἣν νῦν μεταχειρίζομαι, πρῶτος ἁπάντων
> ἐξεῦρον.

> Now pay attention to me already, more than if you were being initiated into the Eleusinian or Samothracian mysteries or some other sacred rite and were wholly present at the things done and said by the hierophants, and hold that this rite here is in no way inferior to those mysteries, and is no less capable of showing forth the wisdom or providence or power of the creator of all living beings; and pay attention mostly, because I was the first of all men to discover this rite that I am now conducting.

---

[60] Cf. Wächter, *Reinheitsvorschriften*, 102. Cf. also *LSS* 108, which lists beans as a source of pollution.

[61] Just as Lucian *Peregr.* 11.

PAUSANIAS had particular interest, not only in the monuments of ancient Greece, but in the religious institutions of which these monuments are often the expressions. On several occasions, he tells us that a τελετή was situated at a certain place, apparently meaning that a certain, often complicated, religious ceremony took place at fixed times. Not only the act in itself, but the institution, the established practice of these special rites, with priests and all those who played a part, is called τελετή. This is nothing new; we have already repeatedly seen this usage, especially of the Eleusinian mysteries. But in Pausanias, this is the principal use. How the author himself feels this distinction between the act and the institution, can be clearly observed in 2.14.1, where he mentions a τελετή dedicated to Demeter at Celeae:

> καὶ τῇ Δήμητρι ἐνταῦθα δι' ἐνιαυτοῦ τετάρτου τὴν τελετὴν καὶ οὐ κατὰ ἔτος ἄγουσιν. ἱεροφάντης δὲ οὐκ ἐς τὸν βίον πάντα ἀποδέδεικται, κατὰ δὲ ἑκάστην τελετὴν ἄλλοτέ ἐστιν ἄλλος σφίσιν αἱρετός, λαμβάνων ἢν ἐθέλῃ καὶ γυναῖκα. καὶ ταῦτα μὲν διάφορα τῶν Ἐλευσῖνι νομίζουσι, τὰ δὲ ἐς αὐτὴν τὴν τελετὴν ἐκείνων ἐστὶν ἐς μίμησιν.

> They celebrate the festival for Demeter there every fourth year, not every year. The hierophant is not appointed for life, but they choose a different one for every festival and if he wants he can even take a wife. In these respects they have different customs from those at Eleusis, but with regard to the sacred act itself, that is an imitation of the one at Eleusis.

Though the line between the different nuances of meaning is fluid, I will first attempt to enumerate the places where the act itself is intended, then those where τελετή is the religious festival as a permanent institution, and finally several other meanings.

A. Ritual act in itself.

1.2.5 mentions the house of Poulytion, where many say that distinguished Athenians (Alcibiades c.s.) imitated the τελετή at Eleusis.[62]

1.37.4. Pausanias comes to speak of the uncleanness of the bean with regard to sacred festivals, such as at Eleusis. He breaks off his argument and says: ὅστις δὲ ἤδη τελετὴν Ἐλευσῖνι εἶδεν, ἢ τὰ καλούμενα Ὀρφικὰ

---

[62] With Hitzig-Blümner we read τὴν ἐν Ἐλευσῖνι παραδρᾶσαι τελετήν for παρὰ τὴν ἐν Ἐλευσῖνι δρᾶσαι τελετήν.

ἐπελέξατο, οἶδεν ὃ λέγω. "Anyone who has seen the ceremony at Eleusis, or has read the so-called Orphic writings, knows what I mean." Cf. Artemidorus, 1.68.

2.14.1, which I cited above, discusses the mysteries at Celeae. It first gives τελετή in the meaning: sacred festival as a permanent institution; this is also confirmed by what immediately follows: δρώμενα for the sacred act at Eleusis. It also tells that the founder, Dysaules, a brother of Celeus, was supposedly banished from Eleusis by Ion. But, Pausanias proceeds to argue, the Homeric Hymn to Demeter that sums up "those who were taught the mystery by the goddess" (τοὺς διδαχθέντας ὑπὸ τῆς θεοῦ τὴν τελετήν) does not mention any Dysaules. He then quotes from the Hymn (474–476):

δεῖξεν Τριπτολέμῳ τε Διοκλεῖ τε πληξίππῳ
Εὐμόλπου τε βίῃ Κελεῷ θ᾽ ἡγήτορι λαῶν
δρησμοσύνην θ᾽ ἱερῶν καὶ ἐπέφραδεν ὄργια πᾶσιν.

To Triptolemus and Diocles, driver of horses, and to mighty Eumolpus and Celeus, leader of the people, she revealed the service of her rites (*hiera*) and taught her mysteries (*orgia*) to them all.

Δρησμοσύνη is synonymous here with τελετή and also with the often used word δρώμενα. In the expression δεῖξεν δρησμοσύνην ἱερῶν, we can see the prototype of τελετὴν καταδεικνύναι and similar expressions, which are later often used in similar contexts. (See below, p. 121).

The same mysteries at Celeae are briefly mentioned in 2.12.5:

πρὸ τῆς τελετῆς ἣν τῇ Δήμητρι ἄγουσιν Ἄραντα καὶ τοὺς παῖδας καλοῦσιν ἐπὶ τὰς σπονδὰς ἐς ταῦτα βλέποντες τὰ μνήματα.

Before celebrating the mysteries for Demeter, the people call Aras and his children to the libations, while looking at these tombs.

2.38.3 discusses the bath that Hera takes in Nauplia every year, by which she restores her virginity.

οὗτος μὲν δή σφισιν ἐκ τελετῆς, ἣν ἄγουσι τῇ Ἥρᾳ, λόγος τῶν ἀπορρή-
των ἐστίν.

This is the story of their secret rites, derived from the sacred act they perform for Hera.

This sacred act consisted of priests bathing the statue of Hera in the source Canathus every year.[63]

---

[63] Cf. Nilsson, *Feste*, 45.

B. Religious festival as a permanent institution.

1.38.3. After the war between Athens and Eleusis, it was determined that Eleusis would be completely subjugated to Athens, but the Eleusinians shall:

> ἰδίᾳ τελεῖν τὴν τελετήν. τὰ δὲ ἱερὰ τοῖν θεοῖν Εὔμολπος καὶ αἱ θυγατέρες δρῶσιν αἱ Κελεοῦ.

> perform the rite independently. Eumolpus and the daughters of Celeus performed the holy rites for the two goddesses.

Cf. Dem. *Neaer.* 104.

In 2.3.4, Pausanias refuses to reproduce the story of Hermes and the ram ἐν τελετῇ Μητρός, although he knows it. There is a difference of opinion about which festival this was.[64]

2.26.8 is about the Epidauria as a part of the Eleusinian mysteries, which are here called τελετή without any further specification.

2.30.2 calls the cult of Hecate on Aegina a τελετή:[65]

> τελετὴν ἄγουσιν ἀνὰ πᾶν ἔτος Ἑκάτης, Ὀρφέα σφίσι τὸν Θρᾷκα κατα-στήσασθαι τὴν τελετὴν λέγοντες.

> They celebrate a festival of Hecate every year, saying Orpheus of Thrace established the festival for them.

2.36.7 and 2.37.2 speak about the Demeter cult at Lerna. Philammon is said to have founded this τελετή (2.36.7). "What they say about these rites (*dromena*) is clearly not ancient."[66] (2.37.2.) The actual ceremony therefore consists of δρώμενα = τελετή.

4.1.5 discusses the history of the τελετή for the Μεγάλοι θεοί at Andania in Messenia. A certain Caucon brought the ὄργια of these gods from Eleusis to Messenia. Many years later, Lycus brought the τελετή to great prosperity. Pausanias tells us that people still call woods where he cleansed the *mystai* after him. Τελεταί is used in this sense several more times:

> 4.1.7: μετεκόσμησε γὰρ καὶ Μέθαπος τῆς τελετῆς ἔστιν ἅ· ὁ δὲ Μέθαπος γένος μὲν ἦν Ἀθηναῖος, τελετῆς δὲ καὶ ὀργίων παντοίων συνθέτης.[67] οὗτος καὶ Θηβαίοις τῶν Καβείρων τὴν τελετὴν κατεστήσατο, κτλ.

---

[64] Cf. Blümner ad locum.

[65] Cf. Nilsson, *Feste*, 398.

[66] τὰ μὲν οὖν λεγόμενα ἐπὶ τοῖς δρωμένοις δῆλά ἐστιν οὐκ ὄντα ἀρχαῖα.

[67] We prefer the reading τελετῆς δὲ καὶ ὀργίων παντοίων συνθέτης (mss.) to Hitzig-Blümner: τελέτης.

For Methapus also reorganized the mysteries. Methapus was an Athenian by birth, a founder of mystery rite and of all kinds of rites (*orgia*). It was he who established the mystery rite of the Cabiri at Thebes, etc.

The first τελετή refers to the Andanian mysteries; the second to mysteries in general; the third to the mysteries of the Cabiri in Thebes.

4.1.9: τοῦτο τὸ ἐπίγραμμα ... δηλοῖ δὲ καὶ τὰ ἐς τὸν Λύκον τά τε ἄλλα καὶ ὡς ἡ τελετὴ τὸ ἀρχαῖον ἦν ἐν Ἀνδανίᾳ. καί μοι καὶ τοῦτο εἰκὸς ἐφαίνετο, τὴν Μεσσήνην μὴ ἑτέρωθι, ἀλλὰ ἔνθα αὐτή τε καὶ Πολυκάων ᾤκουν, καταστήσασθαι τὴν τελετήν.

This inscription also clarifies the rest about Lycus, including the fact that the mystery rite was of old at Andania. And in fact it seemed reasonable to me that Messene should have established the rite where she and Polycaon were living and not elsewhere.

4.3.10 Pausanias again calls these mysteries τελετή. Cf. also Paus. 4.26.8. The Andanian mysteries are mentioned once more in 4.33.5:

τὰ δὲ ἐς τὰς θεὰς τὰς Μεγάλας, δρῶσι γὰρ καὶ ταύταις ἐν Καρναρίῳ τὴν τελετήν, ἀπόρρητα ἔστω μοι· δεύτερα γάρ σφισι νέμω σεμνότητος μετά γε Ἐλευσίνια.

I may not speak about the rites of the Great Goddesses, for it is their mysteries that are celebrated in the Carnasian grove and I consider them as second only to the Eleusinian in sanctity.

4.34.11 mentions the τελετή for Dryops at Asine in Messenia. Nothing is certain about his cult.[68]

In 8.9.8, the annual celebration, a festival for Antinous, is called τελετή:

τούτων ἕνεκα ὁ βασιλεὺς κατεστήσατο αὐτῷ καὶ ἐν Μαντινείᾳ τιμάς, καὶ τελετή τε κατὰ ἔτος ἕκαστον καὶ ἀγών ἐστιν αὐτῷ διὰ ἔτους πέμπτου.

For this reason, the emperor also established his worship in Mantinea, and a *telete* is held every year and a contest in his honour every four years.

Perhaps we may infer from the progression, τιμαί, τελετή, ἀγών, that τελετή is a special ceremony, recurring at regular intervals, whereas ordinary worship is called τιμαί.

8.15.1 Pausanias talks about a branch of Eleusis at Pheneos in Arcadia. The inhabitants possess a temple of Demeter Eleusinia, καὶ ἄγουσι τῇ θεῷ τελετήν, τὰ Ἐλευσῖνι δρώμενα καὶ παρὰ σφίσι τὰ αὐτὰ φάσκον-

---

[68] Cf. Nilsson, *Feste*, 422.

τες καθεστηκέναι ("and they celebrate a mystery rite for the goddess, professing that the Eleusinian rites (*dromena*) have also been established here").

8.15.2–3 discusses the so-called πέτρωμα, where the greater τελετή was celebrated every other year (παρὰ ἔτος). On this occasion, a document inscribed on two stones was read, ἔχοντα ἐς τὴν τελετήν, i.e. containing a precise description of the sacred act. This was done within earshot of the *mystai*. In the rite, a priest put on a mask of Demeter Cidaria and beat the gods of the underworld with switches. (For ἐπιχθονίους MSS., one generally reads ὑποχθονίους).

In 8.15.4, the ceremony for Demeter Thesmia is also called τελετή. Nilsson suspects that these are the Thesmophoria, seen in Arcadia by Herodotus 2.171.[69]

8.23.4. On Mount Cnacalus in Arcadia, a yearly τελετή is celebrated for Artemis. Nilsson remarked: "Wenn das Wort τελετή streng genommen wird, ist diese Feier eines der seltenen Beispiele von Artemismysterien"[70] It is, however, apparent from many examples that, in fact, τελετή indicates any complicated, symbolic act, and certainly does not, in the first place, mean 'mysteries'.

8.29.1 and 8.31.7 mention a τελετή for the Μεγάλαι θεαί at Bathos and in Megalopolis respectively.[71] The δρώμενα of the one in Megalopolis, we are told, are an imitation of those at Eleusis.

8.37.2 mentions that, in the Despoina temple, there is an inscribed plaque containing a description of the sacred act: πινάκιόν ἐστι γεγραμμένον, ἔχον τὰ ἐς τὴν τελετήν.

8.37.8 describes the very special course of action at the cult of Despoina in Lycosura:

τελετήν τε δρῶσιν ἐνταῦθα καὶ τῇ Δεσποίνῃ θύουσιν ἱερεῖα οἱ Ἀρκάδες πολλά τε καὶ ἄφθονα.

The Arcadians perform the mysteries there and sacrifice many and abundant offerings to Despoina.

This is followed by a description of the very special method that is followed in the sacrifice: not the throat, but a leg of the sacrificial victim is cut off. From an inscription found in situ, we know that there were

---

[69] Nilsson, *Feste*, 316.

[70] Nilsson, *Feste*, 231 ("When the word τελετή is taken in the strict sense, this festival is one of the rare examples of Artemis mysteries").

[71] Cf. Nilsson, *Feste*, 342.

many other rules in the temple of Despoina.[72] What the actual τελετή involved, we do not know; according to Pausanias, the true name of Despoina was revealed in it. I believe that the special method of sacrifice and other regulations are a part of the τελετή in the broader sense and can individually also be referred to by this term.

9.25.6. In a passage about the cult of the Cabiri at Thebes, we find the term δρώμενα several times. Pausanias will not reveal their nature to us. The cult is called τελετή:

> Δήμητρος δ' οὖν Καβειραίοις δῶρόν ἐστιν ἡ τελετή. κατὰ δὲ τὴν Ἐπιγό-
> νων στρατείαν καὶ ἅλωσιν τῶν Θηβῶν ἀνέστησαν μὲν ὑπὸ τῶν Ἀργείων
> οἱ Καβειραῖοι, ἐξελείφθη δὲ ἐπὶ χρόνον τινὰ καὶ ἡ τελετή.

> The mystery rite is a gift from Demeter to the Cabiraean men. During the campaign of the Epigoni and the capture of Thebes, the Cabiraeans were compelled by the Argives to migrate; even the mystery rite was abandoned for some time.

Cf. Aristid. *Or.* 53.5.[73]

9.35.3 mentions the τελετή that the Athenians celebrate for the Χάρι-τες. This is ἐς τοὺς πολλοὺς ἀπόρρητος ("not to be spoken about by the multitude").

10.7.2. In an exposition of the most ancient history of Delphi, the first contestants in the games are enumerated. It is said that Orpheus, in his grandiloquence about his ceremonies (σεμνολογίᾳ τῇ ἐπὶ τελεταῖς), did not wish to be tested in a musical competition. Musaeus followed his example. Orpheus was considered an expert in τελεταί.[74]

10.38.3 mentions the τελετή of the Ἄνακτες Παῖδες in Amphissa. According to Pausanias, there is no agreement about who these gods are: "Some say the Dioscuri, others the Curetes and those who think they know more, say the Cabiri."[75]

In 10.31.11, we find the assurance that, with the ancient Greeks, the τελετή at Eleusis was more honoured than the other religious institutions inasmuch as they placed gods above heroes.[76]

---

[72] *Syll.*³ 999 = *LSCG* 68; for a second sacred law (fragmentary) from the same sanctuary, see Lupu, *NGSL* 215–218 no. 8. Cf. also Nilsson, *Feste*, 345.

[73] Mentioning τελεταὶ καὶ μυστήρια for the Cabiri.

[74] Cf. Diod. 1.23.7; E. Maass, *Orpheus* (1895) passim.

[75] Cf. Nilsson, *Feste*, 422.

[76] οἱ γὰρ ἀρχαιότεροι τῶν Ἑλλήνων τελετὴν τὴν Ἐλευσινίαν πάντων ὁπόσα ἐς εὐσέβειαν ἥκει τοσούτῳ ἦγον ἐντιμότερον ὅσῳ καὶ θεοὺς ἐπίπροσθεν ἡρώων.

How τελετή can also have the meaning of 'written exposition of the cult act' was discussed above, p. 20. In Pausanias, we find this usage in 4.26.6–8: the passage about the reinstitution of the mysteries at Andania. A certain Epiteles, warned by a dream, finds a κασσίτερον, a thin rolled-up sheet of lead, in the ground, 4.26.8:

> ἐνταῦθα τῶν Μεγάλων θεῶν ἐγέγραπτο ἡ τελετή, καὶ τοῦτο ἦν παρα-
> καταθήκη τοῦ Ἀριστομένους.

> The rite of the Great Goddesses was inscribed on it, and this was what Aristomenes had stored away.

And in 4.27.5:

> ὡς δὲ ἡ τελετή σφισιν ἀνεύρητο, ταύτην μέν, ὅσοι τοῦ γένους τῶν ἱερέων ἦσαν, κατετίθεντο ἐς βίβλους.

> When the *telete* had been refound, all who were of the priestly family set it down in books.

We should compare to this: *Syll.*³ II, 736 = *IG* V 1, 1390, the famous regulation of the Andanian mysteries.[77] The 'sacred men' (ἱεροί) in this document are certain officials who must promise under oath to manage the affairs of the mysteries faithfully.[78] The regulation shows that these sacred men followed a written manual, which they must deliver to their successors at the termination of their functions (lines 11–12):

> τὰν δὲ κάμπτραν καὶ τὰ | βιβλία ἃ δέδωκε Μνασίστρατος παραδιδόντω οἱ ἱεροὶ τοῖς ἐπικαταστάθεντοις.

> The sacred men are to hand over to their successors the *kamptra*[79] and the books given by Mnasistratus.

This fits well with Pausanias' account of Epiteles' discovery. I believe the original was carefully kept in a box and they had the transcripts in the βί-βλοι for daily use. Perhaps the works entitled Τελεταί, mentioned above at p. 40, were modelled by Stesimbrotus and others after such cult regulations as are mentioned here. We may also compare the aforementioned places, 8.15.2 and 8.37.2, where τὰ ἐς τὴν τελετήν were inscribed in stone.

Finally, there is an example of τελετή in a sense not seen before, personified as a goddess: Paus. 9.30.4. On Mt. Helicon, there are statues of Muses and poets:

---

[77] *LSCG* 65. Cf. Nilsson, *Feste*, 339; Wilamowitz, *Glaube* II, 536 ff.
[78] See below, Chapter XI, no. 35, line 3.
[79] This word appears to mean 'box'; cf. Dittenberger, Sokolowski ad locum.

Ὀρφεῖ δὲ τῷ Θρᾳκὶ πεποίηται μὲν παρεστῶσα αὐτῷ Τελετή.

And Telete is portrayed, standing next to Orpheus from Thrace.

There are several examples of Greek gods arising from cult acts, e.g. Paian, Iacchus.[80]

A few lines on, Orpheus is mentioned as the finder of the τελεταί θεῶν, of purification of irreligious acts, and of healing and warding off the wrath of the gods.

Telete personified as a goddess appears again much later in NONNUS' *Dionysiaca*, where Telete is the daughter of Dionysus and the nymph Nicaea.[81] 16.399–402:

ἐκ δὲ γάμου Βρομίοιο θεόσσυτος ἤνθεε κούρη,
ἣν Τελετὴν ὀνόμηνεν ἀεὶ χαίρουσαν ἑορταῖς,
κούρην νυκτιχόρευτον, ἐφεσπομένην Διονύσῳ,
τερπομένην κροτάλοισι καὶ ἀμφιπλῆγι βοείῃ.

From her union with Bromios blossomed a godsent girl, whom she called Telete: always delighted with religious festivals, girl of nocturnal choral dances, following Dionysus and enjoying the castanets and the double-sided tympanon.

Clearly Telete is here the personification of Dionysiac rites, in particular the choral dances performed at festivals, and not of initiation.

In 48.880, Telete is called χοροπλεκής, a word coined by Nonnus to denote the twisting round in choral dances. 48.880–886:

By your daughter Telete, who twists round in choral dances, I beseech you quickly to lift up my son, lest my implacable Aura kill him with her daring hands. For I know she will kill one of her twin babes in her uncontrollable rage. But you must save Iacchus: protect my better child, so that your Telete may serve both son and father.[82]

---

[80] Cf. K. Latte, *Philologus* 85.2 (1930) 227. For a depiction of Telete in a mosaic from Zeugma, see below, Chapter XI, no. 56.

[81] Nonnus, of course, also uses our term for the rites of Dionysus: 4.271; 7.65; 9.115; 9.127; 14.287; 19.37; 19.41; 28.41; 31.68; 40.152; 46.146; 46.173; 47.730; 48.811; 48.966.

[82] πρὸς Τελετῆς λίτομαί σε, χοροπλεκέος σέο κούρης, | σπεῦσον ἀερτάζειν ἐμὸν υἵέα, μή μιν ὀλέσσῃ | τολμηραῖς παλάμῃσιν ἐμὴ δυσμήχανος Αὔρῃ· | οἶδα γάρ, ὡς διδύμων βρεφέων ἕνα παῖδα δαμάσσει | ἄσχετα λυσσώουσα. σὺ δὲ χραίσμησον Ἰάκχῳ· | ἔσσο φύλαξ ὠδῖνος ἀρείονος, ὄφρα κεν εἴη | σὴ Τελετὴ θεράπαινα καὶ υἵέι καὶ γενετῆρι.

In Polyaenus' *Strategemata*, our term is used for the turbulent rites for the Megaloi Theoi (7.5.1), but also in the more general sense of religious ceremony (8.4.1).

> *Strat.* 7.5.1:
>
> Μίδας προσποιησάμενος τελετὴν ποιεῖν τοῖς Μεγάλοις θεοῖς νυκτὸς ἐξήγαγε τοὺς Φρύγας μετ᾽ αὐλῶν καὶ τυμπάνων καὶ κυμβάλων κρυπτὰ ἔχοντας ἐγχειρίδια. οἱ μὲν πολῖται τῶν οἰκιῶν ἐξῆλθον ἐπὶ τὴν θέαν, οἱ δὲ τυμπανίζοντες καὶ κυμβαλίζοντες τοὺς μὲν θεατὰς κατεφόνευσαν, τὰς δὲ οἰκίας αὐτῶν ἀνεῳγμένας καταλαβόντες Μίδαν τύραννον ἀνηγόρευσαν.
>
> Midas, pretending to hold a ceremony for the Great Gods, lead the Phrygians out by night with auloi and tympana and cymbals, with hidden daggers. The citizens came out of their houses towards the spectacle, but the men playing the tympana and cymbals killed the spectators and seized their open houses and proclaimed Midas king.
>
> *Strat.* 8.4.1:
>
> ὅσαι μέχρι νῦν ἑορταί, θυσίαι, τελεταί, ἱερουργίαι, ταῦτα πάντα Νουμᾶς οἷα δὴ νόμους Νυμφῶν κατεστήσατο.
>
> All the festivals, offerings, religious ceremonies and sacred rituals that have existed up to now, all these things were established by Numa as institutions of the Nymphs.

Flavius Philostratus, the author of the *Life of Apollonius*, recounts, in *VA* 3.32, that a Persian king tells Apollonius how Egyptians who come to his court always belittle the Greeks, while they declare that they themselves are holy men καὶ νομοθέτας θυσιῶν τε καὶ τελετῶν, ὁπόσας νομίζουσιν οἱ Ἕλληνες. This corresponds with the claim of Herodotus and Diodorus that the Greek mysteries were supposed to have come from Egypt.

In *VA* 4.18, Apollonius says that he knows more περὶ τῆς τελετῆς than the hierophant at Eleusis. Perhaps we may read a little more into τελετή here than just the sacred act, and it is this deeper meaning that the wise Apollonius fathoms.

VA 6.20. In a discussion by Apollonius with Thespesion, the leader of the γυμνοὶ σοφοί, the latter disapproves of the practice of subjecting ancient, sacred customs, the origins of which cannot be investigated, to a sober analysis. If we do this, we might as well lay hold of (ἐπιλαβοίμεθα) the τελετή at Eleusis, why it is the way it is and not otherwise; καὶ ὧν Σαμόθρᾳκες τελοῦσιν … καὶ Διονυσίων καὶ φαλλοῦ καὶ τοῦ ἐν

Κυλλήνῃ εἴδους, and so we would impair everything. It is clear how, around 200 AD, the verb τελεῖν, to perform a solemn act, is still heard in the word τελετή. This example also clearly illustrates the respect of the Greeks for religious customs of ancient origin; these are carefully left intact, and not seldom bear the name τελετή.[83] Phallic rites, especially, are also called so, because they have a highly symbolic character.[84] In the Elean town of Cyllene, a phallus was apparently set up as a cult statue (Paus. 6.26.5).

Our term also appears twice in the *Heroicus*, which is traditionally ascribed to Flavius Philostratus, although it may well belong to one of the other Philostrati.

Her. 28.11 describes how Cyrus the Elder was misled by an oracle from Orpheus ("Mine will be yours, Cyrus"), which led him to believe he would conquer the Odrysai and Europe:

> ὡς Ὀδρύσας τε καὶ τὴν Εὐρώπην καθέξων, ἐπειδὴ Ὀρφεύς ποτε μετὰ τοῦ σοφοῦ καὶ δυνατὸς γενόμενος ἀνά τε Ὀδρύσας ἴσχυσεν ἀνά τε Ἕλληνας, ὁπόσοι τελεταῖς ἐθείαζον,

> Since Orpheus, once he had become wise and powerful, swayed power among the Odrysai and the Greeks, who were inspired through *teletai*.

In *Her.* 52.3, the word apparently refers to the institutionalized singing of hymns:

> καὶ μὴν καὶ ὕμνων ἐκ Θετταλίας ὁ Ἀχιλλεὺς ἔτυχεν, οὓς ἀνὰ πᾶν ἔτος ἐπὶ τὸ σῆμα φοιτῶντες ᾖδον ἐν νυκτὶ τελετῆς τι ἐγκαταμιγνύντες τοῖς ἐναγίσμασιν.

> Moreover, Achilles has hymns from Thessaly that people who come to visit his tomb every year sing at night, mixing something of a *telete* in with the *enagismata* (offerings to the dead).

The historian HERODIAN, *Ab excessu divi Marci* 4.2.1, mentions the deification of the emperor, and expresses himself thus: τήν τε τοιαύτην τελετήν[85] ἀποθέωσιν καλοῦσι. He then describes the ceremony, which bore a very special character.[86] For the use of the term τελετή to refer to a cere-

---

[83] E.g. Ar. *Pax* 419 (inter alia the Dipolieia).
[84] Cf. Diod. 4.6.4; Plotinus *Enn.* 3.6.19; cf. also Burkert, *Homo Necans*, 69–72.
[85] Only one manuscript reads τελετήν, the others τιμήν, which Mendelsohn has put in his text. I believe τελετήν is the correct reading.
[86] Cf. E. Bickermann, *Archiv für Religionswissenschaft* 27 (1929) 4.

mony in honour of the deceased, we may perhaps compare Dio Chrysostom 31.80, where there is mention of the τελεταί of heroes, conferred upon certain Rhodians.

Diogenes Laertius tells us, in 1.102, how Anacharsis, the progressive Scythian prince, was killed after his return from Greece. Some say that he was killed performing Greek rites (τελετὰς Ἑλληνικὰς ἐπιτελοῦντα). This refers to the statement in Herodotus 4.76, which says that Anacharsis had seen a festival for the Μήτηρ θεῶν in Cyzicus that Herodotus called ὁρτή and παννυχίς. It was a capricious festival, with deafening music of cymbals, in which Anacharsis, when he imitates it in his homeland, covers himself with amulets.[87]

In 8.2, τελετή perhaps has the meaning of initiation ceremonies. It is said of Pythagoras that he was initiated into the Greek and oriental mysteries (ἐμυήθη τάς θ' Ἑλληνικὰς καὶ βαρβάρους τελετάς).

In 8.33, it is said that Pythagoras believed that ritual purity could be attained through cleansing, lustrations and lustral sprinkling, by staying clean from deaths and births, and abstinence from certain foods. These customs are also recommended by οἱ τὰς τελετὰς ἐν τοῖς ἱεροῖς ἐπιτελοῦντες: "those who perform religious rites in the sanctuaries." I believe it is clear from this that the τελεταί here are nothing else than, or at least of the same nature as, the acts enumerated beside them.[88] For such ritual cleansing, see Wächter, *Reinheitsvorschriften*, 7, where it is apparent that these customs were in fact not limited to the ritual of Orphic and similar ceremonies.

Ps. Oppian, *Cynegetica*, seems to be a work from the beginning of the third century AD.[89] In 4.249, it is told how the nurses of the little Dionysus had put him in a wooden box, had clothed themselves in fawn-skins and vines and had danced τὸ μυστικόν, playing tympana and cymbals, to hide the crying of Dionysus from Hera:

---

[87] Cf. Stein, ad locum.

[88] Zijderveld equates the purification ceremonies with the religious rites in the sanctuaries; I disagree: Since, in Greek religion, purity was a precondition for entering sanctuaries and performing rites there, τελεταί here cannot possibly be cleansing rites but must in fact be religious ceremonies performed in the sanctuaries, e.g. sacrifice, for which purification ceremonies are merely a necessary preparation, FLS. For a listing of Greek sacred laws containing cathartic requirements, see Lupu, *NGSL*, p. 15.

[89] Cf. A. & M. Croiset, *Histoire de la littérature grecque* V (1899) 622.

... πρῶτα δ' ἔφαινον
ὄργια κευθομένῃ περὶ λάρνακι· σὺν δ' ἄρα τῇσιν
Ἀόνιαι λάθρῃ τελετῶν ἅπτοντο γυναῖκες.

They first revealed their rites around the concealed box. And with them,
the Aonian (Boeotian) women secretly took part in the rites.

One sees that in this aetiological myth, the acts of the bacchantes are
called both τελεταί and ὄργια.

It is only natural that PLOTINUS' usage of the term τελετή is very reminiscent of what we saw in Plato. For example, in *Enn.* 1.6.6, he says that
every virtue is a κάθαρσις.

διὸ καὶ αἱ τελεταὶ ὀρθῶς αἰνίττονται τὸν μὴ κεκαθαρμένον καὶ εἰς
Ἅιδου κείσεσθαι ἐν βορβόρῳ, ὅτι τὸ μὴ καθαρὸν βορβόρῳ διὰ κάκην
φίλον.

Therefore the mysteries rightly suggest that he who has not been cleansed
shall lie in the mud even in Hades, because the unclean likes mud because
of its filthiness.

Cf. Plato, *Phaedo* 69c.

In *Enn.* 3.6.19, we again[90] find the notion that the founders of ancient
religious customs were actually philosophers, who e.g.:

μυστικῶς καὶ ἐν τελεταῖς αἰνιττόμενοι Ἑρμῆν μὲν ποιοῦσι τὸν ἀρχαῖον
τὸ τῆς γενέσεως ὄργανον ἀεὶ ἔχοντα πρὸς ἐργασίαν.

hinting through mystic symbolism and in rites, always portray the ancient
Hermes with his genital organ ready for action.

Hermes was worshipped in the shape of a phallus on Mount Cyllene
in Arcadia,[91] so it is possible that Plotinus had that cult in mind with
τελεταί. Cf. also Philostr. *Vita Ap.* 6.20.

His student PORPHYRY, *De abstinentia* 2.49, mentions the fact that a priest
of a certain god is, of course, expert τῆς ἱδρύσεως τῶν ἀγαλμάτων αὐτοῦ
τῶν τε ὀργιασμῶν καὶ τελετῶν καθάρσεών τε καὶ τῶν ὁμοίων ("in
setting up the statues of that deity, and in his rituals and purification rites
and the like"). Here τελεταί are special rites.

---

[90] Cf. Heraclitus, *Quaest. Hom.* 6.
[91]   Cf. Pausanias 6.26.5; see also Wilamowitz, *Glaube* I, 160.

With reference to the doctrine of transmigration of the soul, Stobaeus 1.447 (Wachsmuth) argues that Porphyry said that when we die, we should keep our souls clean from all evil lusts, envy, and such, ὥσπερ ἐν τελετῇ, καθαρεύοντα ("being pure, just as in the initiation rite"). Here, the ritual purity is already regarded as a symbol of moral purity; ἁγνεία δ' ἐστὶ φρονεῖν ὅσια: "purity is to have pious thoughts."[92] Similarly, we see that the regulations for ritual purity as a condition for entry to the sanctuaries are also explained in a moral way.[93]

Augustine, *Civ. D.* 10.9, declares that, according to Porphyry, there are certain "theurgicae consecrationes" called "teletae", by means of which the soul is prepared for seeing ghosts, angels and gods.

In ARISTIDES QUINTILIANUS, *De Musica*, our term is used in different contexts.

In 2.6, the word refers to the Roman *lectisternium*.

ἀλλὰ καὶ ἡ πατρὶς αὐτῶν τοὺς μὲν ἐπὶ Νομᾶ καὶ τοὺς ὀλίγῳ μετ' αὐτὸν ἔτι τυγχάνοντας ἀγριωτέρους μουσικῇ παιδευομένους εἶχε (καθὰ καὶ αὐτός φησιν), ἰδίᾳ τε ἐν εὐωχίαις κοινῇ τε ἐν ἁπάσαις τελεταῖς σφίσι συνοργιαζούσῃ.

But in the time of Numa and a little after him, their country (Rome) managed to educate the men who were still uncivilized, with music—he (Cicero) also says so himself—, both privately at banquets and publicly, celebrating together in all their *teletai*.

The word used by Cicero, to whom Aristides refers, is *pulvinaria* (*Tusc. Disp.* 4.4).[94] *Teletai* here are therefore lectisternia: banquets for the gods. We may recall that Pindar, *Ol.* 3.41, already used the word for theoxenia.

3.25 talks about Bacchic and similar rites:

διὸ καὶ τὰς βακχικὰς τελετὰς καὶ ὅσαι ταύταις παραπλήσιοι λόγου τινὸς ἔχεσθαί φασιν, ὅπως ἂν ἡ τῶν ἀμαθεστέρων πτοίησις διὰ βίον ἢ τύχην ὑπὸ τῶν ἐν ταύταις μελῳδιῶν τε καὶ ὀρχήσεων ἅμα παιδιαῖς ἐκκαθαίρηται.

Therefore they say that Bacchic rites and all that are akin to these have a certain reason, that the passionate excitement of those who, because of

---

[92] Cited as an inscription at the temple in Epidaurus: Porph. *Abst.* 2.19.
[93] Cf. Wächter, *Reinheitsvorschriften*, 8.
[94] I owe this reference to T.J. Mathiesen, *Aristides Quintilianus: On Music* (1983) ad locum.

occupation or fortune, are quite ignorant, may be purified by the melodies and dances in these rites that are accompanied by playfulness.

So *teletai* here are Bacchic and similar rites that have a cathartic character, due to their playful melodies and dances.

In 3.27, the word is used in a metaphorical sense. Philosophy is described as 'making perfect' (τελεσιουργός):

> ἡ μὲν ἀκριβὴς τῷ ὄντι τελετὴ τὸ διὰ τὴν ἐν γενέσει συμφορὰν ταῖς ψυχαῖς ἀποβληθὲν δι᾽ ἀναμνήσεων ἀναπληροῦσα.

> It is accurate because it is an accomplishment (*telete*) that, through recollection, replenishes what was accidentally lost by the souls in creation.

In the *Greek novel*, we repeatedly come across a metaphorical use of the terminology of mysteries for the secrets of love. Aristophanes had already led the way with this, see e.g. *Lys.* 832 where, during the quarrel between women and old men, Lysistrata sees Cinesias approaching and calls out:

> ἄνδρ᾽ ἄνδρ᾽ ὁρῶ προσιόντα, παραπεπληγμένον,
> τοῖς τῆς Ἀφροδίτης ὀργίοις εἰλημμένον.

> A man! I see a man coming, desperate looking, overwhelmed by the mysteries of Aphrodite!

Also 898, where Cinesias says to his wife:

> τὰ τῆς Ἀφροδίτης ἱέρ᾽ ἀνοργίαστά σοι
> χρόνον τοσοῦτόν ἐστιν.

> You have not performed the rites of Aphrodite for such a long time.

We can safely assume that such a metaphor was very common among the people.

In ACHILLES TATIUS,[95] *De Leuc. et Cit.* 1.7, we read that someone is called ἔρωτι τετελεσμένος, and in 4.1 we find τὰ τῆς Ἀφροδίτης ὄργια in the same context. We find τελετή in the same sense in 1.9, where the lovelorn Clitophon turns to an older friend for advice:

> σὺ γὰρ ἀρχαιότερος μύστης ἐμοῦ καὶ συνηθέστερος ἤδη τῇ τελετῇ τοῦ θεοῦ.

> For you are an older initiate than I and already more accustomed to the mysteries of the god (Eros).

---

[95] For when he lived, cf. W. Lehmann, *De Achillis Tatii aetate* (1910).

Without metaphor: you know better how everything works on such occasions. See also 1.2: καὶ γὰρ ὁρῶ σου τὴν ὄψιν οὐ μακρὰν τῆς τοῦ θεοῦ τελετῆς. "For I can tell by your appearance that you are very close to being initiated into the god's mysteries."

In HELIODORUS, *Aethiopica* 2.26, Delphi is called a city, dedicated to ἱερὰ καὶ τελεταί. Perhaps τελεταί here refers to the famous method in which the Pythian oracles were delivered.

9.10. In an Egyptian village, where the Nile festival is about to start, all inhabitants are busy πρὸς θυσίαις τε καὶ τελεταῖς. It is well known how numerous festivals in honour of the Nile are in Egypt.[96] We saw before that Egyptian religious festivals, with their rich and carefully observed ritual, tend to be called τελετή by the Greeks. (Hdt. 2.171; Diod. 1.22.6 etc.)

8.11 gives us an example of τελετή in the sense of miraculous power. Chariclea, the heroine of the story, who once miraculously escaped from death by fire, speaks to her lover, Theagenes, about her γνωρίσματα, the objects given along with an abandoned child. Also among these is a ring with a stone called παντάρβη in which several holy marks are inscribed, καὶ τελετῆς, ὡς ἔοικε, θειοτέρας ἀνάμεστος παρ' ἧς εἰκάζω δύναμίν τινα ἥκειν τῇ λίθῳ πυρὸς φυγαδευτικήν, ἀπάθειαν τοῖς ἔχουσιν ἐν ταῖς φλογώσεσι δωρουμένην. If we translate: "and it is filled, so it seems, with supernatural power and the stone has the power to repel fire, offering protection from the flames to those who wear it", I believe we more or less capture the meaning.

This new use of our term can be explained as follows: τελετή in the context of mysteries, and in particular of Orphism, is, as we saw, a special ritual act, bound by strict laws; he who submits to these rituals, undergoes a profound transformation. But objects, especially rings, could also be subjected to certain ritual acts, to give them a certain power. They are therefore called τετελεσμένοι δακτύλιοι.[97]

To what extent this usage increases, especially in later times, is apparent from the Greek magical papyri from Egypt: the term τελετή is used there several times. That of all places, Egypt has yielded so many magical texts, is of course no coincidence. In this country, magic was particularly

---

[96] Cf. J.H. Breasted, *Development of Religion and Thought in Ancient Egypt* (1912) 8.

[97] Cf. Ar. *Plut.* 883. The Orphic poem attests to magic stones. For the term τετελεσμένος, subjected to a magic act and thus made magic, cf. also: Suidas s.v. Παλλάδιον: τοῦτο ἦν ζῴδιον μικρόν, ὃ ἔλεγον εἶναι τετελεσμένον. It was a gift from the τελεστής Asios.

developed, also in the official cult. It should therefore not surprise us that the people, also in later times, attached much credence to magical practices.

GREEK MAGICAL PAPYRI. The following examples are all derived from the so-called magical papyri. I have adopted the texts from Preisendanz' collection.[98]

PGM 12 (P.Lugd.Bat. J 384 (V)) is dated by Henrichs to ca. 100 AD.[99] In the beginning, a love-charm called πάρεδρος Ἔρως is described (lines 15–17):

Ἔρωτος τελετή, καὶ ἀφιέρωσις καὶ κατασκευή· ποιεῖ δὲ πράξεις ταύτας καὶ ὀνειροπομπείαν· ἀγρυπνίαν ποιεῖ καὶ διαλλάσσει κακοδαίμο-
νος, ἐὰν ὀρθῶς αὐτῷ χρήσῃ καὶ ἁγνῶς, ἔστιν γὰρ ἔχων πᾶσαν πρᾶξιν.

Telete of an Eros—consecration and preparation. He performs the following operations: he sends dreams, causes insomnia and releases you from an evil spirit, if you use him in a proper and holy manner, for he can perform every operation.

This is followed by instructions for creating an Eros doll from wax and other materials, after which it is said: καὶ Ψυχὴν τέλεσον ταὐτὸν ὡς Ἔρωτα ("And make a Psyche of the same kind as Eros"). I can only interpret the words τελετή and τελεῖν here as 'manufacture', though under very specific instructions, minutely prescribed by the papyrus.

After the description of a very complicated sacrifice to Eros that must take place at night, it is prescribed (lines 36–38):

τῇ δὲ γ΄ ἡμέρᾳ ἕτερον νοσσάκιον βωμῷ εἰσθές. ποιῶν τὴν τελετὴν κατά-
φαγε τὸν νεόσσον μόνος, ἄλλος δὲ μηδεὶς συνέστω. ταῦτ᾿ οὖν ποιήσας
ἁγνῶς καὶ καθαρῶς ἁπάντων ἐπιτεύξῃ.

---

[98] In his eagerness to demonstrate the special nature of *teletai*, Zijderveld overemphasized the magical aspect of the word τελετή in the magical papyri. For example, every ritual act is suddenly a 'magic act' and the consecration of an object a 'magical preparation' (e.g., *PGM* 12.36, 209, 211, 311; 4.2205; 5.159; 7.72); invocations of a deity become instances of 'magic use of names' (e.g., *PGM* 4.1596; 5.159). To avoid the charge of knowingly deceiving the reader, I have thought it necessary to bring the translations and interpretation of the magical papyri more in line with current specialist literature and Betz' modern translations, even in cases where this has meant a significant departure from Zijderveld's original interpretation. The expert advice of H.S. Versnel has been instrumental in the revision process. FLS.

[99] *PGM*, ad loc.; Dieterich had dated it slightly later (ca. 200 AD, Dieterich, *Kleine Schriften*, 34, 35).

On the 3rd day, put another chick on the altar. While performing the rite, eat the chick on your own; let no-one else be present. Once you have performed these things in a holy and pure manner, you will be successful in everything.

This is followed by an invocation that must be said at the sacrifice. A touch of magic may be apparent in the fact that success is entirely dependent upon the correct performance of the ritual. Finally, lines 79–95 prescribe the formula that must be written on a piece of papyrus. The formula ends as follows (lines 90–95):

ἧκέ μοι, κλῦθί μου ἐπὶ τήνδε τὴν χρείαν, ἐπὶ τήνδε τὴν πρᾶξιν, μέγιστε Ἀρσαμῶσι μουχα λινουχα ἅρπαξ Ἀδωνεαί· ἐγώ εἰμι, ᾧ συνήντησας ὑπὸ τὸ ἱερὸν ὄρος καὶ ἐδωρήσω τὴν τοῦ μεγίστου ὀνόματός σου γνῶσιν, ἣν καὶ τηρήσω ἁγνῶς μηδενὶ μεταδιδούς, εἰ μὴ τοῖς σοῖς συνμύσταις εἰς τὰς σὰς ἱερὰς τελετὰς ιαρβαθατρα μνηψιβαω χνημεωψ· ἐλθὲ καὶ παράστα εἰς τηνδε χρείαν καὶ συνέργησον.

Come to me, hear me in this service and this ritual, greatest one, *Harsamosi moucha linoucha* robber *Adonai*. I am he whom you met at the foot of the holy mountain and to whom you gave the knowledge of your greatest name, which I shall also guard in a holy manner, imparting it to no-one except your fellow initiates in your holy rites *iarbathatra mnepsibao chnemeops*. Come and assist me in this service and work with me.

In line 202, we find a recipe for a δακτυλίδιον πρὸς πᾶσαν πρᾶξιν καὶ ἐπιτυχίαν: "a little ring for every (magical) operation and for success". You must subject a jasper stone to all kinds of curious treatments and when you have consecrated the stone (τελέσσας τὸν λίθον), wear it in a gold ring. Then, if you are pure, it will provide you with everything you wish (line 209):

τελέσεις δὲ τὸ δακτυλίδιον ἅμα τῇ ψήφῳ τῇ κατὰ πάντων τελετῇ.

You will consecrate the ring, together with the stone, with the rite for all occasions.[100]

Line 211: τελετὴ δὲ ἡ κατασκευὴ ἡ ὑπογεγραμμένη. "The rite consists of the preparation described below." After a meticulous enumeration of the very special preparations for an offering, the text of a prayer follows (lines 216–217):

---

[100] For magic rings, see Ar. *Plut.* 883; *PGM* 5.213–239.

ἐπικαλοῦμαι καὶ εὔχομαι τὴν τελετήν, ὦ θεοὶ οὐράνιοι, ὦ θεοὶ ὑπὸ γῆν,
ὦ θεοὶ ἐν μέσῳ μέρει κυκλούμενοι, γ´ ἥλιοι.

I invoke you and pray for the consecration, celestial gods, gods below the
earth, gods circling in the middle region, 3 suns.[101]

This is followed by magic words: *Anoch Mane Barchuch.*

Line 262. In such a prayer the following words are prescribed among
others:

μηδεὶς δαίμων ἢ πνευμάτων ἐναντιωθήσεταί μοι, ὅτι σοῦ ἐπὶ τῇ τελετῇ
τὸ μέγα ὄνομα ἐπεκαλεσάμην.

No daemon and none of the spirits will oppose me, because I have called
your great name at the consecration.

Line 307 ends a magic spell with the words: ναί, δέσποτα, δέσποτα, τέλει
τελείαν τελετήν. "Yes, master, master, bring to completion a complete
consecration."

In lines 311–312, the ritual that ensures us of the help of a god, is again
called τελετή:

ἐκτελέσαντος δὲ τὴν τελετὴν, καθὼς προσήκει, ἔχε ἀλέκτορα δίλοφον,
ἤτοι λευκὸν ἢ ξανθόν, ἀπέχου δὲ μέλανος, καὶ μετὰ τὴν τελετὴν ζῶντα
τὸν ἀλέκτορα ἀνάπτυζε καὶ ἔνβαλε τὸ ζῳδάριον ἔσω εἰς τὰ σπλάγχνα
τοῦ ἀλεκτόρου.

And when you have completed the consecration rite properly, take a
rooster with a double comb, either white or yellow—keep away from
black—and after the consecration cut the live rooster open and insert the
image between the inner organs of the rooster.

And a few lines on, we read (lines 316–317):

ὁσάκεις ἂν βόλει ἐπιτάσσειν τῷ θεῷ, τὸν μέγιστον Οὐφωρα εἰπὼν ἐπί-
τασσε καὶ τελεῖ· ἔχεις τὴν τελετὴν τοῦ μεγίστου καὶ θείου ἐνεργήματος.

Whenever you wish to command the god, give the command, saying the
greatest name, *Ouphor*, and he will perform it. You possess the power of
the consecration to realize the supreme and divine achievement.[102]

---

[101] Zijderveld interpreted τελετήν as 'magic prayer' here, which makes little sense: one
cannot ἐπικαλεῖσθαι a prayer. Betz has "I invoke and beseech the consecration", which
offers little improvement, for how can one beseech a consecration? Preisendanz has the
correct translation: "Ich rufe euch an und flehe um die Weihe." FLS.

[102] Cf. *PGM* 3.429 (= Pap. Louvre 2391 Mimaut) πράξεως ταύτης μείζων οὐκ ἔστιν.
It should be noted that, in these papyri, πρᾶξις often means the same as τελετή.

PGM 13 (*P.Lugd.Bat.* J 395 (W)) is probably from the same period as the previous one. The text presents itself as the "Sacred Book called Monad." Line 230 marks the beginning of a new topic:

πλήρης ἡ τελετὴ τῆς Μονάδος προσεφωνήθη σοι, τέκνον. ὑποτάξω δέ σοι, τέκνον, καὶ τὰς χρείας τῆς ἱερᾶς βίβλου.

The rite of the Monad has been completely declared to you, child. But for you, child, I will also add the practical uses of this sacred book.

So evidently, the τελετή of the Monad is an act of ritual preparation, which is distinct from the practical applications of the sacred book.

Line 27. In the description of a sacrificial ritual, we find the rule that, twenty-one days prior to the τελετή, one must prepare the seven flowers of the seven stars in a meticulously prescribed way:

ταῦτα τὰ ἄνθη πρὸ εἴκοσι μιᾶς ἡμέρας τῆς τελετῆς λειοτρίβησον εἰς λευκὴν θυίαν καὶ ξήρανον ἐν σκιᾷ καὶ ἔχε αὐτὰ ἕτοιμα εἰς τὴν ἡμέραν ἐκείνην.

Take those flowers twenty-one days before the consecration and rub them fine in a white mortar and lay them to dry in the shade and have them ready for that day.

Lines 889–896 give very precise instructions for a ritual consecration:

τελεῖται ἡλίοις τῆς ιγ΄ αὕτη ἡ τηλητὴ τοῦ χρυσοῦ πετάλου ἐκλειχομένου τε καὶ ἐπιλεγομένου· ιαια ιυ οη ιευοω [κτλ.], εἶτα τελειότερον· αωευη οαι ιο ηυεωα [κτλ.]. ἐν τηλητῇ ταῦτα ἑξάκις λέγεται σὺν τοῖς πᾶσι.

The following rite is performed for the suns on the 13th, when the gold leaf is licked and read: iaia iu oē ieuoō (etc.), then more complete: aōeuē oai io ēueōa (etc.) In the magic preparation this is said six times with the rest of it.

PGM 4 (*P.Bibl.Nat.Suppl.* gr. 574) is the well known Parisian magical papyrus. The ritual described in lines 26–51 is introduced with the title [τ]ελετή (26) and concluded with the assurance: καὶ ἔσει τετελεσμένος (48): "and you will be completely consecrated."

In line 1596, we read: ἔστιν δὲ ἡ κατὰ πάντων τελετὴ ἥδε. πρὸς Ἥλιον λόγος: "This is the rite for all occasions. Prayer to Helios." This is followed by a prayer to Helios, in which, among other things: "I invoke your holy and great and secret name, which you hear with joy."

Line 2205. After a description of the consecration of an iron lamella with three Homeric verses, which one must keep in the wound of a man condemned to death, it is said: ἡ μὲν τελετὴ αὕτη, αἱ δὲ πράξεις αἵδε: "That was the consecration. The (magical) operations are as follows." This is followed by specific applications, e.g. to have a revelation or to overturn racing chariots. So the consecration through which the lamella receives its special power, is called τελετή; the practical applications are called πράξεις.

In lines 2885–2890, we are told how to make a φυλακτήριον τῆς πράξεως ("protective charm for the ritual"): carve a three-faced Hecate on a lodestone, cleanse it and dip it in the blood of someone who has died a violent death. Then, when you have made a food offering, τὸν αὐτὸν λόγον λέγε ἐπὶ τῆς τελετῆς (2889–2890): "say the same spell at the consecration."

PGM 5 (P.Lond. 46, ed. Kenyon). Lines 69–172 contain the invocation of the supreme god with an enumeration of all his names, who is asked to free a person from a certain ghost and to subject all ghosts to him (Kenyon). In line 159, we read:

> τελετὴ τῆς προκειμένης ποιήσεως· γράψας τὰ ὀνόματα (Preisend. τὸ ὄνομα) εἰς καινὸν χαρτάριον καὶ διατείνας ἀπὸ κροτάφου εἰς κρόταφον σεαυτοῦ ἐντύγχανε πρὸς βορέαν τοῖς ϛ´ ὀνόμασι κτλ.
>
> Preparation of the foregoing ritual: having written the names (or: formula) on a new sheet of papyrus and having extended it from one side of your forehead to the other, read the 6 names, facing north …

In line 230, we again have τελετή in the sense of consecration rite: παρακείσθωσαν ἐπὶ τῆς τελετῆς ἄρτοι καθάρειοι καὶ ὅσα ἀκμάζει τῶν ὀπωρῶν. "Let pure loaves of bread lie close at hand at the consecration, and whatever fruits are in season."

PGM 7 (P.Lond. 121) has the term τελετή twice in the lunar spell of Claudianus (lines 862–918). The title of this section is: Κλαυδιανοῦ σεληνιακὸν καὶ οὐρανοῦ καὶ ἄρκτου τε⟨λετὴ⟩ ἐπὶ σεληνιακῶν (862): "Lunar spell of Claudianus and rite of heaven and Bear at lunar offerings." Ten lines on, it reads (line 872):

> καὶ τελέσας αὐτὴν τῇ κατὰ πάντων τελετῇ ⟨ἀπόθου⟩, καὶ ἔσται προτετελεσμένη.
>
> And having consecrated it with the rite for all occasions, put it away and it will be consecrated in advance.

Here we find the same phrase as in PGM 12.209: τῇ κατὰ πάντων τελετῇ.

As we have seen, the word τελετή is frequently used in the magical papyri to indicate a meticulously performed ritual preparation or consecration.

ORPHICA. As was to be expected, the term τελετή occurs very frequently in Orphic literature.

Orph. frag. 578 Bernabé (fr. 31 Kern) is the famous papyrus fragment from Gurôb, *P.Gurôb* 1, from the third century BC.[103] The third line reads: [- - - - -] διὰ τὴν τελετήν, "through (or: because of) the rite." It is not entirely clear what rite is meant here, but the general context is unmistakably Bacchic-Orphic.[104]

Orph. frag. 383 Bernabé (fr. 49 Kern) is a papyrus in Berlin from the second century BC, *P.Berol* 44, where it is said that Musaeus wrote up the hymns of Orpheus and took great care with regard to τελετὰς καὶ μυστήρια καὶ [καθαρμοὺς καὶ] μαντεῖα ("rites and mysteries and purifications and divinations").

Other places where τελετή occurs, classified by Kern as Orphic fragments, have been discussed above: Plato *Phd.* 69c, *Resp.* 364e; Dem. *Aristog.* 1.11.

The *Orphic hymns*[105] often use the term to refer to the secret ceremony celebrated by the Orphics. Several times, the deity is implored to attend this τελετή:

1.9 Hecate: λισσόμενος κούρην τελεταῖς ὁσίαισι παρεῖναι.
  "Beseeching the maiden to be present at the sacred ceremonies."

6.10 Protogonus: βαῖνε γεγηθὼς | ἐς τελετὴν ἁγίαν πολυποίκιλον ὀργιοφάν-
  ταις.
  "Come rejoicing to the very colourful sacred ceremony for priests."

27.11 Mother of the gods: ἔρχεο πρὸς τελετήν, ὦ πότνια, τυμπανοτερπής.
  "Come to the ceremony, mistress who delights in the tympana."

49.7 Hipta: ἔρχεο πρὸς τελετὰς ἱερῶι γήθουσα προσώπωι.
  "Come to the ceremonies, rejoicing with your sacred face."

53.9 Bacchus: βαῖν' ἐπὶ πάνθειον τελετὴν γανόωντι προσώπωι.
  "Come to the all-divine ceremony with a joyous face."

54.7 Silenus: δεῦρ' ἐπὶ πάνθειον τελετὴν Σατύροις ἅμα πᾶσι.
  "Come to the all-divine ceremony with all your Satyrs."

35.7 Leto: βαῖν' ἐπὶ πάνθειον τελετὴν τέλος ἡδὺ φέρουσα.
  "Come to the all-divine ceremony bringing a sweet ritual."

43.10 Horae: ἔλθετ' ἐπ' εὐφήμους τελετὰς ὁσίας νεομύστοις.
  "Come to the auspicious sacred ceremonies for the newly initiated."

---

[103] See also J. Hordern, *ZPE* 129 (2000) 131–140, who presents a new edition of the text, with a very good photograph of the papyrus (Plate III).
[104] See W. Burkert, *Ancient Mystery Cults* (1987) 70–71.
[105] The date of the Orphic hymns is somewhat disputed. They probably date from the third or fourth century AD. See L. van Liempt, *De vocabulario hymnorum Orphicorum atque aetate* (1930); Wilamowitz, *Glaube* II, 514.

7.12 Stars: ἔλθετ᾽ ἐπ᾽ εὐιέρου τελετῆς πολυΐστορας ἄθλους.
     "Come to the very learned contests of the the very sacred ceremony."

42.11 Mise: εὐμενέουσ᾽ ἔλθοις ἀγαθοὺς τελετῆς ἐπ᾽ ἀέθλους.
     "May you come well-disposed to the good contests of the ceremony."

79.12 Themis: ἀλλά μάκαιρ᾽ ἔλθοις κεχαρημένη εὔφρονι βουλῆι |
     εὐιέρους ἐπὶ μυστιπόλου τελετὰς σέο, κούρη.
     "May you come delighted and with favourable will to your very sacred ceremonies of your initiate, blessed maiden."

49.2 Hipta: Ἵππαν κικλήσκω, Βάκχου τροφόν, εὐάδα κούρην |
     μυστιπόλοις τελεταῖσιν ἀγαλλομένην Σάβου ἁγνοῦ.
     "I call on Hipta, nurse of Bacchus, favourable maiden, to come to the ceremonies for the initiates, taking delight in sacred Sabazius."

75.3 Palaemon: κικλήσκω σε, Παλαῖμον, ἐπ᾽ εὐιέροις τελεταῖσιν |
     ἐλθεῖν εὐμενέοντα.
     "I call on you, Palaemon, to come well-disposed to the very sacred ceremonies."

Sometimes the deity is said to have been the first to reveal the τελεταί:

24.10 Nereids: ὑμεῖς γὰρ πρῶται τελετὴν ἀνεδείξατε σεμνήν.
     "You first revealed your solemn ceremony."

38.6 Curetes: ὑμεῖς καὶ τελετὴν πρῶτοι μερόπεσσιν ἔθεσθε.
     "You first instituted your ceremony for humans."

76.7 Muses: αἳ τελετὰς θνητοῖς ἀνεδείξατε μυστιπολεύτους.
     "You revealed the mystic ceremonies to mortals."

79.8 Themis: πρώτη γὰρ τελετὰς ἁγίας θνητοῖς ἀνέφηνας.
     "You were the first to reveal your sacred ceremonies to mortals."

Or the deity is invoked like this:

54.10 Silenus: ὄργια νυκτιφαῆ τελεταῖς ἁγίαις ἀναφαίνων.
     "Revealing, in sacred ceremonies, rites that shine by night."

84.3 Hestia: τούσδε σὺ ἐν τελεταῖς ὁσίους μύστας ἀναδείξαις.
     "May you reveal (i.e. consecrate) these sacred initiates in the ceremonies."

Bacchus is called τελετάρχα, 'leader of the ceremony' (52.3). His foster-father Silenus, too, is given this same epithet (54.4): θιάσου νομίου τελετάρχα: "leader of the ceremony of the rural thiasos."

Finally, *Hymn* 77.9–10 calls on the goddess Mnemosyne to refresh the initiates' memory of the very sacred ceremony:

> ἀλλά, μάκαιρα θεά, μύσταις μνήμην ἐπέγειρε
> εὐιέρου τελετῆς, λήθην δ᾽ ἀπὸ τῶνδ᾽ ἀπόπεμπε.

> Blessed goddess, awaken the memory of the very sacred ceremony for the initiates and send off forgetfulness away from them.

Lithica 726 gives τελετή in a distinctly magical sense. In the mixing of a certain potion (φάρμακον), one must invoke the secret name (ἄρρητον οὔνομα) of the gods:

> ... τέρπονται γάρ, ἐπεί κέ τις ἐν τελετῇσι
> μυστικὸν ἀείδῃσιν ἐπώνυμον οὐρανιώνων.

> For they rejoice when, in ceremonies, someone sings the mystic name of the celestials.

As so often in the magical papyri, here it is the preparation of a magic potion.

In the Orphic *Argonautica* 904, τελετή refers to the mysteries of Hecate.[106] Artemis Hecate guards the Golden Fleece; the poet calls her:

> δεινήν τ' ἀνθρώποισιν ἰδεῖν δεινήν τ' ἐσακοῦσαι
> εἰ μή τις τελεταῖς πελάσει καὶ θύσθλα καθαρμῶν,
> ὅσσα περ ἀρήτειρα καθάρματα μύστις ἔκευθε.

> terrible for men to see and terrible to hear, unless someone will also bring the sacred cleansing implements to the mysteries, precisely the cathartic instruments that the priestess of the mysteries has hidden.

These last two Orphic poems probably date from the fourth and early fifth century AD respectively.

Conclusion

It appears that the more general meaning found in Chapter II: religious act of any nature, is hardly to be found anymore in the period after Alexander. Τελετή is almost always a ceremony of a special nature, sometimes with a symbolical meaning, sometimes secret; in quite a few cases, the magical meaning of the word is evident, especially in the magical papyri.

In Plut. *De Is. et Os.* 369b and Polyaenus, *Strat.* 8.4.1, it is still 'religious ceremony' in a general sense; perhaps also in Aristides 1.44, Musonius Rufus 20 and in the expression τελετή μυστηρίων. Phlegon, *Olymp.* fr. 1.6, uses the word for the festival of the Olympic games. In Paus. 8.9.8, it refers to an annual festival for Antinous.

---

[106] I see no indication of a magic rite here, *contra* Zijderveld, FLS.

Very often it is a ritual act of a special nature. For example:

- peculiar Celtic customs: Strabo 4.4.6;
- Roman lectisternium: Aristid. Quint. 2.6;
- secret rites of the Zoroastrian magi: Dio Chrys. 36.39;
- consecration of the Persian king: Plut. *Artax.* 3 (1012c);
- apotheosis of the Roman emperor: Hdn. *Ab exc. d. Marci* 4.2.1.

Certainly some τελεταί were symbolic acts. For example:

- the usual purification ceremonies at sanctuaries: Porph. *Abst.* 2.49;
- the Egyptian cult acts: e.g. Diod. 4.6.4; Philostr. *Vita Ap.* 6.20.

In particular, however, we should mention here the rites of the mysteries, especially those at Eleusis, that are very often called τελετή (-ταί). Cf. e.g. Diod. 20.110.1; Dio Chrys. 36.33; Plut. *Demetr.* 26 (900e) etc.

Separate parts of these mysteries are also called τελετή: the κερνοφορία are mentioned in this regard by Polemon, in Athenaeus 11.56; and the πομπή to Eleusis: Plut. *Alc.* 34 (210).

Often these rites are shrouded in secrecy, but that this secret nature is not essential to τελεταί, is evident from Diod. 5.77.3.

Written instructions for certain religious customs of a complicated nature, especially mysteries, are referred to as τελεταί: Paus. 4.26.8 (cf. *Syll.*[3] 736). In Philostr. *Her.* 52.3, the word probably refers to the singing of hymns.

The sect or religious community that arises around the τελετή is also called τελετή: Lucian *Peregr.* 11; M. Aur. *Med.* 9.30; see also the Christian authors.

In a pejorative sense: licentious festival of a quasi-religious nature, τελετή is used by Plut. *Cleom.* 33 (820d); cf. Josephus, *Ant. Jud.* 19.1.5.

In a metaphorical sense, to refer to something secret, or something that is only known to certain people, we see τελετή, e.g. Dion. Hal. *Comp.* 25: τελεταὶ λόγου; Lucian *Merc. cond.* 1; Gal. *UP* 448.4; Aristid. Quint. 3.27; Ach. Tatius 1.9 (the τελεταί of love). The usage found in Heraclitus, *Quaest. Hom.* 64, also belongs to this class: allegorical explanation of myths.

When τελεταί refer to mystery rites, one can see magic acts in them, according to some scholars.[107] This magical meaning of τελετή emerges more clearly in Diod. 5.64; Dio Chrys. 4.90; Strabo 7, fr. 18 Cr.; Lucian, *Menippus* 6; and in the magical papyri.

---

[107] See e.g. Deubner, *Attische Feste,* 79.

In Paus. 9.30.4 and Nonn. *Dion.* 16.400 and 48.880 ff., we find Τελετή personified as a goddess.

Finally, we should mention the lost works, Περὶ τελετῶν, by Neanthes and others, which will have had the purpose of explaining special, symbolic rites. We therefore find several aetiological myths in the fragments.

CHAPTER FOUR

ΤΕΛΕΤΗ IN JEWISH AND CHRISTIAN AUTHORS

It is instructive to examine in which cases Jewish and Christian authors avail themselves of the term τελετή, especially when they use it to refer to their own cult practice, which we sometimes know better (or from other sources) than Greek ritual. We already saw that many Egyptian religious ceremonies are τελεταί to the Greeks for the reasons that I have indicated above. It appears that some Jewish and Christian rites also possessed that peculiarity that stamped them as τελεταί for the Greeks.

In SEPTUAGINT, III Kingdoms (Authorized Version: I Kings) 15:12, we read how Asa abolished certain malpractices introduced by his forefathers. Among other things, ἀφεῖλεν τὰς τελετὰς ἀπὸ τῆς γῆς: "He took away the *teletai* from the land." The corresponding word *kadeš* in the Hebrew version means 'male temple prostitute', ἱερόδουλος. So here, τελετή seems to refer, *abstractum pro concreto*,[1] to this familiar figure in Semitic religions.[2] That τελεῖν was used for exactly this type of ritual acts may also be apparent from the use of the words τελεσφόρος and τελισκόμενος in Deut. 23:18, which describe the same concept.

Pagan rituals, too, are called τελετή in Amos 7:9. There, Yahweh speaks to Amos: καὶ ἀφανισθήσονται βωμοὶ τοῦ γέλωτος, καὶ αἱ τελεταὶ τοῦ Ἰσραὴλ ἐρημωθήσονται. "And the altars of laughter will be destroyed and the *teletai* of Israel will be stripped bare." The Hebrew word rendered here as τελεταί is *mikdaš*.[3] This same word is translated as χειροποιητά in Isaiah 16:12, referring to the sanctuaries of Moab. It is noteworthy that in Amos 7:13, the same word is translated as ἁγίασμα, but there it is the priest of these pagan institutions himself who uses the word. Perhaps the word had a certain pagan connotation in this period and the Septuagint,

---

[1] Cf. e.g. III Kgdms. (A.V.: I Kgs.) 14:24, where *kadeš* is translated σύνδεσμος.

[2] For such customs, see e.g. B.D. Eerdmans, *De godsdienst van Israel* I (1930) 118; G.E. Markoe, *The Phoenicians* (2000) 120. In Greece we find temple prostitution in Corinth; it is noteworthy that the scholiast to Lucian *Peregr.* 13, a Christian, refers to these Corinthian customs as τὰς αἰσχίστας καὶ ἐναγεῖς τελετάς.

[3] *Mikdaš* (sanctuary) and *kadeš* (male temple prostitute) are both derived from the root kdš (sacred).

by putting a more neutral word such as ἁγίασμα into the priest's mouth, wished to accentuate that he is condoning the customs.

In the apocryphal text *Wisdom of Solomon*, which was probably written between 100 and 50 BC by an Alexandrian Jew,[4] we find the word τελετή several times. Wisd. 12:4 is a passage from a hymn to Yahweh, who loves his own people more than the pagans, whom he hates:

> ἐπὶ τῷ ἔχθιστα πράσσειν, ἔργα φαρμακειῶν καὶ τελετὰς ἀνοσίους τέ-
> κνων τε φονὰς ἀνελεήμονας καὶ σπλαγχνοφάγον ἀνθρωπίνων σαρκῶν
> θοῖναν καὶ αἵματος, ἐκ μέσου μύστας θιάσου.[5]

> for doing most hateful things, works of witchcraft and unholy rites and merciless murders of children and organ-devouring feasting on human flesh and blood, these initiates from the midst of an unruly cult group.

What context the author has in mind with τελεταί is apparent from the adjacent ἔργα φαρμακειῶν. The author's familiarity with Greek religious terms is clear from the words μύστης and θίασος that her refer to customs of Canaanite peoples conquered by Israel.

Also Wisd. 14:15, where the origin of idolatry is described, τελετή refers to pagan (non-Jewish) rites: a father worships his prematurely deceased son as a god καὶ παρέδωκεν τοῖς ὑποχειρίοις μυστήρια καὶ τελετάς ("and gave his dependents mysteries and rites"). The typically Greek turn of phrase μυστήρια καὶ τελετὰς παραδιδόναι betrays the Hellenized identity of the author.

Wisd. 14:23 deals with pagans who celebrate τεκνοφόνους τελετὰς ἢ κρύφια μυστήρια ἢ ἐμμανεῖς ἐξάλλων θεσμῶν κώμους ("child-murdering rites or secretive mysteries or frantic revellings of deviant institutions"); and so it seems that, as in 12:4, a Moloch cult or something similar is intended.

The pseudo-historic document III Maccabees, which probably dates from the beginning of our era,[6] relates (2:29–30) how Ptolemy IV wanted to make all Jews serfs and give them a brand in the shape of an ivy leaf, as a sign of Dionysus. Yet, so the relevant edict added, if they chose to join those who had been initiatied in the mysteries (τοῖς κατὰ τὰς τελετὰς μεμυημένοις), they would be free citizens (2:30). The Dionysian mysteries that were in vogue in Alexandria will be meant here.

---

[4] Cf. K. Siegfried, in Kautzsch, *Die Apokryphen und Pseudepigraphen des Alten Testaments* I (1900) 479.

[5] The tradition is uncertain. See the critical apparatus of Swete.

[6] Cf. E. Kautzsch, *Die Apokryphen und Pseudepigraphen des Alten Testaments* I (1900) 121.

We establish that, in the Septuagint, the term τελετή is used exclusively for non-Jewish rites, in a disapproving sense.

In the later Jewish authors, however, we find a greater variety in meaning.

PHILO JUDAEUS, the Jewish Hellenist, "steht wie eine wahre Proteus-gestalt vor uns", to use the typical words of Geffcken.[7] It should therefore not surprise us that we find the term τελετή used in all kinds of senses. For example, he uses it:

A. In the sense: pagan, i.e. non-Jewish religious customs, just as the Septuagint.

De mutat. nom. 107 (*CW* III, 175), for instance, mentions people τελε-ταῖς ἀνιέροις ταῖς Βεελφεγὼρ τελεσθέντες ("consecrated in the unholy rites of Baal of Peor"); cf. *LXX* Num. 25:3 καὶ ἐτελέσθη Ἰσραὴλ τῷ Βεελ-φεγώρ: "And Israel was consecrated to Baal of Peor." This Baal of Peor was a rather uncouth local deity connected with Mount Peor in the land of Moab.[8]

De spec. leg. 1.56 (*CW* V, 14) deals with the history, told in Num. 25, of how Phinehas punishes the Israelites who commune with Moabite women. These sexual relations appear to go hand in hand with religious ones. Phinehas, at least, regarded them as τελουμένους τὰς μυθικὰς τελετάς. The adjective μυθικός for orthodox Jews (and Christians) prob-ably has the meaning: irreligious, i.e. derived from pagan myths. We need not think of mysteries of Baal, as we have seen that τελεῖν and τελεταί are certainly not exclusively terms used for mysteries.

De spec. leg. 1.319 (*CW* V, 77), where Philo speaks of pagan customs as mentioned in Deut. 14:1: "Ye shall not cut yourselves, nor make any bald-ness between your eyes." Philo adds that the law furthermore prohibits τὰ περὶ τελετὰς καὶ μυστήρια καὶ πᾶσαν τὴν τοιαύτην τερθρείαν καὶ βωμολοχίαν ("the practice of rites and mysteries and all such deception and buffoonery"). The expression τελετὰς καὶ μυστήρια makes it likely that he has a Greek mystery cult in mind here (cf. Wisd. 14:15, above). Philo proceeds to declare that it is inappropriate that Jews raised in the

---

[7] J. Geffcken, *Der Ausgang des griechisch-römischen Heidentums* (1920) 35 ("stands before us like a true Proteus figure").

[8] See *DDD*[2] s.v. Baal of Peor.

ideal state, i.e. in the theocracy, get involved in the nocturnal, secret rites and concoctions (πλάσματα). He then quotes:

> μηδεὶς οὖν μήτε τελείτω μήτε τελείσθω τῶν Μωυσέως φοιτητῶν καὶ γνωρίμων. ἑκάτερον γάρ, καὶ τὸ διδάσκειν καὶ τὸ μανθάνειν τελετάς, οὐ μικρὸν ἀνοσιούργημα

> "Therefore let none of the followers and disciples of Moses perform or receive such rites." For both the teaching and the learning of mystery rites is no small sacrilege.

The quotation seems to be a variant of the example cited above (*LXX* Deut. 23:18) and an addition that is not in the Hebrew text.[9] So Philo uses these words to refer to Hellenistic mysteries, although actually, as is clear from the original context,[10] they will have referred to the temple prostitution that occurred in Canaan. Philo was perhaps too Hellenized to recognize this. He evidently regards this example as a prohibition to the Jews to subject to Hellenistic mystery cults and perform them themselves.

De spec. leg. 3.40 (*CW* V, 161) is directed against perverted customs such as pederasty. According to Philo, the ἀνδρόγυνοι play a very prominent role in pagan cult, and they can be seen μυστηρίων καὶ τελετῶν κατάρχοντας καὶ τὰ Δήμητρος ὀργιάζοντας ("leading mysteries and ceremonies and celebrating the rites of Demeter"). We might think of the famous *kalathos* processions sung of by Callimachus,[11] were it not that only women were allowed to participate in those.[12] Also, in *De cherubim* 94 (*CW* I, 193), he argues against pagan customs, which are called, among other things, ἀνοργιάστους τελετάς: "profane rites".

B. On the other hand, Philo is strongly influenced by Plato, who, as we saw above, often uses the terminology of the mysteries to explain his notions. For example, Philo, *Quod omnis probus liber sit* 14 (*CW* VI, 4), on the people who have acquired philosophical insight because of Plato:

> ὥσπερ ἐν ταῖς τελεταῖς ἱεροφαντηθέντες, ὅταν ὀργίων γεμισθῶσι, πολλὰ τῆς πρόσθεν ὀλιγωρίας ἑαυτοὺς κακίζουσιν.

---

[9] Cf. Heinemann at this place in the translation.

[10] Cf. the preceding sentence in *LXX* Deut. 23:18: Οὐκ ἔσται πόρνη ἀπὸ θυγατέρων Ἰσραήλ, καὶ οὐκ ἔσται πορνεύων ἀπὸ υἱῶν Ἰσραήλ.

[11] Callimachus, *Hymn.* 6.

[12] Cf. Nilsson, *Feste* 350.

Just like the initiates in the mystery rites, when they have been filled with mysteries, they reproach themselves for their former negligence.

So here the word is not used in the pejorative sense. *De praem. et poen.* 121 (*CW* V, 364) also seems to have been influenced by Plato:

(τὸν νοῦν) μύστην γεγονότα τῶν θείων τελετῶν καὶ συμπεριπολοῦντα ταῖς τῶν οὐρανίων χορείαις καὶ περιόδοις ἐγέραρεν ὁ θεὸς ἠρεμίᾳ.

The mind, having become an initiate in the holy mysteries and dancing together with the heavenly bodies around their orbits, has been honoured by God with quietude.

C. But the ritual customs that the Israelites themselves observed so strictly[13] are understandably also called τελεταί in Philo.

De ebrietate 129 (*CW* II, 195). Aaron and his descendants must abstain from hard liquor:

ἀνάγκη γάρ ἐστιν ἢ ἀρρηφοροῦντα αὐτὸν εἰς τὴν σκηνὴν εἰσιέναι τὰς ἀοράτους ἐπιτελέσοντα τελετὰς ἢ τῷ βωμῷ προσιόντα θυσίας ὑπέρ τε τῶν ἰδίων καὶ κοινῶν χαριστηρίους ἀναγαγεῖν.

For he must either go into the tent (i.e. the tabernacle) himself, serving as Arrhephoros to perform the unseen rites, or, approaching the altar, offer thank-offerings for private and community blessings.

We note here the difference between the τελεταί that take place in the tabernacle and the θυσίαι that take place outside the tabernacle, at the altar. Curious in this context is the use of the very Athenian cult term *arrhephorein*.

In *De vita Mosis* 2.149 (*CW* IV, 235), typically Greek sacral terms are also used for Jewish rites. There Philo says that the so-called fulfilment offering, *LXX* τελείωσις, at the ordination of Aaron and his sons, is rightly called thus: ἐπειδὴ τὰς ἁρμοττούσας θεραπευταῖς καὶ λειτουργοῖς θεοῦ τελετὰς ἔμελλον ἱεροφαντεῖσθαι ("because the sacred acts befitting servants and ministers of God would be revealed to them").

The whole sequence of offerings and ceremonies at the ordination is also called τελετή: *De vita Mosis* 2.153 (*CW* IV, 236):

ὀγδόη δ' ἦν τῆς τελετῆς ἡμέρα καὶ τελευταία, ταῖς γὰρ πρότερον ἑπτὰ ἱεροφαντῶν αὐτόν τε καὶ τοὺς ἀδελφιδοῦς ὠργίαζεν.

---

[13] Cf. Leviticus, passim.

It was the eighth and last day of the celebration; the seven days before, he (Moses) initiated his brother and nephews, acting as their hierophant.

D. We saw above (at B.) that Philo, like Plato, compares those who have acquired a philosophical insight to participants in mysteries. But he also uses the term τελετή (and also μυστήριον) directly, to indicate the revelations of the deity, e.g. those which, according to him, are hidden in biblical stories. E.g. *All.* 3.219 (*CW* I, 162) he explains Gen. 21:7 (where Sarah says: "God hath made me to laugh"):

ἀναπετάσαντες οὖν ὦτα, ὦ μύσται, παραδέξασθε τελετὰς ἱερωτάτας.

So prick up your ears, initiates, and receive the most sacred mysteries.

This is followed by one of his well-known allegorical explanations.

Also *Cher.* 42 (*CW* I, 180). There he commands the δεισιδαίμονες to plug their ears or go away: τελετὰς γὰρ ἀναδιδάσκομεν θείας τοὺς τελετῶν ἀξίους τῶν ἱερωτάτων μύστας ("For we teach the holy mysteries to the initiates who are worthy of the most sacred mysteries"). The use of τελεταί for allegorical explanation also seems to have been used by the Stoics, as we saw above; Heraclitus, at least, seems to have known the word in this sense.

E. But generally, τελετή (and μυστήριον) in Philo often also means: supreme revelation of the deity, divine truth.[14] μυστήριον especially is also used in this way in the New Testament[15] and in Christian authors, and to this day the word 'mystery' still belongs to the language of the church and that of theosophists and freemasons. The following examples illustrate this use by Philo.

Cher. 48 (*CW* I, 182): If you meet one of the τετελεσμένοι who knows a newer τελετή, you must not rest before he has taught it to you. I myself was initiated by Moses, dear to God, into his great mysteries,[16] have later seen the prophet Jeremiah and discovered that he is a capable ἱεροφάντης, and I became his disciple. That is the thrust of Philo's

---

[14] Cf. W. Bousset, *Religion des Judentums im neutestamentlichen Zeitalter* (1903) 426 n. 3. For τελετή in this sense, see also R. Reitzenstein, *Die Hellenistische Mysterienreligionen*[2] (1920) 107.

[15] Cf. H. Ebeling, *Griechisch-deutsches Wörterbuch zum Neuen Testamente*, s.v. μυστήριον. See also *LXX* Dan. 2:18; Tob. 12:7, 12:11.

[16] καὶ γὰρ ἐγώ, παρὰ Μωυσεῖ τῷ θεοφιλεῖ μυηθεὶς τὰ μεγάλα μυστήρια.

argument. One sees that the terms of the mysteries are constantly used. Compare also *De sacrificiis Caini et Abelis* 60 (*CW* I, 226): The soul, τῶν τελείων μύστις γενομένη τελετῶν μηδενὶ προχείρως ἐκλαλῇ τὰ μυστήρια ("having become an initiate of the ultimate mystery rites, will not readily divulge the mysteries to anyone").[17] A similar usage is also found in *De sacr.* 62[18] (*CW* IV, 28); *De somniis* 1.82[19] (*CW* III, 82); *De Abrahamo* 122[20] (*CW* I, 227); *De decalogo* 41[21] (*CW* IV, 278).

It is the deity himself who performs (τελεῖ) the ἱερωτάτας τελετάς in *De gigantibus* 54 (*CW* II, 52), where the meeting of Moses and Yahweh is discussed (Exod. 33:7). Because of this, Moses is not only μύστης, but also ἱεροφάντης ὀργίων and teacher of divine things, which he will teach to those whose ears are pure.

To summarize, we find the following meanings in Philo:

A. Pagan (i.e. non-Jewish) ritual acts, of which he disapproves;
B. (Ritual acts of) Greek mysteries;
C. Jewish ritual acts;
D. Hidden meaning, secret doctrine of the Holy Scripture;
E. Supreme revelation, divine truth.

While a great friend of the Romans, FLAVIUS JOSEPHUS always remained full of enthusiasm for his own people. In *Contra Apionem* 2.22 he expresses his admiration for the theocracy in Israel. No form of government is more sacred, nowhere is God worshipped so constantly, since the entire people is prepared for piety and, furthermore, special care for religion is entrusted to priests, ὥσπερ δὲ τελετῆς τινος τῆς ὅλης πολιτείας οἰκονομουμένης ("while the whole state is regulated as if it were some religious ceremony"). So the whole state forms a τελετή, so to say. What is meant by this is apparent from what follows: "For this situation, which others can only maintain for a few days and which they call μυστήρια καὶ τελετάς, that situation we maintain continually with joy and constant spirit." Josephus will have thought of the Eleusinian mysteries, which lasted several days and which were still famous in his time.

---

[17] Cf. *De praem. et poen.* 121 (*CW* V, 364).

[18] οὐκ ἐξελάλησαν, ἀλλὰ ἐν ἀποκρύφοις αὐτὸν ἐθησαυρίσαντο, οὐκ ἐπαρθέντες τῇ τελετῇ, ὑπενδόντες δὲ καὶ ταπεινωθέντες τὸ αὔχημα.

[19] εὐαγὴς εἰσάπαν οὐδείς ἐστιν, ὡς ταῖς ἁγίαις καὶ ἱεροπρεπέσι χρῆσθαι τελεταῖς, ᾧ τὰς αἰσθητὰς τοῦ θνητοῦ βίου λαμπρότητας ἔτι τετιμῆσθαι συμβέβηκεν.

[20] μήπω τὰς μεγάλας τελεσθεῖσα τελετὰς ἔτι ἐν ταῖς βραχυτέραις ὀργιάζηται.

[21] ὡς μόνον ἑστιᾶν μέλλων καὶ μόνῳ τὸ συμπόσιον εὐτρεπίζεσθαι πρὸς ψυχῆς ἀνάχυσιν ἱεροφαντουμένης, ᾗ θέμις τὰς μεγάλας τελεῖσθαι τελετάς.

In *Ant. Jud.* 19.1.5, there is mention of τελεταὶ μυστηρίων, held by Caligula, in which the emperor himself appeared in women's clothing. Apparently, he had only introduced these quasi-religious secret ceremonies in order to be able to indulge his appetite for excesses. Cf. Plut. *Cleom.* 33 (820d).

The Greek and Jewish realm of ideas together form the spiritual foundation from which nascent Christianity emerged. Of Greek culture, it is the mystery cults in particular that have influenced Christianity, at least outwardly. It is not our intention here to assess to what extent the similarity in terminology covers an adoption of ideas. Much has been written about this subject and there is much diversity of opinion.[22] I will only attempt to examine whether, and to what extent, the meaning of τελετή evolves in the Christian authors.

JUSTIN MARTYR, *Apology* 1.66, after a description of the Christian Eucharist, remarks that, according to some, the same also takes place in the mysteries of Mithras:

> ὅτι γὰρ ἄρτος καὶ ποτήριον ὕδατος τίθεται ἐν ταῖς τοῦ μυουμένου τελεταῖς μετ᾽ ἐπιλόγων τινῶν, ἢ ἐπίστασθε ἢ μαθεῖν δύνασθε.

> For you either know or can learn that bread and a cup of water are set down with certain formulae in the rites of the one who is being initiated.

It is clear that the τελεταί τοῦ μυουμενοῦ mentioned here are the acts performed on those who are being initiated.[23]

CLEMENT OF ALEXANDRIA sharply condemns the Greek mysteries and what took place at them. And yet, we also find several places in his work where he applies their terminology to Christianity.

In *Protr.* 1.2.2 (Stählin), he recommends that those who rage in a τελετῇ βακχικῇ ("Bacchic rite"), should be locked up on Mts. Helicon and Cithaeron, together with all their attributes.

---

[22] Cf. K.H.E. de Jong, *Das antike Mysterienwesen*[2] (1919) 3, where one also finds a list of relevant literature, with additions on p. 432. This scholar argues that the New Testament contains many analogies to the mysteries, but that intentional borrowing by the Christians is out of the question: "Man wird hinsichtlich dieser vielumstrittenen Frage als vorläufiges Ergebnis festzustellen haben, dass im Neuen Testamente zwar was Ausdruck und Anschauung betrifft, manche Analogien an die Mysterien vorkommen, an eine absichtliche Entlehnung seitens der Christen jedoch nicht zu denken ist."

[23] The word μυστήριον is used several times in Justin, as in Philo, in the sense: divine truth (*Apol.* 131; *Exp. ret. fid.* 16).

In *Protr.* 2.12.1, in his famous philippic against the mysteries, Clement will, so to speak, put the gods ὧν αἱ τελεταὶ μυστικαί ("to whom the mystic rites belong") in the limelight by means of a stage machine. Then he tells how the bacchantes τελίσκουσι τὰς κρεονομίας τῶν φόνων ("perform the distribution of the flesh of their victims"): they devour raw the animals that they kill. The sign of the Bacchic rites (ὄργια) is an ὄφις τετελεσμένος, i.e. a serpent that is subjected to certain, in Clement's view magic, acts.

In *Protr.* 2.13.3, he goes on to curse the founder of these false rites, whether it be Dardanus or Eetion, ὁ τὰ Σαμοθρᾴκων ὄργια καὶ τελετὰς καταστησάμενος ("who founded the Samothracian orgies and rites").

In *Protr.* 2.14.2, Clement mentions a festival of Aphrodite on Cyprus: according to him, a grain of salt and a phallus, symbolizing the birth of Aphrodite, are given to those who are initiated into the art of adultery ἐν ταῖς τελεταῖς ταύτης τῆς πελαγίας ἡδονῆς ("in the rites celebrating this pleasure of the sea").

In *Protr.* 2.17.2, Orpheus is mentioned as ὁ τῆς Τελετῆς ποιητής ("the poet of the Rite").[24] This presumably refers to the Orphic document entitled Τελεταί.[25]

In *Protr.* 2.19.4, there is mention of the τελετὴν Καβειρικήν ("Cabiric rite"); 2.22.1 Clement says that ἄξια μὲν οὖν νυκτὸς τὰ τελέσματα καὶ πυρός ("the rites are worthy of night and fire"); and in 2.22.3, he calls all Greek mysteries ἀνοργιάστους τελετάς ("profane rites"); cf. Philo, *Cher.* 94 (*CW* I, 193), who used exactly the same words; Origen *Cels.* 6.33 speaks of ἀτέλεστος τελετή; in the scholion to Lucian *Peregr.* 13, ed. Rabe p. 219, the ἀνέορτος ἑορτή of the Egyptians is reported, also by a Christian.

In *Protr.* 2.24.1, we find the story of the Scythian king Anacharsis, who performed the τελετή of the Mother of the gods: cf. Hdt. 4.76; Diog. Laert. 1.102.

In *Paed.* 2.8.73.1, Christians are dissuaded from the use of floral wreaths, because those who are in Bacchic ecstasy also celebrate their festival with wreaths: ἐπὰν δὲ ἀμφιθῶνται τὰ ἄνθη, πρὸς τὴν τελετὴν ὑπερκάονται: "Once they have put the flowers around themselves, they are exceedingly inflamed for the sacred act."

---

[24] Clement proceeds to mention (2.18.1): τῆσδε τῆς τελετῆς τὰ ἀχρεῖα σύμβολα (...)· ἀστράγαλος, σφαῖρα, στρόβιλος, μῆλα, ῥόμβος, ἔσοπτρον, πόκος, which refer to the Zagreus myth.
[25] See above, p. 20.

In *Strom.* 2.20.106.1, Clement sees a parallel between Greek sacrificial customs and Jewish dietary laws:

> ἐντεῦθεν οἶμαι καὶ τὰς τελετὰς οὐ μόνον τινῶν ζῴων ἀπαγορεύειν ἅπτεσθαι, ἀλλ᾽ ἔστιν ἃ καὶ τῶν καταθυομένων ὑπεξείλετο τῆς χρήσεως μέρη δι᾽ αἰτίας ἃς ἴσασιν οἱ μύσται.

> Hence I believe that the mysteries not only prohibited touching certain animals, but also exclude from use certain parts of the sacrificial victims for reasons which are known to the initiates.

So Clement believes that the Greek custom of eating only certain (parts of) sacrificial victims is explained in the mysteries, which he calls τελεταί.

In *Strom.* 4.22.140.1, Clement connects the word εὐφρόνη (the kindly time, night) with φρονέω, because at night, the soul, no longer receiving sensory impressions, mulls things over and participates more in the φρόνησις. This is also why τελεταί are held at night, because they indicate a withdrawal of the soul from the body. Cf. Plut. *De def. or.* 40 (432c).

In all the places mentioned above, τελετή means: sacred act, performance of rites belonging to the mysteries. Clement always uses it in a pejorative sense, except in the last cited passage.

In *Strom.* 5.4.19.1, Clement states that the Greeks are not yet ready for true salvation, viz. Christianity, just as, at the τελεταί, someone who is still ἀμύητος, and in the χορεῖαι someone who is ἄμουσος, must remain outside the sacred place. It is very clear from the analogy with dances, that sacred performances are intended here. In 20.1 he goes on to argue that τελεταί cannot be shown to just anyone but are revealed by means of καθαρμοί and προρρήσεις. In the last two cited passages, Clement therefore uses mystery terms to explain the revelation of Christianity,[26] despite his fierce attacks on those mysteries which we witnessed above.

HIPPOLYTUS, *Refutatio omnium haeresium* 5.7.1, shows that the Gnostic sect of the Naassenes are nothing but a sort of mixture of all kinds of Greek and non-Greek religious convictions under a Christian guise. When he proceeds to examine these, he says: ἔλθωμεν ἐπὶ τὰς τελετὰς ὅτεν αὐτοῖς οὗτος ὁ μῦθος ("Let us come to the mysteries, whence they have derived this fable"). He then mentions Boeotian, Libyan, Egyptian and Assyrian myths respectively. So τελετή here is religious doc-

---

[26] He even draws a complete parallel between the Christians' path to salvation and the step-by-step progress of initiation in the mysteries: *Strom.* 5.11.70.7.

trine. Cf. also 5.7.9: καὶ πρῶτον ἐπὶ τὰς Ἀσσυρίων καταφεύγουσι τελετάς ("And first they try to find support in the mysteries of the Assyrians").

Haer. 5.7.22. According to the Naassenes, the Egyptians, the most
ancient people after the Phrygians, were the first to preach the τελετὰς
καὶ ὄργια θεῶν πάντων as well as their ἰδέας καὶ ἐνεργείας. The Egyptians are regarded by the Greeks (cf. Herodotus, Diodorus) as particularly
experienced in the knowledge of religious things, because of the impressive form of their religious monuments and institutions and because of
the exotic and secretive nature of their religion. As mentioned above,
almost any Egyptian religious ceremony could have been called τελετή
(or ὄργιον) by the Greeks.

Haer. 5.9.12. The Naassenes connect the word νάας (Hebrew for serpent) with ναός, temple. They say that every sanctuary, πᾶσαν τελετὴν
καὶ πᾶν μυστήριον ("every rite and every mystery") is dedicated to this
νάας. For one never finds a τελετή without a corresponding ναός. The
word τελετή can mean cult here, perhaps also religion.

In *Haer.* 5.20.4, Orpheus is mentioned as the one who, in particular,
τὰς τελετὰς καὶ τὰ μυστήρια κατέδειξε ("revealed the rites and the
mysteries"). As we saw before, τελεταί Ὀρφέως are to be considered
as religious acts (whether transmitted in writing or not) performed by
Orphic priests. A certain doctrine concerning the womb, the serpent
and the navel that is also supported by the Sethians, appears literally in
Orpheus' Βακχικά:

> τετέλεσται δὲ ταῦτα καὶ παραδέδοται ἀνθρώποις πρὸ τῆς Κελεοῦ καὶ
> Τριπτολέμου καὶ Δήμητρος καὶ Κόρης καὶ Διονύσου ἐν Ἐλευσῖνι τελε-
> τῆς.

> This was already performed and handed down to mankind before the
> sacred act of Celeus, Triptolemus, Demeter, Kore and Dionysus at Eleu-
> sis.[27]

From the five cited passages, it appears that Hippolytus uses the word as
1) sacred act, 2) cult, 3) doctrine.

In ORIGEN, these meanings return. In *Contra Celsum* 1.12, he says of the
Persians:

---

[27] For the serpent as a symbol of the Gnostics, cf. H. Leisegang, *Die Gnosis* (1924)
111 ff.

παρ' οἷς εἰσι τελεταί, πρεσβευόμεναι μὲν λογικῶς ὑπὸ τῶν παρ' αὐτοῖς
λογίων συμβολικῶς δὲ γινόμεναι ὑπὸ τῶν παρ' αὐτοῖς πολλῶν καὶ ἐπι-
πολαιοτέρων.

Among them are rites, conducted rationally by the learned among them,
but understood symbolically by the multitude and the more superficial
among them.

This clearly shows that τελεταί are complex rituals. The learned priests,
who understand their significance, perform them in a scholarly way;
laymen, who do not understand them, regard them as symbolic. Origen
remarks that the same is true for Syrians and Indians and all those who
have myths and literature.

In *Cels.* 4.10, Βακχικαὶ τελεταί probably refers to Orphic rites: these
rites, in which φάσματα καὶ δείματα are conjured up, are compared to
Christianity by Celsus. Cf. Dio Chrys. 4.90.

Cels. 8.67. If Athena had been a mortal woman who lived long ago,
for whom her descendants handed down μυστήρια καὶ τελετάς in her
memory, then one should certainly not worship her as a goddess. We
know that Pindar called the Panathenaea the τελεταί of Athens. Also
compare, however, *LXX* Wisd. 14:15, where we find similar words in a
similar context.

In *Cels.* 3.34, Origen challenges Celsus, who claims that Jesus is to be
put on a par with Zalmoxis, Mopsus and Amphilochus, each of whom
also appeared to the people after their deaths. Origen assumes that this
kind of δαιμόνια are tied to certain places, either having always had
their seat there, or having been brought there διά τινων τελετῶν καὶ
μαγγανειῶν ("by certain rites and magic charms"). The ritual act that
is meant here by τελετή, is possibly the consulting and giving of oracles,
which Origen would, of course, regard as μαγγανεία, mumbo-jumbo. Cf.
Plato, *Leg.* 738c.

In *Cels.* 3.36, we find the same hendiadys. Here it refers to the reason
for the foundation of the Antinous cult.

Likewise *Cels.* 5.38, end. This discusses the Sarapis cult, which was
founded by Ptolemy I. Here we see that it is not only sculptors who make
gods, but also magicians and the likes, μετὰ τῶν ἀτελέστων τελετῶν καὶ
τῶν καλουσῶν δαίμονας μαγγανειῶν ("with profane rites and magic
charms invoking demons"). With regard to ἀτέλεστοι τελεταί, one could
think of Ptolemy's dream and what follows.[28]

---

[28] Cf. Plut. *De Is. et Os.* 28 (361f–362b); Tacitus, *Hist.* 4.83–84.

In all these places, τελεταί are pagan rites, which Origen detests. But he also uses τελετή to refer to Christian cult practice. For example, in 3.59, he describes an argument by Celsus, who says that those who call people to other τελεταί, demand purity of action and words, whereas Christians, on the contrary, turn to all kinds of bad people. Origen concedes this point, but adds that those bad people are first taught a better way of life by means of the word (λόγος); only then καλοῦμεν αὐτοὺς ἐπὶ τὰς παρ᾽ ἡμῖν τελετάς ("do we invite them to our mysteries"). So here, τελετή is the most sacred act, or: the highest revelation of Christianity. The term that Celsus apparently used, is taken over by Origen without objection. He adds a quotation from Paul (I Cor. 2:6): σοφίαν γὰρ λαλοῦμεν ἐν τοῖς τελείοις ("For we speak wisdom among them that are perfect").[29]

In *Cels.* 6.24, there is also mention (by Celsus) of the comparison of a τελετή of the Christians and one of the Persians.[30]

In two places, τελετή means the doctrine contained in a ritual act: in 6.22, a passage of Celsus is cited, where he says that Christian conceptions of the afterlife correspond to those of the Persians: αἰνίττεται ταῦτα καὶ ὁ Περσῶν λόγος, καὶ ἡ τοῦ Μίθρου τελετή, ⟨ἣ⟩ παρ᾽ αὐτοῖς ἐστιν. ("For these things are hinted at by the account of the Persians and the rite of Mithras, which is celebrated among them.") Celsus here seems to have equated the sect of the Ophites with Christianity. Origen repudiates their doctrine and in 6.33 calls them an ἀτέλεστος τελετή ("profane rite").

Eusebius also uses τελετή, both in the pagan and the Christian sense. In the pagan sense, e.g. *Vita Const.* 4.25, where it is told how Constantine prohibited all sorts of pagan customs:

μὴ θύειν εἰδώλοις, μὴ μαντεῖα περιεργάζεσθαι, μὴ ξοάνων ἐγέρσεις ποιεῖσθαι, μὴ τελετὰς κρυφίους ἐκτελεῖν.

To offer sacrifice to idols, consult diviners, erect images, perform secret rites.

It is possible that τελεταί κρύφιοι summarizes the preceding pagan customs.[31]

---

[29] We must assume that Paul himself only used these and other terms derived from the mysteries in order to be better understood by his contemporaries. The Gnostics gave Christianity the appearance of a Hellenistic mystery cult, also with regard to content. Cf. W. Bousset (ed.), *Die Schriften des Neuen Testaments* II (1917) 84.

[30] Cf. Justin, *Apol.* 1.66.

[31] Zijderveld believed that ξοάνων ἐγέρσεις ποιεῖσθαι might refer to the daily rite of waking the god at the Serapeum in Rome: cf. Porph. *Abst.* 4.9, where the priest, standing

Christian cult acts—or the Christian doctrine—are referred to as τελετή: *Vita Const.* 3.43. Constantine's mother founded a temple at the Mount of Olives near Jerusalem, because it was said that the Saviour ἐν αὐτῷ ἄντρῳ τοὺς αὐτοῦ θιασώτας μυεῖν τὰς ἀπορρήτους τελετάς ("in that very cave, initiated his disciples in the secret mysteries"). It is difficult to determine what is meant here: is the idea that Christ subjected his followers to certain rites in this cave—baptism, Eucharist?—or does τελετή here mean revelation, divine truth, as in Philo and Origen?

In *Oratio Const.* 19, extensive quotations from Virgil's fourth Eclogue are adduced in Greek translation. In this eclogue, the poet is supposed to have alluded to the coming of Christ: ἠπίστατο γὰρ οἶμαι τὴν μακαρίαν καὶ ἐπώνυμον τοῦ σωτῆρος τελετήν. This I can only translate as: "He knew the beatific *doctrine* named after the Saviour", i.e. Christianity.

The prologue of his panegyric on Constantine (*Laus Constantini*) is full of terms derived from the mysteries. Among other things, he expresses the hope that the prophecies of holy inspiration may be as teachers to us:

> τῶν τελετῶν ἡμῖν γενέσθωσαν διδάσκαλοι ἀμφὶ βασιλείας αὐτῆς ἀμφί τε βασιλέως τοῦ ἀνωτάτω δορυφορίας τε θείας ἀμφὶ τὸν πάντων βασιλέα τοῦ τε καθ᾿ ἡμᾶς βασιλικοῦ παραδείγματος.

> Let them be our teachers of the mysteries, about kingship itself, about the highest king and the divine guard around the king of all, and about the example of a king to us.

So here, τελεταί have the sense of 'highest knowledge'. If we thus behold this holiest knowledge (τὰς θεοπρεπεῖς τελετὰς ἱεροφαντούμενοι) we will attain to divine consecration (θείων ὀργίων ἐφαψόμεθα).

In the ORACULA SIBYLLINA, 5.496 (Geffcken) we find a prophecy, presumably originating from a Christian source, of the decline of the Sarapis cult. One day people will realize that those who held πομπὰς καὶ τελετάς for stone and clay gods, were out of their minds. So this is another example of τελετή for an Egyptian rite.

In later Christian authors, we find the word in the meaning of: sacrament. For example, JOHN CHRYSOSTOM calls the Eucharist "a most horrible mystery rite" φρικωδεστάτη τελετή (*De sacerd.* 3.4). In *Homily*

---

on the threshold, awakens (ἐγείρει) the god in the native tongue of the Egyptians. Since Eusebius is talking about wooden statues, the second meaning in *LSJ*, 'raising', seems more to the point here than 'awakening', FLS.

7 on I Cor. 2:6–7, he also takes much trouble to explain why Christianity is so often referred to with words like μυστήριον, τελετή and such.

Moreover, in his *Ecclesiastical hierarchy* 3.1 (Migne, *PG* III, 424), the sixth-century convert DIONYSIUS THE AREOPAGITE, in whose work the influence of the Neoplatonist school can be readily discerned, speaks of the Eucharist as the τελετῶν τελετή ("rite of rites"); and also of τὴν ἱερωτάτην τῆς θεογενεσίας τελετήν ("the holy rite of divine rebirth"), which refers to baptism.

It is noteworthy that MAXIMUS CONFESSOR, *ad Dion. Areop. Ep.* 8.6, says about the pagan τελεταί:

> μάλιστα γὰρ τὰ μυστήρια τινος τῶν ψευδονύμων αὐτῶν θεῶν τέλη καὶ τελετὰς ἐκάλουν, ὡς τελειούσας καὶ εἰς τὸ τέλειον ἀγούσας τοὺς τελουμένους.

> It is mostly the mysteries of one of the false gods that are called *telos* and *telete*, since these allegedly make perfect and lead to the perfection of those who undergo the ceremonies.

Plato already seemed to suggest this same explanation (*Phdr.* 249c).

Conclusion

When we briefly examine the use of τελετή in Jewish and Christian authors, it appears that the Septuagint uses the term to refer to Canaanite cult customs, especially temple prostitution. The Apocrypha, written in Hellenistic and later times, often have the hendiadys τελεταὶ καὶ μυστήρια, to indicate Greek mystery rites.

In Philo, we see a varied use. It is used for Canaanite, Greek, but also Jewish customs (*De ebrietate* 129, *De vita Mosis* 2.153). Moreover, τελεταί seem to be the hidden meanings retrieved by allegorical explanation of biblical stories (e.g. *All.* 3.219); and also, under the influence of Plato: supreme divine revelation, divine truth (*De sacr.* 60).

Flavius Josephus calls the whole Jewish form of government as a theocracy a τελετή (*Ap.* 2.22).

In Christian authors, we initially find τελετή mostly in the pejorative sense, of pagan rites. And yet, Clement of Alexandria already draws a parallel between Christian customs and those of the μυστήρια (*Strom.* 5.11.70.7) and likewise uses τελεταί (5.4.19.1) metaphorically for Christianity.

Hippolytus uses the term several times in the sense of: doctrine (e.g. *Haer.* 5.7.1), and also: complicated cult practice, e.g. of the Egyptians (*Haer.* 5.7.22).

The same is true for Origen, who used the term τελεταί for complex rituals but also for the doctrine of Christianity itself (*Cels.* 3.59).

In Eusebius it is suggested that Christ initiated his disciples in the secret τελεταί (*Vita Const.* 3.43) and Christianity is spoken of as the τελετή named after its saviour (*Or. Const.* 19). In later authors τελετή, and also μυστήριον, is used for: sacrament. (Dion. Areop., John Chrys.)

In my opinion, the attitude of Christianity towards the term τελετή developed as follows. Initially, the Christians detest everything that is called τελετή, as belonging to the pagan religions. They will not have approved of Lucian calling their community a τελετή (*Peregr.* 11). And yet, Paul already avails himself of the terminology of the mysteries to explain Christian doctrine;[32] he, and also Philo Judaeus, were followed in this regard by later authors. Certain sects, like the Ophites, assimilated themselves, also with regard to content, to Hellenistic mysteries. The Orthodox Church confined itself to the adoption of certain terms.

---

[32] Cf. K.H.E. de Jong, *Das antike Mysterienwesen*[2] (1919) 3; C. Clemen, *Der Einfluss der Mysterienreligionen auf das älteste Christentum*, RGVV 13.1 (1913) 81.

CHAPTER FIVE

SUMMARY

Whereas, in the preceding chapters, the term τελετή was, as far as possible, traced chronologically through Greek literature, I shall now endeavour to summarize the results of this investigation by placing separately the various meanings found, at the same time bearing in mind the probable development of those meanings.

1. The original meaning of τελετή, being a nomen actionis of τελεῖν, to achieve, to perform, must have been: *achievement, performance*, in a neutral and very wide sense. As far as I know this general, non-sacral meaning occurs, however, only once, viz. *Batrachom*. 305, where the end of the battle is described thus: καὶ πολέμου τελετὴ μονοήμερος ἐξετελέσθη. "And the performance of the battle, having lasted one day, was ended." All other places I found, have the word τελετή in a religious sense.

At first, the term is used for all *religious ceremonies*, whatever their nature, just like τέλος, one of the meanings of τελεῖν being: to perform solemnly (τελεῖν τάφον *Il.* 24.660; ἐκτελεῖν γάμον *Od.* 4.7; τελεῖν θυσίαν etc.). Examples of this general use of τελετή, by which any sacral act may be described, are: Pind. *Ol.* 3.41, where τελεταί denote the *theoxenia*, offered to the Dioscuri by the kings of Acragas. Τελετή means 'sacrifice': Ar. *Vesp.* 876; *Pax* 413. In Pind. *Ol.* 10.53, where Heracles is sung of as the founder of the Olympic games, some gods are said to be present ταυτᾷ ἐν πρωτογόνῳ τελετᾷ, and so the performance of the games is described by τελετά. In Pind. *Pyth.* 9.97, it is the Panathenaea that are thus described: τελεταὶ ὥριαι Παλλάδος. Cf. *Nem.* 10.34.

Although from the earliest period of Greek literature there has been a tendency to limit the use of τελετή to certain rites which I shall enumerate below, traces of the original, wider meaning have remained through all times: the meaning of solemn performance is still heard in the fairly current expression: ἡ τῶν μυστηρίων τελετή: and when Aristotle, *Rhet.* 2.24.2, says: τὰ γὰρ μυστήρια πασῶν τιμιωτάτη τελετή, he obviously uses the word in this more general sense.

2. We may notice that, from the earliest time, τελετή is preferably used to denote *religious acts of a special kind*, which deviated in some

way or other from the prevailing practices in Greece and hence drew attention. Thus we find denoted by τελετή: the *nocturnal Bacchanalian rites*, which, owing to their ecstatic character, form such a contrast to the Greek σωφϱοσύνη. Cf. e.g. Pind. fr. 70b Maehler; Eur. *Bacch.* 22, 200, 465; Strabo, 10.3.10; Lucian, *Bacch.* 5.

As a good example of τελετή in this sense of religious act deviating from the prevailing custom, we may quote Eur. *IT* 958, where the Choes festival, celebrated on the second day of the Anthesteria, is called τελετή. As an aetiology of the peculiar use of many mixing-bowls at this festival instead of a single one in common use, we read there the story of Orestes who is shunned by the Athenians, being stained with blood-guilt. Ps. Demosthenes, *Neaer.* 104, a clan cult is called τελετή in a decree of the Athenian people, according to which the Plataeans obtain Athenian civic rights and are made the equals of the Athenians in every respect πλὴν εἴ τις ἱεϱωσύνη ἢ τελετὴ ἐστιν ἐκ γένους. Compare also Dio Chrys. 21.80 (the hero-cult is called τελετή); Herodian, *Ab exc. div. Marci* 8.4.2.1 (τελετή is the apotheosis of the Roman emperors); Plut. *Artax.* 3 (τελετή is the consecration of a Persian king); etc.

3. It is difficult to find out to what extent the ceremonies of the previous group were *symbolic acts*; there are, however, a great number of τελεταί, undoubtedly of symbolic character, which serve as repositories of more or less conscious dogmas. As such we should first consider the *Eleusinian mysteries*. Although we are not accurately acquainted with the nature of the performance in the Eleusinian *telesterion*, we can confidently assume that, by certain sacred acts, hopes for a better lot were raised in the participants.—It is noteworthy that those mysteries were originally an Eleusinian clan cult. (Cf. Dem. *Neaer.* 104).—Thus the whole complex of ceremonies formed by the Eleusinian mysteries is called τελετή (Andoc. *De myst.* 15; Isoc. *Paneg.* 28; Paus. 1.37.4; Alciphr. 4.18.16; Diod. 1.29.2–3, etc.). But the various functions separately are also called τελετή (Plut. *Alc.* 34: τελετή is πομπή) and the τελετὴ κατ᾽ ἐξοχήν is the principal sacred act, that was anxiously kept secret.[1] (Cf. e.g. Paus. 1.37.4: ὅστις δὲ ἤδη τελετὴν Ἐλευσῖνι εἶδεν ... οἶδεν ὃ λέγω). This is well in keeping with the words of Theon of Smyrna, who (*Util. math.* 14.26) mentions ἡ τῆς τελετῆς παϱάδοσις as the second grade of the initiation. We should, perhaps, also think of this when reading the often occurring phrase: τῆς τελετῆς μετέχειν, μεταλαμβάνειν. (Cf. Diod. 5.49.5; Plut. *Erot.* 27.20;

---

[1] From Diod. 5.77.3, it is evident that when the word τελετή is used, something secret need not always be thought of.

Lucian, *Pseudol.* 5, etc.) This highest stage of initiation was revealed by the goddess Demeter herself at Eleusis, when a mortal saw it for the first time (cf. *Hymn. Dem.* 470–482); later by the hereditary priests of the Eumolpidae and Kerykes.

This revelation of the holiest rites by Demeter is described in the hymn (473–479) in the following words:

> (Δημήτηρ) βασιλεῦσιν δεῖξε …
> δρησμοσύνην θ' ἱερῶν, καὶ ἐπέφραδεν ὄργια πᾶσιν
> σεμνά, τά τ' οὔπως ἐστὶ παρεξέμεν οὔτε πυθέσθαι
> οὔτ' ἀχέειν· μέγα γάρ τι θεῶν ἄγος ἰσχάνει αὐδήν.

Demeter showed the kings the service of her rites (*hiera*) and taught them all her solemn mysteries (*orgia*), which no-one may in any way transgress or inquire into or utter, for great awe of the gods checks the voice.

I believe it is this same act of showing the holiest, secret acts of the mysteries that is described by expressions like:

> τὴν τελετὴν διδάσκειν: Hdt. 2.171; Dion. Hal. 1.68.3; Paus. 2.14.1; Philo, *De spec. leg.* 1.319;
> τελετὰς ἀναδιδάσκειν: Philo, *Cher.* 42;
> τὰς τελετὰς καταδεικνύναι: Ar. *Ran.* 1032; Dem. *Aristog.* 1.11; Diod. 1.20.6; 3.64.7; 3.65.2; 3.74.1; Plut. *Pomp.* 24.5 (631c);
> τὴν τελετὴν παραδεικνύναι: Diod. 5.48.4;
> τὰς τελετὰς ἀναδεικνύναι: *Hymn. Orph.* 24.10;
> τὰς τελετὰς ἀναφαίνειν: *Hymn. Orph.* 79.8; ὄργια νυκτιφαῆ τελεταῖς ἀναφαίνειν: *Hymn. Orph.* 54.10;
> τελετὰς παραδιδόναι: Dion. Scytobr. fr. 7 Jacoby = Diod. 3.55.9; Diod. 5.75.4.

Those to whom the rites are revealed are said to μανθάνειν τὰς τελετάς Diod. 3.56.6; διδάσκειν καὶ μανθάνειν τελετάς Philo, *De spec. leg.* 1.319.

Besides the Eleusinian mysteries, other secret cults, like that of Samothrace, may have contained symbolic acts. An indication of this is the occasional occurrence of the phrase that the τελεταί denote some wisdom in an occult manner (αἰνίττεσθαι). Cf. Plato, *Phaedo* 69c; Plot. *Enn.* 1.6.5; 3.6.13. Here also lies the explanation that the Thesmophoria (Hdt. 2.171) and phallic ritual (Diod. 4.6.4; Philostr. *Vita Ap.* 6.20), undoubtedly being fertility rites, are indicated by our term.

Nor need we be surprised at Egyptian religious ceremonies being called τελεταί.[2] For it is well known that they were of a typical symbolic nature, which is partly due to the existence of a centuries-old order of professional priests. Rites of this kind were, as we have seen, preferably called τελεταί by the Greeks. In some of them, Herodotus saw the Greek Thesmophoria (2.171), which he regarded as being of Egyptian origin;[3] in accordance with him, some modern scholars think that the Eleusinian mysteries had also been imported from Egypt. It seems doubtful, however, whether we may speak of Egyptian mysteries in the same sense as of those of Greece. According to Egyptologists, gradual initiation is out of the question; as far as we know, a word denoting mystery is unknown in Egyptian. Naturally priests must have possessed a deep knowledge of theologian theories, which were inscrutable to the layman; but this does not differ from our own days, impossible as it is, in matters of religion, for us to talk of mysteries in the Greek sense of the word. In my opinion, every Greek attending an Egyptian religious ceremony would give it the name τελετή, or perhaps even μυστήριον, because in Greece only those ceremonies, which were of a peculiar, often symbolic or dogmatic character, were generally called thus.

Hence we can quite understand why some patriarchs use our term to denote baptism and holy communion (Dion. Areop. *EH* 3.1).

4. A religious act with a certain dogmatic nature (τελετή) often becomes the centre of a group of participants, which in its turn may be called τελετή, and so we meet with some passages where τελετή seems to signify: exclusive *religious community, sect*. I think this is the case in M. Aurelius 9.30; Lucian *Peregr.* 11 (calling Christianity a τελετή); Hippol. *Haer.* 5.7.1; Orig. *Cels.* 6.33.

5. Psychologically, it is quite conceivable that a symbolic religious act, always performed according to strict rules, gets a *magical meaning* for a certain group of people, that is to say: if the precepts are strictly adhered to, a certain result is thought to be inevitable. We may here denote as such τελεταί, the καθαρμοί, if not all, at any rate those we find with the Orphic mendicant priests. See Plato, *Resp.* 364e: those ἀγύρται καὶ μάντεις say that καθαρμοί and λύσεις exist in order to redeem us from our unlawful deeds, ἃς δὴ τελετὰς καλοῦσιν, αἳ τῶν ἐκεῖ κακῶν ἀπολύουσιν ἡμᾶς. Cf. also Paus. 9.30.4. The τελεταί of the Corybantes are of a similar nature (e.g. Ar. *Vesp.* 121; Pl. *Euthyd.* 277d; Plut. *De aud.* 16 (47a)).

---

[2] Cf. Diod. 1.20.6; Plut. *De Is. et Os.* 361d; Heliod. *Aeth.* 9.10.
[3] Cf. Diod. 1.20, 21, 22; Plut. *De Is. et Os.* passim; Clem. Al. *Strom.* 1.15.66.2; Orig. *Cels.* 1.12.

Magic acts are undoubtedly meant when Hippoc., *Morb. sacr.* 1.71, speaks of a magician who pretends to be able to fetch the moon down from the skies and similar miracles εἴτε καὶ ἐκ τελετέων εἴτε καὶ ἐξ ἄλλης τινὸς γνώμης καὶ μελέτης. We find the term repeatedly in the *magical papyri*, denoting the minutely prescribed acts, mostly of a very bizarre nature, for preparing a charm.

In this shade of meaning, the stress is strongly laid on the result of the act. Likewise, I think that Plato uses τελετή in a figurative sense, to denote the wonderful, as it were magic, influence the world of Ideas has on the human soul. Cf. *Phdr.* 249c: On account of the memory of Ideas, he once beheld an ἀνὴρ, τελέους ἀεὶ τελετὰς τελούμενος, τέλεος ὄντως μόνος γίγνεται. We are not sure as to which τελεταί Plato is alluding to here; in Athens τελεταί fairly often denote the Eleusinian mysteries, whose mighty influence on present life and the afterlife is renowned.[4] As a second instance of this metaphorical use in Plato may be mentioned *Phdr.* 253c, where τελετή can be translated by: uplifting influence, namely of Eros on the soul of the lover. From the passage quoted above, *Phdr.* 249c, it seems to follow that Plato saw a relation between τελετή and τέλειος, so that τελετή is the same as τελείωσις, which explanation has been put forward more emphatically by some patriarchs, when speaking of Christian sacraments.

6. The *figurative meaning* of the word 'mystery' for things known only to few persons is nowadays quite current and already existed in antiquity. As it often designated the secret act of mysteries, τελετή was used in the same manner. Cf. Dion. Hal. *Comp.* 25 τελεταὶ λόγου: the mysteries of eloquence. Cf. Gal. *UP* 448, 3. For the secrets of love, too, these sacral terms are usurped. Cf. Ar. *Lys.* 832 ὄργια ἔρωτος; Achill. Tat. *De Leuc. et Cit.* 1,9 μύστης … συνηθέστερος τῇ τελετῇ τοῦ θεοῦ (sc. Ἔρωτος).

When Chrysippus (fr. 42 Arnim) calls the τελεταί the last stage of philosophy (final doctrine, cf. metaphysics, τὰ μετὰ τὰ φυσικά) it is possible that he alludes to the *allegorical explanation* of myths, which is called τελεταί by Heraclitus, *Quaest. Hom.* 64. Another author who employs the term in this sense is Philo, *All.* 3.219: when about to give an explanation of Gen. 21:7, he says: ἀναπετάσαντες οὖν ὦτα, ὦ μύσται, παραδέξασθε τελετὰς ἱερωτάτας. Cf. *Cher.* 42. But also in general, τελετή, just as μυστήριον in Philo as well in the Christian authors, may mean: *supreme revelation, divine truth.* (*De sacr.* 60; *De somn.* 1.82.)

---

[4] Cf. *Hymn. Dem.* 480–482.

7. In antiquity, several *writings* appear to have existed entitled Τελεταί (or Περὶ τελετῶν). Just like the works Περὶ θυσιῶν, Περὶ μυστηρίων, they must have been theological treatises, trying to explain certain religious acts, the symbolism of which was no longer understood, in consequence of their old age.

8. Finally, mention should be made of the rare occurrence of Τελετή personified as a *goddess* in Paus. 9.30.4 and Nonn. *Dion.* 16.400 and 48.880 ff.

PART TWO

ΟΡΓΙΑ IN LITERARY SOURCES

CHAPTER SIX

INTRODUCTION

As is evident from the lexica—the most comprehensive modern lexicon of Liddell and Scott is no exception—the following development of the meaning of ὄργια is generally presumed:

ὄργια are 1) secret rites performed by initiates;
            2) rites in general; sacrifices;
            3) secrets and mysteries outside the realm of religion.

The fact that this scheme is adhered to, shows that modern lexicographers were not satisfied with the connection between ὄργια and ἔρδω, ῥέζω, ἔργον, ὄργανον. Instead, they still more or less trailed in the footsteps of ancient lexicographers, who had completely forgotten about this connection.[1] Only F. Muller's *Grieksch Woordenboek* mentions the derivation without further ado. Liddell and Scott merely assigned a probability to it.

Professor Bolkestein, on the other hand, expressed as his opinion that ὄργια is, in fact, a synonym of τελετή and that the development of the meanings of both terms runs parallel.[2] From 'religious act' in general, the meaning narrows to 'sacrifice' as the religious act par excellence, and subsequently to 'rites in honour of certain deities', until the term finally acquires the meaning 'mystery cult'.

The correctness or incorrectness of these opinions is best tested by a broad survey of the available material. Before giving an overview of the places where the term ὄργια occurs in its different meanings, we would first like to report some explanations by ancient etymologists.

ETYMOLOGICUM MAGNUM gives s.v. ὄργια: τὰ μυστήρια· κυρίως δὲ τὰ Διονυσιακά, διὰ τὸ ἐν ταῖς ὀργάσιν αὐτοῦ ἐπιτελεῖσθαι. ἢ διὰ τὸ ὀργᾶν καὶ ἐπιθειάζειν ἢ παρὰ τὸ ὀρέγω, τὸ ἐπιθυμῶ: "Mysteries, chiefly the Dionysiac mysteries, because of his worship in meadows, or because of the excitement and the conjuring up of the god, or because of the yearning, the longing." So we are offered a choice here between three possible derivations:

---

[1] Cf. Wilamowitz, *Glaube* II, 71.
[2] Bolkestein, *Charakter der Deisidaimonia*, 55.

1) from ἡ ὀργάς: the meadows where the ὄργια took place;
2) from ὀργάω: to be eager, be excited;
3) from ὀρέγω: to yearn for, strive for.

ETYMOLOGICUM GUDIANUM only gives the third derivation:

> ὄργια σημαίνει τὰ μυστήρια, παρὰ τὸ ὀρέγειν τὸ ἐπιθυμεῖν· δύο γὰρ σημαίνει, τό τε ἐκτείνω τὰς χεῖρας, καὶ τὸ ἐπιθυμῶ· ὀρέγω ὀργύια καὶ ὄργια· τοῖς γὰρ ἐπιθυμοῦσι μυστήρια οἱ θεοὶ μυοῦνται.

> *Orgia* means 'mysteries', after *oregein*: to long for. It means two things: to stretch out your arms and to long for something: *orego* is *orguia* (the length of the outstretched arms) and *orgia* (mysteries). After all, the gods are celebrated with mysteries by those who long for them.

SERVIUS, *ad Verg. Aen.* 4.302, gives two more explanations: "sane sciendum ὄργια apud Graecos dici sacra omnia, sicut apud Latinos caeremoniae dicuntur, sed iam abusive sacra Liberi ὄργια vocantur, vel ἀπὸ τῆς ὀργῆς, id est a furore, vel ἀπὸ τῶν ὀρέων, ex silvis."[3] The fact that Servius states that in Greek, ὄργια can denote *all* things sacred, is noteworthy.[4]

The best parallel for Servius' derivation is CLEMENT OF ALEXANDRIA, *Protr.* 2.13.1: καί μοι δοκεῖ τὰ ὄργια ... δεῖν ἐτυμολογεῖν ... ἀπὸ τῆς ὀργῆς τῆς Δηοῦς τῆς πρὸς Δία γεγενημένης· "I also believe the terms *orgia* must be derived from Demeter's anger (*orge*) towards Zeus."[5] The difference between the two is that in Servius, ἡ ὀργή denotes Bacchic frenzy, whereas Clement recognizes the rage and anguish of Demeter in the word and appears to be thinking first and foremost of the Eleusinian mysteries.

It is also noteworthy that, in the ANECD. OX. (Cramer) II 307, we find the remark: ὅρκος καὶ ὄργια τὰ μυστήρια δασύνεται, "*horkos*; also *horgia*, mysteries, is aspirated." In other words: the correct spelling is with a rough breathing, because of the derivation from ὅρκος. Apparently the idea was that the word referred to ceremonies in which, under oath, one pledged oneself to secrecy.

Since we will also include several cognate words in our research, we finally wish to mention some explanations of these in the ancient lexica.

---

[3] "It is important to know that the Greeks say ὄργια for all things sacred, in the same way as the Latins say *caeremoniae*, but the rites of Liber are also erroneously called ὄργια, either ἀπὸ τῆς ὀργῆς, i.e. from rage, or ἀπὸ τῶν ὀρέων, from woodlands."

[4] Incidentally, Suidas, Photius, Hesychius and the *Anecd. Bach.* also give μυστήρια and ἱερά for ὄργια.

[5] This passage is also quoted by Euseb. *Praep. evang.* 2.3.9.

SUIDAS, s.v. ὀργεῶνες, explains ὀργιάζειν as τὰ τῶν θεῶν ὄργια τελεῖν, τουτέστι μυστήρια καὶ νόμιμα: "to perform the rites of the gods,
that is mysteries and religious customs." And s.v. ὀργιάζων: θύων, ἐπι-
τελῶν: "sacrificing, worshipping."

HESYCHIUS, s.v. ὀργιάζειν: τελεῖν Διονύσῳ: "to worship Dionysus."

HARPOCRATION, s.v. ὀργεῶνας: ὀργιάζειν γάρ ἐστι τὸ θύειν καὶ τὰ
νομιζόμενα δρᾶν, ἤτοι παρὰ τὸ ὀρέγειν τὼ χεῖρε, ἢ παρὰ τὰ ὄργια, ἢ
διὰ τὸ ἐν ταῖς ὀργάσι καὶ τοῖς ἄλσεσι τὰ ἱερὰ δρᾶν: "because *orgiazein*
is to sacrifice and to perform the customary rites, either from stretching
out both arms, or from the rites, or because of the performing of sacred
rites in meadows and groves."

PHOTIUS, s.v. ὀργιασταί: οἱ τὰ μυστήρια ἐπιτελοῦντες: "they who
perform mysteries."

CHAPTER SEVEN

THE USE OF ΟΡΓΙΑ UP TO ALEXANDER

The so-called LAW OF SOLON, mentioned by Gaius, *Dig.* 47.22.4, but apparently originating from the time before Cleisthenes,[1] may be regarded as the oldest place where we find ὄργια. In this law, legal force is given to various regulations and decrees made by private persons, ἐὰν μὴ ἀπαγορεύσῃ τὰ δημόσια γράμματα ("if the public laws do not forbid it"). All kinds of 'communities' are mentioned in a motley variety, among other things, ἱερῶν ὀργίων ⟨κοινωνοί⟩.[2] So ὄργια here apparently refers to a cult of a special, private nature, alongside the public religion.

We do not find ὄργια in Homer, but the word appears twice in the HOMERIC HYMN TO DEMETER, referring to the Eleusinian mysteries. In verse 273, Demeter has just revealed herself as a goddess to Metanira and has ordered a temple to be built for her at Eleusis:

ὄργια δ' αὐτὴ ἐγὼν ὑποθήσομαι ὡς ἂν ἔπειτα
εὐαγέως ἔρδοντες ἐμὸν νόον ἱλάσκοισθε.

And I myself will teach my mysteries, so that hereafter by performing them righteously you may placate my heart.

The combination of ὄργια and ἔρδειν is noteworthy.

So the Eleusinian mysteries are meant here, as in verse 476, where Demeter gives the necessary instructions for her worship:

δεῖξε Τριπτολέμῳ τε Διοκλεῖ τε πληξίππῳ,
Εὐμόλπου τε βίῃ Κελεῷ θ' ἡγήτορι λαῶν,
δρησμοσύνην θ' ἱερῶν καὶ ἐπέφραδεν ὄργια πᾶσι,
σεμνά, τά τ' οὔ πως ἔστι παρεξίμεν οὔτε πυθέσθαι,
οὔτ' ἀχέειν· μέγα γάρ τι θεῶν σέβας ἰσχάνει αὐδήν.

To Triptolemus and Diocles, driver of horses, and to mighty Eumolpus and Celeus, the leader of the people, she revealed the service of her rites and

---

[1] See Dareste, Haussollier and Reinach, *Inscr. Jur.* II, 207 ff. and J.H. Lipsius, *Leipziger Studien* 16 (1894) 162.

[2] We supplement κοινωνοί after P.J.T. Endenburg, *Koinoonia en gemeenschap van zaken bij de Grieken* (1937) 164 ff.

taught her mysteries (*orgia*) to them all, solemn mysteries, which no-one may in any way transgress or inquire into or utter, for great awe of the goddesses checks the voice.

We again see an interesting combination: δρησμοσύνη (: δρᾶν) and ὄργια.³

In the HOMERIC HYMN TO APOLLO, we find a unique occurrence of the noun ὀργιών (gen. ὀργιόνος), apparently used to designate priests (verse 389):

> καὶ τότε δὴ κατὰ θυμὸν ἐφράζετο Φοῖβος Ἀπόλλων
> οὕς τινας ἀνθρώπους ὀργιόνας εἰσαγάγοιτο
> οἳ θεραπεύσονται Πυθοῖ ἔνι πετρηέσσῃ.

> Then Phoebus Apollo pondered which people he could take there as priests to worship him in rocky Pytho.

The word ὄργια occurs several times in *lyric poetry*. In the fragments of PINDAR we find ὀργίοις: fr. 140a Maehler, verse 78. Unfortunately, the context is insufficient to determine with certainty what ὄργια are meant there. PHILODAMUS, the author of the *Paean to Dionysus* (340/39 BC), used the word: see below, Chapter XII, no. 69.

We also find the word in two anonymous, undated fragments in Page, *PMG*. Fr. 975c (fr. adesp. 57) mentions the ὄργια of white-armed Cytherea. So here, the word is used in a metaphorical sense for the rites of love. Fr. 985b (fr. adesp. 67) the word ὀργιασμοί refers to special, secret rites:

> ἢ καλλίπαις δι' ὀργιασμῶν
> Λῆμνος ἀρρήτων ἐτέκνωσε Κάβειρον.

> Lemnos, blessed with beautiful children, produced Cabirus through secret rites.

AESCHYLUS, *Sept.* 179, gives us an example of the use of ὄργια for religious rites in general. The chorus is praying to the tutelary deities of Thebes:

> φιλοθύτων δέ τοι πόλεως ὀργίων
> μνήστορες ἐστέ μοι.

---

³ Zijderveld rightly observed that δεῖξεν ... δρησμοσύνην ἱερῶν is the prototype of the often used τελετὴν καταδεικνύναι "to reveal the sacred rite" (see above, p. 78). That he considered δρησμοσύνη a synonym of τὰ δρώμενα is less accurate.

Please remember our city's rites, performed with an abundance of sacrifices.

Clearly πόλεως ὀργίων refers to the public cult in honour of the tutelary gods.

In Aeschylus fr. 57 N², ὄργια is again used for the cult of a special deity:

σεμνὰ Κοτυτοῦς ὄργι' ἔχοντες.

celebrating the solemn rites of Cotyto.

So ὄργια here are the rituals of the Thracian goddess Cotys or Cotyto, which were closely connected to the cult of Dionysus.[4] We will see below that Euripides uses the word several times for the frenzied rites of Dionysus.

SOPHOCLES uses ὄργια only a few times and exclusively in the sense of 'sacrifice'.

In *Ant.* 1013, Tiresias tells Creon of the bad portents he received. First he heard strange noises of birds fighting: eerie cries and a vicious flutter of wings. When next he tried a burnt sacrifice, the omens were inauspicious:

Ἥφαιστος οὐκ ἔλαμπεν, ἀλλ' ἐπὶ σποδῷ
μυδῶσα κηκὶς μηρίων ἐτήκετο
κἄτυφε κἀνέπτυε, καὶ μετάρσιοι
χολαὶ διεσπείροντο, καὶ καταρρυεῖς
μηροὶ καλυπτῆς ἐξέκειντο πιμελῆς.
Τοιαῦτα παιδὸς τοῦδ' ἐμάνθανον πάρα,
φθίνοντ' ἀσήμων ὀργίων μαντεύματα.

Hephaistos gave no flame, but dank juices, oozing from the thighs, dripped upon the embers, smoking and sputtering; the gall was scattered to the winds; and the fat covering the thighs fell down so they lay bare. Thus I learnt from my boy the dwindling presages of the sacrifice that gave no sign.

In *Trach.* 765, Hyllus tells his mother, Deianira, about the effect of the magic robe that she had given Heracles. Heracles was making a sacrifice:

καὶ πρῶτα μὲν δείλαιος ἵλεῳ φρενὶ
κόσμῳ τε χαίρων καὶ στολῇ κατηύχετο·
ὅπως δὲ σεμνῶν ὀργίων ἐδαίετο
φλὸξ αἱματηρὰ κἀπὸ πιείρας δρυός,

---

[4] Cf. Nilsson, *Feste*, 433.

ἱδρὼς ἀνῄει χρωτὶ καὶ προσπτύσσετο
πλευραῖσιν ἀρτίκολλος, ὥστε τέκτονος,
χιτὼν ἅπαν κατ' ἄρθρον.

And at first my poor father recited the prayers, gentle and happy with the elegance of his robe. But as the flame of the solemn sacrifice began to flare up because of the blood and the resinous wood, a sweat broke out upon his skin and the garment folded itself close around his sides, clinging tightly around his whole body, as if made by a sculptor.

The φλὸξ σεμνῶν ὀργίων here is the flame of the solemn sacrifice. The same sacrifice is referred to by the words πολύθυτοι σφαγαί in verse 756.

EURIPIDES uses ὄργια once to refer to the Eleusinian rites, in *HF* 613, where Heracles, after his return from Hades, tells Amphitryon how he defeated Cerberus:

μάχῃ· τὰ μυστῶν δ' ὄργι' εὐτύχησ' ἰδών.

In a fight: I was lucky because I had seen the rites of the *mystai*.

The story that Heracles participated in the Eleusinian mysteries before his journey into the Underworld is also known from other sources.[5]
Bacch. 78 mentions the ὄργια of Cybele:

ὦ μάκαρ, ὅστις εὐδαίμων
τελετὰς θεῶν εἰδὼς
βιοτὰν ἁγιστεύει καὶ
θιασεύεται ψυχὰν
ἐν ὄρεσσι βακχεύων
ὁσίοις καθαρμοῖσιν,
τά τε ματρὸς μεγάλας ὄρ-
για Κυβέλας θεμιτεύων,
ἀνὰ θύρσον τε τινάσσων,
κισσῷ τε στεφανωθεὶς
Διόνυσον θεραπεύει.

O blessed is he who, fortunate and knowing the rites of the gods, lives a pure life and joins the thiasos with his soul, revelling in the mountains in hallowed purifications, and who, complying with the mysteries of the great mother, Cybele, brandishing the thyrsus, wreathed with ivy, serves Dionysus.

---

[5] See e.g. Apollod. 2.5.12.

There are also numerous places in this tragedy where ὄργια refers to the cult of Dionysus.

In *Bacch.* 34, Dionysus says of the Theban girls and women:

σκευήν τ᾽ ἔχειν ἠνάγκασ᾽ ὀργίων ἐμῶν,
καὶ πᾶν τὸ θῆλυ σπέρμα Καδμείων, ὅσαι
γυναῖκες ἦσαν, ἐξέμηνα δωμάτων.

I have made them bear the emblem of my rites; the whole female population of Cadmus' city, every last woman, I have sent raving from their homes.

In *Bacch.* 262 Pentheus scolds Teiresias:

εἰ μή σε γῆρας πολιὸν ἐξερρύετο,
καθῆσ᾽ ἂν ἐν βάκχαισι δέσμιος μέσαις,
τελετὰς πονηρὰς εἰσάγων· γυναιξὶ γὰρ
ὅπου βότρυος ἐν δαιτὶ γίγνεται γάνος,
οὐχ ὑγιὲς οὐδὲν ἔτι λέγω τῶν ὀργίων.

If your grey old age did not protect you, you would be sitting in the dungeon with your bacchantes for introducing depraved rites: for wherever women have the sparkle of wine at their banquet, no good can come, I tell you, from their rites.

In *Bacch.* 470, 471, 476 and 482, Pentheus interrogates the Stranger about the god and his rites:

Πε. πότερα δὲ νύκτωρ σ᾽ ἢ κατ᾽ ὄμμ᾽ ἠνάγκασεν;
Δι. ὁρῶν ὁρῶντα, καὶ δίδωσιν ὄργια.
Πε. τὰ δ᾽ ὄργι᾽ ἐστὶ τίν᾽ ἰδέαν ἔχοντά σοι;
Δι. ἄρρητ᾽ ἀβακχεύτοισιν εἰδέναι βροτῶν.
Πε. ἔχει δ᾽ ὄνησιν τοῖσι θύουσιν τίνα;
Δι. οὐ θέμις ἀκοῦσαί σ᾽, ἔστι δ᾽ ἄξι᾽ εἰδέναι.
Πε. εὖ τοῦτ᾽ ἐκιβδήλευσας, ἵν᾽ ἀκοῦσαι θέλω.
Δι. ἀσέβειαν ἀσκοῦντ᾽ ὄργι᾽ ἐχθαίρει θεοῦ.
Πε. τὸν θεὸν ὁρᾶν γὰρ φὴς σαφῶς, ποῖός τις ἦν;
Δι. ὁποῖος ἤθελ᾽· οὐκ ἐγὼ 'τασσον τόδε.
Πε. τοῦτ᾽ αὖ παρωχέτευσας εὖ κοὐδὲν λέγων.
Δι. δόξει τις ἀμαθεῖ σοφὰ λέγων οὐκ εὖ φρονεῖν.
Πε. ἦλθες δὲ πρῶτα δεῦρ᾽ ἄγων τὸν δαίμονα;
Δι. πᾶς ἀναχορεύει βαρβάρων τάδ᾽ ὄργια.

PE. Did he possess you in a dream or in plain sight?
DI. We were face to face as he gave his rites.
PE. These rites of yours: what form do they have?
DI. It must not be told to the uninitiated.

PE. And what advantage is there for those who worship?
DI. It is not for you to learn, but it is worth knowing.
PE. A nice trick, to arouse my curiosity.
DI. His rites detest a man practising impiety.
PE. So you say you saw the god clearly: what was he like?
DI. Just as he chose to be. I had no say in that.
PE. Again you avoid the question nicely without saying a thing.
DI. Wise words will never seem insightful to a fool.
PE. Is this the first place where you have introduced this god?
DI. Every foreigner dances these rites.

In *Bacch*. 998, the chorus of Lydian women describes how Pentheus is speeding towards his doom:

ὃς ἀδίκῳ γνώμᾳ παρανόμῳ τ’ ὀργᾷ
περὶ σὰ, Βάκχι’, ὄργια ματρός τε σᾶς
μανείσᾳ πραπίδι
παρακόπῳ τε λήματι στέλλεται,
τἀνίκατον ὡς κρατήσων βίᾳ.

With criminal intent and lawless rage about your rites, Bacchic one, as well as those of your mother, he sets out with furious heart and frenzied spirit to conquer by force that which is invincible.

In *Bacch*. 1080, Pentheus is sitting high up in the tree, when a voice from the sky commands the women:

ἄγω τὸν ὑμᾶς κἀμὲ τἀμά τ’ ὄργια
γέλων τιθέμενον· ἀλλὰ τιμωρεῖσθέ νιν.

I bring you the man who wants to ridicule you and me and my rites. Now punish him!

Finally, *Bacch*. 415 has the verb ὀργιάζειν, said of the Bacchic rites. The chorus begs to be taken to Pieria where the Muses live:

ἐκεῖ Χάριτες, ἐκεῖ δὲ Πόθος·
ἐκεῖ δὲ βάκχαις θέμις ὀργιάζειν.

There are the Graces and Desire; there the bacchantes are allowed to celebrate their rites.

ARISTOPHANES uses ὄργια in three places to denote the cult of Demeter, alluding to Eleusis.

In *Ran*. 384, the chorus (χορὸς μυστῶν) invokes Demeter in a solemn song, apparently in imitation of existing religious songs:

Δήμητερ, ἁγνῶν ὀργίων
ἄνασσα, συμπαραστάτει,
καὶ σῷζε τὸν σαυτῆς χορόν.

Demeter, lady of pure rites, stand beside us and protect your own chorus.

In *Thesm.* 948, the leader of the chorus calls the women to the choral dance:

ἄγε νυν ἡμεῖς παίσωμεν ἅπερ νόμος ἐνθάδε ταῖσι γυναιξίν,
ὅταν ὄργια σεμνὰ θεοῖν ἱεραῖς ὥραις ἀνέχωμεν.

Come, let us do a cheerful dance, as is customary for the women here, when we celebrate solemn rites for the two goddesses in the holy season.

Thesm. 1151 again mentions the ὄργια σεμνὰ θεοῖν. In both places, solemnity is the characteristic element of the ὄργια. It is worth noting that there was also mention of ὄργια σεμνὰ in Aesch. fr. 57 N² and Soph. *Trach.* 765, as well as *Hymn Dem.* 476–478.

In *Ran.* 356, the leader of the χορὸς μυστῶν commands in a solemn πρόρρησις:

εὐφημεῖν χρὴ κἀξίστασθαι τοῖς ἡμετέροισι χοροῖσιν,
ὅστις ἄπειρος τοιῶνδε λόγων ἢ γνώμην μὴ καθαρεύει,
ἢ γενναίων ὄργια Μουσῶν μήτ᾽ εἶδεν μήτ᾽ ἐχόρευσεν.

Let whoever has neither seen nor danced the rites of the noble Muses be silent and stay away from our choral dances.

In *Lys.* 832, we find another instance of metaphorical use:

ἄνδρ᾽, ἄνδρ᾽ ὁρῶ προσιόντα, παραπεπληγμένον,
τοῖς τῆς Ἀφροδίτης ὀργίοις εἰλημμένον.

A man! I see a man coming, desperate looking, overwhelmed by the mysteries of Aphrodite![6]

And in the same comedy, *Lys.* 898, Cinesias pleads with his wife:

τὰ τῆς Ἀφροδίτης ἱέρ᾽ ἀνοργίαστά σοι
χρόνον τοσοῦτόν ἐστιν. οὐ βαδιεῖ πάλιν;

And what about the rites of Aphrodite? You haven't performed them for such a long time! Won't you come home?

---

[6] U. von Wilamowitz, *Aristophanes Lysistrate erklärt* (1927) remarks ad locum: "ὄργια sind eigentlich heilige Handlungen; hier die Einwirkungen der Göttin, wobei wir an ὀργᾶν denken sollen." For this metaphorical use of the terminology of the mysteries for "the mysteries of love", cf. Zijderveld, above, p. 90.

HERODOTUS calls certain rites ὄργια in three places, in each case in honour of a different deity.

Discussing the Egyptian origin of Greek gods, oracles and festivals, Herodotus tells us that the ithyphallic Hermes did not come from the Egyptians but from the Pelasgians (2.51):

> ὅστις δὲ τὰ Καβείρων ὄργια μεμύηται, τὰ Σαμοθρήικες ἐπιτελέουσι παραλαβόντες παρὰ Πελασγῶν, οὗτος ὡνὴρ οἶδε τὸ λέγω· τὴν γὰρ Σαμοθρηίκην οἴκεον πρότερον Πελασγοὶ οὗτοι οἵ περ Ἀθηναίοισι σύνοικοι ἐγένοντο, καὶ παρὰ τούτων Σαμοθρήικες τὰ ὄργια παραλαμβάνουσι. ὀρθὰ ὦν ἔχειν τὰ αἰδοῖα τἀγάλματα τοῦ Ἑρμέω Ἀθηναῖοι πρῶτοι Ἑλλήνων μαθόντες παρὰ Πελασγῶν ἐποιήσαντο. οἱ δὲ Πελασγοὶ ἱρόν τινα λόγον περὶ αὐτοῦ ἔλεξαν, τὰ ἐν τοῖσι ἐν Σαμοθρηίκῃ μυστηρίοισι δεδήλωται.

> Anyone who has been initiated into the mysteries of the Cabiri, which are celebrated by the Samothracians, who received them from the Pelasgians, knows what I am talking about. Those Pelasgians, who became fellow-inhabitants of the Athenians, used to live on Samothrace before and the Samothracians received the mysteries from them. So the Athenians were the first of the Greeks to make those statues of Hermes with erect member, having learnt this from the Pelasgians. The Pelasgians have a sacred tale about him, which is revealed in the mysteries on Samothrace.

In 2.81, he mentions that, among the Egyptians, it is forbidden to wear wool during worship, or to be buried in a woollen garment:

> ὁμολογέουσι δὲ ταῦτα τοῖσι Ὀρφικοῖσι καλεομένοισι καὶ Βακχικοῖσι, ἐοῦσι δὲ αἰγυπτίοισι, καὶ τοῖσι Πυθαγορείοισι· οὐδὲ γὰρ τούτων τῶν ὀργίων μετέχοντα ὅσιόν ἐστι ἐν εἰρινέοισι εἵμασι θαφθῆναι. ἔστι δὲ περὶ αὐτῶν ἱρὸς λόγος λεγόμενος.

> This corresponds with the so-called Orphic and Bacchic rites, which are Egyptian in origin, and with the Pythagorean. It is forbidden for a member of these rites to be buried in woollen clothes. There is a sacred tale about this.

So here, it is Orphic-Pythagorean customs and rites that are referred to as ὄργια.

In 5.61, we find ὄργια again, this time used for the cult of Demeter Achaia. Herodotus is talking about the Gephyraeans, who, according to him, were of Phoenician descent and had settled in Boeotia under the leadership of Cadmus. Having fled from there to Attica, they occupied a special position and were excluded from normal cult practice.

ἄλλα τε κεχωρισμένα τῶν ἄλλων ἱρῶν καὶ δὴ καὶ Ἀχαιίης Δήμητρος ἱρόν τε καὶ ὄργια.

And besides other temples that are different from the others they also had a temple and rites for Demeter Achaia.[7]

In Herodotus, we therefore only find ὄργια used for rites of a special, deviating character.

ISOCRATES, on the other hand, again uses ὀργιάζειν for performing religious rites in a more general sense.

Areop. 29 mentions the excellent conditions that prevailed in all areas at the time of Solon and Cleisthenes. The cult was carefully maintained:

καὶ πρῶτον μὲν τὰ περὶ τοὺς θεούς, ἐντεῦθεν γὰρ ἄρχεσθαι δίκαιον, οὐκ ἀνωμάλως οὐδ' ἀτάκτως οὔτ' ἐθεράπευον οὔτ' ὠργίαζον.

And in the first place with regard to things concerning the gods, for it is right to start with these, people were not irregular or disorderly in service or cult.

It is difficult to distinguish between the meaning of θεραπεύειν and ὀργιάζειν: both verbs indicate the fulfilment of one's ritual duties.

PLATO does not use the noun ὄργια, but the verb ὀργιάζειν occurs in several places.

In *Phdr.* 250c, Plato presents his thoughts on the human soul in a myth. It saw τὰ ὄντα by nature but there are only few souls who have a sufficient memory of them, so that the ὁμοίωμα (resemblance) of the Ideas brings them into a strange kind of euphoria. The difference with celestial pre-existence is strong, for then the souls rejoiced in the beatific sight of the Ideas.

καὶ ἐτελοῦντο τῶν τελετῶν ἣν θέμις λέγειν μακαριωτάτην, ἣν ὠργιάζο-μεν ὁλόκληροι μὲν αὐτοὶ ὄντες καὶ ἀπαθεῖς κακῶν ὅσα ἡμᾶς ἐν ὑστέρῳ χρόνῳ ὑπέμενεν.

And they underwent the rite, which one may rightly call the most beatific of all, in which we participated in unblemished condition, not having experienced the bad things that lay in store for us in later times.

It is clear that Plato has a mystery cult in mind here, and he is probably thinking in particular of the Eleusinian mysteries, in which the viewing

---

[7] This cult is discussed by Nilsson, *Feste*, 325 ff.

(the ἐποπτεία) had a powerful effect on the participants. The construction of ὀργιάζειν with the cult as object deserves special attention in this context.

In *Phdr.* 252d, Socrates says that every soul, to the best of his ability, honours that deity whose χορευτής he was, and tries to find an ideal on earth that reminds him of that deity,

> τόν τε οὖν Ἔρωτα τῶν καλῶν πρὸς τρόπου ἐκλέγεται ἕκαστος, καὶ ὡς θεὸν αὐτὸν ἐκεῖνον ὄντα ἑαυτῷ οἷον ἄγαλμα τεκταίνεταί τε καὶ κατακοσμεῖ, ὡς τιμήσων τε καὶ ὀργιάσων.

> In accordance with his character, everyone chooses the object of his love from among the beautiful, and, as if it were god itself, he erects it as a statue for himself and decorates it in order to honour and worship it.

Here we find ὀργιάζειν used next to τιμᾶν, so that (inward) worship is placed next to (outward) honours.

In *Leg.* 717b, it is argued that the first duty of *eusebeia* is the worship of the Olympian gods, the tutelary gods of the polis and the chthonian gods,

> μετὰ θεοὺς δὲ τούσδε καὶ τοῖς δαίμοσιν ὅ γε ἔμφρων ὀργιάζοιτ᾽ ἄν, ἥρωσιν δὲ μετὰ τούτους. ἐπακολουθοῖ δ᾽ αὐτοῖς ἱδρύματα ἴδια πατρῴων θεῶν κατὰ νόμον ὀργιαζόμενα, γονέων δὲ μετὰ ταῦτα τιμαὶ ζώντων.

> After these gods, the wise man will also worship *daimones*, and heroes after those; next private sanctuaries for family gods may follow, in which the cult is celebrated according to custom, and after that the honours for the parents, while they are still alive.

So here we find ὀργιάζεσθαι, construed with the dative in the sense of 'worship', and ὀργιάζειν with the place of worship as object for 'celebrating the cult'.

We find another example of this last usage in *Leg.* 910c, where measures against the devaluation of the religion of the polis are enumerated:

> μὴ κεκτῆσθαι θεῶν ἐν ἰδίαις οἰκίαις ἱερά, τὸν δὲ φανέντα κεκτημένον ἕτερα καὶ ὀργιάζοντα πλὴν τὰ δημόσια, ... ὁ μὲν αἰσθανόμενος καὶ εἰσαγγελλέτω τοῖς νομοφύλαξιν.

> The possession of shrines of gods in private houses is prohibited. If anyone is shown to possess other shrines or worship in other than public shrines, he that notices it shall inform the law wardens.

Finally, we find an example in the pseudo-Platonic *Epinomis* (985d), where there is mention of gods who are ἀνοργίαστοι, in other words:

τιμὰς μὴ δεχομένοι τὰς προσηκούσας αὐτοῖς ("who do not receive the honours befitting to them").

The *Ethica Eudemia*, attributed to ARISTOTLE, discusses the nature of κοινωνία. In the relationship soul-body, master-slave and so on one cannot speak of κοινωνία (1241b.24):

> αἱ δ' ἄλλαι κοινωνίαι εἰσὶν μόριον τῶν τῆς πόλεως κοινωνιῶν, οἷον ἡ τῶν φρατέρων ἢ τῶν ὀργίων, ἢ αἱ χρηματιστικαὶ ἔτι πολιτεῖαι.

> But the other kinds of community are a part of the community of the city, for example, that of phratries or cults (*orgia*), or even associations with a financial objective.

We are strongly reminded here of the so-called Law of Solon (see above) where a similar enumeration is given.

In *Pol.* 1342a, we find the compound ἐξοργιάζειν. It discusses a homeopathic[8] cure of those who are in a state of Corybantic frenzy:

> οἷον ἔλεος καὶ φόβος, ἔτι δ' ἐνθουσιασμός· καὶ γὰρ ὑπὸ ταύτης τῆς κινή-σεως κατοκώχιμοί τινές εἰσιν, ἐκ τῶν δ' ἱερῶν μελῶν ὁρῶμεν τούτους, ὅταν χρήσωνται τοῖς ἐξοργιάζουσι τὴν ψυχὴν μέλεσι, καθισταμένους ὥσπερ ἰατρείας τυχόντας καὶ καθάρσεως.

> Some people are capable of being possessed by this form of arousal, such as pity and fear, and also being inspired by the god. Because of sacred melodies, we see these people, when they use melodies that excite the soul, brought into a state like that of having received medical treatment and purification.

We find the adjective ὀργιαστικόν used in this same sense a couple of times: *Pol.* 1341a, where he says of the oboe:[9]

> ἔτι δὲ οὐκ ἔστιν ὁ αὐλὸς ἠθικὸν ἀλλὰ μᾶλλον ὀργιαστικόν, ὥστε πρὸς τοὺς τοιούτους αὐτῷ καιροὺς χρηστέον ἐν οἷς ἡ θεωρία κάθαρσιν μᾶλ-λον δύναται ἢ μάθησιν.

> The oboe is not an ethical but rather an exciting thing, so that it should be used for such occasions when the viewing has the effect of purification rather than instruction.

---

[8] See Rohde, *Psyche* II, 48 n. 1.

[9] I have corrected here and passim the common mistranslation of 'flute' for αὐλός, which was, in fact, a wind instrument with a double-reed mouthpiece, i.e. an oboe, not a flute, FLS.

and *Pol.* 1342b, where he speaks of the Phrygian mode and the oboe:

> ἔχει γὰρ τὴν αὐτὴν δύναμιν ἡ φρυγιστὶ τῶν ἁρμονιῶν ἥνπερ αὐλὸς ἐν τοῖς ὀργάνοις· ἄμφω γὰρ ὀργιαστικὰ καὶ παθητικά.

> For the Phrygian mode has the same effect as the oboe among instruments, for both are exciting and passionate.

In the final sentence of HIPPOCRATES, *Lex* 5 (4.642 Littré), the term ὄργια is used metaphorically:[10]

> τὰ δὲ ἱερὰ ἐόντα πρήγματα ἱεροῖσιν ἀνθρώποισι δείκνυται· βεβήλοισι δὲ, οὐ θέμις, πρὶν ἢ τελεσθῶσιν ὀργίοισιν ἐπιστήμης.

> The sacred things are shown only to sacred persons, but it is not permitted for the profane to know them before they have been initiated into the rites of science.

Conclusion

If we look again briefly at the material found thus far, we may start by listing the places where our term is used for religious rites in general.

In Aesch. *Sept.* 179, the religion of the polis was called πόλεως ὄργια. In Isoc. *Areop.* 29, ὀργιάζειν was used for 'performing religious rites', to which we may compare Plato, *Phdr.* 252d, where we find the combination τιμᾶν τε καὶ ὀργιάζειν τινα.

The following may be mentioned as special constructions: ὀργιάζεσθαί τινι for 'worshipping a deity' (Plato *Leg.* 717b) and ὀργιάζειν with ἵδρυμα as its object (*ibid.*) or ἱερά (Plato *Leg.* 910c) for 'performing the cult in a sanctuary'.

The people chosen to conduct the worship of Apollo at Delphi are called ὀργιόνες: *Hymn. Ap.* 389.

We find the adjective ἀνοργίαστος in ps. Plato, *Epin.* 985d, said of a deity 'without worship' and in Ar. *Lys.* 898, of Ἀφροδίτης ἱερά 'that are not performed' (used figuratively).

In the sense of 'sacrificial rite' or 'sacrifice', we find ὄργια twice in Sophocles: *Ant.* 1013 and *Trach.* 765.

The ὄργια that exist alongside the public religion provide a special κοινωνία (the 'Law of Solon' and Arist. *Eth. Eud.* 1241b).

---

[10] J. Jouanna, *Hippocrates* (1999) 396, dates this work to the fourth century BC (just after *The Oath*).

In addition, there are numerous places where ὄργια etc. refer to rituals of a special character.

In Euripides' Bacchae, we find the cult of Dionysus indicated by ὄργια (passim) as well as the verb ὀργιάζειν (Bacch. 415).

Eleusinian Mysteries: Hymn. Dem. 273 (with the combination ὄργια ἔρδειν) and 476. Eur. HF 613 (τὰ μυστῶν ὄργια). Ar. Ran. 384, Thesm. 948 and 1151.

Perhaps alluding to Eleusis: the combination τὴν τελετὴν ὀργιάζειν in Plato, Phdr. 250c.

The worship of Cybele is called ὄργια Κυβέλας in Eur. Bacch. 79 and the cult of Cotyto Κοτυτοῦς ὄργια in Aesch. fr. 57 N².

Herodotus mentions ὄργια in the Samothracian cult of the Cabiri (2.51), the Orphic-Pythagorean cult (2.81) and the cult of Demeter Achaia (5.61).

We find ὄργια used *metaphorically* in Ar. Lys. 832 and Ran. 356, Hippoc. Lex. 5 and PMG 975c.

Aristotle has the compound ἐξοργιάζειν 'to bring to ecstasy' (Pol. 1342a) as well as the adjective ὀργιαστικός 'exciting' (Pol. 1341a and 1342b).

The combinations of certain verbs with ὄργια are also worth mentioning:

Revelation of the ὄργια by a deity is expressed by:

ὄργια ἐπιφράζειν (Hymn. Dem. 476),
ὄργια διδόναι (Eur. Bacch. 470).

To participate in the celebration of the ὄργια is called:

ὄργια ἔρδειν (Hymn. Dem. 273),
ὄργια ἔχειν (Λcзch. fr. 57 N²),
ὄργια ὁρᾶν (Eur. HF 613; Ar. Ran. 356),
ὄργια θεμιτεύειν (Eur. Bacch. 79),
ὄργια ἀνέχειν (Ar. Thesm. 948),
ὄργια χορεύειν (Ar. Ran. 356),
ὄργια ἀναχορεύειν (Eur. Bacch. 482),
ὄργια ἐπιτελεῖν (Hdt. 2.51),
ὀργίων μετέχειν (Hdt. 2.81),
ὀργίοισι τελεῖσθαι (Hippoc. Lex 5).

It appears that, outside the Ionic idiom of Herodotus and the language of tragedy (and comedy, insofar as it was influenced by tragedy), the word ὄργια gradually lost ground to μυστήρια and τελεταί. The verb ὀργιάζειν, on the other hand, continued to be widely used.[11]

---

[11] See W.G. Rutherford, 'The Growth of the Attic Dialect' (Introduction to his edition of the grammarian Phrynichus, London 1881).

CHAPTER EIGHT

THE USE OF ΟΡΓΙΑ AFTER ALEXANDER

APOLLONIUS RHODIUS has the term ὄργια in two places.

In *Argon.* 1.920, it is used to indicate the Samothracian mysteries, in which the Argonauts participated in order to be able to sail more safely:

ἑσπέριοι δ᾽ Ὀρφῆος ἐφημοσύνῃσιν ἔκελσαν
νῆσον ἐς Ἠλέκτρης Ἀτλαντίδος, ὄφρα δαέντες
ἀρρήτους ἀγανῇσι τελεσφορίῃσι θέμιστας
σωότεροι κρυόεσσαν ὑπεὶρ ἅλα ναυτίλλοιντο.
τῶν μὲν ἔτ᾽ οὐ προτέρω μυθήσομαι, ἀλλὰ καὶ αὐτὴ
νῆσος ὁμῶς κεχάροιτο καὶ οἳ λάχον ὄργια κεῖνα
δαίμονες ἐνναέται, τὰ μὲν οὐ θέμις ἄμμιν ἀείδειν.

In the evening, they landed at Orpheus' behest on the island of Electra, Atlas's daughter, (i.e. Samothrace) to be taught secret customs in sacred rites and then sail on safely over the icy-cold water. I shall say no more about these things, but I say farewell to the island and the gods who dwell there, who obtained those rites about which I may not sing.

In *Argon.* 4.1020, Medea beseeches Queen Arete not to extradite her to the Colchians and swears that she did not leave her native land of her own volition:

ἴστω ἱερὸν φάος Ἠελίοιο,
ἴστω νυκτιπόλου Περσηίδος ὄργια κούρης.

Let holy sunlight, let the rites of Perses' daughter who roams by night (i.e. Hecate) be my witness.

In *Argon.* 2.907, we find the verb ὀργιάζειν used for the celebration of the rites of Dionysus. The Argonauts have reached the estuary of the river Callichorus:

ἔνθ᾽ ἐνέπουσι Διὸς Νυσήιον υἷα,
Ἰνδῶν ἡνίκα φῦλα λιπὼν κατενίσσετο Θήβας,
ὀργιάσαι, στῆσαί τε χοροὺς ἄντροιο πάροιθεν
ᾧ ἐν ἀμειδήτους ἁγίας ηὐλίζετο νύκτας.

They say that the son of Zeus from Nysa (i.e. Dionysus), having visited the tribes of India and returning to Thebes, celebrated his rites and installed his choral dances in front of a cave in which, unsmiling, he spent sacred nights.

THEOCRITUS, *Id.* 26.13, tells how Autonoe cried aloud upon seeing Pentheus, who was spying on the bacchantes:

σὺν δ' ἐτάραξε ποσὶν μανιώδεος ὄργια Βάκχῳ,
ἐξαπίνας ἐπιοῖσα, τά τ' οὐχ ὁρέοντι βέβαλοι.

With her feet she disturbed (or: stirred up) the *orgia* of maddening Bacchus, suddenly charging at him; they are not to be seen by the profane.

Because of the addition of ποσίν, one can hardly interpret this as a disturbance of the rites, so ὄργια must have the concrete meaning 'sacred objects' here.[1]

CALLIMACHUS, *Aet.* fr. 63, uses ὄργια for the Thesmophoria:

τοὔνεκεν οὔπως ἐστὶν ἐπ' ὄθμασιν οἷσιν ἰδέσθαι
παρθενικαῖς Δηοῦς ὄργια Θεσμοφόρου.

Therefore the rites of Demeter Thesmophoros are not at all for maiden eyes to see.

As Pfeiffer noted in his commentary, Thesmophoria, without the addition of a placename, refers to the Athenian festival.

DIODORUS SICULUS, 3.65.6, refers to the rituals in the cult of Dionysus as τὰ κατὰ τὰς τελετὰς ὄργια, which Dionysus taught to the Thracian king Charops, in gratitude for his rescue. It is said that Orpheus, the grandson of Charops, πολλὰ μεταθεῖναι τῶν ἐν τοῖς ὀργίοις, "made many changes in the rites."

The word appears in the same sense in 4.82.6:

τὸ δὲ τελευταῖον μυθολογοῦσιν αὐτὸν εἰς Θρᾴκην παραβαλόντα πρὸς Διόνυσον μετασχεῖν τῶν ὀργίων, καὶ συνδιατρίψαντα τῷ θεῷ πολλὰ μαθεῖν παρ' αὐτοῦ τῶν χρησίμων.

---

[1] C.A. Lobeck, *Aglaophamus* (1829) 56 interpreted the ὄργια as the ἱερὰ πεποναμένα mentioned in verse 7, which the maenads took ἐκ κίστας and placed on the altars: "liborum genera varia, una cum malis punicis, ferulisque et papaveribus." Albert Henrichs, on the other hand, has argued that ὄργια συνταράσσειν is 'to stir up (i.e. commence) the rites', A. Henrichs, *ZPE* 4 (1969) 228 n. 15; cf. W. Vollgraff, *BCH* 48 (1924) 141: "elle commença la danse orgiastique, la course extatique des Bacchantes." If this interpretation is correct, the addition of ποσίν clarifies that it is with her feet, i.e. by chasing after Pentheus, that Autonoe starts the Bacchic rites that will culminate in his *sparagmos*, FLS.

And finally, the myths say that he (Aristaeus) visited Dionysus in Thrace and participated in his mysteries and while spending time with the god, he learned much useful knowledge from him.

The verb ὀργιάζειν with the dative is found in 5.50.4, where it is told that pirates:

περιέτυχον ταῖς Διονύσου τροφοῖς περὶ τὸ καλούμενον Δρίος τῷ θεῷ ὀργιαζούσαις ἐν τῇ Φθιώτιδι Ἀχαΐᾳ.

happened upon the nurses of Dionysus, who were celebrating rites for the god around the place called Drius in Achaea Phthiotis.

Furthermore, rites in the cult of Dionysus are called τὰ περὶ τοὺς ὀργιασμούς in 1.22.7:

διὸ καὶ τοὺς Ἕλληνας, ἐξ Αἰγύπτου παρειληφότας τὰ περὶ τοὺς ὀργιασμοὺς καὶ τὰς Διονυσιακὰς ἑορτάς, τιμᾶν τοῦτο τὸ μόριον ἔν τε τοῖς μυστηρίοις καὶ ταῖς τοῦ θεοῦ τούτου τελεταῖς τε καὶ θυσίαις, ὀνομάζοντας αὐτὸ φαλλόν.

And for this reason, the Greeks, too, having received the celebrations of orgies and Dionysiac festivals from Egypt, honour that member in mysteries and rites and offerings of that god, calling it 'phallus'.

Also in 3.74.2:

ἐνεργῆσαι δ' ἐπὶ πλέον καὶ τὰ περὶ τοὺς ὀργιασμούς, καὶ τελετὰς ἃς μὲν μεταθεῖναι πρὸς τὸ κρεῖττον, ἃς δὲ ἐπινόησαι.

He went above and beyond in performing the celebration of orgiastic rites and, with regard to mysteries, he improved some and invented others.

Orphic ceremonies are mentioned 1.96.4, where it is said that Orpheus brought from Egypt:

τῶν μυστικῶν τελετῶν τὰ πλεῖστα καὶ τὰ περὶ τὴν ἑαυτοῦ πλάνην ὀργιαζόμενα καὶ τὴν τῶν ἐν ᾅδου μυθοποιίαν.

most of his mystic ceremonies and the orgiastic rites that accompanied him on his journey and the story of what happened in Hades.

We also find the rites of the Mother of the gods referred to by ὀργιάζειν in 5.49.1, where, in the description of the wedding gifts presented at the wedding of Cadmus and Harmonia, it is told what Electra, Harmonia's mother, gave to her daughter:

τὰ τῆς μεγάλης καλουμένης Μητρὸς τῶν θεῶν ἱερὰ μετὰ κυμβάλων καὶ τυμπάνων καὶ τῶν ὀργιαζόντων.

the sacred rites of the so-called Mother of the gods with cymbals and tympana and the celebrants.

The word ὀργιάζοντες here refers to the Galli, the priests of Cybele.

DIONYSIUS OF HALICARNASSUS uses the word ὀργιάζειν in several places, again in a very general sense.

In *Ant. Rom.* 2.22.1, he tells how Romulus decreed that women were to perform certain rites:

> εἴ τι μὴ θέμις ἦν ὑπ' ἀνδρῶν ὀργιάζεσθαι κατὰ νόμον τὸν ἐπιχώριον, ταύτας ἐπιτελεῖν καὶ παῖδας αὐτῶν τὰ καθήκοντα λειτουργεῖν.
>
> If, according to the law of the land, it was not permitted for a certain ritual to be performed by men, they would perform it and their daughters would perform the appropriate religious services.

So ὀργιάζειν here has as its object τι, a certain rite. In *Ant. Rom.* 8.38.1, on the other hand, we find ὀργιάζειν with the deity as its object. Priests were sent to Coriolanus:

> ἔχοντας ἅμ' αὐτοῖς τῶν ὀργιαζομένων τε καὶ θεραπευομένων θεῶν τὰ σύμβολα.
>
> having with them the symbols of the gods they honoured with rites and worship.

Ant. Rom. 7.70.4. From fear that non-Greeks will not make any changes περὶ τοὺς ὀργιασμοὺς τῶν θεῶν, unless under duress.

Whereas the examples mentioned above omit any reference to a particular cult, *Ant. Rom.* 1.61.4, discussing the origin of the cult of Mother of the gods in Phrygia, mentions how Idaeus, a son of Dardanus, ἔνθα μητρὶ θεῶν ἱερὸν ἱδρυσάμενος ὄργια καὶ τελετὰς κατεστήσατο ("having built a sanctuary, established *orgia* and *teletai* there to the Mother of the gods").

In *Ant. Rom.* 2.19.5, there is also mention of the Cybele cult, at which Dionysius remarks that not a single Roman participates in the rites or processions in her honour:

> οὔτε ὀργιάζει τὴν θεὸν τοῖς Φρυγίοις ὀργιασμοῖς κατὰ νόμον καὶ ψήφισμα βουλῆς.
>
> or worships the goddess with Phrygian rites, in accordance with a law and decree of the Senate.

Finally, Dionysius has a couple of places where the terms ὀργιάζειν and ὀργιασμοί are used in reference to the cult of the Megaloi Theoi:

Ant. Rom. 1.69.4. Dionysius tells that the *hiera*, brought to Italy by Aeneas:

τῶν τε Μεγάλων θεῶν εἰκόνας εἶναι, οὓς Σαμοθρᾷκες Ἑλλήνων μάλιστα ὀργιάζουσι, καὶ τὸ μυθευόμενον Παλλάδιον.

are statues of the Great Gods, whom the Samothracians honour most of the Greeks, and said Palladium.

Ant. Rom. 2.22.2. Romulus derived many cult regulations from Greek customs:

ὅσα δὲ παρὰ Τυρρηνοῖς καὶ ἔτι πρότερον παρὰ Πελασγοῖς ἐτέλουν ἐπί
τε Κουρήτων καὶ Μεγάλων θεῶν ὀργιασμοῖς οἱ καλούμενοι πρὸς αὐτῶν
κάδμιλοι, ταῦτα κατὰ τὸν αὐτὸν τρόπον ὑπηρέτουν τοῖς ἱερεῦσιν οἱ
λεγόμενοι νῦν ὑπὸ Ῥωμαίων κάμιλοι.

Everything that those they called Cadmili celebrated with the Tyrrhenians and, even earlier, with the Pelasgians in the cult of the Curetes and the Great Gods, those now called camilli by the Romans perform in the same manner as acolytes to the priests.

In *Comp.* 4, Dionysius quotes a fragment from Euphronius' *Priapea*:

οὐ βέβηλος, ὦ τελέται τοῦ νέου Διονύσου

. . . .

κἀγὼ δ᾽ ἐξ εὐεργεσίης ὠργιασμένος ἥκω.

Not profane, performers of the rites of young Dionysus ...
I, too, come initiated as a result of kindness.

While its precise meaning is obscure, the fragment appears to hint at a prohibition to celebrate rites uninitiated (βέβηλος). The speaker therefore professes that he is initiated (ὠργιασμένος).

APPIAN uses ὀργιαστής and ὀργιάζειν for the priesthood of Isis, *B.Civ.* 4.6.47. During the proscriptions of the second triumvirate, the aedile Volusius was declared an outlaw:

Οὐολούσιος δὲ ἀγορανομῶν προεγράφη καὶ φίλον ὀργιαστὴν τῆς Ἴσι-
δος ἔχων ᾔτησε τὴν στολὴν καὶ τὰς ὀθόνας ἐνέδυ τὰς ποδήρεις καὶ τὴν
τοῦ κυνὸς κεφαλὴν ἐπέθετο καὶ διῆλθεν οὕτως ὀργιάζων αὐτῷ σχήματι
ἐς Πομπήιον.

The aedile Volusius was proscribed and since he had a friend who was a priest of Isis, he asked for his robe and donned the linen garment that reached to his feet and put on the dog's head and so he went to Pompey, disguised as a priest.

Strabo, in fr. 18 of book 7, gives a rather unfriendly description of the figure of Orpheus, whom he calls:

> ἄνδρα γόητα, ἀπὸ μουσικῆς ἅμα καὶ μαντικῆς καὶ τῶν περὶ τὰς τελετὰς ὀργιασμῶν ἀγυρτεύοντα τὸ πρῶτον, εἶτ᾽ ἤδη καὶ μειζόνων ἀξιοῦντα ἑαυτὸν καὶ ὄχλον καὶ δύναμιν κατασκευαζόμενον.

> a sorcerer who first begged by music and also by divination and (exalting) rites in his magic routine, and then also deemed himself worthy of other things and was able to acquire a mass (of followers) and influence.

From the fact that Orpheus is called a γόης ('sorcerer') it is apparent that, by οἱ περὶ τὰς τελετὰς ὀργιασμοί, Strabo means rituals of a magical character.

Beside these Orphic magic practices, Strabo also refers to rites in the cult of Cybele as ὀργιασμοί.

In 10.3.7, there is mention of the sacred rites (ἱερουργίαι) of Cybele:

> (περὶ) τοὺς τῆς Μητρὸς τῶν θεῶν ὀργιασμοὺς ἐν τῇ Φρυγίᾳ καὶ τοῖς περὶ τὴν Ἴδην τὴν Τρωικὴν τόποις.

> connected with the rites in honour of the Mother of the gods in Phrygia and in the districts around Trojan Ida.

The performance of this cult is also called ὀργιάζειν in 10.3.12:

> οἱ δὲ Βερέκυντες Φρυγῶν τι φῦλον καὶ ἁπλῶς οἱ Φρύγες καὶ τῶν Τρώων οἱ περὶ τὴν Ἴδην κατοικοῦντες Ῥέαν μὲν καὶ αὐτοὶ τιμῶσι καὶ ὀργιά-ζουσι ταύτῃ.

> But the Berecyntes, a tribe of Phrygians, and the Phrygians in general, and those of the Trojans who live round Ida, also honour Rhea and worship her with orgiastic rites.

Crete is mentioned in 10.3.11, where Strabo compares the Curetes to Satyrs in the worship of Dionysus:

> ἐν δὲ τῇ Κρήτῃ καὶ ταῦτα καὶ τὰ τοῦ Διὸς ἱερὰ ἰδίως ἐπετελεῖτο μετ᾽ ὀργιασμοῦ καὶ τοιούτων προπόλων οἷοι περὶ τὸν Διόνυσόν εἰσιν οἱ Σάτυροι· τούτους δ᾽ ὠνόμαζον Κουρῆτας.

> In Crete, both these (rites) and, in particular, those sacred to Zeus were performed with a ritual and such attendants as are in the entourage of Dionysus, the Satyrs; and they call them Curetes.

He concludes his discussion with the words:

> οἱ μὲν οὖν Ἕλληνες τοιοῦτοι περὶ τοὺς ὀργιασμούς.

> Such were the Greeks with respect to orgiastic rites.

Indeed, Strabo only uses ὀργιασμός and ὀργιάζειν for religious rites of this wild and ecstatic type.

In 10.3.10, Strabo mentions the orgiastic experience in the same breath as Bacchic, choral, and mystic affairs:

> οἱ μὲν οὖν Ἕλληνες οἱ πλεῖστοι τῷ Διονύσῳ προσέθεσαν καὶ τῷ Ἀπόλ-
> λωνι καὶ τῇ Ἑκάτῃ καὶ ταῖς Μούσαις καὶ Δήμητρι, νὴ Δία, τὸ ὀργιαστι-
> κὸν πᾶν καὶ τὸ βακχικὸν καὶ τὸ χορικὸν καὶ τὸ περὶ τὰς τελετὰς μυστι-
> κόν.

> Most Greeks therefore ascribed to Dionysus, Apollo, Hecate, the Muses, and especially to Demeter—by Jove!—everything orgiastic, Bacchic or choral, and also the mystic element in the rites.

PAUSANIAS, who was very interested in religious institutions, is a rich source for our knowledge of many local cults. He refers to several of those cults by the term ὄργια.

We find ὄργια as a general term for cult forms of a special, deviating character in 4.1.7, where the Athenian Methapus is mentioned as an ὀργίων παντοίων συνθέτης (a founder of various rites).

The cult of Demeter is called ὄργια in 10.28.3. In Polygnotus' painting in the *lesche* of the Cnidians in Delphi, in which the Underworld is represented, Charon's boat is depicted with Tellis and Cleoboea. About this last figure, Pausanias remarks:

> Κλεόβοιαν δὲ ἐς Θάσον τὰ ὄργια τῆς Δήμητρος ἐνεγκεῖν πρώτην ἐκ
> Πάρου φασίν.

> They say that Cleoboea first introduced the rites of Demeter to Thasos from Paros.

Here we have an example of the Thesmophoria that were popular all over the Greek world.[2]

In the description of Messenia, the mysteries of the Megalai Theai are repeatedly mentioned and these, too, are called ὄργια. They are the famous mysteries of Andania, that supposedly originated in Eleusis.

4.1.5. The first to rule Messenia were Polycaon and his wife Messene:

> παρὰ ταύτην τὴν Μεσσήνην τὰ ὄργια κομίζων τῶν Μεγάλων θεῶν
> Καύκων ἦλθεν ἐξ Ἐλευσῖνος.

> It was to this Messene that Caucon came and brought the mysteries of the Great Goddesses from Eleusis.

---

[2] Cf. Nilsson, *Feste*, 314. The sanctuary of Demeter Thesmophoros at Paros is mentioned, for example, in Hdt. 6.134.

4.2.6. Later, Lycus, the son of Pandion, came to Aphareus, the founder of Arene in Messenia:

καὶ τὰ ὄργια ἐπέδειξε τῶν Μεγάλων θεῶν Ἀφαρεῖ καὶ τοῖς παισὶ καὶ τῇ γυναικὶ Ἀρήνῃ· ταῦτα δέ σφισιν ἐπεδείκνυτο ἀγαγὼν ἐς τὴν Ἀνδανίαν, ὅτι καὶ τὴν Μεσσήνην ὁ Καύκων ἐμύησεν ἐνταῦθα.

He revealed the mysteries of the Great Goddesses to Aphareus and his children and his wife Arene; he revealed these things to them at Andania because Caucon had initiated Messene there.

4.14.1. After the first Messenian war, many Messenians fled, to Eleusis among other places:

ἐς Ἐλευσῖνα δὲ οἱ τοῦ γένους τῶν ἱερέων καὶ θεαῖς ταῖς Μεγάλαις τελοῦντες τὰ ὄργια.

And the members of the clan of the priests who celebrated the mysteries for the Great Goddesses went to Eleusis.

4.15.7. In the second Messenian war, however, they returned again from Eleusis:

ἐξ Ἐλευσῖνός τε, οἷς πάτριον δρᾶν τὰ ὄργια τῶν Μεγάλων θεῶν.

and from Eleusis, those who traditionally celebrated the mysteries of the Great Goddesses.

Pausanias also repeatedly calls the rites celebrated in various places in honour of Dionysus, ὄργια.

8.6.5. About seven stades from Mantinea, at Melangea, is the so-called source of the Meliasts:[3]

οἱ Μελιασταὶ δὲ οὗτοι δρῶσι τὰ ὄργια τοῦ Διονύσου.

Those Meliasts perform the rites of Dionysus.

8.26.2. At Heraea in Arcadia there are two temples of Dionysus and a building ἔνθα τῷ Διονύσῳ τὰ ὄργια ἄγουσιν ("where they celebrate the rites for Dionysus").[4]

In 8.37.5, it is said of Onomacritus:

παρὰ δὲ Ὁμήρου Ὀνομάκριτος παραλαβὼν τῶν Τιτάνων τὸ ὄνομα Διονύσῳ τε συνέθηκεν ὄργια καὶ εἶναι τοὺς Τιτᾶνας τῷ Διονύσῳ τῶν παθημάτων ἐποίησεν αὐτουργούς.

---

[3] Cf. Nilsson, *Feste*, 299.
[4] Cf. Nilsson, *Feste*, 300.

He derived the name of the Titans from Homer[5] and in the rites which he instituted in honour of Dionysus, he represented the Titans as the effectors of his sufferings.

This passage brings us into the realm of Orphism.[6]

9.20.4. The women of Tanagra descend to the sea for a ritual purification before the rites of Dionysus: πρὸ τῶν Διονύσου ὀργίων.

10.4.3. The Attic θυιάδες go to Mt. Parnassus every other year (παρὰ ἔτος):

αὐταί τε καὶ αἱ γυναῖκες Δελφῶν ἄγουσιν ὄργια Διονύσῳ

and they themselves and the women of Delphi perform the rites of Dionysus.[7]

10.6.4. Some say that the name θυιάδες is derived from a certain Thyia, of whom it is said:

ἱερᾶσθαί τε τὴν Θυίαν Διονύσῳ πρῶτον καὶ ὄργια ἀγαγεῖν τῷ θεῷ.

that Thyia was the first priestess of Dionysus and first performed the rites for the god.

In 10.33.11, there is mention of a cult of Dionysus at Amphiclea in Phocis. The place is corrupt,[8] but in any case, it appears to say: Διονύσῳ δρῶσιν ὄργια ("They perform rites for Dionysus").

We find ὄργια used for the cult of Cybele in 7.17.9. When Attis had reached manhood, he travelled to Lydia καὶ Λυδοῖς ὄργια ἐτέλει Μητρός ("and performed the rites of the Mother to Lydians"), according to the story by Hermesianax.

Finally, there is also mention of ὄργια in the Theban cult of the Cabiri, 9.25.7. During the raid of the Epigoni and the capture of Thebes, the Καβειραῖοι were expelled and the τελετή was not celebrated for some time:

Πελαργὴν δὲ ὕστερον τὴν Ποτνιέως καὶ Ἰσθμιάδην Πελαργῇ συνοικοῦντα καταστήσασθαι μὲν τὰ ὄργια αὐτοῦ λέγουσιν ἐξ ἀρχῆς, μετενεγκεῖν δὲ αὐτὰ ἐπὶ τὸν Ἀλεξίαρουν καλούμενον.

---

[5] Hom. *Il.* 16.279.
[6] Cf. Rohde, *Psyche* II, 118.
[7] Cf. Nilsson, *Feste*, 284.
[8] Cf. Nilsson, *Feste*, 286.

It is said, however, that later, Pelarge, the daughter of Potneus, and her husband, Isthmiades, initially established the rites here, but then transferred them to a place named Alexiarous.

PHILO JUDAEUS uses ὄργια (and ὀργιάζειν) in various contexts. They are Greek religious rites in *Legatio ad Gaium* 78, where Philo tells how the emperor Gaius regarded lesser gods and their rites as far inferior to his own divinity:

> ἤρχετο γὰρ ἐξομοιοῦν τὸ πρῶτον τοῖς λεγομένοις ἡμιθέοις ἑαυτόν, Διο-
> νύσῳ καὶ Ἡρακλεῖ καὶ Διοσκούροις, Τροφώνιον καὶ Ἀμφιάραον καὶ
> Ἀμφίλοχον καὶ τοὺς ὁμοίους χρηστηρίοις αὐτοῖς καὶ ὀργίοις χλεύην
> τιθέμενος κατὰ σύγκρισιν τῆς ἰδίας δυνάμεως.

> For he began to liken himself to the so-called demigods: Dionysus and Heracles and the Dioscuri, and he considered lesser gods like Trophonius, Amphiaraus, Amphilochus and their oracles and rites as a joke in comparison with his own power.

In *De spec. leg.* 3.40, ὀργιάζειν is the celebration of mysteries. *Androgunoi* (men dressed as women) can be seen:

> μυστηρίων καὶ τελετῶν κατάρχοντας καὶ ⟨τὰ⟩ Δήμητρος ὀργιάζοντας.

> leading the mysteries and ceremonies and celebrating the rites of Demeter.

These *androgunoi* are apparently Galli, castrated priests of the Mother of the gods.

Philo uses ὄργια in a metaphorical sense for philosophical wisdom in *Quod omnis probus liber sit* 14:

> οἱ δὲ ὥσπερ ἐν ταῖς τελεταῖς ἱεροφαντηθέντες, ὅταν ὀργίων γεμισθῶσι,
> πολλὰ τῆς πρόσθεν ὀλιγωρίας ἑαυτοὺς κακίζουσιν.

> And when, just like initiates in the celebrations, they have been filled with the mysteries, they reproach themselves for their former negligence.

Similarly, he uses it for divine truth in *De sacr.* 60. He explains the need to keep it secret:

> καὶ τῶν τελείων μύστις γενομένη τελετῶν μηδενὶ προχείρως ἐκλαλῇ τὰ
> μυστήρια, ταμιευομένη δὲ αὐτὰ καὶ ἐχεμυθοῦσα ἐν ἀπορρήτῳ φυλάττῃ·
> γέγραπται γὰρ ἐγκρυφίας ποιεῖν, ὅτι κεκρύφθαι δεῖ τὸν ἱερὸν περὶ τοῦ
> ἀγενήτου καὶ τῶν δυνάμεων αὐτοῦ μύστην λόγον, ἐπεὶ θείων παρα-
> καταθήκην ὀργίων οὐ παντός ἐστι φυλάξαι.

> And having become an initiate of the ultimate mysteries, she (Sarah/Virtue) will not divulge the mysteries to anyone off-hand, but will store them

up and guard them in silence and secrecy. For it is written: "Make concealed loaves (i.e. bread baked in the ashes)", because the sacred story about the unborn god and his powers must be concealed, since not everyone can guard the entrusted deposit of holy rites.

Also *De Abrahamo* 122. Some souls have been initiated into the great mysteries, but others have not:

ὅταν μήπω τὰς μεγάλας τελεσθεῖσα τελετὰς ἔτι ἐν ταῖς βραχυτέραις ὀργιάζηται καὶ μὴ δύνηται τὸ ὂν ἄνευ ἑτέρου τινὸς ἐξ αὐτοῦ μόνου καταλαβεῖν, ἀλλὰ διὰ τῶν δρωμένων, ἢ κτίζον ἢ ἄρχον.

When, not yet having been initiated into the great mysteries, it (the soul) still worships in the lower rites and cannot grasp the concept of 'the one who is' (i.e. God) from itself alone without anything else, but through its actions, either creating or ruling.

Philo uses ὀργιάζεσθαι in a distinctly pejorative sense for the celebration of pagan rites in *De spec. leg.* 1.319:

πρὸς τούτοις ἔτι τὰ περὶ τελετὰς καὶ μυστήρια καὶ πᾶσαν τὴν τοιαύτην τερθρείαν καὶ βωμολοχίαν ἐκ τῆς ἱερᾶς ἀναιρεῖ νομοθεσίας, οὐκ ἀξιῶν τοὺς ἐν τοιαύτῃ πολιτείᾳ τραφέντας ὀργιάζεσθαι καὶ μυστικῶν πλασμάτων ἐκκρεμαμένους ὀλιγωρεῖν ἀληθείας καὶ τὰ νύκτα καὶ σκότος προσκεκληρωμένα μεταδιώκειν παρέντας τὰ ἡμέρας καὶ φωτὸς ἄξια.

Furthermore, he also removes the practice of rites and mysteries and all such deception and buffoonery from sacred legislation. He would not allow those raised in such a community to conduct mummeries and, clinging to mystic concoctions, hold the truth in low esteem and pursue things associated with night and darkness, disregarding those things worthy of daylight.

On the other hand, he also adopts the language of Greek mysteries for Jewish rites. The following three passages are about the divine rites of Jewish religion, as taught by Moses.

De gigantibus 54:

προσκυνεῖν τὸν θεὸν ἄρχεται καὶ εἰς τὸν γνόφον, τὸν ἀειδῆ χῶρον, εἰσελθὼν αὐτοῦ καταμένει τελούμενος τὰς ἱερωτάτας τελετάς. γίνεται δὲ οὐ μόνον μύστης, ἀλλὰ καὶ ἱεροφάντης ὀργίων καὶ διδάσκαλος θείων, ἃ τοῖς ὦτα κεκαθαρμένοις ὑφηγήσεται.

He (Moses) begins to worship God and, having entered darkness, the invisible region, he stays there, while he undergoes the holiest ceremonies. And he becomes, not only an initiate, but also a hierophant and teacher of divine rites, which he will teach to those whose ears are pure.

De vita Mosis 2.153:

> Μωυσῆς μὲν εἰς τὴν σκηνὴν εἰσέρχεται τὸν ἀδελφὸν ἐπαγόμενος· ὀγδόη δ' ἦν τῆς τελετῆς ἡμέρα καὶ τελευταία, ταῖς γὰρ πρότερον ἑπτὰ ἱεροφαντῶν αὐτόν τε καὶ τοὺς ἀδελφιδοῦς ὠργίαζεν.

> Moses enters the tent (i.e. the tabernacle), taking his brother with him. It was the eighth and last day of the celebration; the seven days before, he initiated his brother and nephews, acting as their hierophant.

De plantatione 26:

> τοιγαροῦν Μωυσῆς ὁ ταμίας καὶ φύλαξ τῶν τοῦ ὄντος ὀργίων ἀνακεκλήσεται· λέγεται γὰρ ἐν Λευιτικῇ βίβλῳ "ἀνεκάλεσε Μωυσῆν".[9]

> Therefore Moses, master and guardian of the mysteries of 'the one who is' (i.e. God), will be called on, for it is said in the book of Leviticus: "He called unto Moses".

The next two passages also refer to the rites of Jewish religion.
De fuga et inventione 85:

> ἐλαύνετε οὖν, ἐλαύνετε, ὦ μύσται καὶ ἱεροφάνται θείων ὀργίων, τὰς μιγάδας καὶ σύγκλυδας καὶ πεφυρμένας.

> So drive off, initiates and hierophants of holy mysteries, drive off the mixed and motley crowd.

Quod deterius potiori insidiari non instat 143. Philo argues that people suffer their greatest harm when they lose the chance to redeem themselves. For irreligious people, this is when they are permanently excluded from religiousness:

> οὐχ ὅταν εὐσέβεια τῶν ἰδίων ὀργίων ἀποσχοινίσῃ;

> Is it not when religion shuns them from its own rites?

Finally, we find several attestations of the word ἀνοργίαστος ('uninitiated' or 'profane'). In *De ebrietate* 146, in his explanation of the name Hannah ('Grace'), Philo describes the state of mind of a θεοφόρητος, a person possessed by God:

> χάριτος δ' ἥτις ἂν πληρωθῇ ψυχή, γέγηθεν εὐθὺς καὶ μειδιᾷ καὶ ἀνορχεῖται· βεβάκχευται γάρ, ὡς πολλοῖς τῶν ἀνοργιάστων μεθύειν καὶ παροινεῖν καὶ ἐξεστάναι ἂν δόξαι.

---

[9] *LXX* Lev. 1:1.

When the soul is filled with grace, it immediately rejoices and smiles and
dances, for it revels, so that to many of the uninitiated it may seem to be
drunken with wine and to have lost its wits.

Also in *De sacr.* 32. If someone becomes a φιλήδονος, a pleasure-lover,
he will, among many other things, become ἀνοργίαστος: "profane". In
De cherubim 94, Philo argues against pagan customs, which are called,
among other things, ἀνοργιάστους τελετάς: "profane rites".

CORNUTUS, *De Nat. Deor.* 30, mentions the sound of the rhoptra and
tympana of the bacchantes, ἃ παραλαμβάνουσιν εἰς τὰ ὄργια αὑτῶν
("which they take with them to their rites").

MARCUS AURELIUS uses the word ὄργια only once, *Med.* 3.7:

> ὁ γὰρ τὸν ἑαυτοῦ νοῦν καὶ δαίμονα καὶ τὰ ὄργια τῆς τούτου ἀρετῆς
> προελόμενος τραγῳδίαν οὐ ποιεῖ, οὐ στενάζει, οὐκ ἐρημίας, οὐ πολυ-
> πληθείας δεήσεται.

> For he who has chosen above all else his own mind and divine protector
> and the worship of its excellence does not make a tragedy, does not moan,
> and will require neither solitude nor profusion.

So the word is here used in a metaphorical sense.

MAXIMUS OF TYRE, *Diss.* 24.5, is convinced that farmers were the first to
establish festivals and rites for the gods:

> πρῶτοι δὲ μὲν ἐπὶ ληνῷ στασάμενοι Διονύσῳ χορούς, πρῶτοι δὲ ἐπὶ ἅλῳ
> Δημητρὶ ὄργια, πρῶτοι δὲ τὴν ἐλαίας γένεσιν τῇ Ἀθηνᾷ ἐπιφημίσαντες,
> πρῶτοι δὲ τῶν ἐκ γῆς καρπῶν τοῖς δεδωκόσιν θεοῖς ἀπαρξάμενοι.

> For they were the first to perform choral dances for Dionysus at the
> winepress, the first to celebrate threshing rites for Demeter, the first to
> attribute the creation of the olive to Athena, and the first to dedicate fruits
> of the field to those who have given them, the gods.

Diss. 32.7 discusses the pleasures associated with the worship of Dionysus:

> πάντα ταῦτα Διονύσου ἡδονῶν σχήματα ἐν μυστηρίοις ὀργιαζόμενα.

> "All these forms of pleasures of Dionysus are celebrated in mysteries."

In *Diss.* 26.2, we find τελετὰς καὶ ὀργιασμούς used in a metaphorical
sense for philosophical doctrine.[10]

---

[10] See Zijderveld, above, p. 74.

POLYAENUS uses ὄργια as well as the verb ὀργιάζειν.

Strat. 1.1.1. When Dionysus went to India to establish his worship there, he equipped his army, not with normal weapons, but with fawn-skins and thyrsi. Giving his enemies a taste of wine, he led them to dance and to all the other Bacchic rites: καὶ ὅσα ἄλλα βακχικὰ ὄργια.

Strat. 8.53.4 describes how Artemisia captured Latmos. She concealed her armed forces:

> αὐτὴ δὲ μετὰ εὐνούχων καὶ γυναικῶν καὶ αὐλητῶν καὶ τυμπανιστῶν ἐς τὸ ἄλσος τῆς Μητρὸς τῶν θεῶν ἀπέχον τῆς πόλεως ἑπτὰ στάδια παρῆλθεν ὀργιάζουσα.

> And she herself arrived, celebrating rites with eunuchs and women and people and oboists and tympanists at the sacred grove of the Mother of the gods, at a distance of seven stades from the city.

When the Latmians came out to see what Artemisia was up to, her hidden army captured the city. So the verb ὀργιάζειν is here used for the celebration of the rites of Cybele.

PLUTARCH uses the term ὄργια for religious rites of various nature. The rituals in the cult of Dionysus are called οἱ περὶ τὸν Διόνυσον ὀργιασμοί more than once,[11] of which a few examples follow here:

In *Alex.* 2 (665d), it is said of Macedonian women:

> ὡς πᾶσαι μὲν αἱ τῇδε γυναῖκες ἔνοχοι τοῖς Ὀρφικοῖς οὖσαι καὶ τοῖς περὶ τὸν Διόνυσον ὀργιασμοῖς ἐκ τοῦ πάνυ παλαιοῦ.

> that all these women were, of old, devotees of Orphic and Dionysiac rites.

This expression recurs in almost the same form in *Crass.* 8 (547e), concerning the Thracian wife of Spartacus: μαντικὴ δὲ καὶ κάτοχος τοῖς περὶ τὸν Διόνυσον ὀργιασμοῖς ("a prophetess and devotee of Dionysiac rites").

In *De Is. et Os.* 364e, Plutarch expounds how the rites at the funeral of the Apis bull are entirely similar to those of the Dionysus cult:

> οἱ ἱερεῖς ... νεβρίδας περικαθάπτονται καὶ θύρσους φοροῦσι καὶ βοαῖς χρῶνται καὶ κινήσεσιν ὥσπερ οἱ κάτοχοι τοῖς περὶ τὸν Διόνυσον ὀργιασμοῖς.

> The priests wear fawn-skins, carry thyrsi and shout and move about just like the devotees of the Dionysiac rites.

---

[11] Conversely, they are called ὄργια only once, fr. 212 Sandbach.

Likewise, *Cons. ad ux.* 611d mentions τὰ μυστικὰ σύμβολα τῶν περὶ τὸν Διόνυσον ὀργιασμῶν ("the mystic symbols of the Dionysiac rites").

In *Quaest. conv.* 636e, the author argues that all animal species originate from an egg:

> ὅθεν οὐκ ἀπὸ τρόπου τοῖς περὶ τὸν Διόνυσον ὀργιασμοῖς ὡς μίμημα τοῦ τὰ πάντα γεννῶντος καὶ περιέχοντος ἐν ἑαυτῷ συγκαθωσίωται.

> And therefore, it was not inappropriate that it was made into a sacred object in the cult of Dionysus, as a representation of that which produces everything and is contained within itself.

With a minor nuance, we find the combination βακχικοὶ ὀργιασμοί in *Amat.* 758f:

> τὰ γὰρ μητρῷα καὶ πανικὰ κοινωνεῖ τοῖς βακχικοῖς ὀργιασμοῖς.

> The festivals in honour of Cybele and Pan are of the same nature as Bacchic rites.

We also find the verb ὀργιάζειν several times, concerning the cult of Dionysus.

Anim. an corp. 501f. The confused crowd on the forum around the rostra did not gather Διονύσῳ βεβακχευμένον θύσθλον ἱεραῖς νυξὶ καὶ κοινοῖς ὀργιάσοντες κώμοις ("to celebrate, in holy nights and public revels, the rite in Dionysus' honour").

In *Quaest. conv.* 671f, it is argued that even the celebration of the sabbath is not completely unrelated to Dionysus:

> Σάβους γὰρ καὶ νῦν ἔτι πολλοὶ τοὺς Βάκχους καλοῦσιν καὶ ταύτην ἀφιᾶσι τὴν φωνὴν ὅταν ὀργιάζωσι τῷ θεῷ,

> For many even now call the followers of Bacchus Sabi and utter that cry when they celebrate the god.

Apparently, the pagans believed that the Jewish sabbath was somehow connected to Dionysus Sabazius.

Plutarch speaks of τὰ Διονύσου ὄργια only once, but in such a way that it is clear he did not use it specially for the cult of Dionysus. The place in question is fr. 212 Sandbach, where it is said about Orpheus:

> εἰς Αἴγυπτον ἀφικόμενος τὰ τῆς Ἴσιδος καὶ τοῦ Ὀσίριδος εἰς τὰ τῆς Δηοῦς καὶ τοῦ Διονύσου μετατέθεικεν ὄργια.

> Having arrived in Egypt he changed the *orgia* of Isis and Osiris to those of Demeter and Dionysus.

So the rites in the cult of Isis and Osiris and the cult of Demeter are here called ὄργια, like the rites of Dionysus.

In connection with this usage, ἱερὰ ὀργιάζειν (beside ἱερὰ δρᾶν) is said of Thracian, Egyptian and Phrygian religious ceremonies.

De def. orac. 415a argues that, in attempting to explain the creation, one would do better—rather than adopt Plato's notion of a στοιχεῖον—to speak of the race of δαίμονες (who are situated between gods and men):

> εἴτε μάγων τῶν περὶ Ζωροάστρην ὁ λόγος οὗτός ἐστιν εἴτε Θράκιος ἀπ' Ὀρφέως εἴτ' Αἰγύπτιος ἢ Φρύγιος, ὡς τεκμαιρόμεθα ταῖς ἑκατέρωθι τελεταῖς ἀναμεμιγμένα πολλὰ θνητὰ καὶ πένθιμα τῶν ὀργιαζομένων καὶ δρωμένων ἱερῶν ὁρῶντες.

> This doctrine may come from the Zoroastrian magi or be a Thracian doctrine from Orpheus, or Egyptian, or Phrygian, as we can judge from the fact that, in each of those countries, mixed in with the rites (*teletai*) are many things concerning death and mourning from the celebrated and performed sacred rites (*hiera*).

So one can ὀργιάζειν ἱερά in *teletai*, and likewise, in *De fac.* 944d, it is said of the souls of the pious that have become δαίμονες, who live on the moon, that when they descend to earth, they ταῖς ἀνωτάτω συμπάρεισι καὶ συνοργιάζουσι τῶν τελετῶν, κτλ. ("are present and participate in mystery rites of the highest order").

De daed. Plat. (fr. 157 Sandbach; Euseb. *Praep. evang.* 3.1). The hidden character of the old φυσιολογία is apparent in the Orphic poems and Egyptian and Phrygian stories.

> μάλιστα δὲ οἱ περὶ τὰς τελετὰς ὀργιασμοὶ καὶ τὰ δρώμενα συμβολικῶς ἐν ταῖς ἱερουργίαις τὴν τῶν παλαιῶν ἐμφαίνει διάνοιαν.

> But the rites at mystery ceremonies and symbolic acts in religious service in particular, show the persuasion of the ancients.

In *De anima* (fr. 178 Sandbach), it is argued that the soul, having entered the body, is destroyed by its entire transformation. It does not notice this until death approaches, for then it undergoes an experience οἶον οἱ τελεταῖς μεγάλαις κατοργιαζόμενοι, "like those who participate in great initiations (μεγάλαι τελεταί, at Eleusis?)."[12] Among other things, the mysteries will have served as a *memento mori*.

---

[12] Zijderveld, above, p. 62, considers Orphic ceremonies, but I believe there is more reason to think of Eleusis here.

It has already become clear from the examples discussed, how Plutarch uses ὄργια and its cognates to refer to all kinds of rituals: Dionysian, but also Orphic, Egyptian and Phrygian, as well as rites of various *teletai*, of which the character is often not specified.

Purification rites, such as the Plynteria in Athens, are also called ὄργια, *Alc.* 34.1 (210b). This rite is celebrated in honour of the goddess Athena, whose ancient image was washed on this occasion.[13] The following details are mentioned:

> δρῶσι δὲ τὰ ὄργια Πραξιεργίδαι Θαργηλιῶνος ἕκτῃ φθίνοντος ἀπόρ-
> ρητα, τόν τε κόσμον ἀφελόντες καὶ τὸ ἕδος κατακαλύψαντες.

> The Praxiergidae perform these rites in secret on the twenty-fifth of Thar-
> gelion, having taken away all adornment (from the goddess) and having
> covered the statue.

In this context, we should also mention the places where the performance of purification rites is referred to by the verb κατοργιάζειν.

Sol. 12.9 (84e) describes the vigilance of Epimenides, who made the city of Athens obedient and harmonious:

> ἱλασμοῖς τισι καὶ καθαρμοῖς καὶ ἱδρύσεσι κατοργιάσας καὶ καθοσιώσας
> τὴν πόλιν.

> having consecrated and sanctified the city by means of certain propitia-
> tions, purifications and the building of temples.

In *De def. or.* 418a, the stories of Apollo's battle with the Python over the possession of the Delphic oracle are considered to be in violation of the ἱερὰ ἁγιώτατα. To the question as to which *hiera* are meant, the answer is:

> οἷς ἄρτι τοὺς ἔξω Πυλῶν πάντας Ἕλληνας ἡ πόλις κατοργιάζουσα
> μέχρι Τεμπῶν ἐλήλακεν.

> those in which the city made all Greeks west of Thermopylae participate,
> and which it extended up to Tempe.

This apparently refers to the so-called Septerion or Stepterion, the purifi-cation festival celebrated every eight years, of which the official cult leg-end is disputed here,[14] and which, according to *Quaest. Gr.* 12 (293c), consisted of "a representation of Apollo's fight against the Python and the flight and pursuit to Tempe after the fight."

---

[13] Cf. Deubner, *Attische Feste*, 17 ff.; M. Christopoulos, *Kernos* 5 (1992) 27–39.
[14] Cf. *RE* s.v. Septerion (Pfister); Nilsson, *Feste* 150–157.

The Roman cult of Bona Dea is also referred to as ὄργια several times, and ὀργιάζειν is used for the performance of her rites.

Caes. 9.6 (711e). It is forbidden for men to enter the cult house during the performance of the ceremonies (τῶν ἱερῶν ὀργιαζομένων).

Caes. 10.3 (712b). When Clodius ignored this prohibition and caused a great stir among the women present:

> ἡ Αὐρηλία τὰ μὲν ὄργια τῆς θεοῦ κατέπαυσε καὶ συνεκάλυψεν.

> Aurelia adjourned the rites and covered the sacred objects.[15]

So here, τὰ ὄργια are, at the same time, rites and sacred objects.[16]

Cic. 19.4 (870b). At nightfall, Cicero was compelled to go to a friend's house:

> ἐπεὶ τὴν ἐκείνου γυναῖκες κατεῖχον ἱεροῖς ἀπορρήτοις ὀργιάζουσαι θεόν, ἣν Ῥωμαῖοι μὲν Ἀγαθήν, Ἕλληνες δὲ Γυναικείαν ὀνομάζουσι.

> since his own house had been occupied by the women celebrating secret rites of the goddess called Bona Dea by the Romans and Goddess of women by the Greeks.

So we here find ὀργιάζω with, as its object, the deity in whose honour ὄργια are performed. We also find the verb used thus for the worship of a sacred statue:

Cam. 20.6 (139b) mentions the Palladium, of which some say:

> Δάρδανον μὲν εἰς Τροίαν ἐξενεγκάμενον ὀργιάσαι καὶ καθιερῶσαι κτίσαντα τὴν πόλιν.

> that Dardanus had brought it to Troy and had worshipped it as a sacred object after the founding of the city.

We could compare the aforementioned place, *Anim. an corp.* 4 (501f), where we saw the phrase θύσθλον ὀργιάζειν. The word θύσθλον there is, however, usually explained as the festival itself, not 'sacred object'.

The combinations ἱερὰ ὀργιάζειν, τελετὰς ὀργιάζειν etc. are frequent indeed.

For example, in *Numa* 8.3 (64e), it is said of the king that he wanted to soften the character of the Roman people by means of religious customs:

> τὰ μὲν πολλὰ θυσίαις καὶ πομπαῖς καὶ χορείαις, ἃς αὐτὸς ὠργίασε καὶ κατέστησεν.

---

[15] Yet another example of the taboo character of the *orgia*, cf. Theoc. *Id.* 26.14.
[16] Cf. Catull. 64.259–260.

For the most part with sacrifices, processions and choral dances, which he himself caused to be celebrated and established.

We do not find the combination μυστήρια ὀργιάζειν, but there is mention of μυστηρίων ὀργιασταί:

In *Cor.* 32 (228f), the expression probably refers to augurs:

ὅσοι γὰρ ἦσαν ἱερεῖς θεῶν ἢ μυστηρίων ὀργιασταὶ καὶ φύλακες ἢ τὴν ἀπ᾽ οἰωνῶν πάτριον οὖσαν ἔκπαλαι μαντικὴν ἔχοντες.

All the priests of the gods and the celebrants and custodians of the mysteries and those who, of old, practised traditional divination from bird omens.

The same expression is used for δαίμονες in *De def. or.* 417a:

δαίμονας νομίζωμεν ἐπισκόπους θείων ἱερῶν καὶ μυστηρίων ὀργιαστάς.

Let us believe that *daimones* are active as overseers at divine ceremonies and as performers of mystery rites.

Shortly before, the warning was given, *De def. or.* 417a:

ἡμεῖς δὲ μήτε μαντείας τινὰς ἀθειάστους εἶναι λέγοντας ἢ τελετὰς καὶ ὀργιασμοὺς ἀμελουμένους ὑπὸ θεῶν ἀκούωμεν.

Let us not lend our ear to those who claim that there are oracles without divine inspiration or that religious ceremonies and rites remain unnoticed by the gods.

Another aspect of the ὀργιασμοί emerges in *De superst.* 169d, where they are seen from the human point of view:

ἥδιστα δὲ τοῖς ἀνθρώποις ἑορταὶ καὶ εἰλαπίναι πρὸς ἱεροῖς καὶ μυήσεις καὶ ὀργιασμοὶ καὶ κατευχαὶ θεῶν καὶ προσκυνήσεις.

The most pleasant things for men are festivals, banquets at temples, initiations, religious rites, prayer and adoration of the gods.

The same notion returns in a different form in *Non posse* 1101e. Nothing we do or say pleases us more than what we see of the gods and perform in their honour:

ὀργιάζοντες ἢ χορεύοντες ἢ θυσίαις παρόντες καὶ τελεταῖς.

whether we celebrate religious rites or hold choral dances or are present at sacrifices or festivals.

De anima (fr. 178 Sandbach) describes what happens to the 'complete initiate' (ὁ παντελὴς ἤδη καὶ μεμυημένος) in the afterlife:

περιὼν ἐστεφανωμένος ὀργιάζει καὶ σύνεστιν ὁσίοις καὶ καθαροῖς ἀν-
δράσι.

Going around wreathed, he celebrates festivals and enjoys the company of
pure and holy men.

If, with this last example, we have already left the actual field of cult in
its many worldly forms, there are a few more places that demand our
attention, where there is mention of ὄργια, ὀργιάζειν, and ὀργιαστής in
a metaphorical sense.

In *Aem.* 3.7 (256e), the serious and meticulous attitude of Aemilius
Paulus in the army is described:

ὥσπερ ἱερεὺς ἄλλων ὀργίων δεινῶν τῶν περὶ τὰς θυσίας ἐθῶν ἐξηγού-
μενος ἕκαστα.

Directing everything like a priest of other awesome rites concerning the
sacrificial customs.

Similarly, ὀργιαστής is also used outside the religious realm for 'follower'
or 'devotee'.

In *Quaest. conv.* 717d, Carneades is called ἄνδρα τῆς Ἀκαδημίας
εὐκλεέστατον ὀργιαστήν, "a very famous disciple of the Academy".

Adv. Col. 1107f, mentioning Aristodemus from Aegium, says of him:

οἶσθα γὰρ τὸν ἄνδρα τῶν ἐξ Ἀκαδημείας οὐ ναρθηκοφόρον ἀλλ' ἐμμα-
νέστατον ὀργιαστὴν Πλάτωνος.

For you know that the man is not a narthex-bearer[17] of the people from
the Academy, but a most fervent disciple of Plato!

Adv. Col. 1117b, using the same metaphor, refers to the Epicurean school
as τὰ Ἐπικούρου ὡς ἀληθῶς θεόφαντα ὄργια: "the mysteries of Epicu-
rus, which are truly the revelation of a god."

Besides these adherents of philosophical schools, we several times find
Ἔρωτος ὀργιασταί:

Amat. 762a:

ὅθεν ἀγαθὸν μέν, ὦ ἑταῖρε, τῆς ἐν Ἐλευσῖνι τελετῆς μετασχεῖν, ἐγὼ δ'
ὁρῶ τοῖς Ἔρωτος ὀργιασταῖς καὶ μύσταις ἐν Ἅιδου βελτίονα μοῖραν
οὖσαν.

So while it is a good thing, my friend, to participate in the rite at Eleusis, I
observe that followers and initiates of Love have a better fate in Hades.

---

[17] Cf. Pl. *Phd.* 69c: "Many are narthex-bearers, but bacchi are few."

De Amore 1 (fr. 134 Sandbach). The common spirit that inspires all of Menander's plays is ἔρως. He is therefore μάλιστα θιασώτης τοῦ θεοῦ καὶ ὀργιαστής, "very much a devotee of the god and an initiate in his cult."

Finally, κατοργιάζεσθαι is also used for 'being initiated' in a figurative sense for the learning of a secret or being admitted to a public office.

In *De garr.* 505e, it is said that Leaena took part in the conspiracy of Harmodius and Aristogiton:

> καὶ γὰρ αὕτη περὶ τὸν καλὸν ἐκεῖνον ἐβάκχευσε κρατῆρα τοῦ ἔρωτος καὶ κατωργίαστο διὰ τοῦ θεοῦ τοῖς ἀπορρήτοις.

> For she, too, had revelled around Eros' beautiful mixing bowl and through the god had been 'initiated' into their secrets.

Amat. 766b tells that, in the afterlife, the true lover:

> ἐπτέρωται καὶ κατωργίασται καὶ διατελεῖ περὶ τὸν αὐτοῦ θεὸν ἄνω χορεύων καὶ συμπεριπολῶν.

> has grown wings and has been initiated and continuously dances upwards around his god and flies around with him.

In *An seni* 792f, it is said to the old Athenian Euphanes that it is not permitted for him:

> ἀφεῖναι τὰς τοῦ Πολιέως καὶ Ἀγοραίου τιμὰς Διός, ἔκπαλαι κατωργια-σμένον αὐταῖς.

> to give up your honours (i.e. civil obligations) of Zeus Polieus and Ago-raios, in which you have been initiated for so long.

Dio Chrysostomus confines himself to the use of ὄργια in a metaphor-ical sense.

Or. 4.101 mentions ὁ τὰ τῆς ἡδονῆς ἀναφαίνων ὄργια: "he who displays the rites of pleasure."

In *Or.* 36.35, the poets after Homer and Hesiod are accused of having presented their own wisdom:

> ἀμύητοι ἀμυήτοις πολλάκις ἐξέφερον ἀτελῆ παραδείγματα ὀργίων.

> Uninitiated themselves, they have often disclosed incomplete samples of rites to the uninitiated.

Aelius Aristides, too, only uses ὄργια in a metaphorical sense when, in reproaching the Asiani, he asks them, *Or.* 34.56 (50 Df), whether they do not lose all claim to recognition:

ὑμεῖς τοίνυν ὅταν εἰς ψαλτρίας τάττησθε καὶ τὰ τῶν Μουσῶν ὄργια
χραίνητε.

when you join the female cither players and pollute the rites of the Muses.

Apart from this, he uses ὀργιασμός once to refer to the cult of Palaemon-
Melicertes on the Isthmus of Corinth, which ceremonies went hand in
hand with mourning: In *Or.* 46.40 (3 Df), he says it is good καὶ τῆς
τελετῆς ἐπ᾽ αὐτῷ καὶ τοῦ ὀργιασμοῦ μετασχεῖν: "to participate in the
ceremony in his honour and in his sacred rite."[18]

The poet Mesomedes, who was a contemporary of Aristides, wrote a *Hymn
to Isis.*[19] The first four verses run as follows:

εἷς ὕμνος ἀνά τε γᾶν
ἀνά τε νηῦς ἁλιπόρους
ἄδεται, πολυτρόποις
ἓν τέλος ἐν ὀργίοις.

One hymn is sung throughout the land and on the sea-cleaving ships; one
rite (is celebrated) in the much-travelled mysteries.

So ὄργια here are the mystery rites of Isis.

Aelian, *Varia Historia* 2.31, says that all peoples τελετὰς τελοῦσι καὶ
ὀργίων φυλάττουσι νόμον ("perform religious ceremonies and maintain
a set custom in their rites").

In *De natura animalium* 9.66, Aelian uses the word in a metaphorical
sense, when he describes the curious copulation of a viper with a sea-eel:

ὅταν δὲ τὰ τῆς ἀφροδισίου σπουδῆς τελέσωσι μετ᾽ ἀλλήλων ὄργια, ἣ μὲν
ἐπί τε τὰ κύματα καὶ τὴν θάλατταν ὥρμησεν, ὃ δὲ ἀναρροφήσας τὸν ἰὸν
αὖθις ἐς τὰ ἤθη τὰ οἰκεῖα ἐπάνεισιν.

And when they have completed the rites of lovemaking with each other,
she rushes towards the waves and the sea, while he gulps down his poison
again and goes back to his own lair.

Achilles Tatius, *De Leuc. et Cit.* 4.1 uses the word in the same sense:

καὶ ὡς εἴσω παρῆλθον, περιπτυξάμενος αὐτὴν οἷός τε ἤμην ἀνδρί-
ζεσθαι. ὡς δ᾽ οὐκ ἐπέτρεπε, "μέχρι πότε," εἶπον, "χηρεύομεν τῶν τῆς
Ἀφροδίτης ὀργίων;"

---

[18] Cf. Nilsson, *Feste*, 439.
[19] Powell, *Coll. Alex.* fr. 36; Heitsch, *Griech. Dichterfr.* fr. 5.

And as I went in, I put my arms around her and wanted to have my way with her. But since she would not let me, I said: "How long are we to be deprived of the rites of Aphrodite?"

We have seen quite a similar plea in Ar. *Lys.* 898.

LUCIAN uses ὄργια for the Eleusinian mysteries in *Demon.* 11, where Demonax says that if the mysteries were something trivial, he would still not be silent to the uninitiated, ἀλλ' ἀποτρέψει αὐτοὺς τῶν ὀργίων ("but would keep them away from the ceremonies").

In *Astrol.* 10, Orphic rites are called ὄργια. Orpheus was the first to bring astrology to the Greeks, but not clearly and openly: πηξάμενος γὰρ λύρην ὄργιά τε ἐποιέετο καὶ τὰ ἱερὰ ἤειδεν ("for having built a lyre, he created religious rites and sang sacred songs").

Symp. 3 talks about the ὄργια of Dionysus and asks: εἴ τινα τῶν αὐτοῦ ὀργίων ἀτέλεστον καὶ ἀβάκχευτον περιεῖδεν ("whether he allows anyone to remain *atelestos* and *abaccheutos* of his mysteries").

In *Syr. D.* 16, it is argued that Dionysus is most likely the founder of the temple at Hierapolis, and the author continues:

ἐρέω δὲ καὶ ἄλλ' ὅ τι ἐστὶν ἐν τῷ νηῷ Διονύσου ὄργιον.

And I shall also mention something else that is in the temple and is a sacred object of Dionysus.

We see a rare occurrence of the singular ὄργιον here. A few lines on, Lucian explains that it was a bronze statuette with a big phallus.

The ceremonies celebrated at Byblos and Hierapolis are repeatedly called ὄργια.

Syr. D. 6:

εἶδον δὲ καὶ ἐν Βύβλῳ μέγα ἱρὸν Ἀφροδίτης Βυβλίης, ἐν τῷ καὶ τὰ ὄργια ἐς Ἄδωνιν ἐπιτελέουσιν· ἐδάην δὲ καὶ τὰ ὄργια. λέγουσι γὰρ δὴ ὧν τὸ ἔργον τὸ ἐς Ἄδωνιν ὑπὸ τοῦ συὸς ἐν τῇ χώρῃ τῇ σφετέρῃ γενέσθαι, καὶ μνήμην τοῦ πάθεος τύπτονταί τε ἑκάστου ἔτεος καὶ θρηνέουσι καὶ τὰ ὄργια ἐπιτελέουσι.

In Byblos, I saw a great temple of Aphrodite of Byblos, in which they also perform the rites for Adonis, and I learnt those rites. They say that what was done to Adonis by the boar happened in their land and, in memory of his suffering, they beat themselves every year and lament and perform the rites.

Syr. D. 7:

> εἰσὶ δὲ ἔνιοι Βυβλίων οἳ λέγουσι παρὰ σφίσι τεθάφθαι τὸν Ὄσιριν τὸν
> Αἰγύπτιον, καὶ τὰ πένθεα καὶ τὰ ὄργια οὐκ ἐς τὸν Ἄδωνιν ἀλλ᾽ ἐς τὸν
> Ὄσιριν πάντα πρήσσεσθαι.

> But some inhabitants of Byblos say that Egyptian Osiris was buried there
> and that the mourning and the rites are not performed in honour of Adonis
> but of Osiris.

Incidentally, the combination ὄργια πρήσσεσθαι is noteworthy.

Syr. D. 15. A sacred tale in Hierapolis calls the goddess identical to Rhea
and says that the temple is the work of Attes:

> Ἄττης δὲ γένος μὲν Λυδὸς ἦν, πρῶτος δὲ τὰ ὄργια τὰ ἐς Ῥέην ἐδιδάξατο.
> καὶ τὰ Φρύγες καὶ Λυδοὶ καὶ Σαμόθρακες ἐπιτελέουσιν, Ἄττεω πάντα
> ἔμαθον. ὡς γάρ μιν ἡ Ῥέη ἔτεμεν, βίου μὲν ἀνδρηίου ἀπεπαύσατο,
> μορφὴν δὲ θηλέην ἠμείψατο καὶ ἐσθῆτα γυναικηίην ἐνεδύσατο καὶ ἐς
> πᾶσαν γῆν φοιτέων ὄργιά τε ἐπετέλεεν καὶ τὰ ἔπαθεν ἀπηγέετο καὶ
> Ῥέην ἤειδεν. ἐν τοῖσιν καὶ ἐς Συρίην ἀπίκετο. ὡς δὲ οἱ πέρην Εὐφρήτεω
> ἄνθρωποι οὔτε αὐτὸν οὔτε ὄργια ἐδέκοντο, ἐν τῷδε τῷ χώρῳ τὸ ἱρὸν
> ἐποιήσατο.

> Attis was a Lydian by birth and first taught the rites of Rhea (Cybele).
> And all the rites that Phrygians, Lydians and Samothracians perform, they
> learnt from Attis. For when Rhea castrated him, he ceased life as a man and
> changed into a feminine form and dressed in women's clothing. Roaming
> about to every land, he performed rites and told of his sufferings and sang
> about Rhea. Eventually, he also arrived in Syria and since the people across
> the Euphrates did not accept him or his rites, he founded the sanctuary
> here in this land.

Syr. D. 50. On certain days, the crowd gathers in the temple:

> Γάλλοι δὲ πολλοὶ καὶ τοὺς ἔλεξα, οἱ ἱροὶ ἄνθρωποι, τελέουσι τὰ ὄργια,
> τάμνονταί τε τοὺς πήχεας καὶ τοῖσι νώτοισι πρὸς ἀλλήλους τύπτονται.

> And many Galli and the sacred persons that I mentioned perform the
> rites and cut their forearms and knock against each other with their
> backs.

Syr. D. 51. Many are then seized by rage and castrate themselves, ἐπεὰν
γὰρ οἱ ἄλλοι αὐλέωσί τε καὶ ὄργια ποιέωνται ("while the rest play the
oboe and perform rites").

On the model of the Eleusinian mysteries, Alexander Pseudomantis
had instituted a τελετή in which there were δᾳδουχίαι καὶ ἱεροφαντίαι.

The ceremonies lasted three days. These same ceremonies are called ὄργια in the πρόρρησις, that was proclaimed on the first day in this form (*Alex.* 38):

εἴ τις ἄθεος ἢ Χριστιανὸς ἢ Ἐπικούρειος ἥκει κατάσκοπος τῶν ὀργίων, φευγέτω· οἱ δὲ πιστεύοντες τῷ θεῷ τελείσθωσαν τύχῃ τῇ ἀγαθῇ.

If any atheist or Christian or Epicurean has come to spy on the rites (*orgia*), let him be off, and let those who believe in the god perform the mysteries with good fortune.

In *De saltatione* 15, we find ὄργια used in a very general sense for mystery rites. It notes how it is clear from the word ἐξορχεῖσθαι, 'imitating and profaning the mysteries', that these festivals were accompanied by dancing. This is followed by the remark: τὰ μὲν ὄργια σιωπᾶν ἄξιον τῶν ἀμυήτων ἕνεκα: "One is to remain silent about the rites, on account of the uninitiated."

With this, we leave the domain of cult rites and look at a few places where ὄργια and related verbs are used metaphorically. In the following passages, attacks of podagra are spoken of as mystery rites.

In *Trag.* 112, the podagra patient asks the chorus about the goddess Podagra:

τίσιν δὲ τελεταῖς ὀργιάζει προσπόλους;

With what sacred rites does she accept devotees into her service?[20]

In *Trag.* 125, the patient complains:

εἷς ἆρα κἀγὼ τῶν κατωργιασμένων
ἔλαθον ὑπάρχων;

Was I, too, one of the initiated without knowing it?

In *Trag.* 189, the goddess rouses the chorus to honour her, the invincible goddess, with hymns:

ἀλλ᾽ εἶα μύσται πάντες ὀργίων ἐμῶν,
γεραίρεθ᾽ ὕμνοις τὴν ἀνίκητον θεάν.

Come then, all initiates of my rites, honour your invincible goddess with hymns.

---

[20] Cf. Zijderveld, above, p. 68, who translates ὀργιάζειν as 'to enrapture'.

Finally, we find the word ὄργια in the spurious work *Philopatris* 10:

ἀλλ᾽ οὐκ ἐγίνωσκες τὴν ἐπῳδὴν καὶ τὰ ὄργια;

But you did not learn about his incantation and rites?

We have not seen ἐπῳδή and ὄργια together before.[21]

CLEMENT OF ALEXANDRIA uses our terms mostly in a pejorative sense for Orphic, Bacchic and mystery rites. There are two exceptions presented at the end of this section.

In *Protrepticus* 1.3.1, Clement claims that Orpheus, Amphion and Arion were frauds:

προσχήματι μουσικῆς λυμηνάμενοι τὸν βίον, ἐντέχνῳ τινὶ γοητείᾳ δαιμονῶντες εἰς διαφθοράς, ὕβρεις ὀργιάζοντες, πένθη ἐκθειάζοντες, τοὺς ἀνθρώπους ἐπὶ τὰ εἴδωλα χειραγωγῆσαι πρῶτοι.

Under the guise of music they ruined lives and, through some sort of artful sorcery, they were possessed by demons to bring about destruction. They celebrated violent acts, worshipped sorrows, and were the first to lead mankind to idolatry.

Protr. 2.12.2 talks about the Bacchic mysteries:

Διόνυσον μαινόλην ὀργιάζουσι βάκχοι ὠμοφαγίᾳ τὴν ἱερομανίαν ἄγοντες καὶ τελίσκουσι τὰς κρεονομίας τῶν φόνων ἀνεστεμμένοι τοῖς ὄφεσιν, ἐπολολύζοντες Εὐάν δι᾽ ἣν ἡ πλάνη παρηκολούθησεν· καὶ σημεῖον ὀργίων βακχικῶν ὄφις ἐστὶ τετελεσμένος.

His followers worship raving Dionysus with orgies, celebrating their sacred madness with a banquet of raw flesh. Wreathed with snakes they perform the distribution of the portions of their victims, crying "Eva", after that Eve who caused the world to go astray. And the symbol of Bacchic mysteries is a consecrated snake.

This is followed by a remark that the Hebrew word for a female snake is *hevia*, which, with a little imagination, almost sounds like Eva (Eve), which in turn resembles the Bacchic cries εὐοῖ/εὐαί/εὐάν.

A few lines on, *Protr.* 2.13.1, Clement introduces yet another freshwater etymology:[22]

καί μοι δοκεῖ τὰ ὄργια καὶ τὰ μυστήρια δεῖν ἐτυμολογεῖν, τὰ μὲν ἀπὸ τῆς ὀργῆς τῆς Δηοῦς τῆς πρὸς Δία γεγενημένης, τὰ δὲ ἀπὸ τοῦ μύσους τοῦ συμβεβηκότος περὶ τὸν Διόνυσον.

---

[21] Cf. Lucian, *Menip.* 6: ἐπῳδαῖς καὶ τελεταῖς.
[22] I.e. an obviously false etymology.

I also believe that the terms *orgia* and *mysteria* must be derived, the one from Demeter's anger (*orge*) towards Zeus and the other from the pollution (*mysos*) with regard to Dionysus.

In *Protr.* 2.13.3–4, Clement curses the founder of these false rites:

ὄλοιτο οὖν ὁ τῆσδε ἄρξας τῆς ἀπάτης ἀνθρώποις, εἴτε ὁ Δάρδανος, ὁ Μητρὸς θεῶν καταδείξας τὰ μυστήρια, εἴτε Ἠετίων, ὁ τὰ Σαμοθράκων ὄργια καὶ τελετὰς ὑποστησάμενος ... [4] οὐ γάρ με ὁ Κύπριος ὁ νησιώτης Κινύρας παραπείσαι ποτ' ἄν, τὰ περὶ τὴν Ἀφροδίτην μαχλῶντα ὄργια ἐκ νυκτὸς ἡμέρᾳ παραδοῦναι τολμήσας, φιλοτιμούμενος θειάσαι πόρνην πολίτιδα.

So to hell with whoever started this deception for mankind, whether it be Dardanus, who revealed the mysteries of the Mother of the gods, or Eetion, who founded the Samothracian orgies and rites. In no way could the islander, Cinyras of Cyprus, fool me, when he had the audacity to transfer the celebration of the lascivious orgies of Aphrodite from night to day, eager to deify a whore from his island.

In *Protr.* 2.14.2, still more of the same:

ἤδη δέ, καὶ γὰρ καιρός, αὐτὰ ὑμῶν τὰ ὄργια ἐξελέγξω ἀπάτης καὶ τερατείας ἔμπλεα.

But now, and it is high time, I will prove that your orgies themselves are filled with deceit and hocus-pocus.

In *Protr.* 2.19.1, Clement gives his version of the story of the Corybantes, εἰ θέλεις δ' ἐποπτεῦσαι καὶ Κορυβάντων ὄργια: "in case you also wish to view the mysteries of the Corybantes".

Protr. 2.22.3–4. The mysteries of the serpent are a mere custom, an empty, deceitful notion worshipped by men when they go to τὰς ἀνοργιάστους τελετὰς: "those profane ceremonies". The mystic box contains, among other things, δράκων, ὄργιον Διονύσου Βασσάρου: "a serpent, the mystic object of Dionysus Bassaros".[23]

Protr. 2.22.7. Let the night hide the mysteries and σκότει τετιμήσθω τὰ ὄργια: "let the orgies be honoured by darkness."

In *Protr.* 7.74.3, Clement speaks about Orpheus in a more benign tone:

ὁ δὲ Θράκιος ἱεροφάντης καὶ ποιητὴς ἅμα, ὁ τοῦ Οἰάγρου Ὀρφεύς, μετὰ τὴν τῶν ὀργίων ἱεροφαντίαν καὶ τῶν εἰδώλων τὴν θεολογίαν, παλινῳδίαν ἀληθείας εἰσάγει.

---

[23] This passage is also quoted by Euseb. *Praep. evang.* 2.3.39.

The Thracian hierophant, who was at the same time a poet, Orpheus, son of Oeager, after his revelation of mysteries and his story of idols, brings forward a recantation.

In *Paed.* 2.8.73.1, Clement observes that people also use wreaths when they ὀργιάζουσιν:

οἱ μὲν γὰρ βαϰχεύοντες οὐδὲ ἄνευ στεφάνων ὀργιάζουσιν· ἐπὰν δὲ ἀμφιθῶνται τὰ ἄνθη, πρὸς τὴν τελετὴν ὑπερϰάονται.

For revellers do not perform their rites without wreaths: once they have put the flowers around themselves, they are even more ardent towards the sacred act.

In the next two places, Clement uses the word ὄργια to refer to the Christian doctrine and sexual intercourse respectively.

Protr. 12.119.1. In a visionary passage, Clement uses the word ὄργια for the Mysteries of the Word (i.e. Christian doctrine), which should replace the Greek mysteries. There is a mountain beloved by God, not the basis for tragedies like Cithaeron, but devoted to dramas of truth, a wineless mountain, shaded by hallowed groves.

βαϰχεύουσι δὲ ἐν αὐτῷ οὐχ αἱ Σεμέλης τῆς ϰεραυνίας ἀδελφαί, αἱ μαινά-δες, αἱ δύσαγνον ϰρεανομίαν μυούμεναι, ἀλλ' αἱ τοῦ θεοῦ θυγατέρες, αἱ ἀμνάδες αἱ ϰαλαί, τὰ σεμνὰ τοῦ λόγου θεσπίζουσαι ὄργια, χορὸν ἀγεί-ρουσαι σώφρονα.

On that mountain it is not the sisters of thunder-smitten Semele, the maenads who are initiated into the unholy distribution of raw flesh, who revel, but the daughters of God, those beautiful lambs, who declare the solemn rites of the Word, assembling a chaste chorus.

Paed. 2.10.96.2. Even married people require a pedagogue, ὡς μὴ μεθ' ἡμέραν τὰ μυστιϰὰ τῆς φύσεως ἐϰτελεῖσθαι ὄργια: "so that they do not perform the mystic rites of nature by day". This clearly refers to the consummation of marriage.

In HIPPOCRATES, *Epistulae* 27.195 (9.420 Littré), which purports to be written by one of Hippocrates' sons but most likely dates from the Roman imperial period,[24] we find the hendiadys μυστήρια ϰαὶ ὄργια used for the Eleusinian mysteries:

---

[24] They are certainly spurious, see J. Jouanna, *Hippocrates* (1999) 397.

μυήσαντες τὰ Δήμητρος καὶ κόρης μυστήρια καὶ ὄργια καὶ τὸν πατέρα καὶ ἐμὲ δημοσίᾳ.

having initiated my father and me in public in the mysteries and rites of Demeter and Kore.

GALEN, *De usu part.* 2.448 (Helmreich), uses the word in a metaphorical sense when he compares nature's ὄργια to the mysteries of Samothrace and Eleusis.[25]

We now wish to include several important authors from the third century, followed by attestations in Orphic literature.[26]

PHILOSTRATUS, the author of the *Life of Apollonius* and the *Lives of the Sophists*, uses ὄργια (and ὀργιάζειν) for a variety of cults. In the following two places, it refers to the revels of Dionysus.

VA 2.8:

ὀργιάζοντος δὲ αὐτοῦ καὶ σείοντος τὴν Νῦσαν ἀκούουσιν αἱ πόλεις αἱ ὑπὸ τῷ ὄρει καὶ ξυνεξαίρονται.

When Dionysus revels and shakes Nysa, the cities at the foot of the mountain hear him and are excited all at the same time.

VA 2.9. Some Indians claimed that Greek Dionysus was an impostor, while the real Dionysus was the son of the river Indus:

ᾧ φοιτήσαντα τὸν ἐκ Θηβῶν ἐκεῖνον θύρσου τε ἅψασθαι καὶ δοῦναι ὀργίοις, εἰπόντα δέ, ὡς εἴη Διὸς καὶ τῷ τοῦ πατρὸς ἐμβιῴη μηρῷ τόκου ἕνεκα, Μηρόν τε εὑρέσθαι παρ᾽ αὐτοῦ ὄρος [...] οὗ καὶ Ἀλέξανδρος ὀργιάσαι.

Having visited him, this Dionysus from Thebes got hold of a thyrsus and devoted himself to revels. Claiming that he was the son of Zeus and that he had lived inside his father's thigh in order to be born, he found a mountain called Meros ('Thigh'), where Alexander, too, would revel.

The combination δοῦναι ὀργίοις is noteworthy.

In the next four places, ὄργια and ὀργιάζειν are used for various cults.

VA 3.14 talks about a hill in India where they worship a fire: πῦρ τε ἐπ᾽ αὐτοῦ ὀργιάζουσιν. A hymn is sung to it every day towards noon.

VA 6.1 says that the Indus and the Nile were both equally renowned for their sacred rites: λόγοι τε ὀργίων ἐπ᾽ αὐτοῖς ἴσοι. So ὄργια here refers to rites connected with the worship of these rivers.

---

[25] See Zijderveld, above, p. 76.

[26] This material was left out by Van der Burg, who only included sources up to 200 AD.

VA 7.32 mentions flowerpots that the Assyrians make for the rites of Adonis: οὓς Ἀδώνιδι Ἀσσύριοι ποιοῦνται ὑπὲρ ὀργίων.

VS 543 describes a statue of Polemon ὡς ἐπὶ τῆς τριήρους ὠργίαζεν: "dressed the way he was when he worshipped on board the trireme." This trireme was the famous ship of Dionysus, set up in the Agora for the Anthesteria festival. Polemon had been awarded the rare privilege of setting foot on this ship[27] and it was this event that was commemorated by the statue.

The *Imagines*, which may have been written by the same Philostratus, contain two very interesting occurrences of our terms. *Imag.* 1.19.1 describes a painting of two ships, one with Dionysus and one with Tyrrhenian pirates. On the first ship, Dionysus revels (βακχεύει) and the bacchantes answer his call:

> ἁρμονία δέ, ὁπόση ὀργιάζει, κατηχεῖ τῆς θαλάττης.
>
> And music, entrancing as it is, sounds over the sea.

On the other ship, the pirates go mad and are quite literally transformed by the powerful presence of Dionysus. So we have a rare occurrence here of the word ὀργιάζειν, used in the sense: to excite, to entrance.

Imag. 2.16.3 describes special rites for Palaemon Melicertes:

> ὁ μὲν οὖν τῆς θυσίας λόγος καὶ ἡ τῶν θυσάντων ἐσθὴς καὶ τὰ ἐναγίσματα, ὦ παῖ, καὶ τὸ σφάττειν ἐς τὰ τοῦ Παλαίμονος ἀποκείσθω ὄργια.
>
> The meaning of the sacrifice, the attire of those conducting the sacrifice, their offerings to the dead (*enagismata*), dear boy, and the slaughter, must be reserved for the rites of Palaemon.

The ὄργια in question were very secret rites. Aelius Aristides already spoke of a τελετὴ καὶ ὀργιασμός for Palaemon.[28]

HERODIAN, *Ab excessu divi Marci* 1.11.2, mentions the cult of Cybele in Pessinous:

> ἐν δὲ τῷ προειρημένῳ Πεσσινοῦντι πάλαι μὲν Φρύγες ὠργίαζον ἐπὶ τῷ ποταμῷ Γάλλῳ παρραρέοντι, ἀφ' οὖ τὴν ἐπωνυμίαν φέρουσιν οἱ τῇ θεῷ τομίαι ἱερωμένοι.

---

[27] *VS* 531.
[28] *Or.* 46 K 40 (3 Df).

In said place, Pessinous, the Phrygians long ago celebrated their orgiastic rites on the banks of the river Gallus, from which eunuchs, dedicated to the service of the goddess, get their name (Galli).

In 5.5.4, he describes how the emperor Elagabalus indulged in the worship of the sun god El Gabal:

προῄει τε ὑπὸ αὐλοῖς καὶ τυμπάνοις, τῷ θεῷ δῆθεν ὀργιάζων.

He went forward, accompanied by oboes and tympana, really worshipping the god.

5.7.2 the emperor Elagabalus had become so preoccupied with his religious duties that he could not be bothered with affairs of state:

βακχείαις καὶ ὀργίοις τοῖς τε θείοις ἔργοις ἀνακείμενον.

being devoted to his ecstatic and orgiastic rites and divine duties.

Ps. Oppian uses ὄργια and τελεταί for the secret rites of the bacchantes, *Cynegetica* 4.249:

... πρῶτα δ' ἔφαινον
ὄργια κευθομένη περὶ λάρνακι· σὺν δ' ἄρα τῇσιν
Ἀόνιαι λάθρῃ τελετῶν ἅπτοντο γυναῖκες.

(The nurses of Dionysus) first revealed their rites around the concealed box. And with them, the Aonian (Boeotian) women secretly took part in the rites.

The word is not found in Plotinus, but the work of his student, Porphyry, contains two interesting places.

Abst. 2.49. The priest of the supreme god is expert in the making of his cult statues and in purifications and other rites by which he is connected to the god:

ὥσπερ ὅ τινος τῶν κατὰ μέρος θεῶν ἱερεὺς ἔμπειρος τῆς ἱδρύσεως τῶν ἀγαλμάτων αὐτοῦ τῶν τε ὀργιασμῶν καὶ τελετῶν καθάρσεών τε καὶ τῶν ὁμοίων.

just as a priest of one of the particular gods is expert in setting up cult statues of this god, and in his rituals and purification rites and such.

Abst. 4.16 discusses the Mithraic mysteries:

ὡς τοὺς μὲν μετέχοντας τῶν αὐτῶν ὀργίων μύστας λέοντας καλεῖν, τὰς δὲ γυναῖκας λεαίνας, τοὺς δὲ ὑπηρετοῦντας κόρακας.

For example, they call the initiates who participate in their rites 'lions' and the women 'lionesses' and the servants 'ravens'.

In his *Life of Pythagoras*, IAMBLICHUS uses ὀργιασμοί in a metaphorical sense for 'initiations' through learning:

VP 17.74 mentions "initiations derived from so much learning": τοὺς ἐκ τῶν τοσῶνδε μαθημάτων ὀργιασμούς.

VP 32.228 explains what happens when the soul is disciplined "by the initiations of learning": διὰ τῶν μαθηματικῶν ὀργιασμῶν.

In *VP* 17.77, the expression μαθήμασιν ὀργιάζεσθαι is used in the same sense. Clouded are the hearts and minds "of those who have not been properly initiated by knowledge": τῶν μὴ καθαρῶς τοῖς μαθήμασιν ὀργιασθέντων.

VP 28.146 answers the question of where Pythagoras learnt the things he wrote in his treatise on the gods:

λόγος ὅδε περὶ θεῶν Πυθαγόρα τῷ Μνημάρχω, τὸν ἐξέμαθον ὀργια-
σθεὶς ἐν Λιβήθροις τοῖς Θρακίοις, Ἀγλαοφάμω τελεστᾷ μεταδόντος, ὡς
κτλ.

This is the treatise *On the Gods* by Pythagoras, son of Mnemarchus. I learnt it thoroughly when I was initiated in Thracian Libethra, while the priest Aglaophamus shared with me …

So in this last context, ὀργιάζεσθαι refers to an actual religious rite performed on Pythagoras.

ARISTIDES QUINTILIANUS, *De Musica* 2.6, discussing the role of music in educating men, uses the verb συνοργιάζειν:

ἰδίᾳ τε ἐν εὐωχίαις κοινῇ τε ἐν ἁπάσαις τελεταῖς σφίσι συνοργιαζούσῃ.

both privately at banquets and publicly celebrating together in all their *teletai*.

In 3.21, we find the word ὀργιασταί:

δηλοῦσι δὲ τοῦτο καὶ οἱ ταύτης μυστιπόλοι τε καὶ ὀργιασταί.

Those who solemnize mysteries and celebrate the rites of the moon also make this clear.

ORPHICA. There are a handful of attestations in Orphic literature.
Orph. frag. 350 Bernabé (fr. 232 Kern), found in Damascius' commentary *ad Plat. Phaed.* 1.11:

ἄνθρωποι δὲ τεληέσσας ἑκατόμβας
πέμψουσιν πάσησιν ἐν ὥραις ἀμφιέτησιν
ὄργιά τ' ἐκτελέσουσι λύσιν προγόνων ἀθεμίστων
μαιόμενοι· σὺ δὲ τοῖσιν ἔχων κράτος, οὕς κε θέλησθα
λύσεις ἔκ τε πόνων χαλεπῶν καὶ ἀπείρονος οἴστρου.

> And people will send perfect hecatombs in every season every year and will perform rites, seeking deliverance from their forefathers' unlawful behaviour. And you (Dionysus), having power over them, will deliver whomever you wish from hard toil and boundless agony.

So here, ὄργια are the special rites of Dionysus in his capacity of a delivering god. Damascius explains: "Dionysus is responsible for deliverance and for this reason the god is called *Lyseus* (Deliverer)."

Argonautica 31 mentions ὄργια Πραξιδίκης ("rites of Praxidike") among various mystery cults. Praxidike ('exactor of justice') is an epithet for Persephone.

Hymn 52.5 invokes Dionysus under many different names, among which, ὄργιον ἄρρητον ('secret mystery'). The singular, ὄργιον, is quite rare—we have only seen it in Lucian, *Syr. D.* 16 and Clem. Al. *Protr.* 2.22.4, who both mention an ὄργιον Διονύσου. To find it used as a name for the deity is even more unusual.

Hymn 6.4. Among the epithets of the Orphic god Protogonus, we find πολυόργιον ('worshipped with many rites').

Two hymns contain the word ὀργιοφάνται (lit.: 'displayers of rites'). *Hymn* 6.10–11 to Protogonus calls on the god to attend the sacred ceremony:

βαῖνε γεγηθὼς | ἐς τελετὴν ἁγίαν πολυποίκιλον ὀργιοφάνταις.

Come rejoicing to the very colourful sacred ceremony for the orgiophants.

And in *Hymn* 31.5, the Curetes are invoked, among other things, as ὀργιοφάνται. So here, the Curetes themselves are imagined as the displayers of rites. We may compare this to *Hymn* 54.10, which describes Silenus as:

ὄργια νυκτιφαῆ τελεταῖς ἁγίαις ἀναφαίνων.

revealing rites that bring light in the night in sacred ceremonies.

Conclusion

In summarizing the material from this period, which is much more variegated than the data from the pre-Hellenistic era, it is first of all apparent that our term is used most frequently in the cult of Dionysus.

We have ὄργια in the sense of 'rites' or 'revels' in this cult: Diod. 3.65.6. and 4.82.6.; Paus. 8.6.5 and 8.26.2, 9.20.4, 10.4.3, 10.6.4 and 10.33.11; Cornut. *De Nat. Deor.* 30; Plut. fr. inc. 133; Lucian *Symp.* 3; Philostr. *VA* 2.9; [Oppian] *Cyn.* 4.249.

Bacchic cult objects appear to be called ὄργια in Theoc. *Id.* 26.13, while the singular, ὄργιον, is found in the same sense in Lucian *Syr. D.* 16.

Ὀργιασμοί is also a frequently used term in this cult: Diod. 1.22.7 and 3.74.2; Plut. *Alex.* 2, *Crass.* 8, *Is. et. Os.* 35 (364e), *Cons. ad ux.* 10 (611d), *Quaest. conv.* 2.3.2 (636e), *Amat.* 16 (758f).

The verb ὀργιάζειν usually indicates the performance of his sacred rites: Ap. Rhod. 2.907; Diod. 5.50.4; Plut., *Anim. an corp.* 501f, *Quaest. conv.* 671f; Philostr. *VA* 2.8, 2.9, *VS* 543. We find the verb used in the sense of 'to put into a trance' in Philostr. *Imag.* 1.19.1. Someone who has been initiated into the Dionysiac cult may be called ὠργιασμένος, Dion. Hal. *Comp.* 4.

We find Orphic-Bacchic ὄργια: Paus. 8.37.5; *Orph. frag.* 350 Bernabé. The word also refers to Orphic rites in Lucian *Astr.* 10. These are called ὀργιασμοί by Strabo 7 fr. 18; Diod. 1.96.4 uses the verb ὀργιάζειν for their performance.

The rites in the cult of Mother of the gods (Cybele) are called ὄργια: Dion. Hal. *Ant. Rom.* 1.61.4; Paus. 7.17.9 and Lucian *Syr. D.* 15. They are called ὀργιασμοί: Dion. Hal. *Ant. Rom.* 2.19.5 and Strabo 10.3.7, while we find the verb ὀργιάζειν: Dion. Sic. 5.49.1; Dion. Hal. *Ant. Rom.* 2.19.5; Strabo 10.3.12; Hdn. 1.11.1.

The rites of the Eleusinian mysteries are called ὄργια: Lucian, *Demon.* 11; Hippoc. *Ep.* 27.195; those of Andania several times in Pausanias: 4.1.5, 4.2.6, 4.14.1 and 4.15.7. The word is used for the Samothracian mysteries in Ap. Rhod. *Argon.* 1.920. Dion. Hal. *Ant. Rom.* 1.69.4 uses the verb ὀργιάζειν for this cult and id. 2.22.2 ὀργιασμός.

Paus. 9.25.7 mentions ὄργια in the cult of the Theban Cabiri. In the cult of Hecate, we find the term in Ap. Rhod. *Argon.* 4.1020. Furthermore, in the cult of Demeter: Paus. 10.28.3 (Thesmophoria on Paros and Thasos), Callim. *Aet.* fr. 63 (Thesmophoria in Athens), and Plut. fr. inc. 133 (τῆς Δηοῦς ὄργια).

In connection with the Cretan cult of Zeus, Strabo 10.3.11 speaks of an ὀργιασμός. Aristid. 46.40 uses the same word for the ritual of Palaemon-Melicertes. Philostr. *Imag.* 2.16.3 refers to the special rites for Palaemon as ὄργια.

Philostr. *VA* 7.32 uses ὄργια for the rites of Adonis. Lucian, *Syr. D.* 6, also mentions ὄργια several times in connection with the cult of Adonis, but *Syr. D.* 7 adds that, according to some, these rites were actually in honour of Osiris. The ceremonies of Isis are called ὄργια in Mesomedes,

Hymn. Is. 4 and Plut. fr. inc. 133, while Appian, *B.Civ.* 4.6.47, speaks of ὀργιάζειν and ὀργιαστής in connection with the Isis cult. The Mithraic mysteries are called ὄργια by Porph. *Abst.* 4.16. Alexander Pseudomantis also established ὄργια in Lucian *Alex.* 38.

In connection with the Roman cult of Bona Dea, we also find our terms used: Plutarch speaks of ὄργια: *Caes.* 10, and of ὀργιάζειν: *Caes.* 9 and *Cic.* 19.

In Plut. *Cor.* 32, μυστηρίων ὀργιασταί probably refers to the *augures*. Plutarch calls the worship of the Palladium ὀργιάζειν (*Cam.* 20) and also uses this verb for Roman cult practice in general (*Numa* 18).

The ὀργιάζειν of Thracian, Egyptian and Phrygian ἱερά also occurs in Plutarch. Cleansing rituals can also be called ὄργια: Plut. *Alc.* 34 (said of the Plynteria), and the celebration of these rites κατοργιάζειν: Plut. *Sol.* 12 and *De def. or.* 15 (418a).

Herodian uses ὀργιάζειν and ὄργια for the worship of Elagabalus (El Gabal): 5.5.4, 5.7.2; and for the cult of Cybele in Pessinous: 1.11.2.

Our terms are, however, also used for religious ceremonies *in general*, as is evident from Ael. *VH* 2.31 (ὄργια), Porph. *Abst.* 2.49 (ὀργιασμοί), and also the use of ὀργιάζειν in Dion. Hal. *Ant. Rom.* 2.22.1 and 8.38.1; Plut. *Non posse* 21 (1101e) and fr. *De anima*.

We also found several places where mystery cults (or participation in them) are referred to, but it cannot be determined exactly which are meant. E.g. Plut. *De fac.* 30 (944d), fr. *De daed. Plat.*, fr. *De anima* (possibly Eleusis), *De def. or.* 13 (417a), *De superst.* 9 (169d), and Lucian, *Salt.* 15.

The rites called ὄργια in Paus. 4.1.7 also appear to have a special character, but it is hard to say of what it consists.

The adjective ὀργιαστικός is found only once in this period: Strabo 10.3.10.

The *metaphorical* use of our terms deserves separate mention. Ael. *NA* 9.66 and Ach. Tatius 4.1 use ὄργια for the 'rites' of lovemaking (cf. Ar. *Lys.* 898). Marcus Aurelius 3.7.2 mentions τὰ ὄργια τῆς ἀρετῆς, and Plutarch gives us a series of examples where it is clear how non-sacral use developed from sacral use. For example, Plutarch talks about ὀργιασταί of certain philosophical schools (*Quaest. conv.* 717d and *Adv. Col.* 1107f), and about τὰ Ἐπικούρου ὄργια (*Adv. Col.* 1117b). In addition, he uses κατοργιάζειν several times for 'accepting', 'initiating' into offices (*An seni* 792f) and secrets (*De garr.* 505e). Likewise, Iamblichus talks about 'initiations' of learning as μαθημάτων ὀργιασμοί and μαθήμασιν ὀργιάζεσθαι. Finally, Dio Chrys., *Or.* 4.101, speaks of τὰ τῆς ἡδονῆς ὄργια and Aristid., 34.56, of τὰ τῶν Μουσῶν ὄργια, while Lucian, *Trag.* 112, uses the word to refer to attacks of podagra.

It is of interest to note that the verb ὀργιάζειν is again used frequently in this period, both intransitive and connected with various objects.

First, we find the deity, in whose honour the ceremonies take place, as the direct object of ὀργιάζειν: Dion. Hal. *Ant. Rom.* 1.69.4, 2.19.5, 8.38.1; Plut. *Cic.* 19. Next, the cult object: Plut. *Cam.* 20 (the Palladium); Philostr. *VA* 3.14 (a sacred fire).

Ὀργιάζειν τινι we find in Diod. 5.50.4; Strab. 10.3.7; Plut. *Quaest. Conv.* 671f and Hdn. 5.5.4.

Ὀργιάζειν, with the rites (ἱερά, τελετάς etc.) as direct object, we find in Dion. Hal. *Ant. Rom.* 2.22.1 and in several places in Plutarch: *Numa* 8, *Caes.* 9, *Anim. an corp.* 4 (501f) and *De def. or.* 10 (415a).

We find participants of the ceremony as the object of ὀργιάζειν in Lucian, *Trag.* 112, with a construction and in a sense that is very common for the compound κατοργιάζειν.

In conclusion, we draw attention to several combinations of verbs with ὄργια.

For the establishment of ὄργια, we find ὄργια καθίστασθαι (Paus. 9.25.7), ὄργια ποιεῖσθαι (Lucian, *De astr.* 10) and ὄργια συντίθεσθαι (Paus. 8.37.5), which last expression may be compared to the combination ὀργίων συνθέτης (Paus. 4.1.7).

Pausanias several times mentions the handing down of ὄργια. He writes ὄργια φέρειν (10.28.3), ὄργια κομίζειν (4.1.5), ὄργια μεταφέρειν (9.25.7).

The revelation of ὄργια is called διδάσκειν τὰ ὄργια (Diod. 3.65.6),[29] ὄργια διδάσκεσθαι (Lucian, *Syr. D.* 15), ὄργια ἐπιδεικνύναι (Paus. 4.2.6),[30] and ὄργια ἀναφαίνειν (*Hymn. Orph.* 54.10).

For performance of the ὄργια, several expressions are used. We found ὄργια δρᾶν most often (Paus. 4.15.7, 8.6.5, 10.33.11; Plut. *Alc.* 34). In

---

[29] Compare the expressions τελετὴν διδάσκειν (Hdt. 2.171; Dion. Hal. 1.68.3; Paus. 2.14.1; Philo, *De spec. leg.* 1.319); τελετὰς ἀναδιδάσκειν (Philo, *Cher.* 42).

[30] Compare the expressions τελετὰς ἀναδεικνύναι (*Hymn. Orph.* 24.10); τελετὰς καταδεικνύναι (Ar. *Ran.* 1032; Dem. *Aristog.* 1.11; Diod. 1.20.6; 3.64.7; 3.65.2; 3.74.1; Plut. *Pomp.* 24.5 (631c)); τὴν τελετὴν παραδεικνύναι (Diod. 5.48.4).

addition, we find ὄργια τελεῖν (Paus. 4.14.1, 7.17.9; Lucian, *Syr. D.* 50), ὄργια ἐπιτελεῖν (Lucian, *Syr. D.* 6 and 15), ὄργια ποιεῖσθαι (Lucian, *Syr. D.* 51), ὄργια ἄγειν (Paus. 8.26.2, 10.4.3, 10.6.4) and ὄργια πρήσσειν (Lucian, *Syr. D.* 7).

CHAPTER NINE

SUMMARY

An overview of all the evidence gathered, now gives us the opportunity, briefly to summarize the meanings of ὄργια and its cognates and to review the development of the meaning.

In contrast to most of the Lexica, which place the meaning 'secret custom', 'secret rite' in the forefront, I believe we can follow the representation given by Prof. H. Bolkestein, that ὄργια is, in fact, a synonym of τελετή and that the development of the meanings of both terms runs parallel. Consequently, we envisage the development of the meaning of the word ὄργια as follows:

1. The oldest meaning is the most general one: religious ceremonies, e.g. πόλεως ὄργια (Aeschylus), religious acts in general (Aelian). Sometimes also, occupying a special position alongside the religion of the polis (in a 'Law of Solon' and in Aristotle).
2. Ceremonies in honour of specific gods:
   a. Rites in the cult of Dionysus (Eur., Diod., Paus., Cornutus, Plut., Lucian, Philostr., ps. Oppian). In Theoc., ὄργια appear to be cult implements and Lucian also mentions an ὄργιον in this sense.
   b. Rites in the cult of Cybele (Eur., Dion. Hal., Paus., Lucian).
   c. Rites in the cult of Demeter (Hdt., Callim., Paus., Plut.).
   d. Rites in the cult of Hecate (Ap. Rhod.).
   e. Rites in the cult of Isis and Osiris (Plut., Lucian, Mesomedes).
   f. Rites in the cult of the Theban Cabiri (Paus.).
   g. Rites in the cult of Palaemon-Melicertes (Philostr.).
   h. Rites in the cult of Adonis (Lucian, Philostr.).
   i. Rites in the cult of Bona Dea (Plut.) and cult implements (id.).
3. Purification ceremonies, e.g. the Plynteria (Plut.).
4. Ceremonies in mystery cults:
   a. Rites in the Orphic-Bacchic mystery cult (Hdt., Paus.).
   b. Rites in the Eleusinian mystery cult (*Hymn. Dem.*, Eur., Ar., Lucian, Hippoc.).
   c. Rites in the Samothracian mystery cult (Hdt., Ap. Rhod.).

    d. Rites in the mysteries of Andania (Paus.).

    e. Rites in the Mithraic mystery cult (Porph.).

    f. Rites in mystery cults in general (Plut.) and in the false mysteries of Alexander of Abonouteichos (Lucian).

5. The word is also repeatedly used in a metaphorical sense, e.g. ὄργια Μουσῶν (Ar., Aristid.), τῆς Ἀφροδίτης ὄργια (Ar., Ach. Tatius), ὄργια ἐπιστήμης (Hippoc.), ὄργια τῆς ἀρετῆς (M. Aur.), τὰ Ἐπικούρου ὄργια (Plut.), τῆς ἡδονῆς ὄργια (Dio Chrys.), and said of attacks of gout (Lucian).

Ὄργιον in the singular is found in Lucian (*Syr. D.* 16), where it refers to a cult implement in the sanctuary at Hierapolis, and in *Hymn. Orph.* 52, where it is used as an epithet of Dionysus.

The verb ὀργιάζειν in the general sense of 'performing cult acts' is used all the time (Isoc., Plat., Dion. Hal., Plut.).

Furthermore, for performing rites in the cult of:

- Dionysus (Eur., Ap. Rhod., Diod., Plut., Philostr.),
- Cybele (Diod., Dion. Hal., Strab., Hdn.),
- Isis (Appian, Plut.),
- Bona Dea (Plut.),
- the Trojan Palladium (Plut.),
- a sacred fire (Philostr.).

Also in the Orphic-Bacchic mystery cult (Strab., Plut.), and in the Eleusinian and Samothracian mystery cults (Dion. Hal.).

Ὀργιασμοί are found in non-Greek cults in general (Dion. Hal., Plut., Porph.), in mystery cults (Plut.) and also, in particular, in the cult of Cybele (Dion. Hal., Strab.), of Dionysus (Diod., Plut.), Orphic cult (Strab.), the Cretan cult of Zeus (Strab.) and the cult of Palaemon-Melicertes (Aristid.).

Ὀργιαστής is found in the cult of Isis (Appian), in mystery cults in general (Plut.), and is used in metaphorical sense of followers of a philosophical school (Plut.).

The Roman augurs are probably called μυστηρίων ὀργιασταί by Plutarch (*Cor.* 32).

Finally, we mention three special usages.

The verb κατοργιάζειν occurs in Plutarch in the sense of: to perform purification ceremonies, initiate into mysteries, and (used figuratively) admit into secrets and offices. In a similar fashion Dion. Hal. uses ὠργι-ασμένος for someone who has been initiated.

In Aristotle, we find ἐξοργιάζειν: 'to excite', as well as the adjective, ὀργιαστικός: 'exciting'. Likewise, the verb ὀργιάζειν can be used for 'to put into a trance' (Philostr.).[1]

Ἀνοργιαστός is 'neglected', said of the rites of Aphrodite (Ar.), and of a deity (ps. Plato).

---

[1] Perhaps also Lucian, *Trag.* 112.

CHAPTER TEN

ORGIA IN LATIN LITERATURE

It may be instructive to look at the places where the loanword *orgia* is used in Latin literature. The word appears almost exclusively in poetry.[1] It occupies the first or fifth foot in a dactylic hexameter; in a pentameter, it can be found at the beginning of either hemiepes.

In Latin, the word *orgia* refers to the rites of Dionysus in nearly all instances. Servius even claims this is the only proper use of the word.[2] In the remaining cases, the word refers to various rites and sacred objects or is used in a metaphorical sense.

CATULLUS, 64.259–260, says of the Thyiades that accompany Dionysus:

> pars obscura cavis celebrabant orgia cistis,
> orgia quae frustra cupiunt audire profani.

> Some worshipped *orgia* hidden in hollow baskets, *orgia* which the uninitiated in vain long to hear.

So *orgia* refers both to the sacred objects of the mysteries of Dionysus (kept in baskets) and to the secrets associated with them (which may not be heard by the uninitiated).

VERGIL uses the word for the wild rites of Bacchus, performed by the god's female devotees. It has a distinctly negative connotation.

Georg. 4.521, recounting the *sparagmos* of Orpheus, specifies that it occurred in the context of Dionysiac orgies:

> inter sacra deum nocturnique orgia Bacchi
> discerptum latos iuvenem sparsere per agros.

---

[1] The rare prose attestations in Apuleius, Ammianus Marcellinus and Macrobius are found towards the end of this chapter.

[2] Serv. *Aen.* 6.657: "paeana proprie Apollinis laudes [...], abusive omnium deorum, sicut orgia proprie Liberi, abusive omnium deorum sacra." By contrast, the original Greek word ὄργια could refer to all sacred things, Serv. *Aen.* 4.302: "sane sciendum ὄργια apud Graecos dici sacra omnia [...] sed iam abusive sacra Liberi ὄργια vocantur."

Rent apart amid the sacred rites and nocturnal orgies of Bacchus,[3] the young man's body was scattered across the fields.

In *Aen.* 4.303, Dido senses that Aeneas is about to leave her:

> saevit inops animi totamque incensa per urbem
> bacchatur, qualis commotis excita sacris
> Thyias, ubi audito stimulant trieterica Baccho
> orgia nocturnusque vocat clamore Cithaeron.

> At her wits' end, she raged and roamed about the whole city like a Thyiad, excited by the display of sacred objects, when the orgies arouse her upon hearing the call of Bacchus at the triennial[4] festival, and nocturnal Cithaeron calls her with its cries.

It is noteworthy that the *orgia* are presented here as being celebrated in the context of institutionalized worship of Dionysus.

In *Aen.* 6.517, Deiphobus tells Aeneas how Helen aided the Greeks:

> cum fatalis equus saltu super ardua venit
> Pergama et armatum peditem gravis attulit alvo,
> illa chorum simulans euhantis orgia circum
> ducebat Phrygias.

> When the fateful horse had entered Troy's high walls and in its pregnant belly had brought in the armed infantry, she, feigning a choral dance, led the Trojan women round in jubilating orgies.

So Helen uses the proper form of worship, the choral dance, as a pretext for inappropriate rites which are referred to here as *orgia*.

Aen. 7.403 Amata, the wife of King Latinus, tears off into the woods and urges the Latin mothers to join her in ecstatic rites:

> si qua piis animis manet infelicis Amatae
> gratia, si iuris materni cura remordet,
> solvite crinalis vittas, capite orgia mecum.

> If you still have any love in your faithful hearts for unfortunate Amata, if you still care about the right of a mother, loosen your headbands and celebrate orgies with me.

---

[3] "Nocturni orgia Bacchi" is an enallage for "nocturna orgia Bacchi", cf. Serv. *Georg.* 4.520.

[4] I.e. celebrated every two years, since the ancient Romans used inclusive reckoning; see also Censorinus, *DN* 18: "idque tempus trieterida appellabant, quod tertio quoque anno intercalabatur, quamvis biennii circuitus et re vera dieteris esset; unde mysteria, quae Libero alternis fiunt annis, trieterica a poetis dicuntur."

OVID, *Met.* 4.1, we also find the word used for the rites of Dionysus. Despite the fate of King Pentheus, Minyas' daughter, Alcithoe, still refuses to worship Bacchus as a god:

> at non Alcithoe Minyeias orgia censet
> accipienda dei, sed adhuc temeraria Bacchum
> progeniem negat esse Iovis.

> But Alcithoe, the daughter of Minyas, did not believe that the god's rites should be accepted, but still rashly denied that Bacchus was the son of Jupiter.

We find *orgia* in the sense of mysteries in *Met.* 11.93. At the beginning of the story of King Midas, the poet relates how Silenus had been captured by Phrygian peasants:

> ad regem duxere Midan, cui Thracius Orpheus
> orgia tradiderat cum Cecropio Eumolpo.

> They took him to Midas, their king, to whom Thracian Orpheus had handed down the mysteries, together with Cecropian (Athenian) Eumolpus.

So here, the word apparently refers both to the Bacchic mysteries taught by Orpheus and to the Eleusinian mysteries revealed by Eumolpus.

PROPERTIUS, *Eleg.* 2.6.32, uses the term metaphorically for the mysteries of love. About the artist who first introduced erotic images to respectable houses, he says:

> ah gemat in tenebris, ista qui protulit arte
>   orgia sub tacita condita laetitia!

> Oh, may he lament in darkness (i.e. go blind), who, with that art, revealed the mysteries hidden under silent delight.

In *Eleg.* 3.1.4, Propertius presents himself as a priest who wishes to enter the sacred grove of Callimachus (he aspired to be a Roman Callimachus):

> primus ego ingredior puro de fonte sacerdos
>   Itala per Graios orgia ferre choros.

> I, priest from a pure source, enter first, conveying Italic *orgia* through Greek dances.

If Propertius is the priest, the Italic *orgia* must be a metaphor for his Latin poems, written in Greek elegiac distichs.

In *Eleg.* 3.3.29, the word refers to mystic instruments of the Muses:

hic erat affixis viridis spelunca lapillis,
    pendebantque cavis tympana pumicibus,
orgia Musarum et Sileni patris imago
    fictilis et calami, Pan Tegeaee, tui.

Here was a cave, lined with green gems, and from the hollow pumice hung tympana, the mystic instruments of the Muses, and a clay image of father Silenus and of your flute, Tegean Pan.

In the tragedies of SENECA, *orgia* are the sacred objects of the Bacchic mysteries.

Oed. 431 describes the Triumph of Dionysus. The god rides in his golden chariot drawn by lions. Silenus sits on an ass.

condita lascivi deducunt orgia mystae.

Wanton initiates carry the hidden *orgia* in procession.

In *Herc. Oet.* 594, the chorus of Aetolian women addresses Hercules' wife, Deianira:

nos Cadmeis orgia ferre
tecum solitae condita cistis,
cum iam pulso sidere brumae
tertia soles evocat aestas.

We always used to carry the *orgia* hidden in Cadmean (Theban) baskets with you, when, as the winter star has fled, the third summer beckons the sun.

These *orgia condita cistis* recall the *obscura cavis orgia cistis* of Catullus. They are clearly the sacred objects of Dionysus.

C. VALERIUS FLACCUS, author of the *Argonautica*, uses the word once. The Lemnian princess Hypsipyle hid her father in the country, thus saving him from the murder of all the men on the island. 2.282:

non similes iam ferre choros (semel orgia fallunt)
audet.

No more does she dare to celebrate similar dances (only once can rites deceive).

COLUMELLA, *Rust.* 10.219, uses *orgia* in a metaphorical sense for the wonders of nature:

impulit ad rerum causas et sacra moventem
orgia naturae secretaque foedera caeli.

It drove him to explore the causes of things and the sacred rites of nature and the secret laws of the heaven.

JUVENAL, *Sat.* 2.91, uses the word for the secret rites of Cotyto.

> talia secreta coluerunt orgia taeda
> Cecropiam soliti Baptae lassare Cotyton.

> They celebrated such rites in secret by torchlight, the Baptae who always exhausted Cecropian (Athenian) Cotyto.

Aeschylus fr. 57 N² also referred to these rites as ὄργια.

STATIUS uses the word several times. *Silv.* 5.5.4 mentions rites in honour of the Muses:

> me miserum! neque enim verbis sollemnibus ulla
> incipiam nec Castaliae vocalibus undis,
> invisus Phoeboque gravis. quae vestra, sorores,
> orgia, Pieriae, quas incestavimus aras?

> Wretched me! For there are no solemn words for me to begin with, no vocal waters of Castalia, since I am hated by Phoebus. What rites of yours, Pieriae, what altars have I violated?

Theb. 4.792 describes how the Curetes attempt to mask the wailing of the infant Zeus:

> illi certantia plaudunt
> orgia, sed magnis resonat vagitibus Ide.

> They beat their *orgia* in rivalry, but Ide resounds with his loud shrieks.

So *orgia* must refer here to the mystic instruments of the Curetes.

In the following places, the word is used for the orgies of Dionysus. In *Theb.* 2.662, Tydeus attacks Menoetes:

> non haec trieterica vobis
> nox patrio de more venit, non orgia Cadmi
> cernitis aut avidas Bacchum scelerare parentes.

> This triennial night, according to old-established custom, does not come to your aid. You see no orgies of Cadmus or mothers eager to defile Bacchus.

Theb. 4.654 relates how Dionysus established his rites in Thrace:

> marcidus edomito bellum referebat ab Haemo
> Liber; ibi armiferos geminae iam sidera brumae

orgia ferre Getas canumque virescere dorso
Othryn et Icaria Rhodopen adsueverat umbra.

Languid Liber brought the war back from conquered Haemus. There he
had already familiarized the warlike Getae to hold orgies for two winters,
and snow-covered Othrys to turn green on its back, and Rhodope to bear
Icarian shade (i.e. of vines).

Theb. 7.687:

marcida te fractis planxerunt Ismara thyrsis,
te Tmolos, te Nysa ferax Theseaque Naxos
et Thebana metu iuratus in orgia Ganges.

With broken thyrsi, languid Ismara mourned you, as did Tmolus and
bounteous Nysa and Theseus' Naxos, and Ganges that had sworn alle-
giance to Theban orgies.

Theb. 12.788:

gaudent matresque nurusque
Ogygiae, qualis thyrso bellante subactus
mollia laudabat iam marcidus orgia Ganges.

The Ogygian (Theban) mothers and maidens rejoice how Ganges, sub-
dued by the warring thyrsus and already languid, praised the womanly
orgies.

Theb. 11.488, Tisiphone reproaches Piety:

ubi tunc, cum bella cieret
Bacchus et armatas furiarent orgia matres?

Where were you when Bacchus waged war and his orgies drove armed
mothers to madness?

In the unfinished *Achilleid*, the term is used twice more for the turbulent
rites of Bacchus:

Achil. 1.593:

lucus Agenorei sublimis ad orgia Bacchi
stabat et admissum caelo nemus; huius in umbra
alternam renovare piae trieterida matres
consuerant scissumque pecus terraque revulsas
ferre trabes gratosque deo praestare furores.

There stood a lofty forest for the rites of Agenor's descendant, Bacchus,
a grove that reached to the sky. In its shade, the pious matrons used to

renew the recurring triennial festival (of Bacchus) and bring livestock rent apart and trees torn from the earth and demonstrate frenzy pleasing to the god.

Achil. 1.813:

> occurrit genitor: quid si aut Bacchea ferentes
> orgia, Palladias aut circum videris aras?

> The father replies: "What if you could see them performing the Bacchic rites, or around the altars of Pallas?"

We find a rare prose attestation in APULEIUS, *Met.* 11.28. Lucius has finally collected enough money to be initiated into the mysteries of Osiris (cf. the attestations of *teleta* in *Met.* 11.22–30):

> ergo igitur cunctis adfatim praeparatis, decem rursus diebus inanimis contentus cibis, insuper etiam deraso capite, principalis dei nocturnis orgiis inlustratus, plena iam fiducia germanae religionis obsequium divinum frequentabam.

> So when everything was fully prepared to satisfaction, I once again abstained from eating flesh for ten days. Then, admitted with shaven head to the nocturnal orgies of the principal god, I attended the religious service with the full confidence that knowledge of a kindred ritual evokes.

The third century is silent with regard to *orgia*, but the fourth century yields several more attestations of the word.

AMMIANUS MARCELLINUS, 22.8.23, uses the word for the orgiastic rites of Bacchus:

> superatis post triennium Indicis nationibus, ad eos tractus Liber reversus, circa huius ripas viridis et opacas orgia pristina reparavit et choros.

> Having conquered the peoples of India after three years, Bacchus returned to those parts, and on the green and shady banks of this river (Callichorus) he restored his former orgies and dances.

AUSONIUS, *Cupido cruciatur* 3, describes the place where deceased heroines dwell:

> aeris in campis, memorat quos musa Maronis,
> myrteus amentes ubi lucus opacat amantes,
> orgia ducebant heroides.

> In the aerial fields, where, as Vergil's muse mentions, a myrtle grove shades insane lovers, heroines were celebrating rites.

While the nature of the rites is not specified further, the characterization of the celebrants as *amentes* could be an indication that Bacchic or similar rites are intended here.

CLAUDIAN uses the word three times. *In Eutropium* 286, it probably refers to the tympana of the Corybantes. Cybele's crown has fallen from her head.

> obstipuere truces omen Corybantes et uno
> fixa metu tacitas presserunt orgia buxos.

> The loud Corybantes stood perplexed at this omen and, transfixed with fear, at once muted their *orgia* and silenced their boxwood oboes.

The word *orgia* could, of course, just mean 'rites' here, but given its juxtaposition to *buxos*, it seems much more likely that, in fact, it refers to the tympana mentioned in verse 281. For this use, also compare Stat. *Theb.* 4.792 (above).

In *IV Cons. Hon.* 604 and *Cons. Stil.* 3.169, *orgia* are the orgiastic rites of Bacchus.

MACROBIUS, *Sat.* 5.17.3, recalls the story, told by Vergil,[5] of the Latin women who joined their queen, Amata, in the woods to celebrate Bacchic rites:

> nec hoc contenta silvas petit accitis reliquis matribus in societatem furoris,
> bacchatur chorus quondam pudicus et orgia insana celebrantur.

> And, not content with this, she goes to the woods, having summoned the rest of the matrons to a fellowship of fury, and the once modest chorus now rages and insane orgies are celebrated.

PRUDENTIUS, *Symm.* 1.187, tells how the story (*fama vel error*) of Mars and Rhea Silvia induced the Romans, among other things:

> utque deum mater Phrygia veheretur ab Ida,
> Bacchica de viridi peterentur ut orgia Naxo.

> to transport the Mother of the gods from Phrygian Ida,
> and fetch the Bacchic rites from green Naxos.

So here we see the familiar use of *orgia* for the rites of Bacchus.

In *Perist.* 2.65, however, the word is used for Christian rite:

---

[5] Verg. *Aen.* 7.385–405.

Hunc esse vestris orgiis
morem que et artem proditum est,
hanc disciplinam foederis,
libent ut auro antistites.

It has been disclosed that your rites have the following custom and style,
the following rule of your brotherhood, that your priests make libations
from a gold cup.

Since these words are put in the mouth of a Roman prefect, who, despite
his calm demeanour, is clearly no friend of the Christians, it is possible
that the word *orgia* has a negative connotation.

Conclusion

In Latin literature, *orgia* is predominantly used to refer to the rites of
Dionysus. It is also used for the (Bacchic and) Eleusinian mysteries (Ov.
Met. 11.93), rites of the Muses (Stat. *Silv.* 5.5.4), and the rites of Cotyto
(Juv. *Sat.* 2.91). In Apul. *Met.* 11.28, it indicates the mystery rites of Osiris.
Prudentius, *Perist.* 2.65, uses the word for the Christian service.

Occasionally, *orgia* refers to sacred objects:

- mystic instruments of the Muses (Prop. *Eleg.* 3.3.29);
- mystic instruments of the Curetes (Stat. *Theb.* 4.792; Claud. *In
  Eutrop.* 286);
- sacred objects of the Bacchic mysteries (Catull. 64.259–260; Sen.
  Herc. Oet. 594; *Oed.* 431).

Finally, we sometimes find it used in a metaphorical sense:

- mysteries of love (Prop. *Eleg.* 2.6.32);
- mysteries of nature (Columella, *Rust.* 10.219);
- mysteries of Latin poetry (Prop. *Eleg.* 3.1.4).

The celebration of *orgia* is expressed with the following verbs:

- orgia celebrare (Catull.; Macrob.);
- orgia capere (Verg.);
- orgia colere (Juv.);
- orgia ducere (Auson.).

We find the following combinations for transmitting and revealing mysteries:

- orgia tradere (Ov.);
- orgia (pro)ferre (Prop.).

To learn the secrets of the mysteries is 'orgia audire' (Catull.).

ΤΕΛΕΤΗ AND ΟΡΓΙΑ IN INSCRIPTIONS

INTRODUCTORY NOTES

Part Three examines the use of the words τελετή and ὄργια in the epigraphical evidence.[1]

Editorial Notes

The inscriptions are presented in the form of a catalogue, not a corpus. Only the relevant lines of each inscription are included. Each text is introduced by a short lemma that lists the nature of the inscription, a readily available edition (usually a corpus or *SEG*), and the approximate date of the document. For brackets and other editorial signs, I follow the Leiden system as revised by Sterling Dow.[2] Mason's errors and such have been relegated to footnotes. As far as commentary is concerned, I have, in general, restricted myself to brief remarks about the religious context. For additional information, bibliography and commentary, the reader is referred to the original editions.

Origin and General Use of the Words

Τελετή and ὄργια are two Greek lexemes that belong to the same semantic field. In the context of the Eleusinian mysteries, they can even be synonymous. The word τελετή is derived from the Proto-Indo-European root tel- and is thus related to τέλος and τελέω.[3] The word ὄργια is derived from the PIE root uerǵ- (with o-ablaut). It is therefore related to the noun ἔργον and the verbs ἔρδω (< uerǵ-ioH) and ῥέζω (< ureǵ-ioH, Schwebeablaut). Ὄργια and τελεταί are therefore originally 'things performed'; the terms are used for ritual acts or performances reserved for certain (religious) occasions, i.e. rites. In addition, τελετή can refer to the occasion on which a rite is performed, i.e. a ceremony or festival; and ὄργια is occasionally used for mystic objects. When we compare the

---

[1] A summary of my findings appeared in *Talanta* 38–39 (2006–2007) 225–238.
[2] S. Dow, *Conventions in Editing* (1969).
[3] See also F.M.J. Waanders, *The History of τέλος and τελέω in Ancient Greek* (1983).

uses of ὄργια and τελετή in inscriptions, the use of ὄργια appears less varied and abstract. Whereas τελετή can denote a rite, a ceremony, or a festival, ὄργια always refers to the actual rite, never to the religious occasion on which it is performed. Both words occur exclusively in a religious context, except where they are used in a metaphorical sense (e.g. 'rites of love'). Neither word is limited, either in meaning or in context, to rituals of mystery religions.

Geography and Date of the Inscriptions

If we look briefly at the geographical distribution of the inscriptions, we find that the inscriptions with ὄργια appear mostly in Asia Minor and at Eleusis, whereas τελετή is also found in other places. Ὄργια appears in inscriptions from Attica (Eleusis), Delphi, Thessaly, Macedonia, Patmos, Ionia, Caria, Lycia and Rome; τελετή in inscriptions from Attica (Athens and Eleusis), Messenia, Arcadia, Macedonia, Thrace, Bithynia, Pontus, Tenos, Amorgos, Cos, Pergamon, Ionia, Caria, Lycia, Pisidia, Commagene, Syria, Sinai and Rome. Inscriptions with ὄργια range from the fourth century BC to the fourth century AD; inscriptions with τελετή range from the mid-fifth century BC to the mid-fifth century AD. In both cases, the majority of extant inscriptions date from the Roman imperial period.

CHAPTER ELEVEN

THE USE OF ΤΕΛΕΤΗ IN INSCRIPTIONS

A complete overview of the use of the word τελετή in inscriptions has long been a desideratum. In his review of Zijderveld's dissertation, Otto Kern already expressed his regret that this important work did not provide a systematic review of all the epigraphical evidence.[1] Subsequent studies have also focused almost exclusively on the literary evidence.[2] This chapter, therefore, gives an overview of where and how τελετή is used in inscriptions. The next chapter will do the same for the term ὄργια.

It will not come as a surprise that τελετή in inscriptions, as in literary testimonia, often refers to mysteries. As seen in Part One, however, the word τελετή was also used in a variety of other meanings. While the distinction between the different shades of meaning of τελετή is not always clear-cut, I believe it is safe to arrange the epigraphical attestations into the following six categories:[3]

A. Religious ritual or ceremony
B. Religious festival
C. Eleusinian mysteries
D. Other mysteries
E. Taurobolium
F. The goddess Telete

Within these categories, I have arranged the inscriptions geographically according to their place of origin.

---

[1] O. Kern, *Gnomon* 15 (1939) 198–202, 200.

[2] See especially G. Sfameni Gasparro, Ancora sul termine telete: osservazioni storico-religiose, in: *Filologia e Forme Letterarie: Studi offerti a Francesco della Corte*, ed. C. Questa, vol. 5 (1987) 137–152; F.M.J. Waanders, *The History of τέλος and τελέω in Ancient Greek* (1983) 156–158 §§ 153–155; K. Dowden, Grades in the Eleusinian Mysteries, *RHR* 197 (1980) 409–427.

[3] My primary aim is not so much to achieve a logically pure and consistent classification as to present the material in a clear and orderly manner, grouping together inscriptions where the term refers to the same (or similar) religious phenomenon.

A. Religious ritual or ceremony

1 Fragmentary cult regulation, found in the so-called Theseum at the edge
   of the Athenian Agora. *IG* II² 1234. End of the fourth century BC. Lines 3–
   5; 8–10:

> [- - - - - - - - -]ειν κατὰ τὰ π[άτρια - - - - - - - - - - -] |⁴ [. τὴν τελε]τὴν ποεῖν ἐν
> τ[- - - - - - - - - - -] | [- - - - - - - - -]ας τὸ διαγεγραμ[μένον - - - - - - - - - - -].

   (to perform/sacrifice vel sim.) according to the traditions … and to perform the *telete* in the … this document …

> [- - - - - - - - - ἔ]καστος αὐτῶν [δραχμὰς- - - - - - - - - - -] | [-- ἐὰν δ]ὲ τὴν
> τελετὴν μ[ὴ ποήσωσι - - - - - - - - - - -] |¹⁰ [- - - - - - - - - - -]τεισάτω ἕκασ[τος
> αὐτῶν - - δραχμὰς - -]

   Each of them (shall pay X drachmas … and if they will not perform) the
   telete … each of them shall pay (X drachmas).

For the expression τελετὴν πο(ι)εῖν, cf. *LSCG* 103.B.11. Cf. also θυσίαν
ποιεῖν (e.g. *LSCG* 59.15; 6.10?; 38.8?; *LSAM* 2.10; 36.22?; *LSS* 85.24–25?),
παννυχίδα ποεῖν (e.g. *LSCG* 33.B.32; *LSS* 6.13).

From Koehler's identification of the document as a decision of a *pagus*
or *gens*, Zijderveld inferred that we may have a clan cult here;[4] he recalls
that the special ritual of a separate clan is indeed called τελετή, cf. Dem.
Neaer. 104. The wording of the document, however, suggests that it is just
an ordinary cult regulation; if it was indeed set up by a gens, this would,
in my opinion, be significant only insofar as it would confirm that cult
practice at clan level could be called τελετή. It would not necessarily shed
much light on the nature of the rituals involved.

2 Fragmentary ephebic decree from Athens. *IG* II² 1042. Ca. 41/0 BC
   (archonship of Nikandros).
      In line c.14, the decree mentions that the ephebes had participated
   (?) [τ]ῶν τε τελετῶν ἁπασ[ῶν ὧ]ν πάτριον ἦν ("in all the traditional
   religious ceremonies"). Clinton accurately observed that these *teletai*
   "ought to include non-initiatory cults, since the only initiation in which
   the ephebes took part occurred at the Eleusinian Mysteria."[5]

---

⁴ Zijderveld, *Τελετή* (1934) 36.
⁵ K. Clinton, Stages of initiation in the Eleusinian and Samothracian Mysteries, in:
M.B. Cosmopoulos (ed.), *Greek Mysteries* (2003) 54.

3 Relief from Cynuria/Thyreatis. *IG* IV 676. Ca. first century AD (stylistic grounds). The inscriptions were perhaps added later. For a description, bibliography and photo of this relief, see Kaltsas, *NMΓλυπτά*, no. 644.

On the right, a woman sits on a throne decorated with a sphinx, facing left. She wears a chiton and himation and has her hair done up in a haircloth. In her right hand, she holds a bowl in her lap; her left elbow rests on the back of the throne. Below her elbow is an inscription on the throne: ἐπί|κτη|σις ('new acquisition').

At her feet is a square block with mouldings at top and bottom: an altar? In the field between the mouldings is an inscription: Εὐθη|νία ('Abundance'). On top of the block stands a small woman, about one third the size of the first woman, holding a basket in her arms.

High above the second woman stands a statue of an Artemis-like goddess on a pillar, with raised left hand. To the right are branches of a large tree. Tied to the middle branch is a ribbon. Below the lowest branch, right in front of the seated woman, the name or word ΤΕΛΕΤΗ is inscribed.

Judging by the difference in size between the two women, the first is probably a heroine or goddess, preparing to pour a libation or receive an offering, while the second is an offerant. It has been suggested that the second figure may be the statue of a woman or goddess, standing on a pedestal. While it might seem difficult to distinguish between depictions of statues and of real gods and humans, if we examine the second and third figure, noting especially the drapery and posture, we find that the artist had no trouble showing the difference.[6] The second figure, therefore, is probably an ordinary woman, bringing a basket of offerings to the deity before her.

Epiktesis is not attested as a name for a goddess; it probably refers to the throne. Euthenia can be the name of a goddess; perhaps we should read a dative: Εὐθη|νίᾳ '(altar/offerings) for Euthenia', referring to the seated deity. While it is true that Telete is occasionally used as the name of a goddess, the seated deity in no way resembles the recently discovered representation of the goddess at Zeugma.[7] All things considered, the most likely explanation is that we here have τελετή in the sense of ritual, more specifically: offering.

---

[6] And if, for the sake of argument, a very lifelike statue had been intended, would it not be strange that it stands at the very edge of its pedestal rather than at the centre?

[7] See below, no. 56; for literary references to the goddess Telete, see Paus. 9.30.4 and Nonn. *Dion.* 16.400, 48.880 ff.

4 Dedication to Pan found in Bouthrotos (Illyria). *SEG* XXXVIII 518.[8] Second century AD.[9] It reads:

> Πανὶ τελε|τάρχῃ Κασι|ανός. *vacat*

> Cassianus for Pan who leads the ceremony.

Ed.pr.'s interpretation of the term τελετάρχης as "celui qui préside aux mystères, qui dirige les initiés"[10] seems tempting. It is, however, by no means certain that this cult of Pan was, in fact, a mystery cult.

5 Dedicatory epigram on a small marble tablet found in Odessus. Broken on the right. *IGBulg* I² 225. Undated. Lines 5–6:

> καὶ κισσὸν περὶ κρατὶ ϑ[εμ - ᴗᴗ - ᴗᴗ - -]
> ἐκ πάσης τελετῆ[ς - ᴗᴗ - ᴗᴗ -]

> with ivy around his head ... from every *telete*.

The meaning of τελετή is uncertain here. Nothing points to a mystery cult. The ivy perhaps suggests a Dionysian context.

The sacred laws that regulated the sales of priesthoods on Cos[11] often contain precise instructions concerning the ἀνάλωμα ἐς τὰν τελετάν, the cost of the ceremony:

6 Regulation concerning the sale of the priesthood of Dionysos Thyl- lophoros. *Iscr.Cos* ED 216. Third or second century BC.[12] A.16–17:

> τὸ δὲ ἀνάλωμα τὸ ἐς τὰν τελετὰν [τοὶ τα]|[μία]ι διδόντω.

> The treasurers shall pay the cost of the ceremony.

Apparently also on the back of the stone, B.15–17:

> [τὸ δὲ ἐς τὰν τελετὰν] γε[νόμενο]ν ἀνάλω|[μ]α καὶ [τ]ὸ ἐς [τὰν στάλ]αν
> κ[αὶ ἀναγρα]φὰν [τᾶς διαγρα]φᾶς ἀπ[ο]|δώσει τοῖς ταμίαις ἁ πριαμένα
> τὰν ἱερωσύναν.

---

[8] Ed.pr. P. Cabanes, *REA* 90 (1988) 385–388 (ph.); *I.Bouthrotos* 182 (non vidi).

[9] Second or early first century BC (letterforms) ed.pr.; corrected by S. Follet, BE 1990, no. 79.

[10] Rather than "a founder of mysteries"; cf. F.M.J. Waanders, *The History of τέλος and τελέω in Ancient Greek* (1983) 159.

[11] For the sales of priesthoods on Cos, see R. Parker & D. Obbink (I), *Chiron* 30 (2000) 415–449; (II) *Chiron* 31 (2001) 229–252.

[12] See also Parker & Obbink (2000) 422: ca. 225 (or ca. 175).

She who buys the priesthood shall pay the cost of the ceremony and the stone and the inscription of this document to the treasurers.

7 Regulation concerning the priesthood of Dionysos Thyllophoros. *LSCG* 166. Late second or first century BC. Lines 74–75:

> [τὸ δὲ] | [ἐς τὰν] τελετὰ[ν γενόμενον ἀνάλωμα].[13]

The sum required for the ceremony.

8 Regulation concerning the priesthood of Zeus Alseios. *Iscr.Cos* ED 215. First century BC. B.12–21:

> [τοὶ] | [δὲ πω]ληταὶ μισ[θω]σάν[τω] τὰγ [τελετὰν τοῦ ἱερέως κατὰ] ||[14]
> τὰ νομιζόμενα καὶ τὰν δ[ι]αγραφὰν τάν[δε ἀνα]|γράψαι εἰς [σ]τάλαν
> λιθίναν καὶ ἀναθ[έμε]γ πα|[16]ρὰ τὸν βωμὸν τὸν τοῦ Διὸ[ς τ]οῦ Ἀλσείου.
> τὸ δὲ γ[ε]|νόμενον ἀνάλωμα [ἐς] τὰ[ς θ]υσία[ς] τὰς συντε[λου]||[18]μένας
> ὑπὸ τῶν προστατᾶν ἐ[πὶ τ]ᾶι π[ρά]σ[ει τᾶς] | [ἱ]ερωσύνας καὶ τὰν
> τελετὰν καὶ τὰν [στ]άλαν [καὶ] |[20] [τ]ὰν ἀναγραφὰν τᾶς δ[ι]αγρ[αφ]ᾶς
> ἀποτελεσ[άν]|[τ]ω τοὶ προστάται.

The *poletai* (leasing officers) shall contract out the ceremony of the priest according to the customs and shall inscribe this document on a stone slab and set it up by the altar of Zeus Alseios. The *prostatai* shall pay the sum required for the offerings performed by the *prostatai* in connection with the sale of the priesthood, and for the ritual and the stele and the inscription of this document.

9 Regulation concerning the priesthood of an Antigonus, probably Doson.[14] *Iscr.Cos* ED 85. Second century BC. Lines 10–12:

> [τὸ δὲ γενόμενον] ἀνάλωμα ἐς [τὰς] | [θυσίας τὰς συντελουμένας ὑπὸ
> τῶν προστατᾶν ἐπὶ τᾶ]ι πράσει τᾶ[ς ἱε]|[ρ]ωσύνας καὶ τὰν τελετὰν
> - - - - -].

The sum required for the offerings performed by the *prostatai* in connection with the sale of the priesthood and for the ritual.

10 Regulation concerning the priesthood of Adrasteia and Nemesis. *Iscr.Cos* ED 144 (*LSCG* 160). Second century BC. Lines 12–14:

> [τὸ δὲ γενόμενον ἀνά]|[λωμα τοῖς προστάταις ἔς τε] τὰν τελετὰν τοῦ
> ἱερέω[ς καὶ ἐς τὰν] | [στάλαν καὶ ἀναγραφὰν τᾶς δι]αγραφᾶς τοὶ ταμίαι
> π[ροτελεσάντω].

---

[13] Sokolowski's commentary ad locum that τελετή "se rapporte à la préparation d'une stèle" is erroneous.
[14] See Parker & Obbink (2000) 423.

The treasurers shall pay in advance to the *prostatai* the sum required for the consecration of the priest and for the stele and the inscription of this document.

In this last inscription, it is very clear that τελετά refers to the consecration of a new priest. No. 8 already showed that these ceremonies can be put out to contract.

11 Regulation concerning the priesthood of Homonoia. Edd.pr. D. Bosnakis & K. Hallof, *Chiron* 35 (2005) 220–233, no. 20 (a recent discovery in the storeroom of the Asklepieion). Second century BC. Lines 57–59:[15]

> τὸ δὲ γενόμενον ἀνάλωμα ἔς τε τὰν | θυσίαν τὰν ἐπὶ τᾶ[ι πράσει τᾶς ἱερωσύν]ας καὶ ἐς τὰν τελετὰν τοῦ ἱερέως καὶ | τᾶς ἱερείας κ[αὶ τὰν στάλαν καὶ τὰ]γ ἀναγραφ[ὰ]ν τᾶς διαγραφᾶς.

The sum required for the offering in connection with the sale of the priesthood and for the consecration ceremony of the priest and priestess and the stele and the inscription of this document.

12 (= D6) Regulation concerning ritual purity. *LSCG* 154. First half third century BC. A.31–32:

> τὰ δὲ τέλεια ἅ κα ἀναλωθῆι ἐς τ[ὰν τελετὰν τᾶς ἱερείας, ἀποδίδωτι ἁ πόλις ἅ]|παντα χωρὶς ἢ ἃ γέγραπται τὰ[ν ἱέρειαν παρέχεν].

The city pays whatever expenses are spent on the ceremony of the priestess, except for what the priestess supplies according to the regulation.

The restoration of τελετάν, already suggested by Herzog, *HGK* 8, seems plausible: the formula would correspond to the ἀνάλωμα ἐς τὰν τελετάν of other Coan sacred laws.

13 Regulation concerning the priesthood of Herakles Kallinikos. *Iscr.Cos* ED 180. Late second or first century BC. The document calls for 50 drachmas to be recorded, lines 33–34:

> ἐπεί κα ἁ τελετὰ τοῦ ἱερέως καὶ τᾶς ἱερείας ἐπιτελῆ|[τ]αι.

seeing to it that the consecration of the priest and the priestess is performed.

---

[15] Similar words are perhaps found in a regulation concerning the priesthood of Aphrodite Pontia, Parker & Obbink (2000) 417 no. 1 (*SEG* L 766) lines 47–50; cf. Bosnakis & Hallof (2005) 232, who give a new restoration of these lines.

14 Regulation concerning the priesthood of the Kyrbanthes (Corybantes). *Iscr.Cos* ED 177. Late third century BC. Lines 10–11:

> γέρη δὲ λαμ̣[βανέ]‖[τω τοῦ μὲν θυο]μένου ἱερείου ἐπὶ τᾶι τελετᾶι.

> At the ceremony, he (the priest) shall take the following parts of the sacrificial animal as gifts.

In this last inscription, the word τελετή is almost synonymous with sacrifice. The priest's share of the sacrificial meat was, of course, one of the important perquisites for a priest.[16]

15 Inscription on a funerary altar from Nicaea (Bithynia). *SEG* LI 1709bis.[17] Undated. We present the full text.

> ['Ε]πικράτης σ[ὺν γα]-
> μετῇ Ἀπφῃ[18] τὸν
> βωμὸν ἀνέστη-
> 4 σαν τέκνῳ Περσῖ
> εὐχαῖς καὶ τελε-
> ταῖς ὁσίαις παρὰ
> Ζηνὶ φανέντα.

> Epikrates with his wife, Apphe, set up this altar for their child, Perseus, displaying it next to Zeus with prayers and sacred rites.

So the very personal and private rites surrounding the dedication of an altar for a deceased child are also called τελεταί.

16 Honorary decree on a limestone block from Cyaneae (Lycia). Heberdey-Kalinka, *Bericht*, no. 28. Hellenistic period, ca. second century BC (letterforms). Lines 5–11 (restorations exempli gratia):

> [τύχηι ἀγαθῆ]ι δεδόχθαι ἐπαινέσαι Ἀντίχαριν Ἀμύντο[υ] Πινα(ρέα) |⁶
> [καὶ στεφανῶσαι αὐτὸν κ]αὶ στῆσαι αὐτοῦ ἐν τῶι τοῦ Ἀπόλλωνος ἱερῶι
> εἰκόν[α] | [χαλκῆν· τελεῖν δὲ τὴ]ν τελετὴν συ[μ]πομπευόντων καὶ τῶν
> ἐφήβων κ[αὶ] |⁸ [θύοντος τοῦ γυμνασι]άρχου βοῦν ἐπὶ τοῦ βω[μ]οῦ τοῦ
> ἀνατεθ[η]σομένου, τ[οῦ] | [δὲ κήρυκος ἐν τοῖς παρ]οῦσιν καλοῦντος

---

[16] See Van Straten, *Hiera Kala* (1995) 154–155.

[17] Edd.pr. Merkelbach-Stauber, *SGO* II 190 no. 09/05/40; cf. A. Chaniotis, *EBGR* 2001, 226–227 no. 120 (in *Kernos* 2004), who corrects the translation.

[18] Edd.pr. read Ἀπφῇ; since it is an indigenous name, it is better left unaccentuated. For other attestations of the name Ἀπφη, see L. Zgusta, *Kleinasiatische Personennamen* (1964) 75 § 66-18.

Ἀντίχαριν Ἀμ[ύ]ντ[ο]υ εἰς προεδρία[ν] |¹⁰ [ἐν τοῖς ἀγῶσι τοῖς ἀ]νδρῶν,
ὁμοίως δὲ καὶ ἀκοντιστ[ῶν] καὶ τοξ[ο]τῶν καὶ [π]ε[λ]|[ταστῶν].

… have decided, with good fortune, to praise Ant* icharis, son of Amyntas,
from Pinara, and to wreathe him and set up a bronze statue of him in the
sanctuary of Apollo, and to perform the rite while the ephebes accompany
him in procession, while the gymnasiarch sacrifices a bovine at the altar
that has been dedicated, and while, among those present, the herald calls
Ant* icharis, son of Amyntas, to the front seat in the games of men and,
similarly, of javelin throwers, archers, and peltasts.

It is possible, though by no means certain, that the rite refers to the
dedication of a statue in the sanctuary of Apollo in the preceding line.

17 Mosaic from Sheikh Zouède in northern Sinai. *SEG* XXIV 1197.[19] See
now A. Ovadiah, C. Gomez de Silva and S. Mucznik, *The Mosaic Pavements of Sheikh Zouède in Northern Sinai*, in *Tesserae: Festschrift für Josef
Engemann* (1991) 181–191, with Pl. 23d–25c. Mid-fourth to mid-fifth
century AD (Ovadiah et al., on stylistic grounds).

The middle panel shows the so-called triumph of Dionysus. At the
end of a merry thiasos, the god himself comes, riding a four-wheeled[20]
chariot drawn by a couple of centaurs, while Eros holds the reins. The two
gods are identified by name inscriptions: Διόνυσος and Ἔρως. Directly
above Eros' name is the word τελετή, which evidently refers to the whole
scene, as it does not correspond to any of the figures in the mosaic.
Quite similarly a mosaic from Sepphoris, also depicting the triumph of
Dionysus, bears the label πομπή (procession).[21] So in this context, τελετή
is the procession, thiasos.

B. Religious festival

18 Choregic dedication from Athens. *SEG* XXX 132.[22] After 130 AD (death
of Antinous). The festival of Antinous is called a τελετή. Lines 2–3
(restored by Peek):

ἐν θυμ[έλαισι δ'] ἅπας πεί[ρατ' ἔδειξε τέχνης]
ἠιθέου [τελετῆι] θεοειδέος Ἀ[ντιν]όο[ιο].

---

[19] Ed.pr. J. Clédat, *ASAE* 15 (1915) 26–27, with Pl. IV.
[20] Since the chariot is depicted from the side, only two wheels are shown.
[21] See R. Talgam & Z. Weiss, *The Mosaics of the House of Dionysos at Sepphoris* (2004)
63–66.
[22] *IG* II² 3117; restored by W. Peek, *ASAW* 69.2 (1980) 13–14 no. 8.

On stage, everyone showed the full extent of his art at the festival of the godlike youth Antinous.

The restoration, though uncertain, seems plausible enough: the yearly festival for Antinous at Mantinea is called τελετή by Pausanias, 8.9.8.

19 Manumission record from Exochi (Macedonia). *SEG* XLVI 745.[23] The document is dated 223 AD (Actian and provincial era, lines 1–2). The festival of the goddess Enodia is called τελετή. Lines 2–12:

> Δύ[υ]σ|τρου δωδεκά|⁴τῃ, οὔσας τε|λετῆς κὲ συ|⁶ναγωγῆς, Αὐρη|λεία Ἰουλεία ἡ |⁸ προχρηματείσα|σα Ἀμύντου ἐχαρι|¹⁰[σ]άμην θεῷ Ἐνοδί|ᾳ ὀνόματει Ἑρμῆν |¹² δοῦλον.

> On the twelfth of Dystros, being a festival and a day of assembly, I, Aurelia Julia, formerly called daughter of Amyntas, have willingly given my slave, by the name of Hermes, to the goddess Enodia.

Lucian *Nav.* 15 also refers to a festival for Enodia at Aegina as τὴν τῆς Ἐνοδίας τελετήν. In the inscription, the word τελετή merely indicates that the day in question is a holiday without elucidating the nature of the festival.

20 Honorary inscription by the corporation of Aphrodisiasts, from Ephesus. *SEG* XLIII 773.[24] Second century BC. Here τελεταί are the festival of an unknown god. Lines 21–25:

> ὅτι τὸ κοινὸν τῶν Ἀφροδισιασ[τῶν στ]εφα|²²νοῖ Δαμοτέλην Ἱπποστρά- το[υ εὐσεβε]ίας | ἕνεκεν καὶ εὐνοίας τῆς εἰς τ[ὸ κοινὸν τ]ῶι |²⁴ τοῦ θεοῦ στεφάνωι ἐν ταῖς τε[λεταῖς] ἐν | ἁπάσαις ταῖς ἡμέραις.

> That the corporation of Aphrodisiasts has crowned Damoteles, son of Hippostratus, with the crown of the god on all the days of the festival, because of his piousness and his good-will towards the corporation.

Edd.pr. note that the masculine, τοῦ θεοῦ (line 24), is surprising here; one would have expected τῆς θεοῦ for Aphrodite.

---

[23] Edd.pr. P.M. Nigdelis & G.A. Souris, *Tekmeria* 2 (1996) 69–80 (ph.) (available at www.tekmeria.org). Cf. M.B. Hatzopoulos, BE 1998, no. 239.

[24] Edd.pr. D. Knibbe, H. Engelmann and B. İplikçioğlu, *JÖAI* 62 (1993) 125–126 no. 17.

21 Dedicatory epigram to Athena, on a marble block from Heraclea by
    Latmus (Caria). Broken on the right. A. Dain, *Inscriptions grecques du
    Musée du Louvre: Les textes inédits* (1933) no. 60. Undated. Line 31:

> [... τᾶ]ς τελετᾶς. ὦ τὰν ἀείμναστο[ν ----------]

> ... of the festival. O, the ever to be remembered ...

The τελετά is a festival for Athena. Louis Robert has emphasized that
there is no question of mysteries of Endymion, who is merely mentioned
as the mythological founder of the city in line 6.[25]

The Panathenaea at Sardis were perhaps also called τελετή: see below,
Appendix A, no. D10.

22 Dedicatory epigram on a marble block from Cyrene. *SEG* XXXVIII
    1898.[26] Third century BC. Lines 1–6:

> μνᾶμα τόδ' Ἑρμήσανδρος |² ὑπὲρ κράνας ὁ Φίλωνος | θῆκε θεᾶι θύσας
> |⁴ Ἀρτέμιδος τελετᾶι, | βοῦς ἑκατὸν κατάγων |⁶ καὶ ἴκατι.

> Hermesandros, son of Philo, dedicated this monument above the fountain-
> house, having sacrificed to the goddess for the festival of Artemis, leading
> 120 cattle to the sanctuary.

Here, τελετά refers to the Artamitia, a local festival of Artemis. There is
nothing to suggest that it was a mystery festival. Cf. also Paus. 8.23.4, who
mentions a τελετή for Artemis in Arcadia.

C. Eleusinian Mysteries

23 Dedicatory epigram on a statue base, originally set up in the vestibule of
    the City Eleusinion, found in the Athenian Agora. *IG* I³ 953. Ca. 450 BC
    (letterforms). Lines 1–3:

> [ἀ]ρρήτο τελετῆς πρόπολος σῆς, πότνια Δηοῖ, | καὶ θυγατρὸς προθύρο
> κόσμον ἄγαλμα τόδε | ἔστησεν στεφάνω Λυσιστράτη.

> As an attendant of the secret ceremony for you and your daughter, Mistress
> Deo (Demeter), Lysistrate set up this statue of two crowns as an ornament
> for your vestibule.

---

[25] L. Robert, *ATAM* 351–353 (cf. *SEG* XXX 1263).
[26] Ed.pr. G. Pugliese Carratelli, *SEC* 162 (text identical to *SEC* 161) with ph.; F. Cha-
moux, *MMAI* 72 (1991) 26–29 with excellent photo of squeeze (cf. *SEG* XLI 1695).

For a detailed discussion of this inscription, see Clinton, *Sacred Officials*, 69 no. 1.

24 Ephebic decree from Athens. *SEG* XXIX 116.[27] 214/3 BC. The ephebes are praised, among other things, for performing their duty at the Eleusinian mysteries. Lines 10–11 (restored by ed.pr.):

> ἔν τε τῆι τ[ελετῆι?] | [τῶμ μυστηρ]ίων ἐλειτούργησαν καλῶς καὶ εὐσε-
> βῶ[ς - -].

> In the ceremony (?) of the mysteries they performed their duties beautifully and religiously.

The restoration seems reasonably secure: ἡ τελετὴ τῶν μυστερίων is a common combination, see Isoc. *Paneg.* 157 (73d); Diod. 5.48.4 (of the Samothracian mysteries); cf. *IG* II² 1304.28; *I.Didyma* 352.8–10 (of the mysteries at Didyma).

25 Honorary decree for Demaenetus, from Eleusis. *IG* II² 1304. From 209 BC (archonship of Aeschron). See now Clinton, *I.Eleusis*, no. 211 with Pl. 110 (ph. squeeze). Demaenetus had, among other things, three times been *strategos* in the area of Eleusis. Lines 28–30:

> ἐπεμελήθη δὲ καὶ | τῆς τῶν μυστηρίων [τε]λετῆς καθ' ἑκάστην στρατη-
> γίαν, ὅπως | μετὰ πάσης ἀσφαλε[ία]ς συντελεσθεῖ.

> And he also took care of the festival of the mysteries during each period of command, so that it could be performed in all safety.

26 (= D12) Fragmentary herm from Athens, set up in honour of a certain Leucius. *IG* II² 3752. Second century AD. Leucius' mother was apparently a priestess in the Eleusinian mysteries, lines 7–8:

> ἀρρήτου τελ[ετῆς ὄργια] | δερκομένη.

> who always beheld the mysteries of the secret rite.

27 Dedicatory epigram on a herm from Athens, set up in honour of a certain Aelius Apollonius. *IG* II² 3764. Ca. 217/8 AD (Apollonius' son, who had the same name, appears in an ephebic inscription of that year). Apollonius' mother had been a priestess, lines 3–4:

---

[27] Ed.pr. S.V. Tracy, *Hesperia* 48 (1979) 174–179.

ἢ τελετὰς ἀνέφαινε θεοῖν | παρ' ἀνάκτορα Δηοῦς.

who displayed the ceremonies for the goddesses by the temple of Deo (Demeter).

The mother was probably P. Aelia Herennia, a hierophantis: see Clinton, *Sacred Officials*, 88 no. 11.

28 Dedicatory epigram for hierophantis Isidote, on a base from Eleusis. *IG* II² 3632. After 176 AD (initiation of M. Aurelius and Commodus). See now Clinton, *I.Eleusis*, no. 502 with Pl. 233 (very good ph. of stone). Lines 18–20:

ἥ τε καὶ Ἀντωνῖνον ὁμοῦ Κομμόδῳ | βασιλῆας | ἀρχομένη τελετῶν ἔστεφε μυστιπόλους.

And starting the ceremonies, she wreathed the emperors Antoninus (i.e. Marcus Aurelius) and Commodus as initiates at the same time.

29 Dedicatory epigram for Praxagora, on a base from Eleusis. *IG* II² 4077. End of second century AD. See now Clinton, *I.Eleusis*, no. 511 with Pl. 243 (ph. stone). Lines 7–10.

ἀλλά με καὶ παίδων κοσ|⁸μεῖ χορός, οἳ τὸ πρὸ μυστῶν | ἄλλων ἐν τελεταῖς στέμ|¹⁰μα κόμαισι θέσαν.

But a chorus of children decorates me, too. In front of the other *mystai* at the ceremonies, they have placed the wreath on my hair.

Given the special treatment she receives, Praxagora was presumably a hearth-initiate: see Clinton, *Sacred Officials*, 111 no. 40.

30 Letter from Emperor Commodus to the Eumolpidae, published at Eleusis. *IG* II² 1110. 183–190 AD. See now Clinton, *I.Eleusis*, no. 513 with Pl. 245 (good ph. of stone). The emperor accepts his appointment as archon of the Eumolpidae, lines 8–10:

ὡς τά τε ἀπόρρητα τῆς κατὰ τὰ | μυστήρια τελετῆς ἐνδοξ|ό|τερόν τε καὶ σεμνότερον.

so that the secrets of the ceremony of the mysteries may be even more splendid and solemn.

Commodus had himself been initiated into the Eleusinian mysteries on a previous occasion: see above, no. 28.

The following three inscriptions have been identified by Kevin Clinton as dedicatory epigrams for Eleusinian hierophant Julius, who saved the *arrheta hiera* during the invasion of the Costobocs in 170 AD.[28]

31 Herm. *I.Eleusis*, no. 494. Dedicated at Eleusis shortly after the invasion (ca. 171–176 AD), later transported to Aegina, now lost. We present the full text:

> ἀρρήτων θησ[αυρὸν ⏑ - ⏑⏑ - ἐ]ς Ἀθήνας
> μυστικὸν ἠ[γαγόμην ἐν π]ολέμωι στυγερῶι·
> τοὔνεκα ταινία[ις ἀνέδησαν Κ]εκροπίδαι με
> 4 καὶ θέσαν ἐν [τεμένει....]ρος[29] ἀεὶ τελετῆς.

I took the mystic treasury of secrets to Athens during the hateful war. For this reason, the Cecropidae have crowned me with headbands and have dedicated me in the sacred precinct (?) of the everlasting ceremony.

32 (= 66) Marble block from Eleusis, presumably belonging to a grave monument. *IG* II² 3639. From 192 AD or shortly after (death of the hierophant).[30] See now Clinton, *I.Eleusis*, no. 515 with Pl. 235 (very good ph. of stone). Lines 3–6 praise the hierophant:

> ὃς τελετὰς ἀνέφηνε καὶ ὄργια πάννυχα μύσταις
> 4 Εὐμόλπου προχέων ἱμερόεσσαν ὄπα,
> ὃς καὶ δυσμενέων μόθον οὐ τρέσεν, ἀλλ᾽ ἐσάωσεν
> ἄχραντα ἀρρήτων θέσμια Κεκροπίδαις.

who displayed the ceremonies and the all-night mysteries to the *mystai*, pouring forth the charming voice of Eumolpus, and who did not flee from the enemy's onslaught, but saved undefiled the secret rites for the Cecropidae.

Zijderveld noted that τελεταί and ὄργια πάννυχα seem to be used as almost equivalent synonyms here.[31]

33 (= 67) Round base from Eleusis. *IG* II² 3411. After 176 AD (initiation of Marcus Aurelius in line 7); probably around the same time as *IG* II² 3639: 192 AD or shortly after. See now Clinton, *I.Eleusis*, no. 516 with Pl. 246–247 (ph. stone). Lines 1–7:

---

[28] See Clinton, *Sacred Officials*, 38–39.
[29] ἐν[γὺς ἔμεν Μητ]ρὸς, Peek, rejected by Clinton.
[30] See Clinton, *Sacred Officials*, 38 n. 202: instead of ca. 170 AD.
[31] Zijderveld, *Τελετή* (1934) 77.

καὶ σοφίῃ κλεινὸν καὶ σεμνῶν φάντορα νυκτῶν
    Δηοῦς καὶ Κούρης ἁγνὸν ὁρᾷς πρόπολον,
ὅς ποτε Σαυρομάτων ἀλεείνων ἔργον ἄθεσμον
4   ὄργια καὶ ψυχὴν ἐξεσάωσε πάτρῃ,
καὶ τελετὰς ἀπέφηνε καὶ ἤρατο κῦδος ὅμοιον
    Εὐμόλπῳ πινυτῷ καὶ Κελεῷ ζαθέῳ,
Αὐσονίδην τε ἐμύησεν ἀγακλυτὸν Ἀντωνῖνον.

You are looking at the displayer of solemn nights, also famous for his
wisdom, the holy attendant of Deo (Demeter) and Kore, who, avoiding
the unlawful work of the Sarmatians,[32] saved the mysteries and his life for
his country and displayed the ceremonies and elevated their reputation
like wise Eumolpus and very holy Celeus and initiated the very glorious
Antoninus of Rome (i.e. Marcus Aurelius).

34 *Prophetes* inscription on a block of grey marble, inscribed on the front.
I.Didyma 216. 70 BC (Lysimachos stephanephoros, line 13). Lines 19–20.

[Κέ]κροπος ἐν γαίᾳ μὲν ὑπείροχον ἱερο[φάντην]
[μυστι]κὸν ἐν νυχίοις[33] Φερ[σεφό]νης τελετα[ῖς]

In Cecrops' land, the eminent mystic hierophant in the nocturnal rites of
Persephone ...

The text must have continued on the next block (below or to the right).
The nocturnal rites of Persephone in the land of Cecrops are, of course,
the mysteries of Eleusis.

D. Other Mysteries

35 The famous regulation of the Andanian mysteries. *IG* V 1, 1390 (*LSCG*
65). 92/1 BC.[34] The officials of the cult, called *hieroi*, take an oath (lines
A.2–5):

ὀμνύω τοὺς θεούς, οἷς τὰ μυστήρια ἐπιτ[ε]|[λε]ῖται, ἐπιμέλειαν ἕξειν,
ὅπως γίνηται τὰ κατὰ τὰν τελετὰν θεοπρεπῶς καὶ ἀπὸ παντὸς τοῦ
δικαίου, καὶ μήτε αὐ|⁴[τ]ὸς μηθὲν ἄσχημον μηδὲ ἄδικον ποιήσειν ἐπὶ
καταλύσει τῶν μυστηρίων μηδὲ ἄλλωι ἐπιτρέψειν, ἀλλὰ κατακολου|θή-
σειν τοῖς γεγραμμένοις, ἐξορκίσειν δὲ καὶ τὰς ἱερὰς καὶ τὸν ἱερῆ κατὰ τὸ
διάγραμμα.

---

[32] I.e. the Costobocs, see Clinton, *Sacred Officials*, 39.
[33] Confusion of gender: one would have expected νυχίαις, but the omicron is clear in
the photograph.
[34] The date can be inferred from lines A.10, 52, which mention year 55 (after 146 BC).

I swear by the gods for whom the mysteries are performed, to take care that the affairs of the ceremony are conducted devoutly and altogether justly, and not to do anything inappropriate or unlawful myself in the guest quarters of the mysteries or delegate to anyone else, but to obey the writings and administer the oath to the holy women and the priest according to the regulation.

See also Zijderveld's brief discussion of this inscription above, p. 83.

36 Honorary decree of the Achaeans found in the pronaos of the Despoina temple at Lycosura. *IG* V 2, 517. Late second or early third century AD. It is a posthumous honorary decree for Saon, son of Polycharmos, from Megalopolis, a hierophant of the Great Goddesses. Lines 8–9 mention that he was:

> γεγονὼς μὲν ἀπὸ τῶν πρώτως τὴν τελετὴν | τῶν Μεγάλων θεῶν παρὰ τοῖς Ἀρκάσι συστησαμένων ἱεροφαντῶν.

> a descendant of those who, as hierophants, first organized the ceremony of the Great Goddesses in Arcadia.

The *telete* established by Saon's forefathers was that of Arcadian Megalopolis. An important source for our study, since it independently confirms that the celebration of the mysteries at Megalopolis, which, according to Pausanias, were modelled after the Eleusinian mysteries, was indeed called a τελετή. Cf. Pausanias 8.31.7:

> καταστήσασθαι δὲ οὗτοι Μεγαλοπολίταις λέγονται πρῶτον τῶν Μεγάλων θεῶν τὴν τελετήν, καὶ τὰ δρώμενα τῶν Ἐλευσῖνί ἐστι μιμήματα.

> And they are said to have first founded the ceremony of the Great Goddesses for the Megalopolitans, and their rituals are an imitation of those at Eleusis.

37 Dedicatory epigram on an architrave block from Tomis. *I.Tomis* 120.[35] First century BC?[36] We present the full text.

> ἁγνὸν ὑπὲρ θιάσοιο πυρίβρομέ σοι τό[δ' ἄγαλμα]
> δῶρον ἀπὸ σφετέρας ὤπασεν ἐργ[ασίας]
> [μ]υστικὸν ἐμ βακχοῖσι λαχὼν στέφος [- ◡◡ - -]
> 4 Πάρμιδος, ἀρχαίην δεικνύμενος τ[ελετήν].

---

[35] Ed.pr. E. Reisch, *AEM* 11 (1887) 48–49 no. 60, with excellent commentary. See also Jaccottet, *Choisir Dionysos*, no. 62.
[36] Jaccottet.

ἀλλὰ σύ, ταυρόκερως, Ἑρμαγένεος χε[ρὸς ἔργον]
[δ]έξαι καὶ Πασοῦς σῶζε ἱερὸν θίασ[ον].

On behalf of the thiasos, [(*proper name*)], son of Parmis, gave you, fire-roaring, this hallowed statue as a gift from their own workmanship, having obtained the mystic wreath at the bacchanals, displaying the ancient ceremony. Now you, bull-horned, receive this work by the hand of Hermagenes and preserve Paso's sacred thiasos!

πυρίβρομος (line 1) is a rare epithet of Dionysus, cf. Nonn. *Dion.* 14.229 (πυρίβρομος Εἰραφιώτης); ταυρόκερως (line 5) is also an epithet of Dionysus, cf. Eur. *Bacch.* 100; *Hymn. Orph.* 52.2; Euphorion fr. 14 (Powell).

The restoration at the end of line 4 seems reasonably secure: δείκνυσθαι τελετήν is a standard expression of the mysteries, see above, p. 121. The words "mystic wreath at the bacchanals" show beyond any doubt that the *telete* was a ceremony performed in the context of a Bacchic mystery cult.

It is noteworthy that, while the thiasos evidently included men (the dedicant is a man: λαχών, not λαχοῦσα), it was apparently led by a woman.

38 Dedicatory epigram for Isia, from the island of Tenos. *IG* XII 5, 972. Second century AD (Hiller, letterforms). Isia is honoured for financing the completion of a building between the temples of Bacchus and Demeter (?). Lines 1–2:

θυσσάδος ἀγροτέρου Βρομ[ίου θέσαν εἰκόνα μύσται]
ἐν τελεταῖσιν Ἀγηνορίδ[αο ◡ - ◡◡ - -].[37]

Of this wild *thyssad* of Bromios the *mystai* (?) set up a statue (?) at the ceremonies of the Agenorid.

Thyssad is another word for thyiad or maenad (from θύσσειν = μαίνεσθαι).[38] The context is therefore clearly Bacchic. The existence of Dionysiac associations on Tenos is further evidenced by *IG* XII 5, 951 (Jaccottet, *Choisir Dionysos*, no. 162), which mentions τῶν τοῦ Διονύσου οἴ|κων (lines 9–10).

---

[37] Ἀγηνορίδ[ῶν, Kaibel; Ἀγηνορίδ[ων, Hiller; Ἀγηνορίδ[αο, Schuddeboom.
[38] See Erotianus, *Vocum Hippoc. collectio* s.v. θύσσειν: μαίνεσθαι, ὡς καὶ Ἀριστοφάνης ὁ γραμματικός.

At the end of the second line, one expects a genitive ending. Kaibel supplied -ιδῶν,[39] without explanation; Hiller substituted -ίδων,[40] "quia Maenades γενεῆς Εἰνοῦς ἄπο Καδμείης sunt (*Inschr. Magn.* 215)." While these readings appear to be epigraphically possible, they are problematic, because, as far as I am aware, a festival or rites of the Agenorids are not attested anywhere else. For this reason, I prefer to read Ἀγηνορίδ[αο: a genitive singular referring to the god Bacchus, who was, after all, a descendant of Agenor (compare e.g. Statius, *Achil.* 1.593: Lucus Agenorei sublimis ad orgia Bacchi | stabat).

39 Cult regulation from Amorgos concerning the cult of the Mother of the gods. *IG* XII 7, 237 (*LSCG* 103). First century BC. Lines b.11–12:

> ἐπὰν δὲ τελετὴν ποιῇ ἡ ἱέρεια, ὁ πέλαν[ος ὁ ἀποδι]|[12]δόμενος ὑπὸ τῶν τε[λ]ουμένων ἱε[ρὸ]ς ἔσ[τ]ω.

> When the priestess has performed the ritual, the *pelanos* paid by those who undergo the ritual shall fall to the goddess.

Without further specification, the *telete* presumably refers to the ritual of the Metroac mysteries. The *pelanos*, originally a cake, is here a sum of money.[41]

40 Dedicatory epigram on a round base from Cos, battered on the right.[42] Late third or early second century BC (letterforms). Lines 3, 8:

> ἐν τελεταῖς Δάμα[τρος - - - - - - - - - - -]

> in the rites of Demeter ...

> καὶ Κούραν νυχ[ίαις - - - - - ἐν τελεταῖς]

> and Kore in the nocturnal (rites).[43]

The 'rites' evidently refer to mysteries of Demeter, apparently celebrated on Cos ('land of the Meropes', line 1).

---

[39] Gen. pl. masc. (of Ἀγηνορίδης).
[40] Gen. pl. fem. (of Ἀγηνορίς).
[41] Cf. Ziehen in *RE* s.v. πέλανος, col. 250.
[42] Ed.pr. R. Herzog, *PhilWoch* 52 (1932) 1013–1017; cf. S. Sherwin-White, *Ancient Cos* (1978) 311, who discusses the inscription and reproduces the text in note 186.
[43] "Zu νυχ[ίαις kann wohl nur ἐν τελεταῖς ergänzt werden. So schließt in schöner und bedeutungsvoller Symmetrie das zweiletzte Distichon mit denselben Worten, mit denen das zweite begonnen hatte. Sie umhegen die Geheimfeier." Herzog, 1015.

41 Inscription on a pediment stele. *I.Didyma* 352. First or second century AD. There were mysteries connected to the oracle and cult of Apollo and Artemis at Didyma. Lines 2–10:

> ὑδροφόρος Ἀρ|τέμιδος Πυθίης |⁴ Συμφέρουσα Ἀπελ|λᾶ πάσας τὰς κατὰ |⁶ νόμον ἐπιτελέσα|σα τῇ θεῷ θυσίας |⁸ καὶ σπονδὰς καὶ τὰς | τῶν μυστηρίων τε|¹⁰λετὰς εὐσεβῶς.

> Hydrophoros of Artemis Pythia, Sympherousa daughter of Apellas, having performed all the prescribed sacrifices and libations and the rites of the mysteries religiously for the goddess.

Other hydrophoros inscriptions simply refer to the rites of the mysteries as τὰ μυστήρια.[44] Hydrophoroi were young priestesses, normally girls from noble families.[45] This was the highest office open to maidens at Didyma.[46]

42 Honorary decree for a gymnasiarch, found in a gymnasium in Pergamum. *IGR* IV 294.[47] The document dates from 138–133 BC (reign of Attalus III, lines 20, 39, 48). The gymnasiarch was apparently in charge of the performance of the mysteries for the Μεγάλοι θεοὶ Κάβειροι (line 6) and he ensured that the ephebes received their *myesis* on time (line 7). In line 8, we read that he did not allow the ephebes:

> τὰ πρὸς τὴν τελετὴν ἀνήκοντα παρ' ἑαυτῶν πάντα προσενε[γκεῖν].

> to contribute all the costs of the ceremony by themselves.

While the fragmentary state of the document does not allow for certainty, it seems likely that τελετή refers to the performance of the mysteries of the Megaloi Theoi.

43 Funerary epigram from Amastris (Pontus). *SEG* XXXV 1327.[48] It is dated 155 AD (225 of the Lucullan era, line 17). Lines 4–5:

> παρ' ἐμπύροις δὲ κῶμον Εὐίῳ Θεῷ | τριετῆρι τελετὴν μυστικῶς ἀνηγα-γον.

> I (Aemilianus) led the procession past the burnt sacrifices at the triennial festival for the god Euios (Dionysus) and led the ceremony like a *mystes*.

---

[44] *I.Didyma* 312, 326, 327, 329, 333, 360, 373, 381, 382.
[45] See L. Robert, *Hellenica* XI–XII (1960) 440, 463 ff.
[46] See J.B. Connelly, *Portrait of a Priestess* (2007) 40.
[47] Ed.pr. B. Schroeder, *AM* 1904, 152 no. 1 (*OGIS* 764).
[48] Ed.pr. C. Marek, *EA* 6 (1985) 137 no. 12.

So here, τελετή presumably refers to a mystery ceremony for Dionysus.

44 Funerary epigram on a limestone block from Patara (Lycia). *TAM* II 2, 418. Undated. It probably belonged to a grave monument (τύμβος, line 4). We present the full text.

> [- - - - - - - - - - - - - - - - - - - τα?] ῖς τελεταῖσιν *vacat*
> [- - - - - - - - - - - - - - - - - - - σ] ὺγ γαμέτῃ ᾧ *vacat*
> [- - - - - - - - - - - - - - νυμφε?] υτή[ϱ]ιος οἶκος *vacat*
> 4 [- - - - - - - - - - - - - - - - - - -] καὶ κλύε τῆς στήλης ὄντινα τύμβος ἔχει.
> [- - - - - - - - - - - - - - - - - - -] τὰς ἱεϱοφαντείους πϱαξάμενος τελετάς.

> ... at (?) the ceremonies ... with my husband, who ... the bridegroom's (?) house ... and hear from the stele whom the tomb holds ... having performed the ceremonies of the hierophant.

The reference to *hierophanteioi teletai* indicates a mystery rite.

45 Funerary epigram on a sarcophagus from Termessus (Pisidia). *TAM* III 922; G.E. Bean, *Belleten* 22 (1958) 71–73 no. 89, presents an improved text (*SEG* XVII 552). Third century AD. Line 10:

> καὶ Βάγχου τελετῶν πολυ[- ‿‿ - ‿‿ - -]

> and of the rites of Bacchus.

This refers to the mysteries of Dionysus. A shepherd's crook, symbol of the mysteries, is depicted on the left of the inscription.

46 Dedicatory inscription on a statue of Mithras Tauroktonos from Sidon, Syria. *SEG* LII 1591.[49] It is dated 390/1 AD (Sidonian era).[50]

> Φλ(άουιος) Γεϱόνιιος ᾳατὴϱ νόμιμος τῶν τελετῶν τοῦ θεοῦ εὐχαϱιστῶν ἀφιέϱωσα τῷ φ´ ἔτει.

> I, Fl(avius) Gerontius, *pater nomimos* of the ceremonies of the god, dedicated this thankfully in the year 500.

The *pater nomimos* was an official in the Mithras cult. The *teletai* can hardly be anything else than the Mithraic mysteries.

---

[49] A. de Ridder, *Catalogue de la collection Louis De Clerq IV. Les marbres, les vases peints et les ivoires* (1906) 59–60 no. 47; republished by F. Baratte in E. Gubel, *Art phénicien* (2002) 89–90 no. 81 (non vidi). Cf. also *CIMRM* I 74 no. 76. For a photograph, see *LIMC* VI s.v. Mithras, no. 166.

[50] Vermaseren incorrectly suggested a date of 188 AD (Seleucid era).

47 (= 53) Funerary epigram on the tomb of Vettius Agorius Praetextatus, from Rome. *CIL* VI 1779. From 384 AD (death of Vettius). On the back of the monument, Paulina speaks to her husband Vettius, lines D.13–15:

> sed ista parva, tu pius m⟨y⟩stes[51] sacris | teletis reperta mentis arcano premis | divumque numen multiplex doctus colis.

> But those things are trivial: you as a pious initiate keep hidden in the secrecy of your mind what was revealed in the sacred rites, and you worship the multifarious divinity of the gods like an expert.

On the front of the tomb, we read (A.5–7) that Vettius was, among other things, an initiate (*sacratus*) of Liber and the Eleusinian goddesses, hierophant, neocorus, and tauroboliatus. The *teletae* will therefore be the secret rites of the mysteries, including, but not limited to, those of Eleusis.

The word occurs again in line D.27 to indicate the taurobolium; see below, no. 53.

E. Taurobolium

In the next six inscriptions, all dating from the fourth century AD, τελετή refers to the remarkable rite of the *taurobolium*.

48 Dedicatory epigram on a taurobolic altar from Athens.[52] *IG* II² 4841. Fourth century AD. It was set up for Attis and Rhea as a thank-offering for the τελετή ταυροβόλος (line 3). Lines 9–12:

> δαδοῦχός με Κόρης βασιλ⟨ηί⟩δος[53] ἱερὰ σηκῶν |[10] Ἥρας κλεῖθρα φέρων βωμὸν ἔθηκε Ῥέῃ | Ἀρχέλεως, τελετῆς συνθήματα κρυπτὰ χαράξας |[12] ταυροβόλου, πρῶτον δεῦρο τελειομένης.

> As daduch, weighing the sacrificial victims of Queen Kore and carrying the door-bars of Hera, Archelaus dedicated this altar to Rhea, having engraved hidden signs of the taurobolium, performed here for the first time.

49 Dedicatory inscription on a taurobolic altar from Athens. *IG* II² 4842. From 386/7 AD (archonship of Hermogenes). The name of the goddess is not mentioned. Lines 3–8:

---

[51] MOVESTES stone, mason's error.

[52] For a general description of the two Athenian altars and photos (not of the inscriptions), see Kaltsas, *NMΓλυπτά*, 368–369 no. 784.

[53] ΒΑCΙΛΑΝΔΙΟC stone, mason's error.

ἀρχ(οντος) Ἑρμογένους ἐτελέσθη |⁴ ταυροβόλιον ἐν Ἀθήναις ὅ|περ
παραλαβὼν Μουσώνιος |⁶ ὁ λαμ(πρότατος) τῆς τελετῆς τὸ σύν|θημα
τὸν βωμὸν ἀναί|⁸θηκα.

When Hermogenes was archon, I was initiated into the taurobolium in
Athens and having undertaken that, I, the most illustrious Musonius,
dedicated this altar as the token of my initiation.

50 (= 77) Dedicatory epigram on a taurobolic altar from Rome. *IGUR* I 126.
Fourth century AD. The altar is dedicated to the Mother of gods by two
priests, Crescens and Leontius, lines 5–7:

ὄργια συνρέξαντε θεᾶι παμμήτορι Ῥείηι | κριοβόλου τελετῆς καὶ ταυ-
ροβόλοιο φερίστης | αἵμασι μυστιπόλοις βωμὸν ὑπερτίθεσαν.

(who), having performed together the rites of the most excellent criobolium and taurobolium ceremony for the goddess Rhea, mother of all,
dedicated this altar where they shed blood as initiates.

51 (= 70) Dedicatory epigram on a taurobolic altar from Rome. *IGUR* I 128.
From 377 AD (consul names in lines 12–13). The altar is dedicated to Attis
and Rhea. Lines 1–11:

σύνβολον εὐ|²αγέων τελετῶν | ἀνέθηκε Σαβῖνα |⁴ Ἄττει καὶ Ῥείῃ βω|μὸν
ἀγηράσιον, |⁶ Λαμπαδίου θυγα|τὴρ μεγαλήτο|⁸ρος, ὄργια Δηοῦς | καὶ
φοβερὰς Ἑκά|¹⁰της νύκτας ἐπι|σταμένη.

As a symbol of the very sacred rites, Sabina, daughter of great-hearted
Lampadius, dedicated this un-aging altar to Attis and Rhea, knowing the
mysteries of Deo (Demeter) and the fearful nights of Hecate.

52 Dedicatory epigram on a taurobolic altar from Rome. *IGUR* I 129. From
370 AD (consul names in line 13). The altar is dedicated to Rhea and Attis
by a priest of Mithras. Lines 4–6:

κριοβόλου τελετῆς ἠ[δ᾽ ἔτι τ]αυροβόλου | μυστιπόλος τελετῶν [ἱερῶν
ἀ]νεθήκατο βωμὸν, | δῶρον Ἀπόλλωνος [τοὔνομ᾽] ἔχων ἐπίκλην.

As an initiate in the sacred rites, the rite of the criobolium and taurobolium, he dedicated this altar, using the name *Doron Apollonos* ('Gift
of Apollo') as a nickname.

Line 6 ἐπίκλην: the dedicant's actual name is Apollodorus (line 7), which
does not fit the metre.

53 (= 47) Funerary epigram on the tomb of Vettius Agorius Praetextatus,
from Rome. *CIL* VI 1779. From 384 AD. Paulina addresses her husband,
Vettius, in lines D.25–29:

te teste cunctis imbuor mysteriis, |²⁶ tu Dindymenes Atteosqu⟨e⟩⁵⁴ anti-
stitem | teletis honoras taureis consors pius |²⁸ Hecates ministram trina
secreta edoces | Cererisque Graiae tu sacris dignam paras.

With you as my witness, I am introduced to all the mysteries; you, my pious
consort, honour me as priestess of Dindymene (Cybele) and Attis with the
rites of the taurobolium; you instruct me in the threefold secret as minister
of Hecate and you make me worthy of the rites of Greek Ceres.

On the front of the monument, Paulina is called initiate (*sacrata*) of Ceres
and the Eleusinian mysteries, initiate of Hecate at Aegina, tauroboliata
and hierophantria (lines A.20–22).

F. Goddess

54 The famous sacrificial calendar of the Marathonian Tetrapolis. *IG* II²
1358 (*LSCG* 20). First half fourth century BC. See also S.D. Lambert, *ZPE*
130 (2000) 43–70, who presents a new text with extensive line-by-line
commentary (*SEG* L 168). A.II.10:

Τελετῆι σπυΔια: ΔΔΔΔ *vacat*

For Telete: (an offering); 40 drachmas.

The most attractive reading for σπυΔια is perhaps σπυ⟨ρί⟩δια (baskets).⁵⁵ In this context, Lambert also draws attention to the appearance of
a basket on the relief from Cynuria (see above, no. 3); the parallel is prob-
lematic, however, since the inscription on that relief is generally regarded
to be secondary and most likely refers to the scene rather than the deity.

55 A round altar, found in the sanctuary of Demeter at Pergamum, is
dedicated to Nyx, Telete and the Automaton.⁵⁶ Second century AD. The
inscription reads:

Νυκτὶ καὶ Τελετῆι |² καὶ τῶι Αὐτομάτωι | Κλαυδία Τελεσφοριανία |⁴
ὑμνήτρια κατ' ὄναρ.

To Nyx and Telete and to the Automaton, Claudia Telesphoriania, singer
of hymns, in accordance with a dream.

---

⁵⁴ ATTEOSQUI stone, mason's error.
⁵⁵ Suggested by S. Sölders, *Die außerstädtischen Kulte und die Einigung Attikas* (Diss.
Lund 1931) 70 (non vidi): see Lambert ad locum.
⁵⁶ Ed.pr. H. Hepding, *AM* 35 (1910) 457–459 no. 40; cf. Robert, *OMS* VII, 573.

Fig. 1. Mosaic from Zeugma, featuring Telete, Dionysus and Skirtos.
Photograph courtesy of Dr. Mehmet Önal, Gaziantep Museum.

Claudia had apparently had quite an interesting dream that inspired
her to dedicate an altar to Night, Rite and Spontaneous Chance.[57] Robert's
proposal that Claudia was perhaps a singer of Orphic hymns is interesting, though the evidence is inconclusive.

56 A mosaic from Zeugma (Commagene),[58] late second or early third century AD, shows Telete, Dionysus and Skirtos (see Fig. 1). The three figures
are identified by name inscriptions (Τελετή, Διόνυσος, Σκίρτος).

The mosaic features the familiar scene of drunk Dionysus. The young,
beardless god stands in the middle with bare upper body. A blue and yellow garment hangs from his back and folds around the hips to cover his
legs. His head, crowned with a diadem, is surrounded by a blue nimbus.
He is supported by Skirtos, a satyr boy wearing a panther skin.[59] Another
animal skin swings from the boy's left upper arm. To the left stands Telete,
dressed in a blue chiton with a yellow robe draped around her hips. Her
hair is wreathed with ivy and in her right hand she holds a thyrsus with
a snake coiled around the upper part. The poses of the figures and the
shadow cast by Skirtos give the scene an air of three-dimensionality.

---

[57] For *kat'onar* inscriptions, see F.T. van Straten, *BABesch* 51 (1976) 1–38.
[58] Ed.pr. M. Önal, Rescue Excavations in Belkıs/Zeugma: The Dionysos Room and the
Pit below its Mosaic Floor, *DM* 13 (2002) 318–319, with Pl. 45–46.
[59] Skirtos is also found in the merry thiasos in the mosaic from Sheikh Zouède (*SEG*
XXIV 1197), see above, no. 17.

57 Another mosaic from Zeugma, *SEG* XLVIII 1832,[60] second or third
century AD, shows a badly damaged figure, beside which is an inscription
ΤΕΛΕΓΕ. Feissel wondered if we should read τελεταί. I would prefer to
read ΤΕΛΕΤΕ as a mistake (or alternative spelling) for ΤΕΛΕΤΗ. Ergeç et
al. mention the mosaic in passing: "Dionysos mit seiner Tochter Telete
umgeben von den Vier Jahreszeiten." If this new interpretation is correct,
we have here a second pictorial representation of the goddess Telete from
the town of Zeugma.

Conclusion

In inscriptions, the word τελετή appears in a variety of meanings. For
example, it can be used for the rites surrounding the private dedication
of an altar, but it can also refer to a public festival of Artemis at which 120
cattle were sacrificed. Just as in the literary sources, the term is frequently
used for the rite or the festival of the mysteries.

A clear development of the meaning cannot be discerned. Our oldest extant inscription, no. 23, uses the word for the ceremony of the
Eleusinian mysteries. The only other inscription from the classical period
is no. 54, the sacrificial calendar of the Marathonian tetrapolis, where
Telete is a goddess, who receives 40 drachmas worth of offerings.

The term can denote very different religious rituals and ceremonies:
public religious ceremonies in which the ephebes participate (no. 2);
an offering (no. 3); special rites surrounding the private dedication of
a funerary altar (no. 15); the thiasos of Dionysus (no. 17). In the sacred
laws from Cos, the word pertains to the consecration of priests (nos. 6–
14). It is unclear which ritual or ceremony is meant in nos. 1 and 5.

In no. 4, the god Pan is called τελετάρχης, 'leader of the ceremony'. Cf.
Silenus in *Hymn. Orph.* 54.4.

The word τελετή is used for festivals of several gods and goddesses:
Artemis (no. 22); Enodia (no. 19); Athena (no. 21; perhaps also D10);[61]
Antinous (no. 18); an unidentified god (no. 20).

---

[60] Ed.pr. R. Ergeç in D. Kennedy (ed.), *The twin towns of Zeugma on the Euphrates*
(1998) 89 (D. Feissel, BE 1999, no. 553; *SEG* XLVIII 1832); unfortunately, the mosaic is
not discussed in S. Campbell's chapter on new mosaics in the same book. Cf. R. Ergeç,
M. Önal and J. Wagner in J. Wagner (ed.), *Gottkönige am Euphrat* (2000) 108.

[61] See below, Appendix A.

It denotes the special rite of the mysteries of Eleusis (nos. 23, 26–34). The expression 'τελετὴ τῶν μυστηρίων', apparently referring to the whole festival, is found in no. 25 (probably also no. 24).

The word refers to the rite of mysteries modelled on those of Eleusis: Andania (no. 35); Megalopolis (no. 36); Cos (no. 40).

It is used for the rites of Dionysian and other mystery cults: Dionysus (nos. 37, 43, 45; probably also 38; perhaps also D8);[62] Mother of the gods (no. 39); Megaloi Theoi (no. 42); Mithras (no. 46); Artemis Pythia (no. 41); an unknown deity (no. 44); various gods (no. 47). The word is also used for the special ritual of the Taurobolium (nos. 48–53).

Finally, Telete occurs personified as a goddess several times (nos. 54–56; perhaps also no. 57).

---

[62] See below, Appendix A.

CHAPTER TWELVE

THE USE OF ΟΡΓΙΑ IN INSCRIPTIONS

The uses of ΟΡΓΙΑ in inscriptions can be categorized as follows:

A. Dionysiac rites
B. Eleusinian mysteries
C. Other religious rites
D. Rites in a metaphorical sense
E. Cult regulations
F. Cult objects
G. Epithet for Isis

Within these categories, I have arranged the inscriptions geographically according to their place of origin.

A. Dionysiac rites

58 Bacchic gold leaf from Pherae (Thessaly). Graf & Johnston, *Ritual Texts for the Afterlife* (2007) 38 no. 28.[1] Late fourth or early third century BC (letterforms). The text reads:

πέμπε με πρὸς μυστῶ⟨ν⟩ θιάσους· ἔχω ὄργια [σεμνὰ]
Δήμητρος Χθονίας ⟨τε⟩ τέλη καὶ Μητρὸς Ὀρεί[ας].[2]

Send me to the thiasoi of the initiates: I have the solemn rites and rituals of Underworld Demeter and the Mountain Mother.

---

[1] Edd.pr. R. Parker & M. Stamatopoulou, *ArchEph* 2004 [2007] 1–32. See also F. Ferrari & L. Prauscello, *ZPE* 162 (2007) 193–202; Bernabé & Jiménez San Cristóbal, *Instructions for the Netherworld* (2008) no. L13a. For the Bacchic/Orphic gold leaves in general, Graf & Johnston (2007) and Bernabé & Jiménez (2008) should be read in conjunction: Bernabé & Jiménez for their critical text edition, thematic arrangement, and extensive commentary per tablet; Graf & Johnston for a better restoration of the Pelinna texts, better translations, a geographical arrangement, and excellent contextualization of this difficult and elusive group of texts.
[2] μυστωχ lamella, scribe's error; [Βάκχου] (end of line 1) contemplated and rejected by edd.pr. (who prefer ἰδοῦσα), adopted nonetheless by subsequent editors but strongly and convincingly rejected by Ferrari & Prauscello; [σεμνὰ] offered as a possibility by edd.pr., preferred by F. Ferrari, *BMCR* 2007.10.15; ⟨τε⟩ τέλη καὶ edd.pr.; τελ⟨έσαι⟩ καὶ Ferrari & Prauscello, which is unnecessary and perhaps too ingenious.

This message is evidently addressed to Persephone, cf. two of the Thurii tablets,[3] where the deceased comes to Persephone as a suppliant: ὥς με πρόφρων πέμψηι ἕδρας ἐς εὐαγέων: "so that she may gladly send me to the seats of the pure."

For the expression ὄργια σεμνὰ ἔχειν, cf. Aeschylus fr. 57 N²: σεμνὰ Κοτυτοῦς ὄργι' ἔχοντες.

Bernabé and Jiménez identify ὄργια as sacred symbols (cf. Theoc. *Id.* 26.13, above). Graf and Johnston, on the other hand, have the more common translation 'rituals'. While there is something to be said for either interpretation, I believe the latter is to be preferred, given the juxtaposition of ὄργια and τέλη.

The mention of τέλη here recalls the last verse of the longer Pelinna tablet:[4] κἀπ⟨ι⟩μέν|ει σ' ὑπὸ | γῆν τέ|λεα ἄσ⟨σ⟩α|περ ὄλ|βιοι ἄλ|λοι: "Below the earth, rites await you just as the other blessed ones (have them)."

The medium of a gold leaf and the reference to thiasoi of *mystai* indicate that these rites of Demeter Chthonia[5] and Meter Oreia were presumably celebrated in the context of a Bacchic-Orphic mystery cult.

59 (= D8) Dedicatory epigram by a Dionysiac association, from Halicarnassus. *SEG* XXVIII 841.[6] Second or first century BC. Lines 5–6:

καὶ σιγᾶν ὅ τι κρυπτὸν ἐπιστάμενος καὶ ἀυτεῖν | ὅσσα θέμις, στείχηις ὄργια ταῦτα μαθών.

and that, knowing to be silent about what is hidden and to proclaim as much as is permitted, you may go having learnt those rites.

The text clearly refers to the mysteries of Dionysus, which were prevalent in Asia Minor.[7]

---

[3] Graf & Johnston, *Ritual Texts*, 14 no. 6–7 (Bernabé & Jiménez L10a–b).

[4] Graf & Johnston, *Ritual Texts*, 36 no. 26a (alii alia, cf. Bernabé & Jiménez L7a).

[5] Incidentally, the epithet Chthonia ('of the netherworld') is not surprising here, given the aim of these rites to ensure a better fate in the afterlife; Demeter's daughter is called Kore Chthonia in Thurii tablet L12.

[6] See also Jaccottet, *Choisir Dionysos*, no. 152.

[7] See W. Quandt, *De Baccho ab Alexandri aetate in Asia Minore cultu* (Diss. Halle 1923); M.P. Nilsson, *The Dionysiac Mysteries of the Hellenistic and Roman Age* (1957) 8–10.

60 (= D15) Regulation concerning the cult of Dionysus, from Miletus. *LSAM* 48.[8] 276/5 BC (Poseidippus stephanephoros, line 10). Lines 13–15:

[-----] δὲ τὴν ἱέρειαν γυναῖκας διδόναι Δ∷ΙΝΛ[-----] | [----- τ]ὰ δὲ τέλεστρα {καὶ τελεστ} παρέχ[ειν ταῖς] | [γυναιξὶν] ἐν τοῖς ὀργί[οις πᾶ]σιν.

The priestess shall give the women … and supply the *telestra* to the women in all the rites.

The *telestra* are 'things needed for the ceremony'.[9] What rites are intended was perhaps specified in the lost line preceding line 13. It is noteworthy that, while both men and women could sacrifice to Dionysus (line 5), apparently only women were allowed participate in the *orgia*.

61 Marble slab from Magnesia on the Maeander. *I.Magnesia* 215.[10] Inscribed first or second century AD (the original document may be older). Lines 27–30 instruct the Magnesians to fetch maenads from Thebes:

αἳ δ᾽ ὑμεῖν δώσουσι καὶ |[28] ὄργια καὶ νόμιμα ἐσθλὰ ᵛ καὶ θιά|σους Βάκχοιο καθειδρύσουσιν |[30] ἐν ἄστει.

They will give you rites and noble customs and will establish thiasoi of Bacchus in the city.

So the *orgia* are contrasted here with other customs and with thiasoi in the city.

62 Decree of a Dionysiac association on a pediment stele from Teos. *SEG* IV 598.[11] Late first century BC. Line 19 mentions ὄργια:

καὶ ὄργια [π]αγτὸς ἱερο[ῦ] τοῦ Διονύσου κατοιχομένου ἔτους.

and *orgia* of every sanctuary of Dionysus of the past year.

So the inscription refers to the *orgia* of the various sanctuaries of Dionysus. The addition "of the past year" suggests that these *orgia* were rites (as opposed to sacred objects).

---

[8] See also Jaccottet, *Choisir Dionysos*, no. 150.
[9] Cf. Sokolowski: "les choses nécessaires pour la cérémonie de l'initation".
[10] See also Jaccottet, *Choisir Dionysos*, no. 146.
[11] *GIBM* IV, 1032; not included in Jaccottet, *Choisir Dionysos*.

63 Funerary epigram of a boy, on a square marble slab from Rome. *IGUR* III 1228.[12] First or second century AD. Lines 6–10:

ἑπτὰ | μόνους λυκάβαντας δύω |[8] καὶ μῆνας ἔζησα ὧν τρεῖς | ἐξετέλουν Διονύσῳ ὄργια βά|[10]ζων.

I lived only seven years and two months, of which I spent three (years) saying mysteries for Dionysus.

Symbols associated with the Dionysiac mysteries are incised at the four corners of the stone: bell, whip, head of a maenad, shepherd's crook (καλαῦροψ). This monument is an interesting testimony that children could participate in the mysteries of Dionysus.[13] The combination ὄργια βάζειν is noteworthy.

64 Dedication to Liber Pater, from Puteoli. *CIL* X 1583.[14] Probably reign of Septimius Severus.[15]

Libero Patri |[2] sacrum | TT(iti) Flavii Ecle|[4]ctianus et Olym-pianus fil(ius) eius sacerdotes orgiophantae.

Dedicated to Liber Pater. Titus Flavius Eclectianus and his son, Titus Flavius Olympianus, priests and orgiophants.

65 Inscription found in the passageway of the Flavian amphitheatre at Puteoli. *AnÉp* 1956, 138.[16] Roman imperial period.[17]

Schola org[iophantarum].

Corporation of the orgiophants.

Maiuri's restoration is convincing: the presence of orgiophants at Puteoli is attested by our previous inscription. Moreover, it would be difficult to find another Latin word starting with *org-* that would fit as well with *schola*. It is interesting, though, that the orgiophants would have an office in the amphitheatre.

---

[12] See also Jaccottet, *Choisir Dionysos*, no. 186.
[13] Cf. also *IGUR* III 1169, discussed by W. Burkert, *Ancient Mystery Cults* (1987) 28.
[14] See also Jaccottet, *Choisir Dionysos*, no. 172.
[15] Cf. *CIL* X 1585.
[16] Ed.pr. A. Maiuri, *MemNap* 3 (1955) 52–53, who, mixing up his declensions, printed org[iophantorum.
[17] Maiuri dates it to the second half of the second century AD (letterforms and stylistic reasons).

B. Mysteries of Eleusis

66 (= 32) Marble block from Eleusis. *IG* II² 3639. From 192 AD or shortly after. See now Clinton, *I.Eleusis*, no. 515. Lines 3–4 praise the hierophant:

> ὃς τελετὰς ἀνέφηνε καὶ ὄργια πάννυχα μύσταις
>   Εὐμόλπου προχέων ἱμερόεσσαν ὄπα.

who displayed the rites and the all-night mysteries to the *mystai*, pouring forth the charming voice of Eumolpus.

67 (= 33) Round base from Eleusis. *IG* II² 3411. Probably ca. 192 AD. See now Clinton, *I.Eleusis*, no. 516. Lines 4–6:

> ὄργια καὶ ψυχὴν ἐξεσάωσε πάτρῃ,
> καὶ τελετὰς ἀπέφηνε καὶ ἤρατο κῦδος ὅμοιον
>   Εὐμόλπῳ πινυτῷ καὶ Κελεῷ ζαθέωι.

He saved the mysteries and his life for the fatherland and displayed the rites and elevated their glory like wise Eumolpus and very divine Celeus.

68 Round base from Eleusis. *IG* II² 3661. Ca. 235 AD (after the death of the hierophant). See now Clinton, *I.Eleusis*, no. 646 with Pl. 296 (ph. stone). Lines 3–4:

> ὄργια πᾶσιν ἔφαινε βροτοῖς φαεσίμβροτα Δηοῦς
>   εἰνάετες, δεκάτῳ δ᾽ ἦλθε πρὸς ἀθανάτους.

For nine years, he displayed to all mortals the light-bringing mysteries of Deo (Demeter), and in the tenth he went to the immortals.

In other words, Glaucus was hierophant of the Eleusinian mysteries for nine years and then he died.

69 Philodamus' Paean to Dionysus.[18] Delphi. Ca. 340/39 BC (archonship of Etymondas). Lines 20–23 of the inscription (verses 32–36 of the paean):

> [ἔθνος ἔνθ᾽] ἅπαν Ἑλλάδος γᾶς ἀ[μφ᾽ ἐ]ννaέταις | [φίλοις] ἐπ[όπ]ταις
> ὀργίων ὁσί[ων ᾽Ια]κχον |²² [κλείει σ]ε, βροτοῖς πόνων ὦιξ[ας δ᾽ ὅρ]μον
> | [ἄμοχθον].

---

[18] Ed.pr. H. Weil, *BCH* 19 (1895) 393–418. I have used the edition of B.L. Rainer, reproduced by A. Stewart in *Macedonia and Greece in Late Classical and Early Hellenistic Times* (B. Barr-Sharrar & E.N. Borza eds. 1982) 216–220, with bibliography at 224 n. 49 (*SEG* XXXII 552).

There every people of Hellas' land, around inhabitants dear to *epoptai* of
the sacred mysteries, calls you Iacchus, and to mortals you revealed a haven
from toils, free from troubles.

The rites in question are, of course, the Eleusinian mysteries. Lines 29–30
locate the scene at "the flowery vales of Eleusis".

70 (= 51) Dedicatory epigram on a taurobolic altar from Rome. *IGUR* I 128.
From 377 AD. The altar is dedicated to Attis and Rhea. Lines 1–11.

> σύνβολον εὐ|²αγέων τελετῶν | ἀνέθηκε Σαβῖνα |⁴ Ἄττει καὶ Ῥείῃ βω|μὸν
> ἀγηράσιον, |⁶ Λαμπαδίου θυγα|τὴρ μεγαλήτο|⁸ρος, ὄργια Δηοῦς | καὶ
> φοβερὰς Ἑκά|¹⁰της νύκτας ἐπι|σταμένη.

As a symbol of the very sacred rites, Sabina, daughter of great-hearted
Lampadius, dedicated this un-aging altar to Attis and Rhea, knowing the
mysteries of Deo (Demeter) and the fearful nights of Hecate.

Without further specification, the mysteries of Demeter presumably refer
to Eleusis. Apparently, Sabina had been initiated into the Eleusinian
mysteries as well as in the cult of Hecate on Aegina before undergoing
the taurobolium.[19]

The following inscription concerns the mysteries of Demeter and Kore at
Miletus. The festival was presumably one of the many imitations of the
mysteries of Eleusis.

71 Marble block found near Miletus. *I.Didyma* 496. Second century AD.
See also W. Peek, *ZPE* 7 (1971) 207–208 no. 8, who gives several new
restorations of the text. B.10–11:

> τοῖσι γὰρ εὐγενίης ζαθέης ἔτι σύμβολα, ῥέζ[ειν]²⁰ | Δηοῦς καὶ κούρης
> Δηωΐδος ὄργια τῇδε.

For to them, it is still a token of very divine nobility to perform the
mysteries of Deo (Demeter) and Deo's daughter here.

Rehm considered the rites of the Thesmophoria, because the priestess
on side A is the priestess of Demeter Thesmophoros. Peek, on the other
hand, restored at the beginning of line 14: [ὄργια τ' Εὐ]μόλποιο: "rites
of Eumolpus". The restoration of the name, Eumolpus, is convincing and
points to an Eleusinian context. Since the inscription specifies that the

---

[19] Cf. the initiations of Paulina, above, no. 53.
[20] ῥέζ̣[ει], Rehm; ῥέζ̣[ειν], Peek.

mysteries are performed here on the spot, however, it presumably refers to a local imitation of the Eleusinian mysteries.

C. Other religious rites

72 Dedication to Zeus Dionysus Gongylus, from the Serapeion at Thessalonica. *IG* X 2.1 259.[21] First century AD. Lines 11–14:

> ὀμνύντων τῶν τε νῦν καὶ |[12] τῶν ἐσομένων μυστῶν τὸν θεὸν καὶ τὰ ὄργια | καὶ τὸ μεσανύκτιον ἄρτου διαφυλάξειν τὴν |[14] ἐπάνο θρησκήαν κατὰ τὴν δόσιν.

> Present and future initiates shall swear by the god and the rites and the midnight ceremony of bread, that they shall observe the above religious worship in accordance with the gift.

The cult of Zeus Dionysus Gongylus is not attested elsewhere. Presumably, it was a local phenomenon, connected to the mysteries of Sarapis at Thessalonica.

73 Dedicatory epigram for Vera, hydrophoros of Artemis Patmia. From Patmos. *SEG* XXXIX 855.[22] Third or fourth century AD. Lines 12–15:

> νῦν δ' ἐρατὴ Βήρα, θυγάτηρ σοφοῦ ἰητῆρος | Γλαυκ⟨ί⟩εω, βουλαῖς Ἀρτέμιδος Σκυθίης |[14] Αἰγαίου πλ⟨ώ⟩σασα ῥόου δυσχείμερον οἶδ⟨μ⟩α, | ὄργια κ(αὶ) θαλίην, ⟨ὡ⟩ς θέμις, ἠγλάϊσεν.[23]

> Now lovely Vera, daughter of the wise physician Glaucias, sailed the very wintry Aegean Sea at the behest of Scythian Artemis and made splendid the rites and the festival, as is fitting.

Apparently, Vera made the trip from Patmos to Didyma in order to help organize the mysteries of Artemis there. For these mysteries, see also *I.Didyma* 352.[24]

---

[21] Corrected by G. Daux, *CRAI* (1972) 478–487 (*SEG* XXX 622). See also Jaccottet, *Choisir Dionysos*, no. 19.

[22] See also E. Samama, *Les médecins dans le monde grec* (2003) 270–271 no. 155. We cannot use the text of *SEG* XXXIX 855, who reproduce a text of T. Grüll (1987) (non vidi), because it is riddled with mistakes (inter alia, incorrect use of brackets). I have therefore based my text on W. Peek, *RhM* 104 (1964) 315–325 (with ph. facing page 317).

[23] Line 14: ΠΛΟοΣΑΣΑ stone, mason's error; οἶδμα, Peek, but M is shaped like H; line 15: οΣ, mason's error.

[24] See above, no. 41.

74 Regulation concerning the sale of the priesthood of the Corybantes, from Erythrae (Ionia). *I.Erythrai* 206 (*LSAM* 23).[25] Late fourth century BC. Lines 1–4:

> ὁ πριάμενος καὶ ἡ πρι[αμένη τὴν ἱερ]|²ητείην τῶγ Κυρβάντων [ἱερήσεται κ]|αὶ τῶι ὀργίωι τῶι Ἔρσης [καὶ ......]|⁴όρης καὶ Φανίδος.

> He or she who buys the priesthood of the Corybantes shall also act as priest (or: assist)[26] in the ritual of Herse and -ore and Phanis.

We see a rare attestation of ὄργιον in the singular here. The priest or priestess of the Corybantes must also tend to the ritual of three other deities. Herse ('Dew') also appears in an inscription from Erythrae, which honours the priestess of Demeter Thesmophoros and Herse.[27] This Erythraean goddess is probably not the daughter of Cecrops in the famous story about Erichthonios. The second deity cannot be identified with certainty.[28] The third goddess, Phanis, is not attested elsewhere.

75 Marble base from Lagina (Caria). *I.Stratonikeia* 541.[29] Second half second century AD.[30] Lines 1–3:

> ὁ δῆμος καὶ αἱ βουλαὶ καὶ ἡ γερουσία | Ἡραῖον ἱερέα Μυωνίδην ὀργιο-φάντην, | πατροκασιγνήτην ἄλοχον σεμνήν τε Τρύφαινα[ν].

> The people and the councils and the *gerousia* (council of elders) (honour) the Heraea priest, orgiophant Myonides, and his cousin and devout wife, Tryphaina.

So, in addition to performing priestly duties at the Heraea, Myonides was an orgiophant, a displayer of rites, presumably at the famous sanctuary of Hecate at Lagina. Line 4 mentions that Myonides and his wife had been wreathed there by Hecate.[31]

76 Square limestone altar found near Tlos (Lycia). *TAM* II 646. Undated. We present the whole text.

---

[25] See also B. Dignas, *EA* 34 (2002) 29–40; P. Herrmann, *Chiron* 32 (2002) 165–167.

[26] [παραστήσετ]|αι, Wilamowitz, followed by Sokolowski.

[27] *I.Erythrai* 69, lines 3–5: ἱέρειαν Δ[ή]|[μη]τρος θεσμοφόρ[ου καὶ] | [Ἔρ]σης.

[28] J. Keil, *JÖAI* 13 (1910) 29, followed by Sokolowski, restored [καὶ Φανναγ]|όρης (cf. *I.Erythrai* 61, line 23).

[29] See also J.H. Oliver, *The Sacred Gerusia* (1941) 152–153 no. 39.

[30] The priest, Myonides, was a contemporary of Marcus Aurelius, see A. Laumonier, *BCH* 61 (1937) 280–282.

[31] At the beginning of this line, I read ἡ δ' with Oliver.

[.......]ς πο|²λυδαίδαλος | καὶ πάντων ἐτὲ|⁴ρος καὶ μακά|ρων ὄργια σε|
⁶μνὰ τελέσσας | Γηράσιμος πι|⁸νυτόφρων ἐν|θάδε κεῖμε |¹⁰ πεντήκον|
[τα ἐτῶν].

Very skilful and friend of all, having performed the solemn rites of the
blessed, I, wise-minded Gerasimus lie here, fifty years old.

It is unclear to what rites the inscription refers. I do not know of any
mystery cult at Tlos, but the reference to μάκαροι is evocative of a
mystery religion. The combination ὄργια σεμνά appears several times
in literature, see our commentary to Ar. *Thesm.* 1151.

77 (= 50) Dedicatory epigram on a taurobolic altar from Rome. *IGUR* I 126.
Fourth century AD. The altar is dedicated to the Mother of the gods by
two priests, Crescens and Leontius, lines 5–7:

ὄργια συνρέξαντε θεᾶι παμμήτορι Ῥείηι | κριοβόλου τελετῆς καὶ ταυ-
ροβόλοιο φερίστης | αἵμασι μυστιπόλοις βωμὸν ὑπερτίθεσαν.

(who), having performed together the rites of the most excellent criobolium and taurobolium ceremony for the goddess Rhea, mother of all,
dedicated this altar where they shed blood as initiates.

This passage clearly shows that the ὄργια are the actual rituals, while
τελετή refers to the religious occasion on which they were performed.

D. Metaphorical use

78 Three-sided tripod base (the 'Sarapion monument') from Athens. *SEG*
XXVIII 225.³² Second century AD. Front, lines 20–24:

[τοῦνε]κα τοῖς ἀπόφαμι θε[όφροσιν ἠδ'] ἀβεβάλοις | [-----]ας τε γαμ
|----- ἰ]ητῆρες |²² |----- ο]ιο κα[ὶ] ὄργια μὴ [ταχ]ὺ λάθην | [-------]
αὐτά τοι ἀ[ρή]γει |²⁴ [...]ασ[-----]ς τέκος, αὖθ[ι] δὲ τέχνα.

Therefore I declare to the godly minded and the pure ... and ... healers
... and sacred rites not perchance secretly to ... this helps ... child ... and
again art.³³

---

³² Ed.pr. P. Maas, *Bulletin of the History of Medicine* 7 (1939) 321–323. See also
E. Samama, *Les médecins dans le monde grec* (2003) 128–130 no. 22; the document is also
included in D. Geagan, *Athenian Agora* XVIII, *Inscriptions: The Dedicatory Monuments*
(forthcoming).
³³ Trans. J.H. Oliver, *Bulletin of the History of Medicine* 7 (1939) 320.

The text describes the duties of a physician, which are likened to sacred acts. Oliver[34] observed: "It was a commonplace in ancient writing to speak of medical work as a divine service and of physicians and their prescriptions as holy and godlike [...], while the training of a physician was represented as an initiation into sacred rites (ὄργια)."

79 Herm of Menander, from Rome. *IGUR* IV 1526. Late second or third century AD. Lines 2–3:

> [οὐ φθόνος ἦ]ν στῆσαι σὺν Ἔρωτι φίλῳ σε, Μένανδ[ρε]
> [οὗ ζώων γ'] ἐτέλεις ὄργια τερπνὰ θεοῦ.

> It was not invidious to set you up with your beloved Eros, Menandros, since you performed this god's delectable rites while alive.

Presumably, these ὄργια do not refer to Menander's own love life (of which we know nothing), but rather to the recurring love theme in his comedies. Love always played a role in Menander's plays.[35] Cf. also Plutarch, *De Amore* 1 (fr. 134 Sandbach), who calls Menander: μάλιστα θιασώτης τοῦ θεοῦ καὶ ὀργιαστής: "very much a devotee of the god (Eros) and an initiate in his cult."

E. Cult regulations

80 Marble stele from Miletus, containing the Orgia of the Molpoi. *LSAM* 50. Late second century BC. Lines 4–5:

> ἔδοξε μολποῖσιν τὰ ὄργια ἀναγράψαντας θεῖναι ἐς | τὸ ἱερὸν καὶ χρῆ-
> σθαι τούτοισιν.

> The Molpoi have decided to inscribe their *orgia* and set them up in the sanctuary and apply them.

Here we have a rare occurrence of *orgia* in the sense of cult regulations. The Molpoi were a religious association, responsible for the singing (μέλπειν, ἡ μολπή) in the cult of Apollo. They decided to publish their *orgia*, which are, in fact, regulations concerning the administration and religious responsibilities of the Molpoi.[36]

---

[34] Ibid. 318–319.
[35] See *OCD*³ s.v. Menander (1).
[36] See Lupu, *NGSL* 102.

F. Cult objects

81 Funerary epigram on a base from Miletus. Peek, *GV* 1344.[37] Third or second century BC. Lines 3–4:

> ὑμᾶς κεῖς ὄρος ἦγε καὶ ὄργια πάντα καὶ ἱρὰ | ἤνεικεμ πάσης ἐρχομένη πρὸ πόλεως.

> She led you to the mountains and carried all *orgia* and sacred things, going for the sake of (or: before?) the whole city.

The subject is a woman named Alcmeionis from Rhodes (lines 5–6); the context is Bacchic (βάκχαι in line 1). Since it is said of the ὄργια and ἱερά that they are carried, it appears that they refer here to cult objects rather than rites.[38]

The preposition πρό is ambiguous: it probably means that Alcmeionis led the thiasos *for* the city, but alternatively, it could mean that she went *before* the whole city. The thought of the whole city going up into the mountains, however, seems an unlikely hyperbole.[39]

G. Epithet for Isis

Finally, we should mention two rare occurrences of Ὀργία (nom. sing. fem.) as an epithet of Isis.

82 Lower part of a marble column from Cenchreae (Corinthia). *SEG* XXVIII 387.[40] Roman imperial period.

> Ὀργία

> (Isis) Orgia.

Scranton's plausible identification of Ὀργία as an epithet for Isis is based on our following inscription. The epithet has not been attested in combination with another deity's name.

---

[37] See also Jaccottet, *Choisir Dionysos*, no. 149.
[38] See also A. Henrichs, *ZPE* 4 (1969) 225–234.
[39] *Pace* Henrichs. For the expression ἱέρεια πρὸ πόλεως, see P. Herrmann, *Chiron* 32 (2002) 170.
[40] Ed.pr. R. Scranton, *Kenchreai: Eastern Port of Corinth. 1. Topography and Architecture* (1978) 73; 125 (ph.).

83 Statue base from Thessalonica. *IG* X 2.1, 103. Roman imperial period. We
present the whole text:

> Εἶσιν Ὀργί|²αν Γ(άϊος) Φολουί|νιος Οὖῆρος |⁴ ὁ ἱερεὺς ἐπι|σκευάσας |⁶
> ἐκ τῶν | ἰδί ᵛ ᵛ ᵛων |⁸ ἀνέθηκεν.

> Isis Orgia. The priest, Gaius Fulvinius Verus, prepared and dedicated from
> his own means.

The epithet Orgia apparently means 'of the mysteries'.

Conclusion

In inscriptions, the word ὄργια is used for various rites:

It refers to the special rites of Dionysus (nos. 59–63). Similarly, in
no. 58, ὄργια are rites of Demeter Chthonia and Meter Oreia, presumably
celebrated in the context of a Bacchic-Orphic mystery cult.

The word denotes the rites of the Eleusinian mysteries (nos. 66–70,
D12?)[41] and also the imitation of these rites at Miletus (no. 71).

The word is used for the mystery rites of several other deities: Artemis
(no. 73); Cybele (no. 77); Herse and others (no. 74); and, last but not least,
the enigmatic Zeus Dionysus Gongylus (no. 72). It is not clear for which
god or goddess the "solemn rites of the blessed" in no. 76 are celebrated.

It is used in a metaphorical sense for the work of physicians (no. 78)
and for the 'rites of love' in Menander's plays (no. 79).

It is also used for cult objects (no. 81) and for cult regulations (no. 80).

Orgiophants of Liber Pater are found at Puteoli (nos. 64, 65). At
Lagina, we find another orgiophant, presumably of Hecate (no. 75).

I did not find ὀργιάζειν or ὀργιασμός in the inscriptions. The femi-
nine nominative singular Ὀργία is used as an epithet for Isis (nos. 82–
83).

---

[41] See below, Appendix A.

APPENDIX A

Falsa et dubia: τελετή

D1 Fragment of a marble base from Eleusis. Broken on all sides except top. *IG* II² 4715. First or second century AD. See now Clinton, *I.Eleusis*, no. 537 with Pl. 255 (ph. stone). Lines 6–16 appear to be metrical.

Kirchner restored in line 15: [- - - - -]ην τὴν ἐν ταῖς [τελεταῖς - - - - -]. While this reading is possible (it fits the metre and the Eleusinian context), it is too uncertain to be included in our catalogue.

D2 (= D14) Funerary epigram from Phthiotic Thebes (Thessaly). Peek, *GV* 694.[1] Third or fourth century AD. On the basis of ed.pr.'s photograph, Peek initially restored lines 3–6:

[Μ]αικιπα τοὔνομ' ἔχον|⁴[τα, πολυστεφάνοιο] δὲ Βάκχ[ου ...] | θνεο-κλόνων κλει[νῶν] τελ[ετ]ῶν νεο[φάν]|⁶την.

Having inspected the stone, he later published a drawing and corrected reading of these lines in *Griechische Vers-Inschriften aus Thessalien* (1974) 31 no. 29:

[Μ]αίκιπα τοὔνομ' ἔχον|⁴[τα, φιλοστεφάνοι]ο δὲ Βάκχ[ου] | θυρσοκλό-νον κλεινὸν [κ]αὶ ὀ[ρ]γ[ια]κῶν ἔο [φ]άν|⁶την.

called Maikeps, renowned thyrsus-shaker of wreath-loving Bacchus, and displayer of his mysteries.

Whether or not the restoration of *orgiakōn* is correct, the correction of previously misread letters makes it impossible to read *teletōn*.

D3 Funerary epigram on a marble stele from northern Thrace. Broken on the left. *IGBulg* III.2 1862 = V 5656. Third century AD. Peek, *GV* 1319, restored the second verse as follows (lines 2–3):

[ἐνθάδε κεῖθ' ἱερ]ῆς μυστιπό|[λος τελετῆς].

Here lies an initiate of the sacred rite.

---

[1] Ed.pr. N.I. Giannopoulos, *ArchEph* 1929, 142–143 no. 10 (with ph. on page 3). See also Jaccottet, *Choisir Dionysos*, no. 11 (who was apparently unaware of Peek's corrections in *GV Thess.*).

When the stone was subsequently removed from the church wall in which it had been encased, more letters became visible:

[- ‿‿ -] μελίθρους μυστιπό|[λος ‿‿ -].

... honey-voiced initiate ...

Mihailov tentatively restores βακχείου at the beginning, and notes that, in that case, the reading τελετῆς is no longer possible.

D4 Dedicatory epigram from Delos. *SEG* XIX 532.[2] First century BC. Lines 14–16 (tentatively restored by Peek):

τρισσὰ δ' Ἐρεχθειδᾶν ἀ[γαγόμαν ἄεθλα], | ἁγνὸν Ἐλευσῖνος πρὸς ἀνάκ[τορον ἀνίκ' ἰδέσθαι] | πενταετῆ Δηοῦς ἦλθον [ἐγὼ τελετάν].

I carried away for myself three prizes of the Erechtheids (Athenians), when I went to the holy temple of Eleusis to see the five year festival of Deo (Demeter).

D5 Regulation concerning the sale of a priesthood, from Cos. *LSCG* 167. Undated.

Paton and Hicks, *I.Cos* 28, in their majuscule copy, print ΕΠΙΤΑΙΓ at the end of line 3 and restore lines 3–4: ἐπὶ τᾶι [τελετᾶι τᾶς] | [ἱερ]ωσύνας. Independently from Sokolowki, I reached the conclusion that we should read instead: ἐπὶ τᾶι π[ράσει τᾶς] | [ἱερ]ωσύνας, which makes better sense and is supported by *Iscr.Cos* ED 2.A.9 and ED 215.B.18.

D6 (= 12) Regulation concerning ritual purity, from Cos. *LSCG* 154. First half third century BC. Sokolowki restored lines A.33–34:

[τὰν δὲ ἐπὶ τᾶι τελετᾶι θυσίαν] | θύει ἁ ⟨ἱ⟩έρεια.

The priestess also conducts the sacrifice at the ceremony.

The restoration appears to be purely conjectural.

D7 Regulation concerning the cult of Adrasteia and Nemesis, from Cos. *Iscr.Cos* ED 62. First half first century BC.[3]

Herzog, *KFF* 26 read lines 2–4: διαγρα[ψάντωι] | [τοὶ ταμίαι τοῖ]ς προστάταις εἰς [τὰν τε]|[λετὰν (δρ.) -]. Sokolowski, *LSCG* 161.B.3–4

---

[2] *I.Délos* 2552; tentatively restored by Peek, *Zeitschrift Halle-Wittenberg* 9 (1960) 199–201.

[3] See Parker & Obbink, *Chiron* 30 (2000) 423: ca. 75 BC, instead of third cent. BC.

read instead: εἰς [τὰν ἐπὶ τᾶι] | [πράσει θυσίαν], whereas Segre read: εἰς [τὰν θυ]|[σίαν (δρ.) .]; cf. also ED 180.31. There appears to be no τελετή here.

D8 (= 59) Dedicatory epigram of a Dionysiac association, found nearby the Mausoleum of Halicarnassus. *SEG* XXVIII 841.[4] Second or first century BC. Peek restored lines 2–4 as follows:

[κ]αὶ μορφὰν Βρομίου τὰς [τελετάς τε θεοῦ,] | ὄφρα σὺ γινώσκηις ἱεροῦ λουτ[ροῖο μετασχών] | πάντα λόγον μύστην παντὸς ἐόντα βίου.

and the appearance of Bromios and the rites of the god, so that you, participating in the sacred bath, may know the whole mystic story your whole life.

The inscription definitely pertains to Dionysiac mysteries (see comm. to no. 59), but the restoration of τελετάς in line 2 is too uncertain to be included in our catalogue.

D9 Dedicatory epigram from the temple of Hecate at Lagina (Caria).[5] Early Roman imperial period?

Şahin, *I.Stratonikeia* no. 543, republishing this inscription, prints in line 2: σῆς ἱερῆς [..].[....] φαιδιμόεντο πόθῳ, and remarks in the app. crit.: "[τελετῆς] Ed.pr., Peek; man könnte auch erwägen [κεφαλῆς]."

Şahin's edition contains several inaccuracies: πόθῳ is a mistake for πόθωι (or ποθῶι); φαιδιμόεντο is a typographical error for φαιδιμό-εντι (or φαιδιμόεν τι, Peek); edd.pr. did not restore anything between ἱερῆς and φαιδιμόεντι; [τελετῆς] was restored by Hula, who was apparently unaware of Hicks' restoration [τιμῆς] (which had yet to be published); Peek reprints Hula's [τελετῆς] in his text but corrects this in his commentary (*GVAK*, 23): "Indem ich das zu spezielle und die Lücke auch wohl überfordernde τελετῆς (mit Hicks) durch τιμῆς ersetze ..." So there appears to be no τελετή in this inscription.

---

[4] *GIBM* IV, 909; W. Peek, *SRKK* II, 694–695 no. 4 (*SEG* XXVIII 841, who print Peek's text and note an alternative restoration by A. Wilhelm). See also Jaccottet, *Choisir Dionysos*, no. 152.

[5] Edd.pr. C. Diehl & G. Cousin, *BCH* 11 (1887) 160–161 no. 70; E.L. Hicks, *CR* 2 (1888) 290; E. Hula, *AEM* 12 (1888) 77–79; Peek, *GVAK* 22–28 no. 11 (*SEG* XXX 1272).

D10 Honorary decree for the gymnasiarch Dionysius, from Sardis. *I.Sardis* 21. Mid-second century BC (stephanephoros). Here we perhaps have τελετή in the sense of festival. Lines 9–12 (restored by edd.pr.):

> τι[θέμενον] |¹⁰ [δὲ καὶ ἄγαλμ]α τῆς Νεικη[φό]|[ρου Ἀθην]ᾶς καὶ ⟨ἐ⟩πὶ τὰς τ[ελε]|¹²[τὰς τῆς θε]οῦ χρυσᾶς εἰκό[νας].⁶

> and because he is now contributing a statue of Athena Nikephoros and for the festival of the goddess gilded statues.

Edd.pr. note that "[t]he restoration is uncertain, though it is fairly plain that these lines record some tribute or gift to Athena of Pergamum, in whose honour the biennial *Nikephoria* were founded there by Eumenes II … and the *Panathenaia* at Sardis." If the restoration is correct, τελετή probably refers to the festival at Sardis.

D11 Dedication to Men Askaenos, from Antioch (Pisidia). Lane, *CMRDM* I 258,⁷ who reproduces the text as interpreted by Ramsay, *JRS* 8 (1918) 133. Roman imperial period.

> Ἰόν(ιος) κατ(ὰ) τελ(ετὴν) | μετ(ὰ) τέκ(νων) | Μην(ὶ) Ἀσκ(αηνῷ) εὐ-χ(ήν).

> Ionios, in accordance with a rite, with his children, to Men Askaenos, a votive offering.

The reading κατ. τελ. is not entirely certain. Lane (IV, p. 7, no. 21) remarks: "I would myself be inclined to read καὶ for the middle word of the first line, and take τελ. as an abbreviated name, but Ramsay's sketch seems to militate against that assumption." The expression κατὰ τελετήν is not attested in other inscriptions, but cf. Max. Tyr. 2.1.

Falsa et dubia: ὄργια

D12 (= 26) Fragmentary herm from Athens, set up in honour of a certain Leucius. *IG* II² 3752. Second century AD. Leucius' mother was apparently a priestess in the Eleusinian mysteries, lines 7–8:

---

⁶ There is space for one letter after εἰκό[νας: perhaps a number, or vacat?
⁷ With additional commentary in *CMRDM* IV, p. 7, no. 21, based on the sketch of this monument in Ramsay, Notebook B, p. 6, no. 76.

ἀρρήτου τελ[ετῆς ὄργια] | δερκομένη.

who always beheld the mysteries of the secret rite.

D13 Statue base from Eleusis, *IG* II² 3508 (lost). First century BC. See now Clinton, *I.Eleusis*, no. 278.[8] Kirchner (following Boeckh, *CIG*) printed the reading by Spon:

> Κτησίκλεια Ἀπολλωνίου |² Ἀχαρνέως ὀργιαστ⟨ὶ⟩ς τὸν | ἑαυτῆς ἄνδρα Σοφοκλῆν |⁴ Ξενοκλέους Ἀχαρνέα δα|δουχήσαντα Δήμητρι καὶ |⁶ Κόρηι δὶς ἀνέθηκεν.

> Ctesiclea, daughter of Apollonius, from Acharnae, celebrant of mysteries, dedicated her own husband Sophocles, son of Xenocles, from Acharnae, who was daduch of Demeter and Kore, twice.

Instead of ὀργιαστ⟨ὶ⟩ς,[9] Clinton prints θυγάτηρ, which is supported by Vernon's reading of *IG* II² 3507. The noun ὀργιαστής (fem. ὀργιαστίς) is not attested elsewhere in Eleusis. Furthermore, it does not fit well in the structure of the sentence. If one compares other Eleusinian statue bases from the same period, the demotic ought to be followed by θυγάτηρ, which was apparently misread by Spon.

D14 (= D2) Funerary epigram from Phthiotic Thebes (Thessaly). W. Peek, *Griechische Vers-Inschriften aus Thessalien* (1974) 31 no. 29. Third or fourth century AD. Lines 3–6:

> [Μ]αίκιπα τοὔνομ' ἔχον|⁴[τα, φιλοστεφάνοι]ο δὲ Βάκχ[ου] | θυρσοκλόνον κλεινὸν [κ]αὶ ὀ[ρ]γ[ια]κῶν ἔο [φ]άν|⁶την.

> called Maikeps, renowned thyrsus-shaker of wreath-loving Bacchus, and displayer of his mysteries.

Apparently, this Maikeps had had an interesting religious life: he was an initiate in the mysteries of Demeter (Δήμητ[ρος] μύστην, line 2) and had been involved in the cult of Bacchus as a 'thyrsus-shaker' and perhaps also as orgiophant. While the word ὀργιακά is not attested elsewhere and ὀργιακῶν φάντης would seem a rather clumsy periphrastic expression for the well-attested term ὀργιοφάντης, epigraphically the reading appears to be possible (if we trust Peek's drawing).

---

[8] Cf. also Vernon's reading of *IG* II² 3507 (*I.Eleusis*, no. 277), which had an identical text (first line now lost).

[9] ΟΡΓΙΑΣΤΗΣ, Spon.

D15 (= 60) Regulation concerning the cult of Dionysus, from Miletus. *LSAM* 48.[10] 276/5 BC. Lines 1–3:

ὅταν δὲ ἡ ἱέρεια ἐπι[.....]ηι τὰ ἱερὰ ὑπὲρ τῆς πόλ[εω]ς | [.....] μὴ ἐξεῖναι ὠμοφάγιον ἐμβαλεῖν μηθενὶ πρότερον | [ἢ ἡ ἱέ]ρεια ὑπὲρ τῆς πόλεως ἐμβάληι.

When the priestess [performs vel sim.] the sacrifices on behalf of the city, it is not allowed for anyone to add a raw victim before the priestess adds one on behalf of the city.

Wiegand's restoration of [ὄργια] in line 2 was rightly rejected by Wilamowitz and by Sokolowski.

---

[10] See also Jaccottet, *Choisir Dionysos*, no. 150.

APPENDIX B

The Proper Name Τελέτη

The proper name Τελέτη appears several times in inscriptions. Since the accent of proper names that have the form of a noun is usually recessive,[1] I have adopted the paroxytone accentuation throughout this Appendix: Τελέτη instead of Τελετή.[2]

N1 *IG* II² 3960, honorary inscription on a herm from Athens.[3] After 127 AD (Council reduced to 500). The inscription was apparently set up by a woman called Telete.

> ψηφισαμένης τῆς βου|²λῆς τῶν φ´ Τελέτη Γλαύ|κου Κηφεισιέως θυ(γά-τηρ) ἀρρη|⁴φορήσασα τὸν ἑαυτῆς υ|[ἱ]ὸν Γλαῦκον Μ[έ]μνονο|⁶[ς ᾿Αν]αφλύστιον αἰτησαμέ|[νου το]ῦ ἀνδρὸς Κλ(αυδίου) ᾿Αττι|⁸[κου -----].

The Council of 500 voted. Telete, daughter of Glaucus from (the deme) Cephisia, having served as Arrhephoros, (set this up to honour) her own son, Glaucus, son of Memnon, from (the deme) Anaphlystios, at the request of her husband, Claudius Atticus.

Only two girls, aged seven to eleven, were chosen from noble families each year to serve as Arrhephoroi, so Telete must have been of noble birth.[4]

N2 *IG* II² 9160, two names inscribed on a little column from Athens.[5] The second inscription dates from the second century AD (letterforms).

> Τελέτη | Μιλησία.

Telete from Miletus.

---

[1] H.W. Smyth, *Greek Grammar* (1956) 41 §178a.
[2] Τελέτη is also the accentuation used by *LGPN*.
[3] Recorded in *LGPN* II s.v. Τελέτη (2).
[4] For the Arrhephoria, see esp. W. Burkert, *Savage Energies* (2001) 37–63.
[5] Not recorded in *LGPN* II s.v Τελέτη.

N3 *ArchDelt* 25A, 1970, 73 no. 15, fragment of a grave stele (?) found in the Roman Agora in Athens.[6] Second or third century AD.

> Τελέτη ἐ[κ - -]|[- -]έων.

> Telete from (?) …

N4 *Iscr.Cos* EF 742. Epitaph on a quadrangular altar from Cos. Roman imperial period.

> Τελέτα Σωκλεῦς | ΚΕΡΥΑΤΙΣ χρησ|τὴ χαῖρε.

> Teleta, daughter of Socles, good woman, farewell.

N5 *TAM* III 803, inscribed on a sarcophagus from Termessus (Pisidia) for Claudius Nymphicus and Claudia Telete. Roman imperial period (imperial treasury in line 9). The first four lines read:

> Κλ(αυδίῳ) Νυμφικῷ καὶ Κλ(αυδίᾳ) Τελέτῃ, |² τροφεῦσιν, τὴν σω|ματο-θήκην ἱερεὺς |⁴ Τι(βέριος) Κλ(αύδιος) Φλῶρος.

> Tiberius Claudius Florus, priest, (prepared) this sarcophagus for his parents, Claudius Nymphicus and Claudia Telete.

This is followed by the familiar prohibition against adding another corpse.

A search of the Epigraphische Datenbank Frankfurt (EDCS) has yielded a dozen instances of the name Telete in Latin inscriptions:[7]

N6 *CIL* VI 4385, from Rome.

> Hateria Telete | vixit ann(os) XXVII | tu pater et mater | lacrumis retinete | dolorem nam fato | raptam non potes eripere.

> Hateria Telete lived for 27 years. You, father and mother, hold back from tears your grief, for you cannot save me, who has been snatched by death.

N7 *CIL* VI 5294, from Rome.

> Telete | Augustae{s} | libertae liberta | vixit an(nos) XIIII.

> Telete, freedwoman of the freedwoman Augusta, lived for 14 years.

---

⁶ Recorded in *LGPN* II s.v. Τελέτη (1).
⁷ Where Clauss gives multiple references for a single inscription, I will refer only to *CIL* or *AnÉp*.

N8 *CIL* VI 12359, from Rome.

> D(is) M(anibus) s(acrum) | Arrecina | Telete Sex(to) | Titio Epitun|cano con|iugi suo | b(ene) m(erenti) fecit et sibi.

> Dedicated to the gods of the underworld, Arrecina Telete made this for her well-deserving husband Titius Epituncanus and for herself.

N9 *CIL* VI 15941, from Rome.

> Cocceia | Parhedri l(iberta) Telete.

> Cocceia Telete, freedwoman of Parhedrus.

N10 *CIL* VI 35069, from Rome.

> Diis Manibus | Curiasia | Telete | liberta.

> To the gods of the underworld, Curiasia Telete, freedwoman.

N11 *CIL* VI 36141, from Rome, lines 5–9:

> Dis Manibus sacrum | Corneliae Telete C(aius) Cornelius | Chresimus coniugi suae bene | merenti et sibi post(erisque) suis in f(ronte) p(edes) XI in | a(grum) p(edes) XII.

> Dedicated to the gods of the underworld, Gaius Cornelius Chresimus for Cornelia Telete, his well deserving wife, and for himself and for their descendants, (a plot) 11 ft wide and 12 ft long.

N12 *AnÉp* 1996, 226, from Rome.

> Q(uintus) Sosius Trophimus Telete coniugi dul[cissimae fecit] | et sibi quem (*sic*) accepi annor(um) XII vixit mecum | defuncta est VIII Febr(u)a-rias Laeliano [et Pastore co(n)s(ulibus)].

> Quintus Sosius Trophimus made this for his dearest wife, Telete, and for himself. I took her in, she lived with me for 12 years and she passed away on the 8th (before the Calends/Ides?) of February, when Laelianus and Pastor were consuls.

N13 *CIL* XIV 1776, from Ostia.

> Vibia L(uci) f(ilia) | Telete | v(ixit) a(nnos) II m(enses) III | d(ies) XXII h(oras) VI.

> Vibia Telete, daughter of Lucius, lived 2 years, 3 months, 22 days, 6 hours.

N14 *CIL* IX 481, from Venusia (Apulia).

> Antoniae M(arci) l(ibertae) | Nymphe | M(arcus) Antonius Eutactus | posuit sibi et | Antoniae Telete.

For Antonia Nymphe, freedwoman of Marcus. Marcus Antonius Eutactus set this up for himself and for Antonia Telete.

N15 *CIL* II 6158, from Barcino (Hispania citerior).

L(ucio) Fabio L(uci) lib(erto) Restituto | Urcitano e[t] Mariae Telete | uxori | ex testamento fec[e]runt.

For Lucius Fabius Restitutus from Urci, freedman of Lucius, and his wife Maria Telete. They made this from their last will.

N16 *CIL* II² 5, 813, from Singilia Barba (Hispania Baetica).

Telete annor(um) XXIII | h(ic) s(ita) e(st) s(it) t(ibi) t(erra) l(evis).

Telete, 23 years old, lies here. May the earth be light for you.

N17 *AnÉp* 1969/70, 854, from Thugga (Africa proconsularis).

Telete | M(arci) Licini | Rufi ser(va) | p(ia) v(ixit) a(nnos) XXVII.

Telete, slave of Marcus Licinius Rufus, dutiful, lived for 27 years.

I have found one additional example in *LGPN* III.A, s.v. Τελέτη(2):

N18 *NotScav* 1897, 326 no. 4, from Brundisium (Apulia).

[V]ibia Tele[te] | vixit annos | XXXV h(ic) s(ita) e(st).

Vibia Telete, lived 35 years, lies here.

BIBLIOGRAPHY

Abel, E., *Orphica* (1885).

Barr-Sharrar, B., E.N. Borza (eds.), *Macedonia and Greece in Late Classical and Early Hellenistic Times* (1982).

Bernabé, A. (ed.), *Poetae Epici Graeci*. II *Orphicorum et Orphicis similium testimonia et fragmenta*. Fasc. 3 (2007).

Bernabé, A., A.I. Jiménez San Cristóbal, *Instructions for the Netherworld: The Orphic Gold Tablets*, RGRW 162 (2008).

Betz, H.D., Magic and Mystery in the Greek Magical Papyri, in: Faraone & Obbink (eds.), *Magika Hiera* (1991) 244–259.

Betz, H.D. (ed.), *The Greek Magical Papyri in Translation* [2](1992).

Bickermann, E., Die römische Kaiserapotheose, *Archiv für Religionswissenschaft* 27 (1929) 1–34.

Bolkestein, H., *Theophrastus' Charakter der Deisidaimonia als religionsgeschichtliche Urkunde*, RGVV 21.2 (1929).

Bonnechere, P., *Le sacrifice humain en Grèce ancienne*, Kernos Suppl. 3 (1994).

Bousset, W., *Religion des Judentums im neutestamentlichen Zeitalter* (1903).

Bosnakis, D., K. Hallof, Alte und neue Inschriften aus Kos II, *Chiron* 35 (2005) 219–272.

Bousset, W. (ed.), *Die Schriften des Neuen Testaments: neu übersehen und für die Gegenwart erklärt*, vol. 2 [3](1917).

Bréal, M., *Essai de sémantique* (1897).

Breasted, J.H., *Development of Religion and Thought in Ancient Egypt* (1912).

Brede Kristensen, W., *Het leven uit den dood: Studiën over Egyptischen en Oud-Griekschen godsdienst* (1926).

Burkert, W., *Homo Necans: The Anthropology of Ancient Greek Sacrificial Ritual and Myth* (1983).

Burkert, W., *Greek Religion* (1985).

Burkert, W., *Ancient Mystery Cults* (1987).

Burkert, W., *Savage Energies: Lessons of Myth and Ritual in Ancient Greece* (2001).

Christ-Schmid-Stählin = W. von Christ, *Geschichte der griechischen Litteratur*, rev. W. Schmid, O. Stählin, vol. 2 (1920–1924).

Christopoulos, M., Orgia aporrheta. Quelques remarques sur les rites des Plyntéries, *Kernos* 5 (1992) 27–39.

Clemen, C., *Der Einfluss der Mysterienreligionen auf das älteste Christentum*, RGVV 13.1 (1913).

Clinton, K., *The Sacred Officials of the Eleusinian Mysteries*, TAPhS NS, 64.3 (1974).

Clinton, K., Stages of initiation in the Eleusinian and Samothracian Mysteries, in: M.B. Cosmopoulos (ed.), *Greek Mysteries* (2003) 50–78.

Clinton, K., *Eleusis. The Inscriptions on Stone: Documents of the Sanctuary of the Two Goddesses and Public Documents of the Deme* [*I.Eleusis*], vol. 1 (2005).

Connelly, J.B., *Portrait of a Priestess: Women and Ritual in Ancient Greece* (2007).

Cosmopoulos, M.B. (ed.), *Greek Mysteries: The Archaeology and Ritual of Ancient Greek Secret Cults* (2003).

Croiset, A., M. Croiset, *Histoire de la littérature grecque*, 5 vols. (1887–1899).

Cumont, F., *Les religions orientales dans le paganisme romain* [3](1929).

Daremberg, C., E. Saglio, *Dictionnaire des antiquités grecques et romaines d'après les textes et les monuments*, 5 vols. (1877–1919).

Dareste, R., B. Haussollier, Th. Reinach, *Receuil des inscriptions juridiques grecques*, 2 vols (1885–1904).

De Jong, K.H.E., *Das antike Mysterienwesen in religionsgeschichtlicher, ethnologischer und psychologischer Beleuchtung* [2](1919).

Deubner, L., *Attische Feste* (1932).

Dieterich, A., *Eine Mithrasliturgie* (1905).

Dieterich, A., *Kleine Schriften* (ed. R. Wünsch) (1911).

Dignas, B., Priestly Authority in the Cult of the Corybantes at Erythrae *EA* 34 (2002) 29–40.

Dillon, M., *Girls and Women in Classical Greek Religion* (2002).

Dow, S., *Conventions in Editing: A Suggested Reformulation of the Leiden System*, GRBS Scholarly Aids 2 (1969).

Dowden, K., Grades in the Eleusinian Mysteries, *RHR* 197 (1980) 409–427.

Ebeling, H., *Griechisch-deutsches Wörterbuch zum Neuen Testamente* [3](1929).

Eerdmans, B.D., *De godsdienst van Israel*, 2 vols. (1930).

Endenburg, P.J.T., *Koinoonia en gemeenschap van zaken bij de Grieken in den klassieken tijd* (Diss. Utrecht) (1937).

Faraone, C.A., D. Obbink (eds.), *Magika Hiera: Ancient Greek Magic and Religion* (1991).

Farnell, L.R., *The Cults of the Greek States*, 4 vols. (1896–1909).

Farnell, L.R., *The Works of Pindar* (1932).

Foucart, P., *Les mystères d'Eleusis* (1914).

Friedländer, L., *Darstellungen aus der Sittengeschichte Roms*, 4 vols. [10](1921–1923).

Geffcken, J., *Der Ausgang des griechisch-römischen Heidentums* (1920).

Gonda, J., *Δείκνυμι: Semantische studie over den Indo-Germaanschen wortel deik-* (Diss. Utrecht) (1929).

Graf, F., Lesser Mysteries—not less mysterious, in: M.B. Cosmopoulos (ed.), *Greek Mysteries* (2003) 241–262.

Graf, F., S.I. Johnston, *Ritual Texts for the Afterlife: Orpheus and the Bacchic Gold Tablets* (2007).

Gronewald, M., Zwei Hypomnemata zu Aristophanes, *ZPE* 45 (1982) 64–69.

Gruppe, O., *Die griechischen Culte und Mythen* (1887).

Hallager, E. et al., New Linear B Tablets from Khania, *Kadmos* 31 (1992) 61–87.

Harrison, J.E., *Prolegomena to the Study of Greek Religion* (1903).

Harrison, J.E., The meaning of the word telete, *Class. Rev.* (1914) 36.

Hastings, J. (ed.), *Encyclopedia of Religion and Ethics*, 13 vols. (1908–1926).

Heinemann, I., *Die Werke Philos von Alexandria in deutscher Übersetzung.* 7 vols. 1909–1938.

Heitsch, E., *Die griechischen Dichterfragmente der römischen Kaiserzeit* (1961).

Henrichs, A., Die Maenaden von Milet, *ZPE* 4 (1969) 223–241.

Henrichs, A., Human Sacrifices in Greek Religion: Three case studies, in: *Le sacrifice dans l'Antiquité* (1981) 195–235.

Herrmann, P., Eine "pierre errante" in Samos: Kultgesetz der Korybanten, *Chiron* 32 (2002) 157–171.

Herter, H., *De Priapo*, RGVV 23 (1932).

Hiller von Gaertringen, F., *IG* XII, fasc. 5, pars ii, *Inscriptiones Teni insulae* (1909).

Hordern, J., Notes on the Orphic Papyrus from Gurôb, *ZPE* 129 (2000) 131–140.

Hornblower, S., A. Spawforth (eds.), *The Oxford Classical Dictionary* [3](1996).

Hughes, D.D., *Human Sacrifice in Ancient Greece* (1991).

Jaccottet, A.F., *Choisir Dionysos: les associations dionysiaques ou la face cachée du dionysisme*, 2 vols. (2003).

Jacoby, F., *Fragmente der griechischen Historiker* (1923–).

Jouanna, J., *Hippocrates* (1999).

Kaibel, G., *Epigrammata graeca ex lapidibus conlecta* (1878).

Kaltsas, N., *Εθνικό Αρχαιολογικό Μουσείο: Τα Γλυπτά* (2001).

Kautzsch, E., *Die Apokryphen und Pseudepigraphen des Alten Testaments*, 2 vols. (1900).

Kennedy, D. (ed.), *The Twin Towns of Zeugma on the Euphrates* (1998).

Kern, O. (ed.), *Orphicorum fragmenta* (1922).

Koets, P.J., *Δεισιδαιμονία: A contribution to the knowledge of the religious terminology in Greek* (Diss. Utrecht) (1929).

Krumbacher, K., *Geschichte der byzantinischen Literatur* (1891).

Lambert, S.D., The Sacrificial Calendar of the Marathonian Tetrapolis: A Revised Text, *ZPE* 130 (2000) 43–70.

Latte, K., Zeus Telesiourgos, *Philologus* 85.2 (1930) 225–227.

Laumonier, A., Recherches sur la chronologie des prêtres de Panamara, *BCH* 61 (1937) 236–298.

Lavecchia, S., P.Oxy. 2622 e il 'Secondo Ditirambo' di Pindaro, *ZPE* 110 (1996) 1–26.

Lavecchia, S., *Pindari Dithyramborum Fragmenta* (2000).

Lehmann, W., *De Achillis Tatii aetate* (1910).

Leisegang, H., Griechische Philosophie als Mysterion, *PhilWoch* Aug. 1932 (= *Festschrift Poland*).

Leisegang, H., *Die Gnosis* (1924).

Lipsius, J.H., Die Phratrie der Demotionidai, *Leipziger Studien* 16 (1894) 161–171.

Lipsius, J.H., *Das Attische Recht und Rechtsverfahren*, 4 vols (1905–1915).

Lloyd-Jones, H., Heracles at Eleusis: P.Oxy. 2622 and PSI 1391, *Maia* 19 (1967) 206–229.

Lobeck, C.A., *Aglaophamus sive de theologiae mysticae graecorum causis libri tres* (1829).

Ludwich, A., *Die Homerische Batrachomachia des Karers Pigres nebst Scholien und Paraphrase* (1896).

Lupu, E., *Greek Sacred Law: A Collection of New Documents*, RGRW 152 (2005).

Maass, E., *Orpheus: Untersuchungen zur griechischen römischen altchristlichen Jenseitsdichtung und Religion* (1895).

Magnien, V., *Les mystères d'Eleusis* (1929).

Makkink, A.D.J., *Andokides' eerste rede* (Diss. Utrecht) (1932).

Markoe, G.E., *The Phoenicians* (2000).

Maspéro, G., *Études de mythologie et d'archéologie égyptiennes*, 8 vols. (1893–1916).

Mathiesen, T.J., *Aristides Quintilianus: On Music* (1983).

Mommsen, A., *Feste der Stadt Athen im Altertum* (1898).

Motte, A., V. Pirenne-Delforge, Le mot et les rites. Aperçu des significations de orgia et de quelques dérivés, *Kernos* 5 (1992) 119–140.

Murray, G., *Four Stages of Greek Religion* (1912).

Nilsson, M.P., *Griechische Feste von religiöser Bedeutung mit Ausschluss der attischen* (1906).

Nilsson, M.P., *The Dionysiac Mysteries of the Hellenistic and Roman Age* (1957).

Önal, M., Rescue Excavations in Belkıs/Zeugma: The Dionysos Room and the Pit below its Mosaic Floor, *DM* 13 (2002) 318–319.

Oliver, J.H., *The Sacred Gerusia* (1941).

Ovadiah, A., C. Gomez de Silva, S. Mucznik, The Mosaic Pavements of Sheikh Zouède in Northern Sinai, in: *Tesserae: Festschrift für Josef Engemann* (1991) 181–191.

Parker, R., D. Obbink, Sales of Priesthoods on Cos I, *Chiron* 30 (2000) 415–449.

Parker, R., D. Obbink, Sales of Priesthoods on Cos II, *Chiron* 31 (2001) 229–252.

Peek, W., Die Hydrophore Vera von Patmos, *RhM* 104 (1964) 315–325.

Peek, W., Milesische Versinschriften, *ZPE* 7 (1971) 193–226.

Peek, W., *Griechische Vers-Inschriften aus Thessalien* (1974).

Pettazoni, R., *I misteri* (1924).

Poland, F., *Geschichte des griechischen Vereinswesens* (1909).

Powell, J.U., *Collectanea Alexandrina* (1925).

Preisendanz, K. et al. (eds.), *Papyri graecae magicae*, 2 vols. [2](1973–1974).

Preller L., *Griechische Mythologie*, rev. C. Robert [4](1894).

Quandt, W., *De Baccho ab Alexandri aetate in Asia Minore cultu* (Diss. Halle) (1923).

Reitzenstein, R., *Die Hellenistische Mysterienreligionen*[2] (1920).

Robert, L., *Hellenica: Recueil d'épigraphie, de numismatique et d'antiquités grecques*, vol. 11–12 (1960).

Robert, L., *A travers l'Asie Mineure* (1980).

Rohde, E., *Psyche: Seelenkult und Unsterblichkeits-glaube der Griechen* (1894).

Roscher, W.H., *Ausführliches Lexicon der griechischen und römischen Mythologie* (1884–1937).

Rouse, W.H.D., *Greek Votive Offerings* (1902).

Rutherford, W.G., *The New Phrynichus, being a revised text of the Ecloga of the Grammarian Phrynichus* (1881).

Şahin, M.Ç., *Die Inschriften von Stratonikeia*, IGSK 21–22 (1981–1990).

Samama, E., *Les médecins dans le monde grec: sources épigraphiques sur la naissance d'un corps médical* (2003).

Schmid, W., O. Stählin, *Geschichte der griechischen Literatur*, vol. 1 (1929).

Schuddeboom, F., Orgia and Telete in the Epigraphical Evidence, *Talanta* 38–39 (2006–2007) 225–238.

Schwenn, F., *Die Menschenopfer bei den Griechen und Römern*, RGVV 15.3 (1915).

Scranton, R., *Kenchreai: Eastern Port of Corinth*. 1. *Topography and Architecture* (1978).

Sfameni Gasparro, G., Ancora sul termine telete: osservazioni storico-religiose, in: *Filologia e Forme Letterarie: Studi offerti a Francesco della Corte*, ed. C. Questa, vol. 5 (1987) 137–152.

Sherwin-White, S., *Ancient Cos: An Historical Study from the Dorian Settlement to the Imperial Period* (1978).

Smyth, H.W., *Greek Grammar* (1956).

Sokolowski, F., *Lois sacrées de l'Asie Mineure* (1955).

Sokolowski, F., *Lois sacrées des cités grecques* (1969).

Sokolowski, F., *Lois sacrées des cités grecques. Supplément* (1962).

Sourdille, C., *Hérodote et la religion de l'Égypte* (Diss. Paris) (1910).

Spengel, L., *Rhetores graeci*, vol. 3 (1856).

Stengel, P., *Die griechischen Kultusaltertümer* [3](1920).

Talgam, R., Z. Weiss, *The Mosaics of the House of Dionysos at Sepphoris* (2004) 63–66.

Tresp, A., *Fragmente der griechischen Kultschriftsteller* (1914).

van der Burg, N.M.H., Ἀπόρρητα - δρώμενα - ὄργια: *Bijdrage tot de kennis der religieuze terminologie in het Grieksch* (Diss. Utrecht) (1939).

van Herwerden, H., De Batrachomyomachia, *Mnemosyne* 10 (1882) 163–177.

van Liempt, L., *De vocabulario hymnorum Orphicorum atque aetate* (Diss. Utrecht) (1930).

van der Toorn, K., B. Becking, P.W. van der Horst (eds.), *Dictionary of Deities and Demons in the Bible* [2](1999).

van der Weiden, M.J.H., *The Dithyrambs of Pindar* (1991).

van Straten, F.T., Daikrates' dream. A votive relief from Kos and some other kat'onar dedications, *BABesch* 51 (1976) 1–38.

van Straten, F.T., *Hiera Kala: Images of Animal Sacrifice in Archaic and Classical Greece*, RGRW 127 (1995).

Versnel, H.S., *Inconsistencies in Greek and Roman Religion. 2. Transition and Reversal in Myth and Ritual*, SGRR 6.2 (1993).

Vollgraff, W., Le péan delphique à Dionysos, *BCH* 48 (1924) 97–208.

Waanders, F.M.J., *The History of τέλος and τελέω in Ancient Greek* (1983).

Wackernagel, J., *Sprachliche Untersuchungen zu Homer* (1916).

Wächter, Th., *Reinheitsvorschriften im griechischen Kult*, RGVV 9.1 (1910).

Wagner, J. (ed.), *Gottkönige am Euphrat* (2000).

Wendland, P., *Die hellenistisch-römische Kultur in ihren Beziehungen zu Judentum und Christentum* (1907).

Wiedemann, A., *Herodots zweites Buch* (1890).

Wilamowitz-Moellendorff, U. von, *Aischylos: Interpretationen* (1914).

Wilamowitz-Moellendorff, U. von, *Der Glaube der Hellenen*, 2 vols. (1931–1932).

Williger, E., *Hagios: Untersuchungen zur Terminologie des Heiligen in den hellenisch-hellenistisches Religionen*, RGVV 19.1 (1922).

Windelband, W., *Geschichte der abendländischen Philosophie im Altertum* [4](1923).

Wolke, H., *Untersuchungen zur Batrachomyomachia* (1978).

Zeller, E., *Grundriss der Geschichte der griechischen Philosophie* [12](1920).

Zgusta, L., *Kleinasiatische Personennamen* (1964).

Zijderveld, C., *Τελετή: Bijdrage tot de kennis der religieuze terminologie in het Grieksch* (Diss. Utrecht) (1934).

INDICES

Numbers of inscriptions are given in bold type.

SOURCE INDEX: ΤΕΛΕΤΗ

1. *Literary Sources and Papyri*

Latin authors are listed at the end of this section.

τέλος

2. Inscriptions

τέλος

SOURCE INDEX: ΟΡΓΙΑ

1. *Literary Sources*

Latin authors are listed at the end of this section.

2. Inscriptions

SUBJECT INDEX

1. *Festivals*

2. *Gods and Heroes*

3. *Mythological Figures*

4. *Biblical Figures*

5. *Men and Women*

6. Geographical Names

7. Provenance of Inscriptions

8. *Other*